The Cambridge Introduction to
Postcolonial Literatures in English

The past century has witnessed an extraordinary flowering of fiction, poetry and drama from countries previously colonised by Britain, an output which has changed the map of English literature. This introduction, from a leading figure in the field, explores a wide range of Anglophone postcolonial writing from Africa, Australia, the Caribbean, India, Ireland and Britain. Lyn Innes compares the ways in which authors shape communal identities and interrogate the values and representations of peoples in newly independent nations. Placing its emphasis on literary rather than theoretical texts, this book offers detailed discussion of many internationally renowned authors, including Chinua Achebe, James Joyce, Les Murray, Salman Rushdie and Derek Walcott. It also includes historical surveys of the main countries discussed, a glossary, and biographical notes on major authors. Lyn Innes provides a rich and subtle guide to an array of authors and texts from a wide range of sites.

C. L. Innes is Emeritus Professor of Postcolonial Literatures at the University of Kent. She is the author of, among other books, *A History of Black and Asian Writing in Britain* (Cambridge, 2002).

Cambridge Introductions to Literature

This series is designed to introduce students to key topics and authors. Accessible and lively, these introductions will also appeal to readers who want to broaden their understanding of the books and authors they enjoy.

- Ideal for students, teachers, and lecturers
- Concise, yet packed with essential information
- Key suggestions for further reading

Titles in this series:

Christopher Balme   *The Cambridge Introduction to Theatre Studies*

Eric Bulson   *The Cambridge Introduction to James Joyce*

Warren Chernaik   *The Cambridge Introduction to Shakespeare's History Plays*

John Xiros Cooper   *The Cambridge Introduction to T. S. Eliot*

Patrick Corcoran   *The Cambridge Introduction to Francophone Literature*

Gregg Crane   *The Cambridge Introduction to The Nineteenth-Century American Novel*

Kirk Curnutt   *The Cambridge Introduction to F. Scott Fitzgerald*

Janette Dillon   *The Cambridge Introduction to Early English Theatre*

Janette Dillon   *The Cambridge Companion to Shakespeare's Tragedies*

Jane Goldman   *The Cambridge Introduction to Virginia Woolf*

Kevin J. Hayes   *The Cambridge Introduction to Herman Melville*

Nancy Henry   *The Cambridge Introduction to George Eliot*

David Holdeman   *The Cambridge Introduction to W. B. Yeats*

C. L. Innes   *The Cambridge Introduction to Postcolonial Literatures in English*

M. Jimmie Killingsworth   *The Cambridge Introduction to Walt Whitman*

Pericles Lewis   *The Cambridge Introduction to Modernism*

Ronan McDonald   *The Cambridge Introduction to Samuel Beckett*

Wendy Martin   *The Cambridge Introduction to Emily Dickinson*

Peter Messent   *The Cambridge Introduction to Mark Twain*

David Morley   *The Cambridge Introduction to Creative Writing*

Ira Nadel   *The Cambridge Introduction to Ezra Pound*

Leland S. Person   *The Cambridge Introduction to Nathaniel Hawthorne*

John Peters   *The Cambridge Introduction to Joseph Conrad*

Sarah Robbins   *The Cambridge Introduction to Harriet Beecher Stowe*

Martin Scofield   *The Cambridge Introduction to the American Short Story*

Emma Smith   *The Cambridge Introduction to Shakespeare*

Peter Thomson   *The Cambridge Introduction to English Theatre, 1660–1900*

Janet Todd   *The Cambridge Introduction to Jane Austen*

Jennifer Wallace   *The Cambridge Introduction to Tragedy*

The Cambridge Introduction to
Postcolonial Literatures
in English

C. L. INNES

CAMBRIDGE
UNIVERSITY PRESS

CAMBRIDGE UNIVERSITY PRESS
Cambridge, New York, Melbourne, Madrid, Cape Town, Singapore,
São Paulo, Delhi, Dubai, Tokyo, Mexico City

Cambridge University Press
The Edinburgh Building, Cambridge CB2 8RU, UK

Published in the United States of America by Cambridge University Press, New York

www.cambridge.org
Information on this title: www.cambridge.org/9780521541015

First published 2007

A catalogue record for this publication is available from the British Library

Library of Congress Cataloguing in Publication data

Innes, Catherine Lynette.
The Cambridge introduction to postcolonial literatures in English / C. L. Innes.
    p.   cm. – (Cambridge introductions to literature)
Includes bibliographical references.
ISBN 978-0-521-83340-0 (hardback) – ISBN 978-0-521-54101-5 (pbk.)
1. Commonwealth literature (English) – History and criticism. 2. Postcolonialism in
literature. 3. Colonies in literature. I. Title. II. Series
PR9080. I55 2007
820.9–dc22 2007032988

ISBN 978-0-521-83340-0 Hardback
ISBN 978-0-521-54101-5 Paperback

Contents

Preface

This book sets out to consider some of the writing that has emerged during the past century from the numerous and complex range of postcolonial societies which were formerly part of the British Empire. It seeks not only to discuss the authors and texts, but also to raise questions about the ways in which they have been thought about under the aegis of postcolonial studies, and to ask what varying meanings postcolonial literature may have in different contexts.

In the first decades of the twentieth century, European states governed more than 80 per cent of the world's territories and people. Of these the British Empire was the most extensive and powerful, claiming as British subjects a population of between 470 and 570 million people, approximately 25 per cent of the world's population, and laying claim to more than ninety territories in Africa, Asia, Europe, North America, the Caribbean, Australasia and the Pacific. Almost all those territories have now evolved and/or combined into independent states, fifty-three of which constitute the 'British' Commonwealth, a voluntary organization which several former colonies such as Burma, Egypt, Ireland, and Iraq declined to join when they gained independence.[1] To a greater or lesser degree, all these territories shared a history of cultural colonialism, including the imposition of the English language, and British educational, political and religious institutions, as well as economic relationships and systems.

Within the context of postcolonial writing, critics have often quoted Caliban's retort to Prospero in *The Tempest*: 'You gave me language, and my profit on't / Is I know how to curse.'[2] Perhaps less frequently quoted, but even more significant, are the lines which display Caliban's eloquence (in the English language) when it comes to describing the island Prospero has taken from him, with a combination of force, magic and the seductions of new learning:

> Be not afeard; the isle is full of noises,
> Sounds and sweet airs, that delight and hurt not.
> Sometimes a thousand twanging instruments
> Will hum about mine ears; and sometimes voices[3]

As George Lamming commented, 'Prospero had given Caliban Language; and with it an unstated history of consequences, and unknown history of future intentions.'[4]

Thus one major and unintended consequence of British colonialism has been an enormous flowering of literature in English by postcolonial authors, presenting the story of colonialism and its consequences from their perspective, and reclaiming their land and experience through fiction, drama and poetry, a representation and reclamation requiring a reinvention of the English language and English literary traditions.

This book cannot attempt to encompass the many literary texts and cultures that are an important feature of the anglophone postcolonial world. Even to try to acknowledge half of those ninety territories or former colonies would result in superficial lists of authors and a blurring of the qualities and issues specific to different colonial and postcolonial histories and cultural contexts. Hence, although there will be occasional reference to writers from other countries such as Canada, the Republic of South Africa, Sri Lanka and Zimbabwe, this book will concentrate on works from just a few former colonies, chosen as examples of particular kinds of colonial and postcolonial structures and traditions. These include Ireland, as England's oldest colony and the testing ground for many of her later colonial policies. More importantly for this study, Ireland's literary revival is acknowledged by many postcolonial writers in other countries as a model for their own construction of a national literature. In addition to Ireland, I have chosen India and West Africa (specifically Ghana and Nigeria) as examples of former colonies administered by indirect rule but with very different indigenous cultures. Kenya and Tanzania, with their varied indigenous populations together with a history of white settlement and occupation of farming land, as well as immigrants from the Indian subcontinent and the Middle East, provide examples of settler colonies in Africa with a multicultural history and population. Australia represents a predominantly white settler colony and postcolony whose identity involves not only two centuries of development and attachment to a natural world perceived as almost the reverse of Britain's, but also its origins as a convict settlement, and its history of brutal dispossession of the continent's Aboriginal peoples. The Caribbean islands of Jamaica, St Lucia and Trinidad provide histories of enforced immigration, enslavement and acculturation, where original languages and traditions were either submerged and/or masked and transformed. Finally, the diasporic communities in contemporary Britain from former colonies provide another point of departure for contrast and comparison with Caribbean and other multicultural or intercultural societies. An Appendix provides brief histories of the selected areas to help orient readers.

These histories have been compiled with considerable assistance from Dr Kaori Nagai, whose careful research and keen intelligence have also contributed to the biographical entries for the main authors discussed, and the glossary of terms. I also wish to acknowledge the contributions of many undergraduate and postgraduate students at Tuskegee Institute, Cornell University, the University of Massachussets, and the University of Kent, whose varied enthusiasms and questions have informed my teaching and writing over the years. This book has benefited from insights and new material brought to my attention by former postgraduate students and I wish particularly to acknowledge Maggie Bowers, Sarah Chetin, Paul Delaney, Eugene McNulty, Kaori Nagai, Elodie Rousselot, Florian Stadtler, Amy Smith, Mark Stein, Monica Turci, and Anastasia Vassalopoulos. Past and present colleagues at the University of Kent and elsewhere to whom I owe a particular debt include Samuel Allen, Ashok Bery, Elleke Boehmer, Denise deCaires Narain, Rod Edmond, Abdulrazak Gurnah, Louis James, Declan Kiberd, Susheila Nasta, Stephanie Newell, Caroline Rooney, Joe Skerrett, Angela Smith, Dennis Walder and my husband, Martin Scofield. Tobias Döring's thoughtful comments on the draft manuscript have been exceptionally helpful, as have been his own publications.

Sections of this book have appeared previously in different versions as journal essays or chapters in books. Since they first appeared, they have been considerably revised, updated and elaborated within different contexts. I acknowledge their publication in earlier form and express my thanks to the editors and publishers of the following:

Howard Booth and Nigel Rigby, eds., *Modernism and Empire* (Manchester: Manchester University Press, 2000).

Clara A. B. Joseph and Janet Wilson, eds., *Global Fissures: Postcolonial Fusions* (Amsterdam and New York: Rodopi, 2006).

Tobias Döring, ed., *A History of Postcolonial Fiction in Twelve and a Half Books* (Trier: WVT, Wiss. Verl. Trier, 2006).

Chapter 1

Introduction: situating the postcolonial

Over the past half-century, postcolonial literatures and postcolonial studies[1] have gained the attention of more and more readers and scholars through-out the world. Writers as diverse as Chinua Achebe and Wole Soyinka from Nigeria, Salman Rushdie and Arundhati Roy from India, Derek Walcott from the Caribbean, Seamus Heaney from Ireland, Margaret Atwood and Michael Ondaatje from Canada, Peter Carey and Patrick White from Australia, and J. M. Coetzee and Nadine Gordimer from South Africa have been prominent when major literary awards such as the Booker Prize or the Nobel Prize have been announced, and their works now appear on numerous school and university syllabuses. Concurrently, their writing has provided the nourishment for a variety of postcolonial theories concerning the nature of such works, approaches to reading them, and their significance for reading and understanding other literary, philosophical and historical works. Indeed, the production of intro-ductions to postcolonial theory has become a major industry.[2] However, this book seeks to focus on the literary texts rather than the theories, and to give a general sense of the issues and choices which inform the writing and reading of those texts. It will discuss the ways in which these issues have changed over the decades, involving questions of genre, form and language, as well as social and political concerns; it will also discuss how these texts may be read and responded to in different contexts.

Although the focus of this book will be on texts rather than theories, and although I will use the adjective postcolonial (without a hyphen) throughout to refer to both the texts and their contexts, it is useful to be aware of the terms and theories that have become current in critical discussion, not least the terms 'postcolonial' and 'post-colonial' themselves, for their usage varies, is far from consistent, and is the subject of considerable debate. For historians, the hyphenated word refers specifically to the period after a country, state or people cease to be governed by a colonial power such as Britain or France, and take administrative power into their own hands. Thus India and Pakistan gained their political independence in 1947 and so became historically 'post-colonial' after 15 August 1947. But within the area of 'Postcolonial Studies', which tends to embrace literary and cultural – and sometimes anthropological – studies, the term is more often used to refer to the consequences of colonialism from the time the area was first colonized. Such studies are generally concerned with the subsequent interaction between the culture of the colonial power, including its language, and the culture and traditions of the colonized peoples. And almost always, the analysis of those interactions acknowledges the importance of power relations in that cultural exchange – the degree to which the colonizer imposes a language, a culture and a set of attitudes, and the degree to which the colonized peoples are able to resist, adapt to or subvert that imposition. I should add that the label 'postcolonial' is rejected by some writers to whom it has been applied. The Indian writer Nayantara Sahgal, for example, dislikes the term because she considers that it implies that colonization by the British is the only important thing that has happened to India, and that it denies the history that precedes British colonization and the continuing traditions stemming from those earlier periods.[3]

Some scholars are also uneasy about the application of the term to such a variety of colonial and postcolonial contexts, and fear that its generalized use obscures the significant differences between different colonies and their histories and cultures. It has been argued that predominantly European colonies such as Australia and Canada, which were settled by British and other European groups over a period of two hundred years, and which now have a relatively small indigenous population, should not be grouped together with settler colonies such as Jamaica and Kenya, where historically a small group of Europeans dominated a majority African population, and where, after the achievement of political independence, indigenous Kenyans and Jamaicans of African descent took over the reins. Indeed, given that indigenous Australian Aborigines and Native Americans have yet to recover their territory and achieve self-government, it has been claimed that countries such as Australia and Canada should be classified as not 'post-colonial' but 'colonial'. As an island settled and governed by the British since the twelfth century, Ireland is seen by some to have a dual status as a postcolonial state in the south while remaining a British colony in the north.

Nations which were historically settler colonies also differ significantly from those which were not settled by Europeans but governed by the British directly from London through the agency of civil servants, police, and soldiers sent not as permanent settlers occupying the land but as administrators and 'peacekeepers' to ensure that the laws and regulations promulgated by the British were enforced. The Indian subcontinent changed over a period of two hundred years from being seen as a series of states whose rulers collaborated, often as a result of military intervention, with the British East India Company, to becoming in the nineteenth century an area governed by the British and subject to its statutes. In both Ireland and India, the British sought to establish an intermediate class of English-speaking people who could act as interpreters, teachers and lower-grade civil servants, and so provide support for British cultural, military and economic domination. Similar policies were followed in African colonies such as Ghana and Nigeria after the allocation of these territories to Britain at the Berlin Conference in 1884.[4]

Although this book will concentrate on literature written in English by members of the colonized groups just before or during the historically postcolonial period in the colonies formerly dominated by Britain – that is, works written in the phase leading up to independence or following the achievement of independence – it is important to bear in mind the differing histories of each former colony and the impact of those differing histories. It is also important to be aware of the development of postcolonial studies and the peculiarities of the discipline, in order not to be confined by its present boundaries and terms, but rather to question and modify them. As Stuart Hall remarks, 'Those deploying the concept must attend . . . carefully to its discriminations and specificities and/or establish more clearly at what level of abstraction the term is operating and how this avoids a spurious "universalisation" . . . Not all societies are "post-colonial" *in the same way* . . . But this does not mean they are not "post-colonial" *in any way*.'[5] In the same essay Hall also insists on the need to view postcoloniality as a process, involving changing relationships and positions with regard to the colonizing culture and the postcolonial subject's identity.

From Commonwealth to postcolonial literary studies

Postcolonial literary studies owe their origin chiefly, of course, to the enormous and exciting efflorescence of creative writing which first came to the attention of readers and critics in the 1950s and 1960s, and coincided with a series of states in Africa, South East Asia and the Caribbean moving from colonial to postcolonial status.[6] Concurrent with the dismantling of the British Empire came the establishment of the British Commonwealth (more recently called the 'Commonwealth of Nations'), a structure grouping together most of the former British colonies. In 1964 A. Norman Jeffares convened the first Commonwealth Literature Conference at the University of Leeds, and courses in Commonwealth literature became a significant part of the curriculum in English departments at various universities in Britain.[7] Later, such courses would also be introduced in Australia, Canada, India, Sri Lanka and the various African countries, though here the emphasis was more often on the country's own writers, rather than a comparative study or survey, and there was often considerable opposition to the introduction of such courses. The Kenyan writer Ngugi wa Thiong'o writes about the absence of any reference to writing by Africans in English departments in Kenya and Uganda, and describes his own struggle to introduce African literature courses at the University of Nairobi.[8]

The study of Commonwealth literature in Britain was reinforced by the presence of many writers and academics from the former colonies. Some, like Kamau Brathwaite, V. S. Naipaul and Wole Soyinka had come in the 1950s and 1960s to study in British universities; others, such as the novelists George Lamming and Samuel Selvon, and the poets Dom Moraes and Peter Porter, sought work and wider opportunities for publication. After World War II, Britain had recruited thousands of people from the West Indies and the Indian subcontinent to sustain the national health and transport systems and to work in the steel and textile factories. As the children of these recruited immigrant workers began to enter the secondary school and university systems in the 1970s, teachers and students alike sought to encourage the study of African, Caribbean and Indian writing.

While Commonwealth literary studies had on the whole striven to remain apolitical, focusing on aspects such as form and style in the novels of Australian authors such as Patrick White, or the use of language in the poetry of Brathwaite and Derek Walcott, sometimes drawing comparisons with works by mainstream British authors, there was also considerable pressure to read and understand these works within a political context. In Britain and the United States, texts by African, Caribbean and Indian authors were often read within the framework of area studies programmes, such as African Studies or Asian Studies, or, especially in the United States, Black Studies or Third World Studies. In North America the Civil Rights and Black Power movements, and in Britain the racist attitudes which kept black and Asian people out of all but the most poorly paid jobs and resented their presence in British cities and suburbs, led to an increasing emphasis on political, psychological and cultural resistance to discrimination on grounds of race and colour. For authors such as Achebe in Nigeria and Brathwaite in the West Indies, as for students and teachers of African descent in Britain, the Caribbean, and the United States, the writing and reading of texts by African and Caribbean authors were seen as a means of restoring dignity and self-respect to people who had suffered from hundreds of years of contemptuous dismissal, exploitation and enslavement by Europeans. Postcolonial literature is concerned above all with the issue of self-representation in two senses of the word, the artistic and the political. Writers from the former colonies wish to speak for themselves, to tell their own stories, including the story of the colonial encounter and its consequences, and so to create the psychological base and historical understanding which will encourage wise choices in self-government. But, as Paul Gilroy and other critics have pointed out, one of the consequences of the colonial encounter has been what the African American writer W. E. B. Dubois described as a double consciousness, the ability to live within and between two cultures and two perspectives (and sometimes more), and with that the creation of a particularly postcolonial form of modernism.[9]

It is the amalgamation of Commonwealth literary studies, Black Studies and Third World Studies that has produced contemporary postcolonial literary studies, and which accounts for some of its peculiar features and the debates within the discipline. From Commonwealth literary studies it derives its embrace of a wide range of European settler colonies as well as predominantly indigenous and former slave colonies. The British Commonwealth category also involved an emphasis on English-speaking countries, writing in the English language (and the exclusion of writing in indigenous languages) and an emphasis on literary texts. Because the Commonwealth was set up in 1948, replacing the political structures and connotations covered by the term 'British Empire' for those ex-colonies which were now self-governing, it excluded former British colonies which had achieved independence and become republics prior to the 1940s, such as Ireland and the United States.

However, the influence of the Black Power and Black Arts movements in the United States, and the combination of Asian and Caribbean radicals in Britain, joining forces under the label 'black British' to contest racial prejudice and discrimination in education, law enforcement, housing and employment, as well as in society as a whole, encouraged an increasing emphasis on issues of identity, racial and cultural difference, and social and economic empowerment particularly with regard to people of African and Asian descent. In Britain and North America, academics and writers whose origins were in Africa, the Caribbean, the Indian subcontinent and Palestine became prominent intellectual leaders elaborating the connections between written discourses and Europe's political domination over the rest of the world. These academics also drew on the thinking of influential European intellectuals such as the philosophers Theodor Adorno, Hélène Cixous, Jacques Derrida and Jean-Paul Sartre, the psychoanalyst Jacques Lacan, and the sociologist Michel Foucault. The emphasis these intellectuals have placed on the power of language and modes of discourse has been particularly significant in the development of postcolonial theory.

Four names appear again and again as thinkers who have shaped postcolonial theory: Frantz Fanon, Edward Said, Homi Bhabha and Gayatri Chakravorty Spivak. Of African descent and born in the French former slave colony of Martinique in 1925, Fanon was taught by the great Martiniquan poet and

Marxist politician Aimé Césaire. He studied medicine and psychiatry in France, where Lacan was one of his teachers, and published his psychological analysis of racism and its effects, Blac k S kin, Whit e M asks , in 1952. This is a remarkable personal account and analysis of the effect of the 'colonial gaze' – of being seen, defined and stereotyped by the Europeans whose culture is deemed to be superior and to have greater authority than the cultures of Africa and the Caribbean. European appearance and culture is assumed to be the norm by which others are judged, making all others 'abnormal' and either exotic or inferior or both. Fanon writes:

> There is a fact: White men consider themselves superior to black men.
> There is another fact: Black men want to prove to white men at all costs, the richness of their thought, the equal value of their intellect.
>   How do we extricate ourselves?[10]

Fanon states his belief that 'the fact of the juxtaposition of the white and black races has created a massive psychoexistential complex,' and his hope that an analysis of that complex will help to destroy it.[11] He also declares that 'what is often called the black man's soul is the white man's artefact'.[12]

Thus Blac k S kin, Whit e M asks is a psychoanalytical study, an attempt to understand the causes of racism, and more importantly, the effects of racism and colonialism on black people and how to overcome or deal with those effects. In short, Fanon believes that to a greater or lesser extent black people had internalized the racism of those who ran the society, and either accepted an inferior status or felt the necessity to prove themselves fully human and equal – but in the white man's terms. He discusses various ways in which black intellectuals have sought to challenge racist attitudes. One chapter discusses and reluctantly rejects neg rit ude , an ideology dramatized in his poetry by Césaire and developed more extensively in essays and poetry by the Senegalese poet and politician Léopold Senghor. Senghor argued that African culture was completely distinct from but equal and complementary to European culture. Drawing on examples from the writing of Harlem Renaissance writers such as Langston Hughes, Claude McKay and Jean Toomer, as well as the cultures of his native Senegal, he claimed that rhythm, emotion and humour were the distinctive qualities of African writing, that 'emotion is completely Negro, as reason is Greek', and that Africans understood the world through intuition rather than objective analysis.[13] Senghor and other African intellectuals such as Cheikh Anta Diop also turned to precolonial African cultures and histories to illustrate the achievements of Africans ignored by modern Europeans. They wrote about the significance of Timbuktu as a centre of learning in the Middle Ages (as defined by European historians), and of the prestige accorded kingdoms such as Mali by medieval Europe. They also reclaimed Egypt and its past artefacts and monuments as part of a continental African civilization.

Fanon acknowledged the psychological importance of this historical reclamation, but he saw neg rit ude as an ideology trapped within the terms of a European dialectic, and unable to break away from the essentialism inherent in colonialist and racialist thinking. He accepted Jean-Paul Sartre's description of the movement as a necessary but passing phase in that dialectic. Sartre had written, in his Preface, entitled 'Black Orpheus', to an anthology of francophone African poetry edited by Senghor:

> In fact, Négritude appears to be the weak stage of a dialectical progression: the theoretical and practical application of white supremacy is the thesis: the position of Négritude as antithetical value is the moment of negativity. But this negative moment is not sufficient in itself and the blacks who employ it well know it; they know that it serves to pave the way for the synthesis or the realization of a raceless society. Thus Négritude is dedicated to its own destruction, it is passage and not objective, means and not the ultimate goal. At the moment the black Orpheus most directly embraces this Eurydice, he feels her slip away from between his arms.[14]

While neg rit ude was an important movement, influencing the works of many writers and scholars in the Caribbean and the United States as well as Africa, Fanon's work has perhaps had a longer-lasting effect, and has been given new impetus in the work of postcolonial theorists and writers. However, it is important to remember that Fanon is writing from a particular position at a particular time – that is, a multiracial Caribbean colony ruled by the French, where the language is entirely French or French patois, and as one of the few black intellectuals studying in France. His situation was very different from that of Ghanaians, Nigerians or Senegalese living in societies which retained their own languages and continuing traditions. Nevertheless, many anglophone African writers shared Fanon's scepticism regarding Senghor's promotion of neg rit ude . The Nigerian playwright Soyinka expressed his view that it was superfluous for Africans to broadcast their African identity, pointing out that a tiger does not need to proclaim his tigritude.[15] And Achebe was adamant that precolonial Africa must be presented honestly, not as 'some glorious technicolour idyll'.[16]

Fanon's experience working with Algerians fighting to liberate their country from French colonialism led to the publication of other essays and books, of which The W retche d of the E ar th (L es D amn es de la te rre, published in French in 1961 and in English in 1965) has become the most widely read. In this work he continues his psychological study of the colonized, but also describes the psychology of the colonizers.[17] He asserts that in order to justify their rule and occupation of the natives' territory, settlers and administrators create and define a 'Manichean Society'; that is, they classify the world of the 'native' as the opposite of everything the European supposedly represents: civilization, morality, cleanliness, law and order, wholesome masculinity.[18] So the native is by definition uncivilized or barbaric, childlike, feminine, unable to rule himself, superstitious. He is deemed to have no historical monuments, no literature, and hence no history.

Indeed, a recurring European view of Africa was that it is a place which has no history, and that history does not become significant there until the European comes on to the scene. Thus the German philosopher G. W. F. Hegel in his *Introduction to the Philosophy of History* (1837) expresses an attitude shared by many European historians even in the mid-twentieth century:[19]

> Africa proper, as far as History goes back, has remained shut up . . . The negro [*sic*] as already observed exhibits the natural man in his completely wild and untamed state. We must lay aside all thought of reverence and morality – all that we call feeling – if we would rightly comprehend him; there is nothing harmonious with humanity to be found in this type of character.
>
> At this point we leave Africa never to mention it again. For it is no historical part of the world; it has no development or movement to exhibit. Historical movement in it – that is its northern part – belongs to the Asiatic or European world. What we properly understand by Africa, is the Unhistorical, Undeveloped Spirit, still involved in the *condition of mere nature* and which has to be presented here as on the threshold of the World's History.[20]

Attitudes such as Hegel's were used to justify colonization, since it was argued that Europeans brought civilization and progress, and thus history, to Africa, or India, or Ireland, for the first time. At the same time, Africans and other colonized peoples were seen as mentally and physically adapted only for menial labour or routine clerical positions. Such justifications had been used throughout the seventeenth, eighteenth and early nineteenth centuries to justify the enslavement of millions of Africans to work in the sugar and cotton plantations of the Americas; colonial settlers and governments continued to maintain that the people they colonized were incapable of self-government or of putting their land and its resources to good use. In *The Wretched of the Earth*, Fanon maintained that European interests in retaining their hold on the lands and resources they had occupied made it almost impossible for them to change their attitudes, as Senghor hoped the *négritude* movement could. Fanon believed that settlers and colonial governments could be uprooted only by violence. Moreover, Fanon argued, such violence was a means of destroying the mental colonization and sense of racial inferiority he had analysed in his earlier work.

While Fanon had focused mainly on the relationship between colonizer and colonized in Africa and the Caribbean, the literary and cultural critic Edward Said, who was born in Palestine, concentrated more on portrayals of Asia, including India, and the Middle East. In his influential and much-debated book *Orientalism* (1978), Said is concerned with the ways in which knowledge is governed and owned by Europeans to reinforce power, and to exclude or dismiss the knowledge which natives might claim to have.[21] Drawing on Foucault's work, and his notion of systems of discourses controlled by those in power which define the 'truths' by which we live and judge others, Said refers to anthropology, history, linguistics and literary criticism as well as European literary works as a network of 'discourses' which establish a particular view of 'orientals' as a people to be governed rather than as equals who are capable of self-government. In this case, he argues, the writers about the East (or the Orient) acknowledge monuments, but only those which belong to the distant past – they are ruined monuments, and the cultures are seen as degenerate. Scholars also acknowledge writings from India and Egypt, for example, but writings in the ancient languages – Sanskrit or Egyptian cuneiform script – not contemporary writers in Arabic or Bengali or Urdu, for example. In any case, contemporary oriental societies were perceived to be in need of civilizing, and that meant European civilization. Said stresses that Orientalism refers not to a place but to an idea, and can be seen as a 'Western style for dominating, restructuring, having authority over the Orient'. He contends that:

> without examining Orientalism as a discourse one cannot possibly understand the enormously systematic discipline by which European culture was able to manage – *and even produce* – the Orient politically, sociologically, militarily, ideologically, scientifically and imaginatively during the post-Enlightenment period. . . . European culture gained in strength and identity by setting itself off against the Orient as a sort of surrogate and even underground self.[22]

Said has been criticized on the grounds that his discussion of orientalist discourse moves too readily across time and geography and does not place particular texts precisely enough within particular economic and political contexts. The fact that Said himself is criticizing orientalist discourse on these same grounds, for its lumping together and homogenising of a variety of historical and geographical examples of Eastern culture, does not entirely invalidate his critics. Nevertheless, the existence of such prestigious institutions as London University's School of Oriental and African Studies, where 'Oriental' includes such diverse areas as China, India, Japan, Iran, Iraq, Palestine and Turkey, might substantiate Said's argument.

Culture and Imperialism, which Said published fifteen years after *Orientalism*, responded in part to another criticism of his earlier work for its noninclusion of ways in which native writers had responded to orientalist attitudes, and so implicitly represented the Orient and 'orientals' as silent or silenced subjects. In this work he not only analysed the presence of empire in texts such as Jane Austen's *Mansfield Park* (1814) and Rudyard Kipling's *Kim* (1901), he also referred to writers such as Achebe, Fanon, Salman Rushdie and W. B. Yeats from colonized and postcolonial countries.[23]

Whereas Said in his earlier work had focused on academic research and European ownership of the study of the Orient and its problems, Fanon was more interested in the effects on those who have been conquered and how they should resist. In chapter 3 of *The Wretched of the Earth*, he discusses the various ways in which African and Caribbean intellectuals have responded to European stereotypes, first by internalizing European views of them and their cultures and showing that they can mimic the white man, and behave just like him. A second stage comes when these intellectuals, finding that they are discriminated against despite their demonstrably equal intelligence and educational attainment, begin to protest against this discriminatory treatment, often in terms of the very values which the Europeans have proclaimed – especially equality and justice. Another move by educated Africans seeks to validate their own culture and civilization by rediscovering a buried history and celebrating early achievements, including the Egyptian pyramids, the medieval cities and scholarship found in Timbuktu, Mali and Ghana, the kingdoms of Ashanti and the Zulu King Chaka, the kingdoms and buildings of Benin and ancient Zimbabwe, and so on. These acknowledgements of early African achievements were important, but to some extent they might be seen as accepting and responding to European views and values regarding what is historically significant, what is worth celebrating. And they also left open the question of why these kingdoms and centres of learning or artistic achievement did not survive.

Fanon believed that such restoration of the past was an important factor in giving colonized people the confidence to envision a future without European rule and a nation capable of future achievements. It responded to and negated the European insistence that Africans were incapable of creating a civilization – or anything worth while. Moreover, the writing of an African or Indian history might involve a different view of events already narrated by British historians.

For example, what the British named the 'Indian Mutiny' of 1857 is renamed by some Indian historians as the 'First War of Indian Independence' or the 'Great Indian Uprising'.

But Fanon also insisted that the recovery of the past was not enough. In other words, cultural nationalism of this kind was necessary if one was to restore confidence and create a sense of identity, but it was not sufficient if the land occupied by colonizers was to be retrieved and self-government achieved. Writers and intellectuals would need to be aware of current issues, political and economic concerns, and they would need to be in tune with the people as a whole, not just a small intellectual elite. For some writers, this meant an engagement with 'folk culture', a concern to speak of and for the folk – usually defined as the peasantry or rural population, rather than the urban residents. Fanon believed that it was also necessary for writers to propose a political programme to show the way towards liberation. This might be seen as one of the tasks Raja Rao took on in *Kanthapura* (1938), like Mulk Raj Anand previously in *The Untouchable* (1935) and *Coolie* (1936), and Ngugi in his later works such as *Petals of Blood* (1977) and *Matigari* (1986).

There is also a related historical movement with regard to the rewriting of history, which is referred to as subaltern history or Subaltern Studies. The term 'subaltern' signifies those who are not part of the ruling group, and subaltern history refers to the history of those groups – those who are subordinated by the dominant class, which is usually the author and subject of history. In other words, most historical narratives have traditionally foregrounded the achievements or misdeeds of kings, presidents, prime ministers and the classes and cultures associated with them; subaltern histories might deal with the groups they dominated – perhaps the working class, perhaps women, perhaps members of a lower caste. The study of subaltern groups has been particularly influential in India and has played a significant part in the work of another very influential postcolonial scholar, Gayatri Chakravorty Spivak. Spivak, who was born in Calcutta but rapidly became a prominent academic in the United States after gaining her doctorate at Cornell University and publishing a translation of Jacques Derrida's seminal work *De la Grammatologie* (1967: published in English as *On Grammatology* in 1976), has taken on the difficult task of bringing Marxist, deconstructionist and feminist theory to bear upon her analysis of American, Bengali, British and French texts. Influential essays including 'Three Women's Texts and a Critique of Imperialism' and 'Can the Subaltern Speak?' explore the ignored or distorted presence of colonized women in texts such as Charlotte Brontë's *Jane Eyre* (1847) and in official records maintained by British officials in India regarding *sati*. Spivak also insists that scholars should be self-conscious about the ways in which their own positions as academics in tertiary institutions, most often in the 'First World,' relate to the ways in which their work is produced and received.[24]

A fourth critic and theorist whose name frequently recurs in discussions of postcolonial literary and cultural studies is Homi Bhabha. Drawing on psychoanalytical theory with particular reference to Sigmund Freud and Lacan, Bhabha has elaborated the key concepts of mimicry and hybridity. Whereas Fanon and Said have analysed the oppositions set up in colonialist and anti-colonialist societies, Bhabha has sought to demonstrate that their discourses contain ambivalences and ambiguities. He argues that the 'mimicry' of colonizers by colonized subjects can be a form of subversion, since it makes unstable the insistence on difference ('them' and 'us') which forms the basis of colonialist and nationalist ideologies.[25] Like Said and Spivak, Bhabha celebrates the 'hybridity' of postcolonial cultures, seeing their embrace of European as well as indigenous traditions as a positive advantage which allows their writers and critics to understand and critique the West as both insiders and outsiders.

Until recently, it has been the approaches and concepts developed by Said, Spivak and Bhabha that have dominated postcolonial literary theory and criticism. However, their work has been vociferously rejected by the Indian scholar Aijaz Ahmad, who attacks both Said and the American academic Fredric Jameson for their homogenizing of 'Third World' writing, and their concentration on European and European language texts to the neglect of indigenous language writing in, for example, Arabic, Hindi, Urdu or Yoruba.[26] Ahmad is also fiercely critical of poststructuralism and the abstractions which he sees as a feature of much postcolonial theory, especially the theories elaborated by Bhabha and Spivak. He shares with Benita Parry, another opponent of theories based on poststructuralism, a commitment to Marxism as a basis for analysing the conflicts between colonizing and colonized nations, and for resisting new forms of domination.[27]

While Bhabha, Said and Spivak, and more recently Kwame Anthony Appiah, Paul Gilroy, Edouard Glissant and Stuart Hall, have most strongly influenced the critics of postcolonial literatures, it is Fanon who has perhaps most influenced writers – particularly in Africa and the Caribbean, and particularly in the earlier phases of resistance to colonization and the creation of a national consciousness. (And for this reason this study places particular emphasis on Fanon's analysis of colonialism and its effects.) Ngugi has written about Fanon, and his later fiction and drama follows many of Fanon's precepts regarding the role of a revolutionary writer. Walcott's *Dream on Monkey Mountain* (1970; discussed in the next chapter) can be read as a dramatization of Fanon's analysis of black subjectivity in *Black Skin, White Masks*. Lamming's novel *In The Castle of My Skin* (1953), published one year after Fanon's first book, shows its influence in the title as well as the portrayal of the internalization of racism by Barbadians. Some of Achebe's early essays indicate an acquaintance with Fanon and Sartre's responses to *négritude* as 'an anti-racist racism'.[28] Like Fanon, he writes of the need to restore the self-esteem of African people, to assert that they did not hear of civilization for the first time from Europe; and he declares that the greatest sin of all was the African's acceptance of inferiority. Fanon's work has also inspired Bhabha, who likewise draws on psychoanalytical models to discuss identity, and who has written a substantial introduction to *Black Skin, White Masks*.[29]

My discussion of postcolonial writing will be informed by these theories and concepts, and to other critics who draw on them, though my focus will be on the literary texts rather than the theories. Thus concepts such as hybridity, othering, Creolité, mimicry and the subaltern, will recur frequently in the chapters that follow. But it is important not to assume that 'theory' relevant to postcolonial literary analysis is confined to those three or four names which have become so dominant in the past two decades. Essays by many of the writers, such as Achebe, Lamming, Ngugi, Rushdie and Walcott have been equally influential in providing a framework and an orientation through which to approach not only their own writings but also those of others. Hence I have drawn attention to such essays as they became relevant. And of course much critical discourse which is not limited to postcolonial writing has also informed my thinking about these texts.

In the chapters that follow, each will include detailed analysis of one or more literary texts which relate to a particular concern in postcolonial writing and criticism. However, each chapter will also refer to relevant texts from other geographical areas, and other aspects of the chosen texts will be picked up and referred to in subsequent chapters. Rather than being arranged according to various territories (African, Caribbean, Indian, etc.), the structure of the book is designed in part to enable a sense of the diversity of texts and approaches as well as contexts, and an awareness that no one framework is adequate to all areas or texts subsumed under the postcolonial umbrella. I do not attempt to provide a complete coverage of postcolonial writing in English. As noted in the Preface, instead of skating thinly over many surfaces, I considered it more sensible to concentrate on literary texts from several areas which represent different histories of colonial and postcolonial relationships. Thus I have chosen to refer mainly to writers from the Indian subcontinent, from East and West Africa, from Australia, from the Caribbean, from the black and Asian diaspora communities in Britain, and from Ireland. By focusing on writers mainly but not exclusively from just three different settler postcolonial areas (Australia, East Africa and Ireland), three differing administrative ex-colonies (Ghana,

India and Nigeria), and two areas which contain large and diverse diasporic communities (Britain and the Caribbean), I hope the book will give its readers a fuller and richer sense of the cultural and literary contexts and debates within those communities, as well as the variety of writing which has been produced within and across these postcolonies.

One of the more contentious aspects of this study is the inclusion of Irish writers. While it is the case that because of the development of postcolonial studies from Commonwealth literary studies on the one hand, and Black Studies and Third World Studies on the other, Irish writing has traditionally been neglected in postcolonial literary studies, this situation is rapidly changing. Said includes a long section on Yeats as a nationalist writer in his *Culture and Imperialism*; David Lloyd has consistently written about nineteenth- and twentieth-century Irish writers in the context of postcolonial writing, as have Marjorie Howes and more recently Elizabeth Butler Cullingford.[30] Jahan Ramazani's *The Hybrid Muse: Postcolonial Poetry in English* (2001)[31] begins with a discussion of Irish literature and a chapter on Yeats, and there have been several 'postcolonial' readings of Joyce published in the past decade. Other American, British and Irish academics such as Gregory Castle, Joe Cleary, Terry Eagleton, Jed Esty, Colin Graham, Glenn Hooper, Declan Kiberd and John Nash have found comparisons between Irish and other postcolonial literatures fruitful.

Thus the inclusion of Irish literature under the postcolonial remit takes account of changing perspectives which are to some extent revising the earlier frameworks for viewing postcolonial writing. Such perspectives include a growing awareness of race as constructed rather than given, and an interest in varieties of colonial experience rather than simple binary paradigms along colour lines. In the context of the British Empire and the Darwinian evolutionary theory of the mid-nineteenth century, the Irish were often seen as an in-between race, belonging not only to what Bhabha has defined as the ambivalent world of the 'not quite/not white' but also to the 'not quite/not black',[32] as suggested in a letter written to his wife by the English novelist Charles Kingsley while travelling in Ireland in 1860. He wrote:

> But I am haunted by the human chimpanzees I saw along that hundred
> miles of horrible country. I don't believe they are our fault. I believe
> there are not only more of them than of old, but that they are happier,
> better, more comfortably fed and lodged under our rule than they ever
> were. But to see white chimpanzees is dreadful; if they were black, one
> would not feel it so much, but their skins, except where tanned by
> exposure, are as white as ours.[33]

Postcolonial critics have also drawn attention to Irish literature in the context of making distinctions between the modernisms that were a product of colonial experience and those that were more clearly based in metropolitan centres.[34] Moreover, the Irish cultural renaissance was influenced by comparisons with other nationalist literary movements (especially in India), and in turn became a significant model for later postcolonial writers including Walcott. Some of those interactions will be discussed in later chapters, and especially the next one.

Chapter 2, 'Postcolonial issues in performance', will focus on the role of theatre in various African and Irish contexts, before going on to a more detailed discussion of two plays and the circumstances in which they were first created and performed: Walcott's *Dream of Monkey Mountain* and Brian Friel's *Translations* (1980). These texts and their first productions provide a means of discussing the complex cultural mixtures of Trinidad (and St Lucia) and the politics of (London)Derry and the Field Day project, leading to an exploration of the wider issue of reading the politics of the past through the politics of the present. Both Walcott and Friel interrogate various nationalist myths and notions of cultural purity such as *négritude* and Irishness. Both plays also raise the problem of translating cultures, and finding an appropriate language and idiom to express a culture distinct from the colonial one. The discussion of the Field Day project will also include brief reference to the question of Ireland as a (post)colonial territory and culture (acknowledging that territory and culture may not always overlap). This chapter serves as an introduction to many of the main topics to be explored later with regard to other specific texts, topics such as language, place, mapping, history, cultural hybridity, genre and audience.

Chapter 3 takes up the issue of alternative and subaltern histories, considering early cultural nationalist works, and views of local history and culture 'from the inside' in response to the colonial and Hegelian insistence on a lack of 'native' history. There will be reference to differing histories and cultural contexts and how these affect writing. In addition to 'historical' narratives, there will be analysis of how and to what purpose different writers and groups have invoked myth and legend, and also reworked and appropriated 'European' myths. Here further distinctions will be made between male and female writers and histories. The chapter includes detailed analysis of Achebe's *Things Fall Apart* (1958), Brathwaite's *The Arrivants* (1973), and Aidoo's *Our Sister Killjoy* (1977).

One means of establishing a new starting point for the writing of a national history which is not defined within the terms of the colonialist version of history is autobiography. Chapter 4 explores the prevalence of autobiographical writing in much colonial and early postcolonial literature, analysing the ways in which the story of the individual does and does not provide a base for departing from the collective history imposed by the colonizer on the one hand and the cultural nationalist on the other. Among other works in this chapter I will refer to Miles Franklin's *My Beautiful Career* (1901), as well as poetry and fiction by Joyce and Yeats. These analyses also draw distinctions between the projects of male-authored autobiographical works in relation to the nationalist project, and female ones which often question such constructions of the nation. Lamming's *In the Castle of My Skin* (1953) and Sally Morgan's *My Place* (1987) are considered in greater detail.

As Said remarked with regard to Yeats, geography and the naming of places plays a prominent part in the work of many anticolonial and nationalist writers.[35] Chapter 5 discusses the perceived importance of reclaiming, remapping and revisioning the land, its flora and fauna, particularly in settler colonies. It contrasts the portrayals of landscape and place in the works of early settlers and visitors and those of later postcolonial writers. Here the gendering of land and landscape and its consequence for women writers (as, for example, analysed by Aidoo and Eavan Boland) is noted, but will be developed in more detail in Chapter 8. The topic is explored in greater depth here through essays and selected poems by Walcott (and his view of the writer as 'Adam'), and then through four generations of Australian writers: Henry Kendall, Henry Lawson, Judith Wright and Les Murray.

The question of which language to use and its relation to authentic identity has been a fraught one from the beginnings of postcolonial writing. Chapter 6 outlines the debates over language (vernacular or English, standard or Creole) through a number of different positions, and the debates which took place in Ireland, Africa, and the Caribbean and Ireland. I analyse different attempts to create recognizably national or 'nation languages' in the works of Australian, Caribbean, Indian and Irish authors, and look in particular detail at works by Louise Bennett, Brathwaite, Synge and Walcott. This chapter also includes discussion of 'performance poetry'; the significance of its emphasis on voice, presence and communal response; and the use of oral 'literatures' and performance as a model in much postcolonial writing.

Alongside the issue of language, and whether the English language could adequately express the experience of people whose worlds, attitudes, histories and experiences were very different from those of people whose history was rooted in England, postcolonial authors and critics have debated the question of form and genre. Can the form of the sonnet, developed during the European Renaissance, be adapted to express contemporary Caribbean or Irish thoughts? Seamus Heaney, Walcott and Yeats have used the sonnet and other traditional forms, but have often given them a new significance. The Caribbean novelist

Wilson Harris argued that the traditional form of the novel of manners was inappropriate for societies which needed to break from European assumptions and conventions, and embraced a form of fiction which radically questioned our concepts of realism.[36] Chapter 7 therefore explores questions of genre conventions and expectations, and how they may or may not be appropriate to the aims and concerns of postcolonial writers. It concludes with a detailed study of Rushdie's *Midnight's Children* (1981). The following chapter picks up and elaborates the brief discussions in previous chapters regarding gendered histories, narratives and landscapes, with specific reference to responses by postcolonial women writers to male colonial and postcolonial representations.

Critics have sometimes described postcolonial literatures as very roughly falling into several phases: literature of resistance; literature of national consolidation; literature of disillusion and/or neocolonialism; post-postcolonial literature; and diaspora literature. Although these categories rarely fit neatly, this book will have followed these phases to some extent, discussing literature of resistance and national consolidation in the first chapters. Later chapters deal with the literature by both male and female authors which portrays and opposes neocolonialism, whereby multinational companies and economically powerful nations such as Britain and the United States continue to control the economies and often the politics of newly independent states. Chapter 9 will focus on the sense of disillusion expressed by authors such as Ayi Kwei Armah, Ngugi, Arundhati Roy and Rushdie, who expose the betrayal of the nation and its ideals by its leaders. However, as this chapter will discuss, authors such as Roy and Rushdie are also concerned to make room in their novels for marginalized peoples and groups. Whereas earlier nationalist novels and plays often implied a homogenous national identity, many later writers seek to acknowledge and celebrate a heterogeneous and inclusive nation. In some cases, for example Australia and Canada, this movement also involves increasing acknowledgement of indigenous peoples as writers and speaking subjects, rather than simply subjects for writing. But in all cases there is also a sometimes troubled recognition of the nation as an immigrant nation with a multiplicity of ethnicities and cultures. Here, too, the question of languages and voices becomes significant. In this chapter Abdulrazak Gurnah's novel *Paradise* (1994) is given detailed attention.

Chapter 10 continues this discussion of heterogeneity, but with a specific focus on Britain, exploring the particular relationships of postcolonial writers within the 'heart of empire'. It will cover briefly the changes occurring since the 1950s, responses to the 'mother country', the establishment of communities of writers and audiences, and the development of institutions and publications which encouraged such writing and readerships.

The concluding chapter discusses why and how different kinds of readers respond to postcolonial texts. For example, a Trinidadian reader might read V. S. Naipaul's earlier novels with delighted or dismayed recognition, finding his or her own world portrayed in the work of a fellow national, whereas a reader who has never been to Trinidad may feel he or she is discovering a new and exotic world. But there can also be a complex interplay between these kinds of readings. Readers are also influenced by critics and varying critical approaches, by publishers and cultural institutions (including educational ones and books such as this one), and by state institutions which may censor or ban the works of particular authors. This final chapter refers back to texts previously discussed for examples.

Chapter 2

Postcolonial issues in performance

Drama has played a crucial part in the development of national cultures and audiences, and yet has received relatively little attention in postcolonial literary studies. This is all the more surprising given that dramatic performance raises so many issues that are central to postcolonial cultures – questions of identity, language, myth and history; issues regarding translatability, voice and audience; problems relating to production, infrastructures and censorship. In *The Wretched of the Earth* (1965), it is drama rather than poetry or the novel that Frantz Fanon advocates as the best means of raising the consciousness of people involved in an anticolonial struggle. In cultures where literacy has been confined mainly to a small elite group, and where there is a continuing oral culture with roots in precolonial traditions, drama and performance provide a means of reaching a much wider indigenous audience and tapping into forms and conventions which are already familiar to them. As W. B. Yeats wrote in retrospect in his *Autobiographies* (1926), 'the great mass of our people, accustomed to interminable rhetorical speeches, read little, and so from the very start we felt that we must have a theatre of our own'.[1]

Thus Yeats, Lady Gregory and Edward Martyn set out in 1897 to create an Irish Literary Theatre (using the term 'literary' to emphasize that it would not cater to purely commercial interests). They stated their aims thus:

> We propose to have performed in Dublin in the spring of every year certain Celtic and Irish plays, which whatever be their degree of excellence will be written with high ambition, and so to build up a Celtic and Irish school of dramatic literature. We hope to find in Ireland an uncorrupted and imaginative audience trained to listen by its passion for oratory, and believe that our desire to bring upon the stage the deeper thoughts and emotions of Ireland will ensure for us a tolerant welcome, and that freedom to experiment which is not found in theatres of England, and without which no new movement in art or literature can succeed.

> We will show that Ireland is not the home of buffoonery and easy
> sentiment, as it has been represented, but the home of an ancient
> idealism. We are confident of the support of all Irish people, who are
> weary of misrepresentation, in carrying out a work that is outside all the
> political questions that divide us.[2]

As Christopher Morash points out, this statement of intent was both disingen-
uous and liberating. 'The Irish Literary Theatre came into being by imagining
an empty space where in fact there was a crowded room.' By ignoring the existence of various Irish theatrical traditions going back to at least the seventeenth
century, 'the Irish Literary Theatre was able – indeed, it was compelled – to
imagine afresh its relationship to Irish history', and also to Irish audiences.[3]

In fact, the hopes for a tolerant and supportive audience were soon con-
founded with the inaugural production of the Irish Literary Theatre, Yeats's
Countess Cathleen (1892). This was not only a highly literary play, but ran
counter to the myths, beliefs and oral traditions associated with the Irish famine
(1845–7), when the play is set. Yeats's portrayal of a member of the landlord
class who sells her soul to the devil in order to save the starving peasantry
offended deeply held Catholic beliefs about the priority of spiritual salvation,
as well as their historical experience of landlords as exploiters and dispossess-
ors of the Irish poor rather than their saviours. Four years later, however, Yeats
and Lady Gregory did meet with acclaim for their nationalist play *Cathleen ni
Houlihan* (1902), which drew on folk legend and myth as well as nationalist
desire by invoking a popular representation of Ireland as the 'Shan Van Vocht'
(poor old woman) who is made young and beautiful again by the willingness
of young men to go out and fight for her. The play received an enthusiastic
response, and Stephen Gwynn, who saw it as a young man, later wrote:

> The effect of *Cathleen ni Houlihan* on me was that I went home asking
> myself if such plays should be produced unless one was prepared for
> people to go out to shoot and be shot. Yeats was not alone responsible;
> no doubt but that Lady Gregory had helped him to get the peasant
> speech so perfect; but above all Miss Gonne's impersonation had stirred
> the audience as I have never seen another audience stirred.[4]

The unqualified approval of this play by Irish nationalists meant that Yeats
and Lady Gregory had created a sympathetic audience for the successor to their
Irish Literary Theatre, which was rechristened the Irish National Theatre and in
1904 housed in the now-famous Abbey Theatre. However, that enthusiasm was
soon to be severely tested by another play which drew in a different way on Irish
folk culture, *The Shadow of the Glen* (1905) by J. M. Synge. Its central figure is
Nora, married to a much older and miserly husband, and lonely and unfulfilled

in a remote glen in Co. Wicklow. The play draws on an anecdote Synge heard when he lived among the people of the Aran Islands about a husband who pretends to be dead in order to spy on his wife. At the end of the play, Nora leaves with a tramp who has sought shelter and food in her house, and who offers 'a fine bit of talk' rather than respectability and the certainty of food and shelter.

Those who objected to the play saw it as a 'scandalous slur' on Irish woman-hood, claimed to be 'the most virtuous in the world'. Critics insisted it was not a realistic representation of Irish life, and, noting the resemblances to Henrik Ibsen's play *The Doll's House* (1879), in which another Nora abandons her love-less and unfulfilling marriage, accused the theatre management of importing dangerous foreign influences. In a letter to the *United Irishman* newspaper, Yeats defended the freedom of the National Theatre to stage works which drew on whatever influences the playwrights found inspiring. In return, the socialist political leader James Connolly argued that at this point in its history, that is, while the nation was in formation and yet to become independent, it was necessary to build up an Irish-based drama which both reflected and reflected upon Irish life.[5]

The arguments surrounding the foundation of the Irish National Theatre and the production of Synge's play would be played out again and again not only in later Abbey Theatre productions such as Synge's *The Playboy of the Western World* (1907) and Sean O'Casey's *The Plough and the Stars* (1926), but also in new theatre movements throughout the postcolonial world. In every new nation there have been continuing debates about the role of a national theatre, whether it should focus on reflecting the life and culture of the citizens of the nation 'realistically' or critically, and whether it should bring plays from other parts of the world to 'enlarge' the consciousness of its audiences. Should a national theatre encourage an idealized vision of what the community and its citizens might be (perhaps through enacting examples of heroic resistance and a precolonial past less inglorious than the one described by colonialist narratives), or should it encourage contemporary 'realism' and self-criticism? Given a history of derogatory representation, especially on stage, is it the role of a national theatre to restore self-respect and remind its audience of a heroic history and a tradition of 'ancient idealism'? What language is appropriate, and can English be used to depict the experience and culture of the indigenous population? To what extent can nationalist playwrights borrow forms, conven-tions, and plots from other cultures and still represent and speak to their own society? In many of those debates, the characterization of women becomes a focus for critical consternation, for women are often seen to embody the nation and preserve its traditions.

In Ireland these issues came to the boil in 1907 with the production of Synge's *The Playboy of the Western World* at the Abbey Theatre. The audience was outraged by what its members saw as the loose behaviour and language of the central woman character, Pegeen Mike; they objected to the language of Christy Mahon, the hero, with its liberal sprinkling of oaths; they were offended by the stark realism of the staging, showing Christy's father with a bloody and bandaged head. To many nationalists, the play seemed a travesty of the National Theatre's original aims, showing not 'ancient idealism' but just that 'buffoonery and easy sentiment' which had characterised representations of the Irish for so many years. Heckling and riots broke out, causing Yeats and other members of the management to bring in the police, with the bizarre result that the Irish National Theatre had to be protected by English police.[6]

Despite the controversies surrounding the Irish National Theatre and the Abbey productions and playwrights, they have provided a model and an inspiration for many later postcolonial playwrights and writers. The Australian playwright and poet Louis Esson, now seen by many as the father of Australian drama, was particularly inspired by Synge and Yeats in his attempt to create a national theatre for Australia. In particular, he drew on Synge as a model for a kind of drama which represented 'the folk' and used a modified version of the language and idioms characteristic of Australian rural and working classes[7]. However, his bush vignettes and characters, as in *Dead Timber* (1911) and *The Drover's Wife* (1920), lacked the linguistic vitality and dramatic plots that Synge was able to adapt from the stories and Irish-inflected English he heard among the Irish peasantry. In the 1940s Douglas Stewart was one of a number of artists who used the Irish-Australian outlaw Ned Kelly as a focus for reflecting on Australian identity. Stewart's verse play, *Ned Kelly* (1941), is often reminiscent of Yeats's drama in its style, technique and philosophy, though its realism perhaps owes more to Synge.[8]

Courses on Irish drama taught at Ibadan University College, Nigeria, in the 1950s may well have influenced Nigerian writers such as Wole Soyinka and John (Pepper Clark) Bekederemo, not so much in terms of their style and technique as in encouraging the link between theatre and nationalism. However, both these playwrights were also able to draw on vibrant and continuing West African dramatic traditions, and so to create a distinctive form of theatre, often primarily African in its concerns, conventions, and techniques, but also employing English as its main language and inflected by ancient and contemporary European drama, notably classical Greek tragedy and the epic theatre of Bertolt Brecht. Soyinka established and directed several theatre groups, including 'The 1960 Masks' in Ibadan and the Orisun Theatre Company in 1964 in Lagos. One of Soyinka's earliest plays, *The Lion and the Jewel*, first performed in 1959 at the Royal Court Theatre in London, has several similarities with Synge's *The Playboy of the Western World*. Like *The Playboy*, Soyinka's play dramatizes the desire of a young man, in some ways resembling the caricatures fashioned by English writers, to win in marriage a beautiful rural maiden who also personifies (or is perceived to personify) the nation. Both plays end with the maiden finally rejecting her younger suitor and choosing to live within a patriarchal society. And both plays also involve a contest within their theatrical conventions and ethos between realism and fantasy, or as Synge put it in his Preface to *The Playboy*, between a literature rich in imagination and language and, on the other hand, 'Ibsen and Zola dealing with the reality of life in joyless and pallid words'. 'On the stage,' Synge went on to say, 'one must have reality, and one must have joy.'[9]

In Soyinka's play the acceptance of patriarchal society is presented much more positively than in Synge's, and a reconciliation is sought not only between realism, as a means of representing society, and nonrealistic staging, but also between Western technology and traditional Yoruba customs and values. Lakunle, the young protagonist and suitor of the beautiful maiden Sidi, seeks to turn her into a 'modern' woman, wearing skirts and blouses, covering her breasts and learning to speak 'correctly'. He has much in common with Mister Johnson, the eponymous protagonist of Joyce Cary's 1939 novel, who ardently aspires to be like the British, wears Western clothes, and tries in vain to persuade his young bride to do likewise. (More will be said about this character and the novelist Chinua Achebe's response to him in the next chapter). As in Synge's play (and indeed Cary's novel), clothing has a significant role, together with the identities it symbolizes, as well as the identities that can be put on and cast off. Although Sidi finds Lakunle and his aping of Western customs ridiculous, and rejects him in favour of the aged patriarch and head of the village, Baroka, neither Soyinka nor Baroka reject Western technology and art forms altogether. For just as Christy Mahon in Synge's play sees his reflection in a mirror and admires what he sees, Sidi sees herself captured in a photograph in a fashion magazine, and it is through this image that she is wooed and won by Baroka when he promises to issue a stamp bearing her picture. Thus her image will officially represent her region as it moves into modes of administration and communication made possible and necessary by the implementation of European technology and forms of government. But this combining of Western technology and Yoruba tradition operates not just on a thematic level; one of the achievements of Soyinka's play on stage is the brilliant and energetic choreography, based on Yoruba dance, which mimics the activities of the photographer and also of a cyclist. (Photography also functions dramatically to define and capture identity in Athol Fugard's plays composed jointly with John

Kani and Winston Ntshona, *Statements After an Arrest under the Immorality Act* (1972) and *Sizwe Bansi is Dead* (1972).)

I have drawn attention to certain resemblances between the earlier Irish play and Soyinka's comedy not to suggest that Soyinka borrowed from Synge but rather to suggest themes, issues, tropes and strategies that recur in anti-colonial and postcolonial writing. One could also notice similarities between Yeats's much more solemn verse drama *The King's Threshold* (1904/1922) and Soyinka's *Death and the King's Horseman* (1975). In Yeats's play the poet and protector of tradition Seanchan goes on a hunger strike and dies rather than submit to the King's 'modernizing' decree that the chief poet should no longer have a place on his council, for the King believes that reason and pragmatism must supplant spiritual principles. In Soyinka's play the son of a Yoruba king's horseman wills his own death when his father's ritual suicide, prescribed by tradition, is interrupted by the well-meaning British District Officer. Here, as in the Yeats play, much of the dramatic interest focuses on the conflicting values of a Western secular and pragmatic society (and a prejudiced one), and a traditional society in which spiritual values both add to and supersede the fullness of life in this world. But neither Soyinka's play nor Yeats's (particularly the revised 1922 version) should be viewed as confined to dramatizing the conflict between cultures; both writers are concerned with the role of honour and honourable behaviour as a principal value in societies where self-interest and self-preservation seemed to have brought conflict, civil war and corruption to destroy the utopian dream of a postcolonial nation.

Soyinka had foreshadowed this danger in some of his earlier plays, sometimes comically, as in *The Trials of Brother Jero* (1960), sometimes solemnly, as in *A Dance of the Forests*, the play he was commissioned to write for the Nigerian independence celebrations in 1960. It seeks, as Martin Banham remarks, to be 'both a celebration and a morality play': 'The celebration . . . is of language and culture – the poet speaking with his own voice of his own people. The moral concerns the responsibilities of government, and shows how man too often pursues aims that are selfish and narrow and attempts to further his own interests at the expense of his fellow men.'[10] *A Dance of the Forests* celebrates African culture not only by invoking and elaborating Yoruba mythology through the ancestral figures and the personas of the Forest Father, the god Ogun and the 'wayward cult-spirit' Eshuoro, but also through its employment of some of the conventions of Yoruba opera, including dance, mask, music and the mingling of supernatural and legendary elements. Through the figure of Demoke, once a court poet and now a carver, it also raises the issue of the role of the artist in relation to the traditions of the past, and the future of his community.[11]

A number of critics, African as well as Western, have dismissed Soyinka's drama as too obscure and elitist.[12] Some felt that for these reasons *A Dance of the Forests* was an inappropriate choice for the Nigerian independence celebrations. But as another critic, Annemarie Heywood observes, this and other Soyinka plays appear obscure and incoherent 'only if one's expectations are geared to narrative articulation and character development;' in other words, to the conventions of realist European drama.[13] Rather, the plays should be viewed as surrealist spectacle, produced and plotted 'as masques or cabaret, with characters conceived as masks, dialogue as choral, movement and gesture as emblematic'.[14] However, Soyinka's plays are remarkable not only for his use of spectacle and often exuberant dance, but also for his equally exuberant use of language, and his delight in African proverbs, metaphors and idioms. Later plays such as *The Road* (1965) and *Death and the King's Horseman* include a vibrant mix of speech and verse in English, Yoruba and 'pidgin'. These two plays, like *The Lion and the Jewel*, derive much of their comedy as well as their satirical force, through episodes in which mimicry is highlighted, and here we might call to mind Homi Bhabha's discussion of mimicry as a subversive tool,[15] whether 'sincere' as in the case of Lakunle, or parodic, as in the case of the villagers in that play or the market women in *Death and the King's Horseman*.

The Ghanaian author Ama Ata Aidoo also combines traditional African forms and historic events as a means of raising issues about moral responsibility and the community's future. In 1943 it was in Ghana (then called the Gold Coast) that the first two full-length plays in English by West Africans had been published by J. B. Danquah and F. K. Fiawoo, and in the 1950s theatre was written and promoted by Efua Sutherland, who drew on traditional Akan forms to create a storytelling performance art, involving music and dance as well as language. Following the achievement of independence in Ghana in 1957, Sutherland founded the Experimental Theatre Players, producing work in both English and Akan. Three years later, this group was to have its own building, the Ghana Drama Studio, one of the first modern African theatres to be based on an indigenous model rather than the European model with its platform and proscenium arch. Aidoo also drew on the storytelling performance model for her two early plays, *The Dilemma of a Ghost* and *Anowa* first staged in 1964 and 1969 respectively. As do Soyinka and Achebe, she creates an Africanized form of English for her characters, an English which conveys the impression of speech in Akan. Like *The Lion and the Jewel*, *The Dilemma of a Ghost* deals with the conflict between Western customs and values embraced by a younger generation (in this case Kofi, who has studied in the United States, and his African American wife), and the traditions adhered to by Kofi's parents. And like *A Dance of the Forests*, *Anowa* passes judgement on Ghana's past, in this case its complicity with slavery, as a means of calling for individual and communal responsibility, and a shift away from materialism and self-interest, in the future.

Soyinka and Aidoo both create a hybrid drama, combining Western and African conventions, and both choose the English language as their primary medium for drama, though it is an English mingled with and inflected by indigenous languages. The Kenyan author Ngugi wa Thiong'o also wrote his early plays in English. *The Black Hermit* (1962) was first performed during Uganda's Uhuru (freedom) celebrations, and perhaps less ambivalently and more pessimistically than Soyinka's and Aidoo's first plays, dramatizes the conflict between traditional rural values (mainly represented by the village women) and Westernized urban values (mainly represented by the young male protagonist). Whereas the two West African plays end with the reconciliation of their heroine with her elders, Ngugi's heroine commits suicide in the last act. (As does the eponymous heroine Anowa in Aidoo's second play). In the Preface to the play, published six years after it was first performed, Ngugi remarks on the difference between his views then and in 1968: 'I thought then that tribalism was the biggest problem besetting the new East African countries . . . [that] all we had to do was to expose and root out the cantankerous effects of tribalism, racialism and religious factions.'[16]

During the next decade, Ngugi encountered the writings of Fanon and George Lamming, as well as the theatre of Brecht. Fanon's call to African intellectuals to join forces with the peasantry and write dramas of resistance is echoed in the Preface to *The Trial of Dedan Kimathi* (1976), the play that Ngugi jointly wrote and produced with Micaere Githae-Mugo: 'We believe that good theatre is that which is on the side of the people, that which, without masking mistakes and weaknesses, gives people courage and urges them to higher resolves in their struggle for total liberation.'[17]

This play sought to overturn the representation of the Mau Mau leader Kimathi as merely crazed and brutal in Kenneth Watene's 1974 play of the same name. Ngugi and Githae-Mugo aim to recreate Kimathi as a man committed to the freedom of his country and his people, the courageous hero of folk memory. Although based on the actual transcripts of his trial, the play is not naturalistic but draws on Gikuyu songs, mime and dance, as well as oratory. Like Brechtian theatre, which likewise drew its inspiration from folk song and pageant, the play is epic rather than realistic, calling on the audience to understand the issues, judge and take action. It also intersperses mimed 'scenes from the black man's history', including the enslavement of Africans sold by African chiefs to white traders. The audience response in Nairobi was enthusiastic, with many spectators joining in the final triumphant dance and continuing it in the streets.

Ngugi's experience with this play encouraged him to take theatre further in the direction of community and collaborative theatre, using the language of the rural Gikuyu people. In this play also, he celebrates the role of women in the struggle for liberation. With Ngugi wa Mirrii and members of the community he devised a play, *Ngaahika Ndeenda* (1977; translated as *I Will Marry When I Want*), which revolves around the theft of a labourer's small plot of land by a wealthy Christian businessman, and the seduction and abandonment of the labourer's daughter by the businessman's son. Ngugi described it as depicting 'the proletarisation of the peasantry in a neocolonial society'.[18] Employing mime, song and dance, as well as dialogue and exposition, the play attracted large crowds of people enthusiastic about a performance in Gikuyu and applauding the play's critique of society and call for action. The Kamiruthu Cultural Centre, which had worked with Ngugi on the play, received delegations from other rural Communities asking for advice and help in setting up similar cultural centres and theatrical events. But the play also attracted the attention of the authorities. The Kiambu District Commissioner withdrew the licence for performances and Ngugi was arrested and detained without trial for nearly a year. Ngugi later wrote about the experience in his book *Detained: A Writer's Prison Diary* (1981):

> The six months between June and November 1977 were the most exciting in my life and the true beginning of my education. I learnt my language anew. I rediscovered the creative nature and power of collective work.
>
> . . .
>
> Although the overall direction of the play was under Kimani Gecau, the whole project became a collective community effort with peasants and workers seizing more and more initiative in revising and adding to the script, in directing dance movements on the stage, and in the general organization.
>
> . . .
>
> The rehearsals, arranged to fit in with the working rhythms of the village, which meant mostly Saturday and Sunday afternoons, were all in the open, attracting an ever-increasing crowd of spectators and an equally great volume of running appreciative or critical commentaries. The whole process of play-acting and production had been demystified and the actors and the show were the gainers for it.[19]

His experience with the Kamiruthu Theatre encouraged Ngugi to move from writing in the English language to writing in Gikuyu, and since his release from prison in 1978 he has published several novels and children's stories in that language. Speaking of his decision to abandon English and write in Gikuyu, Ngugi stated:

> Language is a carrier of a people's culture, culture is a carrier of a people's values; values are the basis of a people's self-definition – the basis of their consciousness. And when you destroy a people's language, you are destroying that very important aspect of their heritage . . . you are in fact destroying that which helps them to be themselves . . . that which embodies their collective memory as a people.[20]

The choice between an indigenous language and English is possible for Ngugi, in whose native Kenya a large proportion of the population speaks Gikuyu. Soyinka and Aidoo could also choose between English and Yoruba or Akan, and indeed they have drawn on both languages, but like many other African writers (and similarly Indian subcontinental writers), their reason for choosing English is because it is a common language for the nation as a whole, rather than for specific ethnic or cultural groups within the nation. But for Caribbean writers the English language is the only one they have, and their choice must be between a standard version and one that is inflected by the idioms, pronunciation and vocabulary of Caribbean speakers. However, as with the history of African Americans, the use of 'dialect' or 'patois' has in the past been associated with comic representations of black people in minstrel shows and in writing by white authors about black people. The African American poet Paul Laurence Dunbar lamented the pressure to write 'jingles in a broken tongue', and had been advised by the American critic William Dean Howells to stick to writing in dialect rather than 'correct' English.

Yet most Irish people do not speak like English people; neither do most Africans or West Indians (white and black). And many African Americans do not speak like white Americans. How then can one realistically represent their speech in writing or on stage without reinscribing that history of prejudice regarding their speech and character? Indeed, how can one respect and celebrate that speech, the experience and view of the world it expresses? For the African American critic and poet James Weldon Johnson, and for the West Indian poet and playwright Derek Walcott, it was the Irish playwright Synge who pointed the way.

For other West Indian playwrights also, Irish drama has proved instructive. In the 1950s the Dramatic Society in Mona, Jamaica, produced O'Casey's *Juno and the Paycock* (1925). This play with its urban setting in the Dublin tenements and its delight in language and rhetoric found an appreciative audience in Kingston and Mona. But Walcott sought a drama and a kind of language that resonated with the world of peasants and fishermen in his native St Lucia. Walcott's early plays were written in a poetic standard English, though they focused on Caribbean historical figures such as Henri Christophe, who governed Haiti after it became the first Caribbean island to achieve independence (in 1804). However, the models provided by Synge and Yeats, as poets and dramatists, and particularly Synge's use of Irish-English idioms, proved useful when he tried to develop a Caribbean theatre. In a 1980 interview Walcott spoke of his identification with Irish writers:

> I've always felt some kind of intimacy with the Irish poets because one realised that they were also colonials with the same kind of problems that existed in the Caribbean. They were the niggers of Britain. Now, with all that, to have those outstanding achievements of genius whether by Joyce or Becket or Yeats illustrated that one could come out of a depressed, depraved, oppressed situation and be defiant and creative at the same time.[21]

For Walcott, it was not only the general inspiration given by the achievements of Irish writers, but more specifically Synge's use of language that provided an important model for his early drama:

> And then the whole question of dialect began to interest me. When I read Synge's *Riders to the Sea* I realized what he had attempted to do with the language of the Irish. He had taken a fishing port kind of language and gotten beauty out of it, a beat, something lyrical. Now that was inspiring, and the obvious model for *The Sea at Dauphin*. I guess I knew then that the more you imitate when you're young, the more original you become. If you know very clearly that you are imitating such and such a work, it isn't that you're adopting another man's genius; it is that he has done an experiment that has worked and will be useful to all writers afterwards. When I tried to translate the speech of the St. Lucian fisherman into an English Creole, all I was doing was taking that kind of speech and translating it, or retranslating it, into an English-inflected Creole, and that was a totally new experience for me, even if it did come out of Synge.[22]

While Yeats was to prove major influence for his poetry in his early years, and James Joyce for his verse epic *Omeros* (1990) in his later work, it was Synge who was one of the most important exemplars for the creation of a national theatre. *The Sea at Dauphin* (1966) clearly shows the influence of Synge's *Riders to the Sea* (1904) with regard to both its setting and its use of local patois, while his productions for the Trinidad Theatre Workshop that he helped to found in 1959 and directed for twenty years demonstrate that he had also imbibed

Synge's dictum, 'On the stage, one must have reality and one must have joy', a joy derived in part from the richness of the local language.

In the remaining part of this chapter, I propose to explore in detail two plays, one West Indian and one Irish, both of which build upon the examples provided by Synge and the Abbey Theatre tradition, and which demonstrate particular issues regarding language, community and the performance of identity in a postcolonial context. They are Walcott's *Dream on Monkey Mountain* first performed in 1970, and Brian Friel's *Translations*, first performed in 1980.[23] I am interested in asking questions about the particular role and effect that drama might have – or might be intended to have – in a moment of political transition.

Why these two plays? The choice firstly has to do with the ways in which each work was centrally involved with the project of setting up a community theatre. Walcott's play was written in 1970 for the Trinidad Theatre Workshop. Friel's play was the opening play for the Field Day Theatre in Derry, Northern Ireland. Like Friel, Walcott was influenced by an earlier model of postcolonial theatre, the Abbey Theatre, founded as a means of reaching audiences more open to oral performance than the written word. Indeed, Walcott acknowledges his debt to Synge in pointing the way to a dramatic language which could convey the richness of the local idiom, and overcome the associations of comic inadequacy traditionally evoked by stage Irish or black minstrel performance. In both plays the issue of language is paramount and is closely tied to the question of identity and naming. In *Dream on Monkey Mountain* the conflict is between standard metropolitan English and the regional or creolized English spoken by the people of St Lucia and Trinidad; in *Translations* it is between the English and Irish languages. The voicing of these different languages on stage makes the conflicts particularly pointed and dramatic.

But in terms of the communities for which these plays were written and performed, the issues of language are especially resonant. Like the Abbey Theatre directors, Walcott sought to create a company of actors who could be at ease in their own way of speaking, and their own form of English, whose voices and gestures would identify them with the audience, not with an alien theatrical tradition. Their role was to bring theatre home, and to allow the audience to see and judge their own social attitudes and conflicts.

Dream of Monkey Mountain is epic theatre, in the Brechtian sense of the term, but also influenced by Samuel Becket, Jean Genet and Jean-Paul Sartre, Afro-Caribbean folktale and song, Caribbean carnival, and Fanon's writings. It begins with the imprisonment of an old charcoal burner and ends with a scene in which he is released from prison. In the opening scene he is forced to name himself as Makak (monkey), lampooned by the gaol guard and fellow prisoners as a monkey, and ridiculed for having also named himself the Lion of Judah. In the final scene he is able to name himself as Felix Hobain and is set free to return home to his mountain.

Between the Prologue, where first the old man is imprisoned and named as an animal, and the Epilogue, where he takes his own name and is free, a series of dream visions take place, each inspired by the vision of a white goddess or perhaps a *diablesse*, imaged as a carnival mask of a white woman's face with long black hair. So this image recalls the title of Fanon's first book, *Black Skin, White Masks* (1952), and his argument that the black soul is a white man's artefact. But Walcott's drama also shows that the associations with whiteness are also artefacts of the black man.

Let me quote Makak's first description of this vision:

> Sirs, I am sixty years old, I have lived all my life
> Like a wild beast in hiding. Without child, without wife.
> People forget me like the mist on Monkey Mountain.
> Is thirty years now I have look in no mirror,
> Not a pool of cold water, when I must drink,
> I stir my hands first, to break up my image.
> I will tell you my dream. Sirs, make a white mist
> In the mind; make that mist hang like a cloth
> From the dress of a woman, on prickles, on branches,
> Make it rise from the earth, like the breath of the dead
> On resurrection morning, and I walking through it
> On my way to my charcoal pit in the mountain.
> Make the web of the spider heavy with diamonds
> And when my hand brush it, let the chain break.
> I remember, in my mind, the cigale sawing.
> Sawing, sawing wood before the woodcutter,
> The drum of the bull-frog, the blackbird flute,
> And this old man walking, ugly as sin,
> In a confusion of vapour,
> Till I feel I was God self, walking through cloud,
> In the heaven of my mind. Then I hear this song,
> Not the blackbird flute,
> Not the bull-frog drum,
> Not the whistling of parrots
> As I brush through the branches, shaking the dew,
> A man swimming through smoke,
> And the bandage of fog unpeeling my eyes,
> As I reach this spot,
> I see this woman singing

And my feet grow roots. I could move no more.
A million silver needles prickle my blood,
Like a rain of small fishes.
The snakes in my hair speak to one another,
The smoke mouth open, and I behold this woman,
The loveliest thing I see on this earth,
Like the moon walking along her own road.
    (*During this, the apparition appears and withdraws*)[24]

I have cited this passage in full to illustrate how powerfully Walcott deploys the idiom and voice of the local language, rooted in the local environment, to summon up a world and a vision, despite the fact that the whole event takes place on a bare stage representing a prison cell. This passage also dramatizes the link between Makak's belief in his own ugliness, and thus his literal self-effacement, with his longing for beauty, and for a vision which can give his life meaning.

The subsequent scenes of the play enact the consequences of this vision. In scenes 1 and 2, Makak becomes a local hero, a redeemer and Christlike figure who heals a dying man through his faith and, significantly, through a piece of coal. In scene 3 Moustique, his assistant and friend, impersonates Makak in order to make money, and is beaten to death when the crowd discovers that he is a fraud. Part II presents a Rastafarian dream, with Makak as a powerful African king, the Lion of Judah, destroying all whiteness and, finally – at the behest of Corporal Lestrade, beheading the white-woman mask. It is this act which restores him to his real name and returns him home to Monkey Mountain, for both the vision of black power as a negation of whiteness and of whiteness as a negation of blackness must be discarded before the black man can be at home with himself. Throughout the play, Lestrade, who is of mixed race, represents the schizophrenic world of the Caribbean, taught to aspire to the worlds claimed by white colonizers – of law, order, civilization and culture – and to despise all that is embodied in black people. Caribbean reviewers recognized the significance of the play in its dramatization of Lestrade for themselves. The Trinidadian novelist Earl Lovelace wrote that the play sought to expose 'truths we try to suppress' and so to 'free ourselves of the colonial neurosis'. He saw Corporal Lestrade as an image of 'the native intellectual upholding the white man's law at the expense of his black half-brother'.[25]

Whereas Lestrade's psyche is torn between the worlds supposedly represented by two colours and two races, Friel's characters represent the worlds contained within two different languages. And whereas Walcott's play might be seen as a psychodrama and a dream play, Friel has written a historical drama. However, like *Dream of Monkey Mountain*, *Translations*[26] explores issues of communication between those who are poor and relatively powerless and those who assume power. Here, too, standard English is the language of imperialism, and imperial law.

Both plays are concerned with the power to name oneself and one's world, and with ways of mapping and describing that world, a concern that Edward Said has emphasized as common to postcolonial communities.[27] *Translations* was the first play performed by the Field Day Company and the first play to be opened in Derry (or Londonderry) by a professional company for nearly two hundred years. As such it marked a determination to both initiate and record actual cultural and historical changes with a play which is particularly pertinent to that town's fraught past and present. Originally named Derry (from the Irish 'doire', place of the oaks), it was renamed Londonderry by the English colonizers and mapmakers, and is named thus yet by Northern Irish Unionists, though the Catholic majority city council elected in 1978 had reverted to the older name. When Ireland was finally partitioned in 1922, the boundary line divided 'the province of Londonderry' from Donegal (where the play is set), and the city of Derry was placed just inside the border defining Northern Ireland as part of the United Kingdom. Thus the historical event around which the play is staged, the ordinance survey and mapping and naming of Irish locations by the British in the 1830s, had a particular resonance for the citizens of Derry in 1980. In the 1970s Derry had also been the scene of bitter and violent demonstrations and clashes between Irish nationalists, who continued to oppose the partition of Ireland strongly and saw Northern Ireland as colonized territory, and unionists supported by British troops, who equally opposed the reunification of Ireland and consequent loss of British citizenship and identity.[28]

Friel and Stephen Rea (one of the founders of the Field Day Project and director of the Field Day Theatre) chose members of the Ulster community to play most of the characters, and encouraged the cast not to tone down their strong Ulster accents. Rea stressed the play's resonance for a Northern Irish audience: 'the play has a great deal of political resonance', he commented, and he went on to say, 'If we put it on in a place like Dublin's Abbey Theatre, its energy would be contained within the theatre and its clientele. But its energy is bound to spread much more profoundly through a place like Derry.'[29] As Christopher Morash remarks:

> Performing *Translations* with a largely Ulster cast in a building only a few miles from its Donegal setting allowed the audience to feel the same kind of local pride that the play itself sets against any kind of centralising standardising authority, be it imperial or national. Like the character of Hugh, the audience's experience of the Derry production drew heavily on what he calls 'the *desiderium nostrorum* – the need for our own.'[30]

Like *Dream on Monkey Mountain*, Friel's play begins with a failed attempt by one of the characters to name herself. In the first scene the Irish schoolteacher Manus trying to teach his pupil Sarah to say, 'My name is Sarah.' Sarah has been assumed by the community to be dumb, to have no speech, but Manus believes that she does have the power of self-expression and can name herself. The opening of the play dramatizes powerfully, as no prose fiction could have done, Sarah's struggle to speak and name herself, a struggle which suggests in microcosm the difficulty a colonized people have in representing themselves and having their voices heard, a difficulty explored cogently by Gayatri Chakravorty Spivak in her essay 'Can the Subaltern Speak?'.[31]

The play brings together two acts of colonialism in Ireland: one the action of the troops who set out to map and anglicize place names across the whole of Ireland; the other the replacement of the Irish-speaking schools by a national system of English-speaking schools. So it portrays the transitional moment between a confident and locally based Irish culture and the imposition of a powerful English culture, reinforced by military superiority. At a time when the educational system in the Irish republic was seeking 150 years later to restore an Irish-speaking culture, and when one of the principal signs of resistance among nationalist political prisoners in Northern Irish gaols was the study of the Irish language, the issue of language was particularly relevant. A central figure in the play is the translator and interpreter, Owen, the brother of Manus, who is working for the British army. He might be seen as the equivalent of Walcott's Lestrade, the man caught between two cultures and two worlds, and seduced by the more powerful one. But ironically, Owen also finds himself constantly misnamed by his British employers, who insist on calling him Roland.

Owen's ambivalent role as interpreter and translator is well illustrated in the cynical humour of his version of the speeches of the English Captain Lancey and Corporal Yolland to 'the natives':

> LANCEY: His Majesty's government has ordered the first ever comprehensive survey of this entire country – a general triangulation which will embrace detailed hydrographic and topographic information and which will be executed to a scale of six inches to an English mile.
> OWEN: A new map is being made of the whole country.
>   . . .
> YOLLAND: I think your countryside is – is – is – is very beautiful. I've fallen in love with it already. I hope we are not too – too crude an intrusion on your lives. And I know that I'm going to be happy, very happy, here.
> OWEN: He is already a committed Hibernophile.[32]

The passages above are a tangle of paradoxes: not only does Owen translate Lancey's convoluted Latinate and Greek-based words into simple Anglo-Saxon vocabulary, he also teasingly turns Yolland's linguistically plainer expression into a Latinate one. At the same time, we are aware that his audience is thoroughly at home with Latin and Greek. But the overarching paradox is that although the actors are all speaking in English, the illusion is that some are speaking in Irish and some in English. These passages also compare interestingly with those in Achebe's novels set in colonial Nigeria, where interpreters diplomatically soften the harshness of terms used by British administrators, and where Latinate and literary phrases such as 'The Pacification of the Tribes of the Lower Niger' are used to obscure the reality of the suffering and loss imposed by a colonial administration supported by military force.[33]

The character perhaps most similar to Walcott's Makak in Friel's play is Jimmy Jack, described as 'a bachelor in his sixties . . . [who] never washes, [and whose] clothes, heavy top coat, hat, mittens, are filthy'. While Makak is bewitched by the white goddess figure, and dreams of becoming either a Christlike redeemer figure or a king, Jimmy Jack is bewitched by Homer and the goddess Athena. Thus both plays also reveal the dangers of being caught in myths belonging to a former civilization which at one and the same time seek to give richer meaning to an existence which might seem barren and without significance, but may also prevent one from engaging constructively with the world of 'historical fact'. Or, as Seamus Heaney wrote in his review of *Translations*, they demonstrate 'the need we have to create enabling myths of ourselves and the danger we run if we trust too credulously to those myths'.[34] In that same review Heaney commented that it was time that Friel was 'as it were, translated. I am sure this piece would come home like a remembrance in, for example, Derek Walcott's theatre in Trinidad.'[35]

Towards the end of the play, there is a reference to yet another myth and figure which has played a central role in Irish nationalism and Irish nationalist theatre. Jimmy Jack and Hugh, the father of Manus and Owen, recall how they set out as young men to join in the 1798 rebellion led by Wolfe Tone, the most revered of the risings in Irish nationalist history, and the event that Yeats summons up in his dream-vision play *Cathleen ni Houlihan*. Jimmy Jack and Hugh turn back and return home, however, before reaching the scene of the rising – and in so doing reject not only the call of Cathleen ni Houlihan, but also the Yeatsian version of nationalist theatre. For this particular Yeats play was received as propaganda calling for a military rebellion. Like Walcott, Friel rejects 'the men of violence', with the myths surrounding them, and drama as propaganda. Both playwrights call upon their audiences to reflect and judge through becoming aware of the analogies between the world portrayed on stage and the world they inhabit. Or, in the words of Hugh regarding Jimmy Jack's obsession with the Greek past, 'we must learn . . . that it is not the literal past, the "facts" of history, that shape us, but images of the past embodied in language' and 'that we must never cease renewing those images; because once we do, we fossilize'.[36]

Chapter 3

Alternative histories and writing back

In his chapter on 'National Consciousness' in *The Wretched of the Earth* (1965), Frantz Fanon speaks of the importance of rescuing history from the colonizer's custody. In the face of European denials of any worthwhile native culture or history, he states:

> the claims of the native intellectual are not a luxury but a necessity in any coherent programme. The native intellectual who takes up arms to defend his nation's legitimacy and who wants to bring proofs to bear out that legitimacy, who is willing to strip himself naked to study the history of his body, is obliged to dissect the heart of his people.[1]

That 'Africans did not hear of civilization for the first time from Europeans', as Chinua Achebe declared,[2] is a claim central to many works in the early stages of contesting a colonialist mentality. Achebe sees this as one of the main messages carried in his historical novels, *Things Fall Apart* (1958) and *Arrow of God* (1964), the first of which will be discussed in greater detail below. Perhaps because Africa has been the victim of the greatest denial and contempt, seen as the 'Dark Continent', and, as Fanon puts it, the home of 'barbarism, degradation, and bestiality',[3] the affirmation of its cultural validity, the delineation of a history in its own terms, has been particularly the task of novelists throughout the African continent such as Achebe from Nigeria, Ayi Kwei Armah from Ghana, Assia Djebar from Algeria, Ngugi wa Thiong'o from Kenya and Solomon Plaatje from South Africa.

However, the recovery of a lost or 'subaltern' history, told from the point of view of those who have been ruled and oppressed rather than those who are members of the ruling classes, has also been a concern in other postcolonial areas. The Barbadian poet and historian Kamau Brathwaite produced an epic trilogy, *The Arrivants* (1973), which traces the migrations of African peoples in the African continent, through the terrible sufferings of the Middle Passage and slavery, and further journeys to England, France and the United States in search of economic and psychic survival. The middle section of the trilogy, *Masks*, seeks to recover for African Caribbeans the Ghanaian culture from which many of their ancestors were forcibly torn two or three centuries ago. In this and his later poetry, Brathwaite sought to create a poetry with a redemptive purpose, linking Caribbean peoples to their ancestral roots, tracing the lines of resistance to psychic and spiritual destruction, and transmitting within the Caribbean islands a sense of national identity which supersedes the colonial identification with Britain as 'the mother country'. That sense of group identity and cultural belonging is reinforced by Brathwaite's use of the rhythms and song forms, such as blues, calypso and reggae, developed in the Caribbean, and his ventriloquizing of the idioms and language forms specific to particular West Indian islands. In his role as a historian, Brathwaite had published a book-length study, *The Development of Creole Society in Jamaica, 1870–1920* (1971), and also an influential literary study, *History of the Voice* (1984), both of which focus on the continuation of African cultural expressions, especially through music, dance and oral poetry, in the Caribbean, and the creation of a distinctive hybrid European and African culture. However, Brathwaite's view of a hybrid culture differs from both Homi Bhabha's and Edouard Glissant's in its emphasis on the 'Africanness' of Caribbean customs, traditions and beliefs. Bhabha's formulations tend to focus on language and to present hybridity as consisting of two equally weighted cultures, whose interaction creates an 'in-between' or 'third' space, in which a speaker positions himself or herself,[4] while Glissant (like Stuart Hall) emphasizes the process of interchange and transformation rather than the search for an originary culture.

The Indian novelist Raja Rao declares in the foreword to his first prose fiction, *Kanthapura*, 'There is no village in India, however mean, that has not a rich *sthala-purana*, or legendary history, of its own . . . One such story from the contemporary annals of a village I have tried to tell.'[5] Published in 1938, *Kanthapura* narrates, from the point of view of a spirited and garrulous South Indian grandmother, the effects of Mahatma Gandhi's ideas on the varied inhabitants of a small village in India. The voice of the narrator allows Rao to link traditional oral narrative, myths and legends, and social structures to create an impression of rural India which is also a microcosm of the nation as a whole, and the ways in which the Gandhi movement brings change. It is, as Robert Fraser remarks, 'an early attempt, in Homi Bhabha's words, to "write the nation": to depict in vivid outlines, the writings, the jostlings and the uneasy birth pangs of the Indian collective consciousness'.[6] The following passage from an early section of *Kanthapura* demonstrates Rao's creation of an Indian voice in English, and a consciousness imbued with traditional stories, myths and beliefs:

'Today,' [Jayaramachar] says, 'it will be the story of Siva and Parvati.'
And Parvati in penance becomes the country and Siva becomes heaven
knows what! 'Siva is the three-eyed,' he says, 'and Swaraj too is
three-eyed: Self-purification, Hindu-Moslem unity, Khaddar.' And then
he talks of Dmayanthi and Sakunthala and Yasodha and everywhere
there is something about our country and something about Swaraj.
Never had we heard *Harikathas* like this. And he can sing too, can
Jayaramachar. He can keep us in tears for hours together. But the
Harikatha he did, which I can never forget in this life and in all lives to
come, is about the birth of Gandhiji.[7]

Drawing on the model of the *harikatha*, an oral form of the traditional
purana, to create a hybrid prose fiction, Rao portrays the changes in consciousness of the villagers from identification and divisions in terms of class
and caste, marked by its mapping in terms of the Brahmin quarter, 'a pariah
quarter too, a Potters' quarter, a Weavers' quarter, and a Sudra quarter'.[8] At
first they are horrified by the refusal of Moorthy, Kanthapura's own Gandhi
activist, to acknowledge such divisions, his visiting even the pariah quarters and
his assertions that widows should be allowed to remarry, and that Brahmins
might marry pariahs. But gradually the divisions are broken down and replaced
by a sense of village identity, which in turn allows the villagers to unite against
the British landlord, Skeffington, and his plans to extend his coffee plantation. Thus, as Elleke Boehmer comments, 'Rao has composed a narrative in
which story-line, generic structure, and nationalist resistance politics mutu-
ally reflect upon one another.'[9] A much later postcolonial national narrative,
Salman Rushdie's *Midnight's Children* (1981), chooses multiple voices and narratives, sometimes conflicting, to challenge not only the colonial portrayal of
India, referring among other texts to E. M. Forster's *A Passage to India* (1924),
but also the nationalist histories of India which foreground Gandhi and ignore
other groups. As the Canadian scholar Linda Hutcheon remarks, 'a novel like
Midnight's Children works to foreground the totalising impulse of western –
imperialistic – modes of history-writing by confronting it with indigenous
models of history'. Moreover, 'his intertexts for both writing history and writing fiction are doubled', drawing on Indian legend, film and literature as well
as European models such as *Tristram Shandy* (1759–69) and *The Tin Drum*
(1959).[10] Rushdie explicitly challenges Western concepts of historical narrative
by introducing the metaphor of 'chutnification', suggesting that the contents
will always be flavoured in a particular way by particular cooks or authors in
the pickling or preservation process, and also that the different bits selected for
preservation will blend and mingle to create new flavours.

These literary works by Achebe, Brathwaite, Rao, Rushdie and others can be read as alternative histories which both challenge colonial narratives and give voice to those whose stories have been ignored or overwhelmed by European historians. Many postcolonial texts also implicitly and/or explicitly engage with and 'write back' to colonial novels and histories. Hutcheon uses the term 'historiographic metafiction' to describe novels which include as part of their structure and allusions a dialogue with colonial narratives of history.[11] The concept of 'writing back' is central to one of the most influential postcolonial literary studies, *The Empire Writes Back* (1989) by Bill Ashcroft, Gareth Griffiths and Helen Tiffin, three Australian critics who have been leading academics in Commonwealth literary studies. The title of their book refers to Rushdie's comment, 'The Empire writes back to the centre.'[12] What they discuss, among other things, are the issues that arise in postcolonial reading as well as postcolonial writing and rewriting.

Problems relating to postcolonial reading with reference to texts written by postcolonial writers will be discussed at greater length in chapter 11; here I will focus briefly on readings of colonial and metropolitan texts and responses to them. Many critics had until the 1960s generally assumed that 'intelligent readers' might reach a consensus on how to interpret and respond to a text, but this assumption came under scrutiny with the development of feminist literary theory in the 1970s, and the concept of 'reading as a woman'. Given that in the past many writers presupposed a white male audience or at least assumed that that audience's values and attitudes should be taken for granted, and given that such writers also often assume that the central story should be concerned with a white male protagonist, what happens when you imagine yourself as a female and/or a non-European reader? Take for example a much-debated text, Joseph Conrad's *Heart of Darkness* (1902), one of the most frequently taught novels in English departments. Achebe has written bitterly about his sense of outrage on reading it as a college student and finding how Africans are characterized – as cannibals, as having no speech, as a mass of whirling savages indulging in unspeakable rites, and also as mere background to the story of Marlow and Kurtz.[13] Yet as an African he is particularly aware of the fact that when Conrad's novel was being written, African art and music was making a significant impact on European artists such as Claude Debussy and Pablo Picasso; while African artefacts such as the Benin bronzes were prize possessions of the British Museum and the Palace of the Archbishop of Canterbury. Achebe also recalls the very different response from that of British readers that he and his classmates had to Joyce Cary's *Mister Johnson* (1939), the story of a naive young Nigerian named Mr Johnson, who adores the District Commissioner and the ways of the English, but has to be executed for killing a European. Many

English critics referred to the novel as the best depiction ever of the Nigerian character, seen as humorous and childlike; Achebe tells that when they were asked by the British teacher what they liked best about the novel, one of them replied, 'The shooting of Mr Johnson.' In the Caribbean context Aimé Césaire from Martinique and George Lamming from Barbados have both offered very different readings of Shakespeare's *The Tempest* from those taken for granted by English critics, pointing out that it is Caliban whom they are identified with rather than Prospero. This has led in turn to new readings of the play and an emphasis on Caliban as a colonized native rebelling against the imperial power represented by Prospero. Indeed, it is rare now to see productions of the play which do not relate it to a colonial and political context. Again, Edward Said sparked much controversy by his reading of Jane Austen's *Mansfield Park* (1814), a reading that foregrounds the brief mention of the slave plantations in the West Indies from which Sir Thomas Bertram has gained the wealth which makes Mansfield Park such a pleasant but also a morally corrupt world.[14]

But such rereadings of these canonical works have also involved rewritings. Césaire's version of *The Tempest* (*Une Tempête* (1969)) has Prospero as a Cecil B. de Mille-type film director calling up storms and sound effects, Ariel is cast as an intellectual of mixed race, and Caliban goes around muttering 'Uhuru', the Swahili word for freedom, which Prospero can hear only as 'brutish gabble'. Marina Warner has written a novel called *Indigo* (1992) which features Sycorax as an Amerindian woman with magic powers, who has a child, Caliban, with an escaped slave, and Ariel as her adopted daughter. Achebe began his first novel in order to rewrite Cary's *Mister Johnson*, to tell the story 'from the inside'. What had originally been planned as one novel turned into two, *Things Fall Apart*, which portrays the historical moment of change, the impact of the colonizer's first appearance from an African point of view, and *No Longer at Ease* (1960), which like Cary's novel tells the story of a Nigerian clerk who commits a crime and is dismissed (though not executed) by his English boss. However, in this case the clerk is rooted in a history of cultural and political change; he is the grandson of Okonkwo and the son of Nwoye, whose stories are told in *Things Fall Apart*. Similarly, Abdulrazak Gurnah's novel *Paradise* (1994) provides in some aspects an African variation on Conrad's *Heart of Darkness*, as well as an East African Arab/African version of the colonial encounter narrated in *Things Fall Apart*.

Shakespeare and Conrad have provided two canonical versions of the colonial encounter. Another well-known account is Daniel Defoe's *Robinson Crusoe* (1719). This novel has often been seen as providing a paradigm of the colonial enterprise, especially in the Caribbean and the Pacific. What is most significant here is the immediate assumption that the native must be the white man's servant, despite the fact that Crusoe is an intruder on the island. And, as in *The Tempest*, it is assumed that language does not exist for the 'native' until it is given by the European; until he can speak as a European, he is speechless. Moreover, it is assumed that the story is Crusoe's story (Friday is merely a member of the supporting cast), and that the islands are empty until they are inhabited by Europeans. (Similarly, Australia was declared *terra nullius*, land belonging to no one, despite the presence of aboriginal peoples on that continent for many thousands of years.) *Robinson Crusoe* became a reference point for many African and Caribbean writers, and it is significant also because it is seen as the first major novel in English, and the seminal work for a genre which is distinctively European in its values. Derek Walcott has written a number of poems using Crusoe as a motif, and a witty radio and stage play called *Pantomime*, in which the roles of white master and black servant are reversed.[15]

For women readers and writers in postcolonial countries, there is what has been referred to as a 'double colonization', for they are marginalized and stereotyped on grounds of both colour and gender.[16] In his focus on what he sees as the racist characterization of Africans and Africa in *Heart of Darkness*, Achebe has little to say about the depiction of the women, Kurtz's European and African mistresses. Yet many readers of this novel are likely to feel some disquiet at the portrayal of these women. The 'Intended' is seen as too delicate to be told the truth, while the black mistress is seen as merely a symbol of Africa – savage, barbaric and rather awesome. Neither is given a voice or any 'agency'.

Such fiction, poetry and drama set in Africa, or 'the East', or other areas colonized by European powers, belongs to a long history of representation of these areas as uncivilized, inhabited by inferior peoples – if inhabited at all – and in need of 'development'. These representations have been discussed in the Introduction to this book, and have been analysed by Achebe and Fanon, among others, with reference to Africa, and by Said with reference to 'the Orient'. Roy Foster and L. P. Curtis have written about the depiction of the Irish in the nineteenth century as simian, childlike and effeminate.[17] Australian Aborigines, New Zealand Maoris and native Canadians were regarded as belonging to the 'Stone Age' or simply barbaric, peoples who would inevitably die out and so prove no obstacle to the settlers who were occupying the lands they had inhabited. Only recently did the Australian Supreme Court overturn the ruling by earlier British and Australian governments that Australia was *terra nullius* when Europeans first arrived.[18] There was a further layer of condescension in that metropolitan writers also tended to view the white settlers in these colonies as second-rate people, cast out or unable to succeed 'at home', lacking culture and sophistication. Such attitudes towards those who had emigrated to

Australia were compounded by that country's history as a convict settlement, founded by the British in 1788 to relieve its overflowing prisons.

Fanon argues that the process of colonization involved not only physical occupation of the land and imposition of government on the colonized people, but also mental colonization. 'In the colonial context', Fanon writes, 'the settler only ends his work of breaking in the native when the latter admits loudly and intelligibly the supremacy of the white man's values.'[19] Or, as James McQueen, writing about strategies for British penetration of West Africa, stated in 1821, 'If we really wish to do good in Africa, we must teach her savage sons that the white men are their superiors. By this charm alone can we insure their obedience.'[20] We have seen in *The Lion and the Jewel* (1959) how Wole Soyinka mocks those who have succumbed to such mental colonization, while V. S. Naipaul also satirizes would-be leaders of postcolonial Caribbean states and laments the long-term effects of cultural colonization in his novel *The Mimic Men* (1967). (Some of Naipaul's critics would argue that he himself, in his attitudes towards Africans, West Indians and Indians, is an example of one who 'admits loudly and intelligibly the supremacy of the white man's values'.)

At this point we can examine more closely Achebe's seminal novel, *Things Fall Apart*, which seeks to tell the story of the colonial encounter in Nigeria 'from the inside', and also to remind his readers in Nigeria that 'African peoples did not hear of civilization for the first time from Europeans'.[21] As noted above, Achebe's first novel responds to and contests European depictions of Africa by Cary and Conrad. The title of his novel also alludes and responds to a poem by the Irish poet W. B. Yeats, 'The Second Coming', which begins:

> Turning and turning in the widening gyre
> The falcon cannot hear the falconer;
> Things fall apart; the centre cannot hold,
> Mere anarchy is loosed upon the world[.][22]

Like Yeats, Achebe projects a vision of history, and the beginning of a new cycle in which old customs and beliefs become displaced, and a whole society loses its way. But whereas Yeats saw the twentieth century ending the historical cycle begun two thousand years previously with Christianity and culminating in the hierarchies of class and tradition which typified Renaissance Europe, Achebe's novel narrates how the coming of Christianity and European culture causes a particular African society to fall apart and lose its central and shared values.

Yeats's image of disintegration is echoed and revised in a metaphor which recurs throughout Achebe's novel and is voiced in the passage below by Obierika, one of the wise elders in the village of Umuofia and a friend of the novel's main protagonist, Okonkwo: 'The white man is very clever. He came quietly and peaceably with his religion. We were amused at his foolish-ness and allowed him to stay. Now he has won our brothers, and our clan can no longer act like one. He has put a knife on the things that held us together and we have fallen apart.'[23] Here we have one of the many versions of the colonial encounter that occur in the novel, for Achebe is concerned not so much with historical events as with the narration of those events. As the critic Simon Gikandi writes, 'Indeed, the historical significance of Achebe's works lies in his ability to evolve narrative procedures through which the colonial language which was previously intended to designate and reproduce the colo-nial ideology, now evokes new forms of expression, proffers a new oppositional discourse, thereby countering the "permanence of vision" embedded in colo-nialist discourse.'[24] *Things Fall Apart* offers not only an overall narrative that profoundly questions the European version of its dealings with Africa, but also a series of perspectives within the Igbo community which counter or question one another. Consequently, readers of the novel are frequently encouraged to interrogate each narrator and the purposes and contexts which influence each version we are given.

Differing perspectives and modes of historical narrative are embodied most obviously in the contrast between the first and last paragraphs of the novel. In the opening paragraph we hear the voice of an oral historian, speaking of and to his community:

> Okonkwo was well known throughout the nine villages and even beyond. His fame rested on solid personal achievements. As a young man of eighteen he had brought honour to his village by throwing Amalinze the Cat. Amalinze was the great wrestler who for seven years was unbeaten from Umuofia to Mbaino. He was called the Cat because his back would never touch the earth. It was this man that Okonkwo threw in a fight which the old men agreed was one of the fiercest since the founder of their town engaged a spirit of the wild for seven days and seven nights.[25]

Here we are introduced not only to Okonkwo as a heroic character and fiercely masculine wrestler, but also to a narrative voice profoundly different from that of written colonial discourse. Achebe's oral narrator is encompassed by the world of 'the nine villages from Umuofia to Mbaino'; areas outside these boundaries have little significance as yet, belonging simply to that vague realm 'beyond'. His values are those of his society, recognizing 'solid personal achieve-ments' (rather than status achieved by birth or inheritance), and approving those who bring honour to their village. The stories he records link up with the legends passed on by the old men, their legendary status subtly underscored for the Westernized reader by the recurrence of the number seven, reminding him or her of other traditions in which the number has special significance and in which history and legend, myth and poetry are closely intertwined. And his language echoes the everyday spoken language, the proverbs and allusions that characterize other speakers in this Igbo community.

The opening paragraph also carries the traces of spoken or performed narration in its awareness of the kinship between the speaker and his implicit audience with regard to values and locations which they all share. An acknowledgement of the needs of the audience, its call on the speaker, is implied in the qualities which make both the opening paragraph and the work as a whole, with its numerous digressions and episodic structure, reminiscent of oral composition. Explanations like that concerning the identity of Amalinze and the source of his nickname are inserted as the narrator feels his fictive audience's need for them, not according to a preconceived structure and sense of proportion.

The nature of the story of Okonkwo as oral history, belonging to a specific culture, is contrasted sharply and poignantly with the closing paragraph of the novel, in which the District Commissioner contemplates what is to be his record of the events that the novel has just related:

> The Commissioner went away, taking three or four of the soldiers with him. In the many years in which he had toiled to bring civilization to different parts of Africa he had learned a number of things. One of them was that a District Commissioner must never attend to such undignified details as cutting a hanged man from a tree. Such attention would give the natives a poor opinion of him. In the book which he planned to write he would stress that point. As he walked back to the court he thought about that book. Every day brought him some new material. The story of this man who killed a messenger and hanged himself would make interesting reading. One could almost write a whole chapter on him. Perhaps not a whole chapter, but a reasonable paragraph at any rate. There was so much else to include, and one must be firm in cutting out details. He had already chosen the title of the book, after much thought: *The Pacification of the Primitive Tribes of the Lower Niger.*[26]

This final paragraph emphasizes the contrast between Achebe's District Commissioner and Cary's Mr Rudbeck, who does participate in 'such undignified details' as the execution of an African clerk. Also, and more significantly, it exposes the dismissal and displacement of Igbo culture by British power and language, as well as the displacement of oral history by written history. With this change comes the self-absorbed and self-conscious concern with form, with the nature of the book, its chapters and paragraphs and title. The audience has become distant and impersonal – a vague and passive entity for which 'the story of Okonkwo would make interesting reading'. From now on, the world of this Igbo community will be imprisoned within the language of the District Commissioner whose written record will classify the story of Okonkwo as a mere detail, the story of the massacre at Abame and the destruction of a civilization as 'pacification'.

Yet the contrast between the oral Igbo history of the first paragraph and the written British history which ends the novel conceals a central paradox in the novel as a whole. For after all, *Things Fall Apart* is not spoken but written; it draws on European literary forms such as the novel, and the poetry to which the title refers. Nor is the assurance of the speaker in that first paragraph sustained; the novel reveals other perspectives, tensions and strains within the society it commemorates. Not all members of that community endorse without question the admiration for Okonkwo's assertive masculinity, his dismissal of folktale and music, his preference for histories of war and warlike deeds, the concern he shares with the District Commissioner for not appearing weak in front of others. His son Nwoye, his foster son Ikemefuna, his wives and his closest friend, Obierika, all come to question Okonkwo's dogmatism. Indeed, the ability to acknowledge multiple points of view, to accept the truth of one of Achebe's favourite Igbo proverbs – 'Wherever something stands, there something else also stands' – becomes within the novel a salient feature of the Igbos' relatively democratic culture. He writes with reference to this proverb, 'The Igbo people have a firm belief in the duality of things. Nothing is by itself, nothing is absolute. "I am the way, the Truth, and the Life" would be meaningless in Igbo theology.'[27] Yeats, too, dramatized in his poetry and plays 'the duality of things'. However, Yeats's vision of historical cycles ignores Africa altogether, as did Hegel; Achebe's vision incorporates and plays upon European perspectives and traditions within an African perspective.

Moreover, *Things Fall Apart* is after all a written and very literary commemoration of an oral culture, a novel whose story does in fact counter and outweigh the District Commissioner's fictional and unread account. As David Punter points out, it is Achebe's text which survives, and the District Commissioner's which is 'lost'; in resurrecting an oral culture and recording the destruction of a community, Punter remarks, '*Things Fall Apart*, more than any other work of African fiction, marked the emergence of its own culture into Western consciousness.'[28] It is also true that for many readers, Yeats's lines can no longer be read without Achebe's novel entering into its multiple resonances. But one should also remember the converse, that this novel records the emergence of Western consciousness into African culture, not in this case to overwhelm but to provide a means of survival and understanding, and indeed of marking the difference between African and Western cultures.

That difference, as I have suggested above, involves important divergences in artistic traditions, modes of government and religious beliefs; it also includes disparities in concepts of history – and historical progress. The District Commissioner's projected book implies a version of history which is dictated and controlled by particular men, acting in accord with pragmatism, logic and reason, a belief in absolute truths and a necessary and linear evolution towards European paradigms of civilization and government. Moreover, he did not question the relationship between the discourse – the narration of history – and the 'real' – the 'facts' of history. Achebe's novels repeatedly broach the 'what ifs' of history; the awareness that events and the interpretation of events are all too often matters of the chance convergence of particular people, particular technologies, particular blindnesses within an overall picture.[29] In the historical novels *Things Fall Apart* and *Arrow of God*, the protagonists Okonkwo and Ezeulu seek to control the direction their communities will take, as well as their own personal histories, but each is shown to confuse personal desires and concerns with what they believe to be the interests of their community. Their projected histories and those of other members of the community are often shown to be at odds, and their chief weakness lies in their unwillingness to acknowledge the validity of those alternate histories. Yet even the most admirable characters cannot act in full knowledge and understanding of the context; choices must be made, and made in consensus with others, but one can never know what unforeseen events and convergences might make those choices ineffectual.

Achebe's historical novels also counter Western historiography and narration in that previous historians and novelists frequently portrayed Africa as static, a place devoid of story – a view articulated not only by G. W. F. Hegel in the early nineteenth century, but more recently by the Oxford historian Hugh Trevor-Roper, commenting in 1965: 'Perhaps in the future there will be some African history to teach. But at present there is none, or very little: there is only the history of Europeans in Africa. The rest is largely darkness, like the history of pre-European, pre-Columbian America. And darkness is not a subject for history.'[30]

Trevor-Roper's reference to the 'darkness' of the African past conjures up Conrad's canonical novel, *Heart of Darkness*, whose portrayal of Africans Achebe denounces in his essay, 'An Image of Africa', but also counters in his historical novels. Not only do the articulateness of his characters, their love of oratory, their delight in proverbs, the extended debates which are held at each meeting of the elders, constitute a telling response to Conrad's speechless Africans, he also dramatizes a society in the process of change, aware of its past history and desiring to control its future. One might also compare the humanity of Okonkwo's wives on the one hand, and on the other the priestess Chielo, a woman of immense intelligence and authority, with Conrad's vision of the African woman represented by Kurtz's mistress.

Other African writers have offered counterperspectives to Conrad's *Heart of Darkness*. Ngugi alludes to it in *A Grain of Wheat* (1968) in his portrayal of the District Officer in Kenya, his attitudes and sense of mission, and his resort to torture and 'extermination'. Nadine Gordimer's short story 'The African Magician' (1965) rewrites Conrad's story of a voyage up the Congo, and Gurnah's *Paradise* also carries Conradian echoes, as its protagonist Yusuf (Joseph) journeys into the interior of the African continent. Parallel journeys into the interior of Guyana and Australia have been written by Wilson Harris in *The Palace of the Peacock* (1960) and other novels belonging to his Guyana Quartet, and Patrick White in *Voss* (1957). Here I wish to concentrate on Ama Ata Aidoo's *Our Sister Killjoy: or Reflections from a Black-eyed Squint*[31] (1977), which can be read as a seriously playful and experimental reversal of Conrad's novel that engages with questions of history and its modes of narration. Aidoo shares with Achebe and many other postcolonial writers a commitment to changing and redeeming Africa, a change which can be brought about in part through narration and the retelling of history. In a 1987 interview Aidoo summarized her vision and role as a writer thus: 'I wish, of course, that Africa would be free and strong and organised and constructive, etc. That is basic to my commitment as a writer. That is a basic and consistent part of my vision. I keep seeing different dimensions of it, different interpretations coming through my writing.'[32]

As the first sections of Aidoo's novel make clear, the attempt to change the way things are must also challenge the way things are described, and this includes the forms and language used to portray them. Aidoo's experimental technique revises the form and conventions of the novel as they have been handed down from British writers, and more specifically sets up a series of reversals with regard to narrative form, the assumptions and characterization of African and European, male and female, which make up Conrad's African novel. Like many of his novels, Conrad's *Heart of Darkness* is largely single-voiced and almost unbroken, shaped and held by a European male narrator, Marlow, speaking to other men, seamen like himself, sharing his values and assumptions – about ideas of empire, the essential decency of the British, the relative inferiority of Africans, the need to honour and protect women. As with so many European novels set in Africa, *Heart of Darkness* is a story of a quest, in which white men play the central roles and black men are part of the natural scenery in what often becomes a metaphysical or allegorical landscape. The central narrative concerns Marlow's mission on behalf of the Belgian empire to rescue and bring home Kurtz, an ivory trader who has become 'lost' in the Congo. Whatever is discovered or learnt is brought back to Europe and used for the redemption or development of the European psyche.[33] What Marlow learns is deemed too challenging for a female audience, however, and despite his commitment to truth and honesty, he conceals the truth from Kurtz's 'Intended', whom he judges too delicate and innocent to bear the full story.

Conrad's male narrator travels from Europe to Africa to discover the dark irrationality which lies suppressed in the hearts of European men – a darkness manifested in the 'unspeakable rites', the nameless 'horror', in which Kurtz participates. Aidoo replaces Marlow with Sissie, a character equally distinguished by common sense, but in this case an African woman who travels from Africa to discover the 'heart of whiteness'[34] – a Germany confident of its wholesome civilizing mission in the 1960s, despite the memories of Hitler (the only two German males mentioned in this text are named Adolf), the remnants of concentration camps, the many widows who help tend the plantations of pagan Christmas trees. These things are all spoken and named, as is the true 'horror' at the heart of whiteness – a horror which is both banal and tragic, and which leads Sissie to turn back towards Africa and her 'Intended'. Indeed, it is the figure of Conrad's 'Intended' – that blonde European woman who has no identity other than wife and mother – who haunts the central episode in the novel, with her dazzling white bedroom, her desperate loneliness, and her ignorance of any worlds outside her home, which is a soulless shrine to the sensual and the material.

Aidoo also replaces the hypnotic univocal narration with which Marlow holds his audience spellbound with a fragmented, multivocal fictional structure which Aidoo herself hesitates to call a novel. The narrative is fractured by a series of dialogues and debates with other characters, but also with the narrator herself, so that the main character, Sissie, becomes multivoiced, multidimensional, constantly calling her thoughts and experiences into question. Above all, the seamless cloth woven by Marlow's narrative is cut into small pieces, sometimes unravelled, sometimes pieced together again, and typesetting is Aidoo's chief technique for signalling such fragmenting. The splintering of the narrative and questioning of 'knowledge gained then' through 'knowledge gained since' is related to questioning of the language which comes with empire:

> A common heritage. A
> Dubious bargain that left us
> Plundered of
> Our gold
> Our tongue

Our life – while our
Dead fingers clutch
English – a
Doubtful weapon fashioned
Elsewhere to give might to a
Soul that is already fled.[35]

In the third section of the novel, 'From Our Sister Killjoy', Sissie uses this 'doubtful weapon' to speak and debate political truths. The debate over which she becomes most passionate is literally concerned with a heart of darkness, and its appropriation by white men for their salvation. In the argument over the significance of Dr Christian Barnard's transplant of an African heart into a European body,[36] Sissie finds herself opposing her male colleagues who wish to see assimilation rather than a plurality of cultures, and who insist that scientific knowledge is universal and value-free. The most ardent admirer of Barnard's success in effecting a heart transplant is Kunle, and it is significant that Kunle later becomes a victim of capitalism and Western technology – he is killed when his powerful car crashes, and his family is robbed of all compensation by the insurance company, which interprets the legalistic language of his policy to its own advantage.

But Aidoo's story does not end with the car crash or with the silencing of the female narrator, although her male colleagues do their best to persuade her to keep quiet and 'know her place' as an African woman. The fourth and final section of *Our Sister Killjoy*, 'A Love Letter', seeks to use English for personal communication – a message to Sissie's 'Intended'. As Sissie and Aidoo make clear, personal communication cannot be divorced from sexual politics, nor from the consequences of colonialism which reinforce divisions of class, gender and race while at the same time providing the 'dubious weapon' with which those divisions might be overcome. The problem of language is raised in the opening sentence of the letter:

My Precious Something,
First of all, there is this language. This language . . . Eh, My Love, what positive is there to be when I cannot give voice to my soul and still have her heard? Since so far, I have only been able to use a language which enslaved me, and therefore, the messengers of my mind always come shackled?[37]

Our Sister Killjoy ends with a letter which is not sent, because Sissie realises that its original purpose, reconciliation with her ex-lover, cannot be achieved;

and anyway, that is no longer the point. Unlike Marlow, she does not lie to the 'Intended', but speaks hard truths to him about the complicity of African males who are members of the educated elite with the colonizing powers. Marlow's 'truths' are spoken to his comrades, men who share his assumptions and hence do not encourage him to question those assumptions or himself; Sissie's 'truths' are spoken and written to those with whom she is at odds. Thus her writing, the act of attempting communication, has been a process of self-understanding which has cleared her mind of the 'ticky-tacky', has allowed her to explore and come to terms with the ambivalences in herself, and prepared her for her return to Africa. And it is the aeroplane, that manifestation of Western technology, which carries her back. Like Achebe, even as they contest their consequences, Sissie and Aidoo will seek to use the language, the literary forms, the technology of the colonizer, to bring them back home to an Africa which is not merely a literary or metaphorical construct, but their home – an Africa whose physical reality welcomes and challenges them: 'Besides she was back in Africa. And that felt like fresh honey on the tongue: a mixture of complete sweetness and smoky roughage. Below was home with its unavoidable warmth and even after these thousands of years, its uncertainties.'[38]

Another African woman writer who has taken up and rewritten a colonial story from an African perspective is Bessie Head, whose work also explores the historical consequences of colonization. Head's volume of short stories, *The Collector of Treasures* (1977),[39] is structured in such a way that it moves from stories about the precolonial African past, like Achebe's *Things Fall Apart* drawing on myth and legend and echoing the technique and voice of a village storyteller, to anecdotes about contemporary village and urban life in Botswana, and drawing on a multiplicity of voices, perspectives and modes. One of these stories, 'The Wind and the Boy', involves a fundamental retelling of the story of Robinson Crusoe by an African grandmother, whose Crusoe brings meat, leather and safety to his community by killing an elephant. Her version inspires her grandson, named Friedman (echoing Friday and 'freed man') to wish to emulate Crusoe: '"Grandmother," he whispered, adroitly stepping into the role of Robinson Crusoe, the great hunter, "One day, I'm going to be like that. I'm going to be a hunter like Robinson Crusoe, and bring meat to all the people."'[40]

Among the many other authors who have rewritten Defoe's story are Walcott and J. M. Coetzee. Unlike other postcolonial writers, Walcott's 1965 and 1970 volumes, *The Castaway* and *The Gulf*, include several poems which take not Friday but the figure of Crusoe as their focus. For Walcott, Crusoe's sense of isolation, his attempt to create a life and to survive in a world which is alien and seemingly empty provides a paradigm for the island inhabitants of the New World:

> Upon this rock the bearded hermit built
> His Eden:
> Goats, corn crop, fort, parasol, garden,
> Bible for Sabbath, all the joys
> But one
> Which sent him howling for a human voice.
> Exiled by a flaming sun
> The rotting nut, bowled in the surf.
> Became his own brain rotting from the guilt
> Of heaven without his kind,
> Crazed by such paradisal calm
> The spinal shadow of a palm
> Built keel and gunwale in his mind.[41]

Yet it is Crusoe's language and traditions that the people of the anglophone West Indies inherit, learning first to see themselves and their worlds through the eyes of English novelists such as Defoe, G. A. Henty and Frederick Marryat. Denied an alternative language and traditions through the imposition of slavery, writers in the Caribbean must use the tools they have been given, the leavings of the shipwreck which is the consequence of slavery and the Middle Passage, to fashion a new way of describing and seeing themselves and their world:

> So from this house
> that faces nothing but the sea, his journals
> assume a household use;
> we learn to shape from them, where nothing was
> the language of a race,
> and since the intellect demands its mask
> that sun-cracked bearded face
> provides us with the wish to dramatize
> ourselves at nature's cost.
> to attempt a beard, to squint through the sea-haze,
> posing as naturalists,
> drunks, castaways, beachcombers, . . .[42]

Walcott has commented on the significance of Crusoe for Caribbean artists in his essay 'The Figure of Crusoe'.[43] Another West Indian writer who has commented on Crusoe's meaning as a shipwrecked and isolated castaway is V. S. Naipaul, in his essay, 'Columbus and Crusoe'.[44] The motif of shipwreck echoes through Naipaul's novel about the failures of Caribbean politicians, *The Mimic Men* (1967).

For the South African writer Coetzee, in the novel *Foe* (1986), both Crusoe and Friday become enigmatic figures, Friday most of all, because his story has been lost, and can only be speculated upon. His mystery is figured in the image of his mutilated tongue, torn from its roots, but his untold story, his thoughts, become an obsession not for Crusoe or his creator, Daniel de Foe, but for Coetzee's semi-invented narrator, Susan Barton (hers is the name of a character in another Defoe novel, *Roxana* (1724)), whom he imagines to have been shipwrecked on the same island and who tries to persuade de Foe to tell her story. *Foe* points to the different ways in which histories are suppressed and the consequences of that suppression: the white woman's story is neglected because she herself believes that she lacks the authority or credibility to be heard; the black slave's story has been more brutally suppressed, but also can not be understood because Europeans are incapable of reading the signals he gives. As Elleke Boehmer remarks:

> J. M. Coetzee's *Foe* (1986), a postmodern rewriting of the Robinson Crusoe story, gives a neat symbolic shorthand for this process of self-articulation by the colonized. In this novel, the Friday character, who lacks a tongue, mutely represents the colonized problem of making meaning. He dances in a circle, he plays one tune on the flute, he writes one character only, o, the empty set, the empty mouth. In a situation where there is no access to the media of cultural authority – the voice, the pen, the book – the forms of expression available to Friday are either silent, repetitive, or both. Yet, by enacting his own exclusion, by tracing the circles of interpretation which shut him out – by writing o – Friday begins to signify.[45]

Alongside postcolonial responses to Conrad's *Heart of Darkness*, and Defoe's *Robinson Crusoe*, perhaps one of the most frequently discussed texts is Jean Rhys's revisiting of Charlotte Brontë's *Jane Eyre* (1847). The feminist critics Sandra Gilbert and Susan Gubar published an influential reading of this novel in *The Madwoman in the Attic* (1979), the title of which refers to their argument that the figure of Bertha, Mr Rochester's mad first wife, is an image of the suppressed anger that many nineteenth-century women felt and expressed through such gothic manifestations.[46] Gayatri Chakravorty's Spivak's essay 'Three Women's Texts and a Critique of Imperialism' rejected this mainly psychoanalytical interpretation of the significance of Bertha, with its failure to acknowledge the actuality of colonial attitudes and relationships, and drew attention to Rhys's *Wide Sargasso Sea* (1966), a response to the story from the point of view of the so-called 'madwoman'. Rhys renames her protagonist Antoinette (it is her husband who robs her of her identity by calling her Bertha), and denies the husband a name at all, though readers cannot avoid identifying him with Brontë's Rochester. The first and last of the three sections of the novel are allocated to Antoinette, who reveals the impossibility of her role and class as a displaced white Creole after the emancipation of slaves in the Caribbean. Distrusted by the freed black people (and vilified as 'white cockroaches'), and scorned by wealthier white English entrepreneurs as 'tainted' by their West Indian context, Antoinette and her mother become the victims of violence and callousness from both groups. The burning of their house, Coulibri, causing the death of Antoinette's brother and the derangement of her mother, becomes an event which haunts Antoinette, represents the destruction of her class (the 'Rochester' narrator of the second part of the novel observes 'ruins all over the place'), and also both mirrors and leads to the burning of Thornfield Hall in *Jane Eyre*. Thus, as Fraser observes, 'just as the destruction of Coulibri spelled the end of a slaving plantocracy, the wanton razing of Thornfield Hall epitomizes the decay of the gentrifield class embodied by Rochester'.[47] Rhys's novel also makes clear the dependency of that gentrified class on the colonies, and their economic exploitation of the West Indies. Antoinette is identified with the people, the landscape and the flora of the West Indies by both the author and 'Rochester', who is equally alienated by the sensuality of the island of Dominique and that of Antoinette herself, but he marries Antoinette for the money she can bring to shore up the dwindling fortunes of his family in England.

Just as Achebe has removed Okonkwo and his story from the fictional paragraph assigned to him by the District Commissioner and breathed a full life into him, so Rhys has rescued Bertha Mason from the attic and stereotype to which she was confined by Brontë. 'The madwoman in the attic' is given a history, a sensibility, an alternative text, and as a consequence it will be difficult to see either her or Mr Rochester again solely in terms of Brontë's novel, she as an unfortunate and uncouth obstacle to Jane Eyre's happiness, he as a strong and romantic hero. Another West Indian take on Brontë's work, and in contrast to Rhys's text a deeply misogynist one, is Naipaul's novel *Guerrillas* (1975), which alludes explicitly to *Jane Eyre* by naming two of its central characters Roche and Jane, and expands the allusion to include Emily Brontë through its location in a commune named Thrushcross Grange.

Rhys includes the voices of African Caribbean people, most notably in the person of the black servant Christophine, who is given dignity and independence of mind surpassing that available to Antoinette. But the story is Antoinette's, and hers is the story of the formerly slaveowning class and its disintegration. In other settler fiction often it is the narratives of early settlers that are revisited and retold. Thus Margaret Atwood has written a series of poems which revisit the journals of Susanna Moodie, one of Canada's first published authors. Atwood's novel *Alias Grace* (1996) enlarges and retells the story of Grace Marks, a convicted murderer who was declared insane and whom Moodie visited in prison.

Atwood not only revises Moodie's entirely unsympathetic nineteenth-century account of Grace Marks, but, like Rhys, seeks to question the notion of a single 'true', linear history. One of the motifs that runs through the novel is that of stitching and patchwork, and this relates to a concept of history as a kind of patchwork quilt, containing varied 'limited histories',[48] which can be stitched together to make different patterns. Each of the fifteen sections of the novel begins with a quilt pattern, and the sections are also varied in terms of style, narrative technique and kinds of writing, ranging from newspaper clippings, journal entries, confessions and letters to interviews, monologues and memories, told by the American psychiatrist who is determined to discover 'the truth' as well as by Grace, who remains an enigma to both the doctor and the reader. This novel interrogates and resists earlier colonial and settler attitudes, as well as the continuing neocolonial relationship between Canada and the United States.

Recent postcolonial writers have not only revisited and challenged colonial and settler narratives, some have offered more complex histories of the colonial encounter than those offered in earlier postcolonial fiction and poetry. Thus Gurnah's *Paradise* published almost half a century later, compares interestingly with Achebe's seminal anticolonial account in *Things Fall Apart*. Not only is it set on the other side of the continent, and so contrasts the rather different impact of Europeans (women as well as men) who come as settlers, as well as military occupants (in this case German), it also creates a multilayered series of cultures and settlers, Muslim traders who originate from Yemen, Oman and other Arabic areas, Indian merchants and traders, different groups of African peoples, all with differing responses to the presence of those other groups. This is one of the many ways in which Gurnah's novel departs from the more binary contrast between Africans and Europeans set up in *Things Fall Apart* or *A Grain of Wheat*, as well as in Conrad's *Heart of Darkness*. Gurnah's fiction work, and that of other recent postcolonial writers, will be discussed in chapters 9 and 10.

Chapter 4

Authorizing the self: postcolonial autobiographical writing

The previous chapter discussed texts which challenge and revise the form and content of colonialist histories and narratives as a means of asserting the dignity and validity of the authors' cultures, or simply setting the record 'straight'. But works which enter into dialogue with metropolitan depictions of colonized peoples and places run the risk of becoming caught within the terms defined by the colonizer. Thus Jean-Paul Sartre described the assertions of *négritude* writers such as Léopold Senghor as 'antiracist racism', the antithesis to the colonialists' racist thesis.[1] As I have tried to show, writers such as Chinua Achebe, Margaret Atwood, Jean Rhys and Salman Rushdie have been aware of this danger and have created fictions which question the very process of a single perspective and linear narration which establishes simple categories of good and evil or civilized and barbaric, or makes absolute distinctions between 'them' and 'us'.

Another strategy frequently found in postcolonial writing sidesteps entering into dialogue on the colonizer's terms by grounding the text in autobiography, starting from the self as the central point of reference. Thus, as Chaucer's Wife of Bath challenged the dogma of male clerks and scholars by asserting 'the authority of experience', many postcolonial writers have drawn on their childhood experience sometimes as a means of conveying precolonial culture, a relatively innocent world preceding the impact of foreign educational systems, sometimes conveying the vulnerability of a child to the dictates of colonial power, and at the same time offering a perspective which challenges the premises and beliefs that are taken for granted in the hegemonic culture accepted by adult readers. In these ways postcolonial autobiography is often read differently from autobiographies produced in a metropolitan context. For whereas metropolitan autobiographies are more typically works which seek to explore and assert the writer's individualism, postcolonial autobiographies are often written to portray the author as a representative of his cultural group, as in the case of Camara Laye's *Enfant Noir* (*Dark Child*) (1953), or as the embodiment of a new nation's struggle to come into being and its establishment of a cultural and ideological identity, as in the autobiographies of Mahatma Gandhi, Nelson

Mandela, Jawarhalal Nehru and Kwame Nkrumah. Philip Holden describes works such as these as 'documents of struggles to create new social imaginaries after colonialism through narratives that personify national sovereignty'.[2] In both Nehru's *An Autobiography* (1936) and *Ghana: The Autobiography of Kwame Nkrumah* (1957) the personal and national narratives merge (as the title of Nkrumah's text makes explicit). Nehru writes of India, its people and culture, as a female entity, and his relationship with India is frequently made to parallel his relationship with his wife, Kamala. The state, on the other hand, as Philip Holden notes, is perceived as masculine, and as Nehru portrays it, the role of the state is to discipline and modernize the sometimes recalcitrant and traditionalist nation.[3] Similarly Nkrumah's text, written in 1956 in time for the 1957 independence celebrations, inscribes Ghana as feminine, and parallels the nation with his mother, to whom the autobiography is dedicated.[4] Both autobiographies become iconic texts which are alluded to and questioned in later fictions such as Rushdie's *Midnight's Children* (1981) and *The Moor's Last Sigh* (1995) in the case of Nehru, and, in the case of Nkrumah, *The Beautyful Ones Are Not Yet Born* (1968) by Ayi Kwei Armah and *Anowa* (1970) and *Our Sister Killjoy* (1977) by Ama Ata Aidoo. Women nationalists and political leaders may also make use of the trope of the nation as female as a means of merging their public personas with the nation. Thus Maud Gonne's autobiography, *A Servant of the Queen* (1938) emphasizes her identification with Erin, and her determination to serve not the English Queen but Cathleen ni Houlihan, the symbol of Ireland. And Nehru's daughter, Indira Gandhi, campaigned as leader of the Congress Party on the slogan 'Indira is India'. (This identification is resisted and subverted in Rushdie's *Midnight's Children* and *The Moor's Last Sigh*.) Bapsi Sidwha's autobiographical novel, *Ice-Candy-Man* (1988) (published in the USA in 1991 as *Cracking India*), brilliantly uses a child narrator, closely connected to Sidwha's own situation at the time with her Parsi family in Lahore, to realize the tensions and sufferings experienced by various groups during the partition of the subcontinent into India and Pakistan. The narrator's Ayah, courted by both Muslim and Hindu, becomes a symbol of the continent itself as she is ultimately kidnapped and ravaged. In the film of the novel, *Earth* (1999), the child's lameness caused by polio is made a prominent feature, and the autobiographical element is made evident when Sidwha herself, still limping slightly, appears at the end of the film

In the autobiographies mentioned above, the public figures recount their personal journey as a paradigm which encourages the citizens of the new state to align themselves with them, and thus identify themselves with the nation in formation. In the majority of postcolonial autobiographies, however, the connection between public and private expression may be less explicit, and cannot be taken for granted by readers even before they open the text. Such autobiographies, as Gayatri Chakravorty Spivak points out, may also occur as 'testimonies', in which 'the subaltern [gives] testimony to the less oppressed other'.[5] Many slave narratives belong to this genre. Here one might also consider Frantz Fanon's *Black Skin, White Masks* (1952) as an often autobiographical testimonial, which at the same time contests the author's designation as subaltern. Fanon's work explicitly addresses the issue of the conflict between the identity ascribed by others to him as a representative and stereotyped black body, and the self which asserts an individual subjectivity and identity. Fanon's work is alluded to in semi-autobiographical works such as Aidoo's *Our Sister Killjoy* and Tsitsi Dangarembga's *Nervous Conditions* (1988). In *Our Sister Killjoy* Sissie's experience in Germany of being pointed to by a mother exclaiming, '*Ja, das Schwartze Mädchen* [*sic*]',[6] echoes but also refuses Fanon's example of a sudden sense of imprisonment in his blackness when a French child exclaims, 'Look, a Negro!'[7]

Fanon comments that the colonial denial of the humanity of the colonized drives them 'to ask the question constantly "Who am I?"'.[8] Hence it is not surprising that autobiography and autobiographical fiction and poetry become pervasive modes in postcolonial writing. In Ireland W. B. Yeats foregrounds the construction of self, the struggle to achieve identity, not only in his *Autobiographies* (1926) but also in his poetry and drama. Thus he writes in 'A Dialogue of Self and Soul':

> How in the name of heaven can he escape
> That defiling and disfiguring shape
> The mirror of malicious eyes
> Casts upon his eyes until at last
> He thinks that shape must be his shape?[9]

'That defiling and disfiguring shape' the poet sees mirrored in 'malicious eyes' may refer in part to the portrayal of him by his critics within Ireland; it is likely also to refer to the more general stereotype of Irishmen promulgated by the English, a stereotype which he, Lady Gregory and others sought to destroy when they founded the Irish Literary Theatre with its ambition 'to show that Ireland is not the home of buffoonery and easy sentiment, as it has been represented'.[10]

In his *Autobiographies* Yeats makes explicit the connection between a national and an individual quest for identity and unity:

> Nations, races, and individual men are unified by an image, or bundle of
> related images, symbolical or evocative of a state of mind, which is of all
> states of mind impossible, the most difficult to that man, race or nation;
> because only the obstacle that can be contemplated without despair
> rouses the will to full intensity.[11]

James Joyce's *A Portrait of the Artist as a Young Man* (1916) and *Ulysses* (1922) both draw attention to their status as autobiographical fiction, while at the same time problematizing the issue of physical and mental colonization. Like Yeats, Joyce reveals in *A Portrait* the developing consciousness of his protagonist, Stephen Dedalus, as a divided self, who must steer his way past the institutional dogmas of religion, family and nation in order to become a writer who can 'forge in the smithy of [his] soul the uncreated conscience of [his] race'. Stephen – like Nehru, Nkrumah and Indira Gandhi, like Maud Gonne, Yeats and Padraic Pearse (one of the leaders of the 1916 Easter Rising) – conceives of his country as feminine. Thus in thinking of Emma Cleary, the woman he would like to woo, and who seems not to respond to him, he merges her image with that of Ireland:

> And yet he felt that, however he might revile and mock her image, his anger was also a form of homage. He had left the classroom in disdain that was not wholly sincere, feeling that perhaps the secret of her race lay behind those dark eyes upon which her long lashes flung a quick shadow. He had told himself bitterly, as he walked through the streets, that she was a figure of the womanhood of her country, a batlike soul waking to the consciousness of itself in darkness, and secrecy, and loneliness.[12]

Although *A Portrait of the Artist as a Young Man* is based closely on Joyce's own experience – his family, the school and university he attended, the culture of Dublin in the last twenty years of the nineteenth century – we should be careful not to merge the author completely with Stephen. The critic James Olney maintains that 'any autobiography constitutes a psychological-philosophical imitation of the autobiographer's personality'.[13] In autobiographical fiction the act of imitation of the author's personality in certain periods and in specific contexts is made more evident by the adoption of a pseudonym for the central protagonist, and perhaps the use of indirect free speech, or the sense of an interior monologue, rather than first person narrative to convey the consciousness of its subject. Joyce's subsequent novel, *Ulysses*, portrays a slightly older Stephen, who is much more self-conscious and sceptical about the identification of Ireland with Cathleen ni Houlihan or with other female figures. He also parodies and criticizes forms of Irish nationalism which hark back to a nostalgic precolonial or rural utopia, and which promulgate a singular racial identity. Hence the other major protagonists in *Ulysses* are Leopold and Molly Bloom, who are respectively of Hungarian Jewish and English-Spanish descent. Nevertheless, Joyce's opposition to Britain's colonial rule, as well as to the hegemony of the Roman Catholic Church, was clearly recognized by his contemporaries. Thus the pro-British provost of Trinity College, J. P. Mahaffy, declared that Joyce's writings demonstrated that 'it was a mistake to establish a separate university for the aborigines of the island, for the corner-boys who spit into the Liffey'.[14] Mahaffy's comment illustrates clearly the racial and class distinctions established and maintained by Ireland's ruling elite in this period, and their similarity to the distinctions made by ruling elites in other colonized countries. In both novels, the issue of nationalism and the writer's responsibility to his nation is debated explicitly and implicitly.

Robert Fraser comments on the significance of first person narrative in the postcolonial context as a response to colonial texts which in anthropological mode 'invariably describe the colonised human as "other", and just as invariably in the third person plural'.[15] In this context the 'first person singular, may also become 'the representative I' as Fraser terms it, 'in novels in which the first person singular is explicitly construed as identical, and coterminous, with the nation itself'.[16] But it is also significant that many of the key colonial texts to which postcolonial writers have 'written back' are narrated in the first person – for example, *Robinson Crusoe* (1719), *Jane Eyre* (1847) and *Heart of Darkness* (1902). Each of these novels, like many colonial travel books and anthropological texts, constructs the white European male or female observer/narrator as normative. One function of postcolonial autobiographies is to resituate the central perspective, the seeing 'eye' or 'I', and at the same time dramatize the process of the indigenous speaker's reconstruction or reassertion of his or her identity.

Writing about European autobiographies, Olney has commented that for most readers the particular interest is 'the isolate uniqueness that nearly everyone agrees to be the primary quality and condition of the individual and his experience'.[17] With regard to African writing, however, he argues that community is more important than the individual, the life much more socially oriented, so that he considers 'autobiography from Africa less an individual phenomenon than a social one'.[18] The generalization Olney makes about African writing, whether fictional or explicitly autobiographical, might be disputed, but arguably postcolonial writers are as much concerned with the social context, the political and cultural forces which impinge on their community, as with the individuality of the protagonist. Nevertheless, the individuality, or perhaps the independence of the protagonist is at stake, alongside the independence of the nation to which he claims allegiance. Much early postcolonial writing addresses itself to the dual task of giving both the community and the individual expression, writing 'from the inside' in opposition to the colonial outsider's dismissal of either cultural value or individual subjectivity within that community. But there is also a tension, an ambivalence, inherent in that dual task. In both *A Portrait of the Artist as a Young Man* and *Ulysses*, Joyce vividly, one might claim lovingly, recreates the Dublin he felt he could no longer live in if he were to become a writer. Yeats's autobiographical poetry and prose dramatizes his commitment to Ireland, as he strives to change it and to be true to his own divided and conflicting selves.

In the West Indies C. L. R James's *Beyond a Boundary* (1963) and his early semi-autobiographical novel *Minty Alley* (1936) depict the protagonist's growing awareness of the ways in which colour and class may circumscribe the expansion of the self. George Lamming's influential autobiographical novel *In the Castle of My Skin*, portraying a childhood and adolescence in Barbados, was published in 1953. In later decades, Kamau Brathwaite and Derek Walcott produced poetic autobiographies in *X/Self* (1987) and *Another Life* (1973) respectively, while V. S. Naipaul drew on his father's life to write *A House for Mr Biswas* (1961), and made fiction and autobiography inextricable in *The Enigma of Arrival* (1987). Autobiography and autobiographical fiction and poetry have also been important genres for Caribbean women writers, including Michelle Cliff, Zee Edgell, Lorna Goodison, Jamaica Kincaid, Paule Marshall, Jean Rhys and Olive Senior. Challenging the concept of autobiography as centering on one individual, Sistren, the Jamaican women's collective, has produced a collective autobiography, *Lionheart Gal* (1986), which transfers the oral narratives of working-class women to a single written-text.

Lamming's *In the Castle of My Skin*, like *A Portrait of the Artist as a Young Man*, explores a history of mental colonization which the protagonist seeks to escape through exile. In his Introduction to the novel, written thirty years after its first publication, Lamming wrote of the impact of British colonialism on the psychology of Barbadians during the 1930s and 1940s, a community which on the one hand took pride in its relationship to the 'Mother Country', identifying itself as 'Little England', and on the other hand was aware of the need for an independent economic and cultural existence:

> It was not a physical cruelty. Indeed, the colonial experience of my generation was almost wholly without violence. No torture, no concentration camp, no mysterious disappearance of hostile natives, no army encamped with orders to kill. The Caribbean endured a different kind of subjugation. It was a terror of the mind; a daily exercise in self-mutilation. Black versus Black in a battle for self-improvement.[19]

This mental colonization, linked to a rigid class structure, created in Lamming's view 'a fractured consciousness, a deep split in its sensibility which now raised difficult problems of language and values; the whole issue of cultural allegiance between imposed norms of White Power, represented by a small numerical minority, and the fragmented memory of the African masses: between white instruction and Black imagination'.[20] Although Lamming differs from Joyce in adopting for some episodes a first person narrator, and in marking a relationship between author and protagonist through identifying him simply with the first initial of the author's first name (G.), he takes a similar trajectory and structure to Joyce by enacting the development of his protagonist, G., in successive contexts: family, school, community, adolescent awareness. Thus both authors depict the consciousness of an entire community to which the protagonist is attached, but from which he also seeks detachment. In both novels an ambivalent parting is achieved at the end, as the protagonist rejects a particular call to nationalism based on racial identification, and looks towards departure from the island home. Some readers would argue that at this point Lamming is more distanced from his protagonist than Joyce was from his: Ngugi wa Thiong'o, for example, sees Lamming as endorsing Trumper's support for Black Power and diasporic racial awareness for those of African descent as a means of casting off the cultural and economic 'nets' of British colonialism.[21]

In autobiographical writings by women in Africa, India, and the West Indies, the search for identity and self-fulfilment is even more problematical. One collection of critical and creative writing on colonial and postcolonial women's texts is entitled *A Double Colonisation*,[22] referring to the oppression of 'native' women by both the colonial and the patriarchal local cultures which confine women to domestic and childbearing duties, and discriminate in terms of both gender and ethnicity or colour. As we have seen in the previous chapter, Jean Rhys portrayed the traumatic effects of such double colonization in *Wide Sargasso Sea* (1966); she also revealed the sense of disorientation and loss of identity experienced by her protagonist in her more autobiographical novel, *Voyage in the Dark* (1934). Indeed, many autobiographical works by postcolonial women narrate a descent into disorientation and madness in the face of the impossible demands and denial of worth that they face. These works include Bessie Head's *A Question of Power* (1973), Keri Hulme's *The Bone People* (1984), Janet Frame's *An Angel at My Table* (1984) and Dangarembga's *Nervous Conditions*. In the novels by Head, Hulme and Dangarembga, the women protagonists are assaulted physically and psychologically by men who feel their own fragile status in emerging or newly independent nations threatened, and by conflicting expectations regarding their role and sexual attractiveness, an attractiveness based on Western norms of appearance and behaviour.

Other women writers have avoided the issue of sexuality by focusing on childhood and early adolescence, as do male writers such as Michael Antony, Christopher Drayton and Lamming. Indeed, Alison Donnell argues that although the dominant focus on childhood in canonical Caribbean writing has effectively used the child's vision to expose 'the complex power structures of colonial institutions and power structures . . . through the child's encounter with the school, the church, the cinema and the people of the communities in which they live', this emphasis on childhood experience 'has nevertheless limited the critical response to Caribbean literature in one important way: it has arrested the discussion of sexuality'.[23] Thus Merle Hodge's *Crick-Crack Monkey* (1970), Zee Edgell's *Beka Lamb* (1982) and Jamaica Kincaid's *Annie John* (1986) all portray their protagonists' growing awareness of discrimination in terms of gender, class and colour, but end their narratives before the discovery of sexual identity. One can see a similar pattern in Australian autobiography and autobiographical fiction, though the emphasis on childhood is less prevalent there. One of Australia's best-known autobiographical novels, Miles Franklin's *My Beautiful Career* (1901) focuses mainly on the narrator's early, almost Edenic childhood on a remote bush farm, contrasted with her teenage years in a harsher and poorer environment on a dairy farm, where she feels culturally deprived and oppressed by the expectation that she should forget her ambition to be a writer and marry. Published in 1901, the year the Australian states became united under a federal government, and thus formed a new nation, Franklin's novel both endorses the ardent nationalism that led up to federation and critiques the masculine ethos of that nationalism. Early reviewers of the novel praised its 'Australianness' but were made uneasy by its feminism and romanticism. Thus Henry Lawson, Australia's leading writer in this period, wrote in his Preface to the first edition, 'I don't know about the girlishly emotional parts of the book – I leave that to girl readers to judge; but the descriptions of bush life and scenery came startlingly and painfully real to me, and . . . as far as they are concerned, the book is true to Australia, the truest I ever read.'[24] Another early and influential reviewer, P. R. Stephensen, voices the critical assumption that has informed discussions of women's writing for centuries, that women simply transpose their lives on to the page, writing 'diaries' – seen as a female genre – rather than creative literature. Stephensen considered that, '"Miles Franklin" has simply turned her girlish diary into a book; she has made literature out of the little things that lay around her – and this is what gives the book its value.' However, he also endorsed the book strongly as 'the very first Australian novel', and in an interesting merging of the woman and the country, reminiscent of other nationalist autobiographies discussed above, claimed, '[T]he author has the Australian mind, she speaks Australian language, utters Australian thoughts, and looks at things from an Australian point of view absolutely . . . her book is a warm embodiment of Australian life, as tonic as bush air, as aromatic as bush trees, and as clear and honest as bush sunlight.'[25]

My Brilliant Career has reemerged as a canonical text in various guises – as a nationalist fiction, as an autobiographical document about country life in the 1890s, and in the second half of the twentieth century as a feminist statement.

It is in this role that it was endorsed and republished in 1980 by Virago Press with a Preface by Virago's Australian editor, Carmen Callil. More recently, critics such as Ian Henderson have addressed the apparent inconsistencies in this autobiographical novel and the problem of reconciling Franklin's apparent disdain for 'peasantdom' with her dedication of the book to 'the honest bush folk who toil for their future', or her romantic aspiration for an ideal partner and her 'feminist' refusal of marriage. Henderson argues that earlier readings of her text relate to the gendering of genres and modes, in which realism is seen as masculine, romance as feminine, autobiography where 'a woman finds her voice' as feminist. Instead, he analyses *My Brilliant Career* as a 'performative' text in which Franklin consciously adopts a variety of gendered genres: 'Within *My Brilliant Career* sometimes realism is dominant, sometimes the romance mode, but neither mode is consistent for long, and even while "dominant", each mode's "other" irrupts into the narrative. In the process, then Sybylla delivers a self-conscious performance of her displacement in either gendered mode, preferring to roleplay.'[26]

The performance of gender, and in this case the questioning of notions of a stable sexual identity, are crucial motifs in another Australian semi-autobiographical fiction, Patrick White's *The Twyborn Affair* (1979). Here the protagonist shifts between identities as Eudoxia, Eddie and Eadith. As Eudoxia, Twyborn is a transvestite and 'wife' to his Greek lover Angelo; as Eddie he works, as White himself did, as a 'jackeroo', an apprentice farmer amid an aggressively masculine society; as Eadith Trist, s/he becomes the madam of a sophisticated brothel catering to the English aristocracy in London (this part is *not* autobiographical). In this novel the struggle for national independence and self-validation is paralleled by the quest for acceptance as a homosexual. White's autobiography *Flaws in the Glass* (1981) is explicit about his life as a writer, and his complex identity as an Australian and a homosexual in what was then a homophobic culture.

Robert Fraser sees Franklin's *My Brilliant Career* as typical of many settler colony autobiographical works in its narcissism, and its use of 'the colonial first person singular'.[27] It is also comparable with many other settler autobiographies in its attention to place, its assertion of belonging to a particular locale rather than a particular society, and its refusal to acknowledge the ownership of that locale by indigenous people.

Postcolonial autobiographical writing often plays a significant role in establishing the subject's sense of location and belonging. However, the desire to establish location and belonging may perform differently for settler authors, for indigenous authors, and for writers of mixed race and cultures. Examples of these different functions in autobiographies can be seen in Karen Blixen's *Out of Africa* (1937), Sally Morgan's *My Place* (1987), Bernardine Evaristo's *Lara* (1997), and Michael Ondaatje's *Running in the Family* (1982).

'I had a farm in Africa, at the foot of the Ngong hills': thus Karen Blixen establishes her ownership, stating that the land once belonged to her and asserting her presence and being in that 'colonial singular first person.' Moreover, we are told a few lines on that this was not just a random piece of land; 'it was Africa distilled up through six thousand feet, like the strong and refined essence of a continent'.[28] Nevertheless, the title of this autobiographical work, *Out of Africa*, forewarns the reader that the author no longer belongs. One might read this text as a contest between Blixen and Africa in terms of asserting then rejecting her right to belong, and this perhaps is the narrative entrenched in much settler writing during the nineteenth and early twentieth centuries. In addition to *My Brilliant Career*, one could include here such works as Susanna Moodie's *Roughing it in The Bush* (1852), and more recently, Judith Drake-Brockman's *Wongi Wongi* (2001), written in response to Morgan's *My Place*.

All these works share a lack of interest in the prehistory of the location and the author's family; it is the author who gives the place meaning, and who takes meaning from her presence in that place. Moreover, its significance is contained within the period of the writer's residence. For Blixen, as Gillian Whitlock points out, Africa is represented as the place where a European woman can become herself, powerful and independent. Beyond that period it has no past and no future.[29]

In contrast, Morgan's autobiography begins with a scene in which the author is conspicuously out of place and disempowered, while the affirmative title, *My Place*, suggests a future belonging. This is the opening paragraph:

> The hospital again, and the echo of my reluctant feet through the long, empty corridors. I hated hospitals and hospital smells. I hated the bare boards that gleamed with newly applied polish, the dust-free window-sills, and the flashes of shiny chrome that snatched my distorted shape as we hurried past. I was a grubby five-year-old in an alien environment.[30]

Dust-free, sterile and distorting, the hospital is a place where the self is threatened and dissolved, full of wounded or shell-shocked white males, victims of World War II, all of them incomplete. Here the child Sally is called upon to perform the role of daughter to her white father, of compliant little girl, but cannot. The older Sally writes, 'I felt if I said anything at all, I'd just fall apart. There'd be me, in pieces on the floor. I was full of secret fears.'[31] The alien unnaturalness of the hospital is then juxtaposed with Sally's memories of her grandmother's closeness to nature, another bedside scene where she is woken to hear the sound of a bullfrog and the call of a special bird.[32] The opening contrast, between a self distorted and threatened in a sterile white male world, and a self remembered and sustained in connection with her grandmother and nature, sets up the scheme of the autobiography, and the later scenes where Sally becomes an intermediary between her father and her mother, and between the state and the private worlds of her mother's family. Like the hospital, school, with its rigid and 'unnatural' regulations, presents another public realm in which Sally feels completely alien, whereas her grandmother provides a sympathetic retreat from that world. The autobiography reiterates a contrast between the new, white imposed and unnatural world, and the older 'natural' world associated with her grandmother, a world which draws its sustenance from close attention to birds, animals and the natural environment, a world rooted both in the land and the past.

But the truth about the past and her grandmother remains mysterious, concealed by a 'white lie', as Sally's mother admits when finally confronted about her aboriginal identity. "'All those years, Mum", I said, "how could you have lied to us all those years?" "It was only a little white lie," she replied sadly.'[33] Thus, while Blixen begins her memoir with the affirmation of her 'self' in connection to the land and ends with the dissolution of that fantasy of belonging, Morgan is concerned with the quest for selfhood, and for an identity which locates her biologically, culturally and geographically. And while Kenya allows Blixen to establish herself as an *exceptional* European woman (and indeed also nourishes exceptional European men such as Denys Finch-Hatton), Morgan seeks to construct a communal identity, dissolved into a common strand of aboriginality and connected to a particular place of origin through the voices of 'ordinary' Aborigines. And whereas Blixen's narrative begins with a clearly focused autobiographical 'I' and then disintegrates at the end into a series of fragments as Finch-Hatton dies and she and her community of servants move away into an unknown future, Morgan's work builds to a climax through a series of connected narratives moving back into the past. For Blixen, her presence in Africa must be self-contained, in terms of both time and place, cut off from past or future; for Morgan, her presence and self-realization in Australia, her future, can be achieved only through a series of historical and geographical journeys, which allow a suppressed past and sense of belonging to come to the surface.

While for Blixen a European identity is taken for granted, and there is plenty of reference to all those artefacts which signal her European culture – the fine china, the silverware, the piano, the books, the furniture, the wine – Morgan's text involves the gradual discovery and recognition of aboriginality. In so doing, she constructs a generalized aboriginal identity for the reader. This moves from racial identity, the recognition of the significance of her darker skin, and her grandmother's non-European features, towards cultural identity, through the narration of the experiences of her great-uncle, her mother and finally her grandmother. Through these stories Morgan also moves away from the confines of an urban location in the suburbs of Perth to the former freedom and sense of belonging in Corunna Downs. Thus her great-uncle Arthur remembers Corunna Downs:

> There was some wonderful wildlife on Corunna Downs. There was one little bird, he was a jay or a squeaker, he'd sing out three times and then the rains would come. He was never wrong. While he was there, there was always good feed, but when he was gone, drought! When the little frogs sang out, we knew it was going to rain. They were lovely colours, white and brown with black spots. They were all different, there wasn't one the same. They used to get into the cooler and we'd have to clean it out. They was all natural animals. Wonderful creatures.
>
> There were no insecticides to kill the birds. That's why the blackfellas want their own land, with no white man messin' about destroyin' it.
>
> All the people round there, we all belonged to each other. We were the tribe that made the station. The Drake-Brockmans didn't make it on their own. There were only a few white men there, ones that fixed the pumps and sank wells by contract. The blackfellas did the rest.
>
> I remember seein' native people all chained up around the neck and hands, walkin' behind a policeman. They often passed the station that way.[34]

In this reminiscence Arthur Corunna juxtaposes both the claim to the land and the denial of that claim; the ability to know and read a specific natural world is articulated in detail, as is sense of community and mutual belonging: 'All the people round there, we all belonged to each other. We were the tribe that made the station.' Against this claim is set the dismissed claim of the Drake-Brockmans, and a history of dispossession and captivity – 'native people all chained up around the neck and hands, walkin' behind a policeman'. As Ngugi wa Thiongo's novels dispute Blixen's claim to ownership through their recounting of historical, legendary ties to the land and the experience of dispossession and imprisonment, so Morgan disputes the claims of the Drake-Brockmans and other white settlers. Moreover, Morgan establishes this aboriginal closeness to nature and communal responsibility as a biological inheritance, figured through the recurring reference to a special bird call, heard by her grandmother, her great-uncle, her sister Jill and herself. Morgan's quest, with her mother and sister, leads her to that place of origin, Corunna, and to being claimed as part of the community by the people who live there. In Morgan's words, 'What had begun as a tentative search for knowledge had grown into a spiritual and emotional pilgrimage. We had an Aboriginal consciousness now, and were proud of it.' She also declares, 'How deprived we would have been if we had been willing to let things stay as they were. We would have survived, but not as whole people. We would never have known our place.'[35]

Sally Morgan's quest stems in part from her hidden identity as a mixed-race Australian, whose whiteness is foregrounded to begin with in that white men's hospital, and whose nonwhite identity is a mystery. Bernardine Evaristo, in her autobiographical verse novel *Lara*,[36] begins with an awareness of her racial mixture (Irish and Nigerian), but like Morgan her narrator must experience a geographical and historical journey of discovery before she can fully acknowledge her Nigerian heritage, and so locate herself back in England. Despite significant differences in the contexts and contents of these two works, there are also interesting similarities. In each case their colour is connected with their sense of unbelonging, of being out of place. Both urban Australia and urban England are seen as the worlds of white people, where black people are perceived as belonging elsewhere. Paradoxically, it is only by going elsewhere, by leaving the city, that the authors can claim their place in the city. Thus Lara travels first to Lagos and encounters the world of her father and his relatives, and then to Brazil, where her great-grandfather had been taken as a slave, in order to locate herself in history through its associations with specific places, and then returns to 'London /, [where] Across international time zones / I step out of Heathrow and into my future.' Like Morgan, the artist, she resolves 'to paint slavery out of me, / the Daddy people onto canvas with colour rich strokes', and to 'think of my island, the 'Great' Tippexed out of it- / Tiny amid massive floating continents, the African one / An embryo within me'.[37]

Both these autobiographies by Morgan and Evaristo share certain scenes or tropes with Ondaatje's autobiographical *Running in the Family*. Neluka Silva has commented on the ways in which the emphasis on hybridity and multiculturalism in this text functions as a counter to the discourse of ethnic nationalism which was becoming so virulent in Sri Lanka in the 1970s and early 1980s.[38] Thus the marriage of Ondaatje's partly Tamil father and Burgher mother, the friction between them and their subsequent divorce, has a particular resonance in the context of the ethnic and class tensions in Sri Lanka. As a returnee of mixed race who seeks to retrieve his identity in a Sri Lankan context, Ondaatje must restage those tensions and conflicts, and seek some reconciliation between the attachments to mother and father. There are interesting similarities between the scenes in *My Place* and *Running in the Family* where the child must act as intermediary between a violent alcoholic father and the mother who is the victim of his outbursts. Ondaatje tells how his mother makes her children act out this intermediary role:

> Whenever my father would lapse into one of his alcoholic states she would send the three older children . . . into my father's room where by now he could hardly talk, let alone argue. The three of them, well coached, would perform with tears streaming, 'Daddy, don't drink, daddy if you love us, don't drink,' while my mother waited outside and listened . . . These moments embarrassed my older brother and sister terribly; for days after they felt guilty and miserable.[39]

Likewise, Sally is sent to negotiate with her father whenever the family has had to flee at night from one of his alcoholic rages. It is described as a recurring ritual drama:

> He always knew when I had come, quietly opening his bedroom door when he heard the creak on the back verandah.
> I took up my usual position on the end of his bed and dangled my feet back and forth . . .
> 'Dad, we'll all come back if you'll be good' I stated . . . [H]e responded with his usual brief, wry smile, and then gave his usual answer, 'I'll let you all come back as long as your grandmother doesn't.' He had a thing about Nanna.

The scene continues with the father's attempt to bribe Sally into staying with him, and a demand that she make clear whether her love and loyalty lie with her mother or her father. As in the Ondaatje scenes, the demand for an allegiance to one side rather than another, the staging of the child as negotiator on behalf of the 'wronged' party, is imbued with racial significance (the mother must leave behind her aboriginal parent) and reverberates in the context of the racial politics of the country as a whole. In Evaristo's work also, Lara acts as an intermediary between her white grandmother and her Nigerian father, and also learns to act the penitent in face of her father's harsh beatings; in all three works the father's presence and the tensions between the parents bring fear, pain and guilt for the children.

All three are also hybrid texts in their use of a mixture of genres. In contrast to Blixen's univocal text, told entirely from her perspective and in her authoritative voice, Morgan, Evaristo and Ondaatje deploy a mixture of voices, perspectives and genres. Ondaatje foregrounds the problem of recapturing the past through his fragmentary structure, in which he mingles anecdotes (sometimes conflicting), poems, quotations from past travel writers, memoirs, dialogue and photographs. The borderlines between the factual and the imagined often become blurred, as in the vivid account of his grandmother floating away in the floods or of his father's last train ride. Indeed, the text ends with the poignant admission that the past cannot be truly known, and that he will never 'find' his father, so is unable to see himself in terms of a patriarchal origin and descent. Even the photographs add to this sense of unknowability; rather than confirming the 'reality' of those photographed, and allowing us to 'see' them as they were, the groups in fancy dress, the parents making ape faces, the streets awash with water, all suggest transient or performed identities, moments of instability. Like Franklin and White, and like Naipaul's characters in *The Mimic Men* (1967), Ondaatje's use of a mixture of genres denies the notion of a fixed or stable identity, and suggests rather the performance of identities.[40]

Thinking about these autobiographical works, one is struck by how often travel, the move away from a starting place, becomes in postcolonial autobiography a means of locating oneself back in that land. One can think back to *The Interesting Narrative of Olandah Equiano* (1789), which, after the African prologue, describes a series of journeys to and from England before Equiano finally settles there as an Englishman. Similarly Mary Seacole's *The Wonderful Adventures of Mrs. Seacole in Many Lands* (1857), after her Jamaican starting point, describe two journeys to England, where she is rejected before her triumphant return as 'Mother Seacole'. Naipaul's *The Enigma of Arrival* also begins with his persistent mapping of the Wiltshire countryside, before then describing his journey from the Caribbean, his disorientation in London, and then his sense of belonging in Wiltshire again. Like Naipaul, Ondaatje mingles autobiography and travel writing in his *Running in the Family*. For both Naipaul and Ondaatje, England and Sri Lanka are made familiar and at the same time strange by a tradition of writing about them. They come to these countries with a kind of double vision, recognizing the scenes portrayed in books or advertisements yet finding the written or picture book images slightly out of kilter. Thus Naipaul's image of England is both confirmed and amended by the sight of the black-and-white cows on the Wiltshire hillside, a reminder of the images on the tins of condensed milk he remembered from his childhood. But as Tobias Döring points out, Naipaul also revisions the English landscape in terms of his Trinidadian world: the patterns of snowdrifts remind him of the whorls of sand on the beaches he walked on as a child.[41] In Ondaatje's case, however, the recognition of scenes in Sri Lanka is influenced both by his childhood memories and by the reaction of his Canadian-born children to a world which is for them completely new.

The title of Naipaul's autobiographical 'novel', *The Enigma of Arrival*, encapsulates one aspect of many postcolonial autobiographies. Whereas European

autobiographies traditionally map a journey through life to a point of comple-
tion or arrival, many postcolonial autobiographies, as Linda Anderson points
out, accept a concept of identity which embraces 'contingency, indeterminacy,
and conflict'.[42] For Naipaul, the 'arrival' is always uncertain, enigmatic, possibly
yet another departure. However, autobiographies by diasporic writers such as
Evaristo, Naipual or Ondaatje differ from those of writers like Morgan, who
assert their recovery of self and place in their 'home' country, or Wole Soyinka,
whose trilogy beginning with *Ake* (1981) affirms his origins and belonging in
Yoruba culture.

Chapter 5

Situating the self: landscape and place

The issue of place names runs through the history of every colonized and postcolonial country, often involving the name of the country itself. As Edward Said points out, 'If there is anything that radically distinguishes the imagination of anti-imperialism, it is the primacy of the geographical in it.'[1] Thus the territories which settlers named Rhodesia, to honour the military conquest by Cecil Rhodes, is renamed Zimbabwe when that nation becomes independent in 1980. Similarly, the name of its capital city is changed from Salisbury to Harare. In settler colonies and postcolonies such as Australia, Canada and New Zealand, place names such as Rylstone, Sydney, Victoria, London, Nova Scotia and Wellington indicate the concern to make the land familiar and to mark its ownership by the settlers. Yet these names will be found side by side with indigenous place names such as Mudgee, Wagga Wagga, Saskatchewan and Waikato indicating a continuing consciousness of the connection between the land and the peoples who inhabited it before the settlers.

This double claim also pertains to the flora and fauna of settler countries. The Britons who came to these lands often gave familiar names to birds, animals and plants which bore some resemblance to those they had known in England or Scotland. But Australian magpies, though black and white, belong to a different species than the English magpie, as Australian robins also differ from English ones. However, birds and animals such as the kookaburra and the kangaroo, which bore little resemblance to anything known in Europe, retained the names given them by the indigenous people. Other unfamiliar creatures and plants such as the platypus and the eucalyptus tree became known by the Latin labels assigned them, or were named after their 'discoverers', as in the case of the Banksia tree named after the botanist Sir Joseph Banks.

Brian Friel's play *Translations* (1980), discussed in chapter 2, takes as one of its focal events the British army's mapping of Ireland, its concern to name and rename places so that their significance speaks to the English-speaking occupiers rather than the Irish-speaking indigenous people. The process of reclaiming places as Celtic rather than English is illustrated in many of W. B. Yeats's poems, especially earlier ones. For example, 'The Man Who Dreamed of Fairyland' invokes Drumahair, Lissadell, the well of Scanavin, and the hill of Lugnanall, while 'The Hosting of the Sidhe' insists on the Celtic (rather than English) place names such as Knocknarea and Clooth-na-Bare, names which signify a whole system of traditions rooted in Celtic Irish culture and identity. In these early poems and some later ones, Yeats remaps Ireland as a possession of a distinctively Celtic people. In a different mode, James Joyce insistently maps Dublin in *Dubliners* (1914) and *Ulysses* (1922), but here the fact of dispossession is simultaneously acknowledged with the act of reclamation. In the first story of *Dubliners*, we encounter Great Britain Street and Little Britain Street; *Ulysses* sets its opening episode in a Martello tower, built as part of a British military defence system. The tower, together with the viceregal procession, Nelson's column, the presence of sailors from the HMS *Belle Isle*, and British soldiers in the Night Town episode, is a constant reminder of England's occupation of Ireland. But through the meanderings of Stephen Dedalus and Leopold Bloom, Joyce reclaims the city step by step, revisioning and sometimes renaming it. Thus Nelson's column, intended by the British as a declaration of military might and presence, becomes a mere device for an embryonic *Dubliners'* story, a site from which ordinary Dubliners might view and reclaim their city ('A Pisgah Sight of Palestine'). Nelson is demoted from his identity as victorious admiral to the 'one-handled adulterer', from public hero to private philanderer.

As Seamus Deane has argued, 'Yeats began his career by inventing an Ireland amenable to his imagination [but] ended by finding an Ireland recalcitrant to it.'[2] While Yeats was able to reimagine and reclaim Ireland *geographically* in his early poems, tensions arise when he seeks to confront Ireland's changing historical identity, or to weld together the geographical and the historical. The Easter Rising, the establishment of the Irish Free State and the growing power of the Catholic middle classes were all events which forced him to see Ireland as not only space to be reclaimed, but a state involved in and making contemporary history. Those poems which most powerfully express the tension between space and time, or perhaps more precisely place and change, where a stasis of place provokes a desire to escape out of time and out of history, and which one might see as his most modernist writings, include 'The Tower', 'Easter 1916', 'A Prayer for My Daughter', 'Meditations in a Time of Civil War', 'Coole Park and Ballylee' and 'Sailing to Byzantium'. Each begins with an invocation of a particular place and a particular biographical or historical moment, and each turns to visions of empty space and time, or visions out of space and time, in response to the torment of history. Like Stephen Dedalus, Yeats seeks, in part by stopping time and recreating a static place, to escape 'the nightmare of history' as it has impacted upon Ireland.

For Seamus Heaney, the metaphor of the bog, those very peat bogs which have been used by colonizers to dismiss the Irish as 'bog people', becomes a means of revisiting the interrelationship between place and history. In the volume entitled *North* (1975), he insists on excavating the soil, on depth and rootedness, rather than the manmade and aesthetically constructed landscapes which feature in Yeats's later poems. Although his reference in 'Bog Queen' and 'Grauballe Man' is to the photographs in P. V. Glob's *The Bog People* (1969) of Iron Age corpses preserved in Jutland, the references and analogies to Irish land and history are inescapable. Indeed, the analogy between Irish consciousness or identity and Ireland's peat bogs recurs not only in colonialist writing but also in nationalist writing. Thus the Irish writer and critic Daniel Corkery wrote in 1931, 'Our national consciousness may be described, in a native phrase, as a quaking sod. It gives no footing. It is not English, nor Irish, nor Anglo-Irish.'[3] Heaney's sequence of bog poems culminates and makes the analogies with Ireland and her history of blood-feud and blood-sacrifice in the causes of nationalism and unionism explicit in Section IV of 'Kinship'. There are allusions here also to Yeats's *Cathleen ni Houlihan* (1902), in which Mother Ireland calls for the blood of her young men, and in the fourth stanza to Yeats's yearning question in 'Easter 1916', 'Oh, when may it suffice?' In Heaney's poem 'terrible beauty' is displaced by the image of shaved heads (referring to girls whose heads were shaved for 'collaborating' with British soldiers) and by 'love and terror' swallowed by the goddess:

> And you, Tacitus,
> observe how I make my grove
> on an old crannog
> piled by the fearful dead;
>
> a desolate peace.
> Our mother ground
> is sour with the blood
> of her faithful,
>
> they lie gargling
> in her sacred heart
> as the legions stare
> from the ramparts.
>
> Come back to this
> 'island of the ocean'
> where nothing will suffice.
> Read the inhumed faces

of casualty and victim;
report us fairly,
how we slaughter
for the common good

and shave the heads
of the notorious,
how the goddess swallows
our love and terror.[4]

With reference to poems such as 'Bog Queen', Heaney has been criticized for a kind of voyeuristic, some would say almost pornographic fascination with the violence inflicted on women's bodies. Then again, he has been criticized for evading and aestheticizing the actual violence wrought in Northern Ireland by distancing it through the metaphor of Iron Age sacrificial burials. These two objections are not only at odds with one another, but also ignore the complexity of Heaney's poems. As Declan Kiberd points out:

> [T]here is in Heaney's writing a developed ethical sense which causes him constantly to question his own evasions. So, in ['Punishment'] when the IRA tars and feathers a woman for fraternising with British soldiers, he is reminded not only of a parallel case of a Danish woman sacrificed to the land in an ancient fertility rite but also of the accusing parallel between the IRA and himself, since both are guilty of reducing woman to a cultural totem.[5]

Here we can note how Heaney's use of 'history in the form of geography', to quote Kiberd's apt phrase,[6] contrasts with Yeats. Whereas Yeats invoked hills, towers, constructed landscapes and vistas, Heaney digs beneath the soil in these early poems, acknowledging (like Patrick Kavanagh) his peasant ancestry and his potato-farming father and grandfather, and also acknowledging his complicity in a deeply layered history of violence:

> I can see her drowned
> body in the bog,
> the weighing stone,
> the floating rods and boughs.
>
> Under which at first
> she was a barked sapling
> that is dug up
> oak-bone, brain-firkin:
>
> . . . .

> I almost love you
> but would have cast, I know,
> the stones of silence.
> I am the artful voyeur
>
> of your brain's exposed
> and darkened combs,
> your muscles webbing
> and all your numbered bones:
>
> I who have stood dumb
> when your betraying sisters,
> cauled in tar,
> wept by the railings,
>
> who would connive
> in civilized outrage
> yet understand the exact
> and tribal, intimate revenge.[7]

In later sequences of poems, when Heaney had moved away from a Northern Ireland occupied by British soldiers and torn between a colonial and anticolonial identity, to the Republic of Ireland and the independent South, his focus moves above ground, and embraces a wider and more invigorating landscape. His *Sweeney Astray* (1983) is a translation of the medieval Irish sequence *Buile Suibhne*, which relates in vibrantly detailed lyrics the life of the Irish King Sweeney after he had been cursed and transformed into a bird by the Irish cleric he insulted. Heaney's move from the macabre to the miraculous, grounded in precise language and natural imagery, is marked and perhaps inspired by this sequence. Here are three stanzas from one of the poems Sweeney speaks near the church at Swim-Two-Birds:

> The blackthorn is a jaggy creel
> stippled with dark sloes;
> green watercress in thatch on wells
> where the drinking blackbird goes.
> . . . .
> Low-set clumps of apple trees
> drum down fruit when shaken;
> scarlet berries clot like blood
> on mountain rowan.
>
> Briars curl in sideways,
> arch a stickle back,
> draw blood and curl up innocent
> to sneak the next attack.[8]

Like Yeats in his early poems, Heaney in these later poems returns to a pre-colonial Ireland, its myths and place names, as a means of reclaiming the island. But Heaney is concerned not merely with their resonance as signs of a precolonial culture, but also with revisiting the natural world and the consciousness of it expressed through the Sweeney sequence. One finds a similar strategy in the works of African poets such as Kofi Awoonor from Ghana and Jack Mapanje from Malawi, Christopher Okigbo and Wole Soyinka from Nigeria and Okot p'Bitek from Uganda. For these poets, however, traditional associations between land, nature and myth are less distant; indeed, they would assert that they have never disappeared, and continue as part of an alternative and hybrid culture, despite the domination of English educational syllabuses and literature in these countries. In India poets such as Arun Kolatkar, particularly in his sequence *Jejuri* (1976), combine an almost photographic depiction of a specific landscape with an evocation of the religious and other cultural traditions associated with it. It is striking how frequently the concept of a pilgrimage becomes the framework for a reuniting of landscape and tradition in postcolonial literature. This framework provides the plot for *Jejuri*; it is also what binds together the sequence in Heaney's *Station Island* (1984); provides a central scene in Soyinka's poetic sequence *Idanre* (1967) as well as his first novel, *The Interpreters* (1965) (when Egbo visits the bridge across the Ogun River); and is the plot and governing metaphor for many of Wilson Harris's novels, beginning with *Palace of the Peacock* (1960). In other works the trope of travel and pilgrimage is used not only to revisit the past and a consciousness which derives from the past, but also to contrast it with the consequences of modern technology, as in Soyinka's 'Death in the Dawn':

> Traveller, you must set out
> At dawn. And wipe your feet upon
> The dog-nose wetness of the earth.

> Let sunrise quench your lamps. And watch
> Faint pricklings in the sky light
> Cottoned feet to break the early earthworm
> On the hoe. Now shadows stretch with sap
> Not twilight's death and sad prostration.
> This soft kindling, soft receding breeds
> Racing joys and apprehensions for
> A naked day. Burdened hulks retract,
> Stoop to the mist in faceless throng
> To wake the silent markets – swift, mute
> Processions on grey byways . . . On this
> Counterpane, it was –

Sudden winter at the death of dawn's lone trumpeter. Cascades
Of white feather flakes . . . but it proved
A futile rite. Propitiation sped
Grimly on, before.
The right foot for joy, the left, dread
And the mother prayed, Child
May you never walk
When the road waits, famished.

Traveller, you must set forth
At dawn.
I promise marvels of the holy hour
Presages as the white cock's flapped
Perverse impalement – as who would dare
The wrathful wings of man's Progression . . . .

But such another wraith! Brother,
Silenced in the startled hug of
Your invention – is this mocked grimace
This closed contortion – I?[9]

Soyinka's influence on a younger generation of Nigerian writers is evidenced in Ben Okri's borrowing of the last line of the second stanza of this poem for his prizewinning novel, *The Famished Road* (1991). (Moreover, Soyinka's haunting poem 'Abiku' concerns the belief in the possession of a child by the spirit of another child who has died before puberty, a belief that provides the central metaphor in Okri's novel, and also Toni Morrison's *Beloved* (1987)). But Okri's fiction also shares this potent combination of the physical and the metaphysical, of precisely imaged and evocative natural detail ('The dog-nose wetness of the earth', the grey shapes of people walking towards the markets or their fields) linked to suprahuman forces whose ominous power cannot be propitiated by the traditional sacrifice of a cock. The landscape and the early morning is definitively Nigerian and everyday; it is also uncanny, and haunted by the possibility of an unknown fate, a double sense of possibility and destruction, which derives both from the road (and specifically the horrific accident rate on Nigeria's roads), and the Yoruba god Ogun who is the god of the roads, and Soyinka's personal identification with Ogun. However, together with the explicit and lethal impact of the motor car in the context of Yoruba landscape and myth, there is also a subtle importation of European imagery in the lines 'On this / Counterpane, it was – / Sudden winter at the death of dawn's lone trumpeter'.[10] 'Death at Dawn' can be read alongside *The Road*, Soyinka's 1965 play that elaborates powerfully images of death on the roads, the powerlessness of words to prevent those deaths, and yet at the same time the poetic creativity that the road and the life of truck drivers and travellers inspire.

'The strange scribblings of nature learning how to write'

Soyinka's work expresses a continuing and deeply embedded consciousness of a land given meaning by Yoruba culture, its myths, beliefs and associations. In settler countries such as Australia, New Zealand and the West Indies, many writers express a sense of alienation from or ambivalence towards a landscape and natural world which differ from that of their ancestral homeland and are at odds with the natural imagery implanted in the literary traditions which have accompanied them. The Australian poet Judith Wright has declared this problem of coming to terms with the landscape a central preoccupation in Australian literature, since '[b]efore one's country can become an accepted background against which the poet's and novelist's imagination can move unhindered, it must first be observed, understood, described, and as it were absorbed. The writer must be at peace with his landscape before he can turn confidently to its human figures.'[11]

Chinua Achebe in his third novel, *Arrow of God* (1964), portrays the difference between the consciousness of his indigenous Igbo characters, whose natural world and agrarian way of life is integral to the proverbs, anecdotes and idioms of their everyday speech, forming an organic part of their culture, and that of the English District Commissioner Winterbottom, whose very name imports an alien season, and who is introduced first as an *observer* of nature watching 'the riot of the year's first rain' and acutely uncomfortable in the eastern Nigerian heat. For this Englishman, African nature is romanticized, deceptive and hostile: 'This treacherous beguiling wind was the great danger of Africa. The unwary European who bared himself to it received the death-kiss.'[12] In *The Conservationist* (1973) Nadine Gordimer shows the difference in the consciousness of her main protagonist, the white settler/businessman Mehring, for whom a South African farm is a pastoral retreat, a natural world to be conserved, and the black workers on the farm who see it as a place where food is produced. But Mehring is also haunted by the consciousness of a repressed history of dispossession by white South Africans of the original African owners of the land, a repressed history imaged in the inadequately buried body of an unknown black man on Mehring's farm.

For the first European settlers in Australia, everything was unfamiliar. Its strangeness reinforced the view, held by almost all those first immigrants, and especially the convicts, that it was a place of exile. Here the seasons were reversed, the trees were evergreen, the eucalyptus trees shed their bark rather than their leaves, the skies were unfamiliar, the animals seemed bizarre, the summers glaring and hot, the soil and climate unresponsive to European methods of farming. In his remarkable trilogy, *The Fortunes of Richard Mahony*

(1917–29), Henry Handel Richardson consistently presents the land as harsh, shabby, and ugly, an inhospitable world for its eponymous Irish hero who never ceases to feel himself an exile. What struck these early settlers as the uncanny nature of the Australian bush was summarized by the nineteenth-century novelist and journalist Marcus Clarke, who emigrated to Australia from England in 1864:

> What is the dominant note of Australian scenery? That which is the dominant note of Poe's poetry – Weird Melancholy . . . The Australian mountain forests are funereal, secret, stern. Their solitude is desolation. They seem to stifle in their black gorges a story of sullen despair. No tender sentiment is nourished in their shade. In other lands the dying year is mourned, the falling leaves drop lightly on his bier. In the Australian forests no leaves fall. The savage winds shout among the rock clefts. From the melancholy gums strips of white bark hang and rustle. the very animal life of these frowning hills is grotesque and ghostly. Great gray [*sic*] kangaroos hop noiselessly over the coarse grass. Flights of white cockatoos stream out shrieking like evil souls. The sun suddenly sinks, and the mopokes burst out into horrible peals of semi-human laughter . . .
>
> There is a poem in every form of tree or flower, but the poetry which lives in the trees and flowers of Australia, differs from those of other countries. Europe is the home of knightly song, of bright deeds and clear morning thought . . . In Australia alone is to be found the Grotesque, the Weird, the strange scribblings of nature learning how to write.[13]

Apart from Clarke's mistaken conflation of the mopoke with the kookaburra, it is worth noting his need to 'read' the Australian landscape through a literary medium, and in this case an American rather than a European one. But it is a landscape which is yet to be written or spoken intelligibly: its stories are suppressed or stifled; it is either soundless or emits meaningless shrieks; its nature is undecipherable – 'strange scribblings . . . learning how to write' – in contrast to the knightly songs and 'clear morning thought' of Europe. Clarke suggests that Australia's natural world is both unwritten and unwritable, even as he seeks to write it.

Central to the history of Anglo-Australian literature is that endeavour to find a way of describing and coming to terms with the not-Englishness of Australia's geography, flora and fauna. The narrative of Australian history foregrounds those doomed explorers – Robert O'Hara Burke and William Wills, Ludwig Leichhardt, Charles Sturt, Edmund Kennedy – who sought to know and map the heart of the continent, and perished in the attempt. One of Patrick White's best-known novels, *Voss* (1957), is based on the story of the German explorer Ludwig Leichhardt, who set out to cross the Australian continent from east to west with a group of men. Journeying from the coast and embryonic urban life of Sydney to the bush and isolated cattle and sheep stations, to the desert interior, Voss seeks to impose his will on the Australian landscape, to conquer it by knowing and surviving it. Like Kurtz in Joseph Conrad's *Heart of Darkness* (1902), his idealism is no match for the actuality of physical suffering, isolation and alien cultures. And like Conrad's (or Marlow's) Africa, Australia becomes a metaphor for an existential journey of self-discovery. Nevertheless, as Laura Trevalyn, the novel's heroine and Voss's 'Intended', affirms, 'His legend will be written down, eventually, by those who have been troubled by it.'[14] And although she maintains that 'Knowledge was never a matter of geography. Quite the reverse, it overflows all maps that exist. Perhaps true knowledge only comes of death by torture in the country of the mind',[15] the novel itself creates Australia as a country of the mind, and maps it as physically malign once the explorers move beyond the coastal regions. Like Achebe's District Commissioner Winterbottom, Voss experiences acute discomfort in the heat and humidity, and then aridity, in what for him is an entirely alien landscape.

This response to the Australian landscape as hostile, barren, destructive and alien, a 3,000-mile-wide test of endurance, pervades much Australian fiction of the nineteenth and early twentieth centuries. One finds it in the short stories of Barbara Baynton and Henry Lawson, in the novels of Miles Franklin, Joseph Furphy, Xavier Herbert, Henry Handel Richardson and (in a more popular vein) Ion L. Idriess. Other writers treat the incongruity of European norms and Australia's unnatural nature as comic, or grimly comic, rather than merely grim. Thus Barron Field, one of the continent's first poets, in a pamphlet called *First Fruits*, apostrophizes the kangaroo:

> Kangaroo! Kangaroo!
> Thou spirit of Australia.
> That redeems from utter failure,
> From perfect desolation,
> And warrants the creation
> Of this fifth part of the Earth,
> Which should seem an after-birth,
> Not conceiv'd in the Beginning
> (For God bless'd His work at first,
> And thought that it was good),
> But emerg'd at the first sinning,
> When the ground was therefore curst; –
> And hence this barren wood![16]

In his review of Field's poems, published in 1819, Charles Lamb expressed a fairly prevalent view of Australia as a place of deformed morals, as well as deformed nature, where literary efforts were also warped by their dependency on English literary models. After mentioning that Field had left England 'to go and administer tedious justice in inauspicious and unliterary Thiefland' (Field was a judge in Australia), Lamb goes on to say:

> The First Fruits consist of two poems. The first ['Botany Bay Flowers'] celebrates the plant epacris grandiflora; but we are no botanists, and, perhaps, there is too much matter mixed up in it from the Midsummer Night's Dream to please some readers. The thefts are, indeed, so open and palpable, that we almost recur to our first surmise, that the author must be some unfortunate wight, sent on his travels for plagiarisms of a more serious complexion . . . We select for our readers the second poem; and are mistaken if it does not relish of the graceful hyperboles of our elder writers. We can conceive it to have been written by Andrew Marvell, supposing him to have been banished to Botany Bay, as he did, we believe, once meditate a voluntary exile to Bermuda.[17]

A conflict between a European tradition of nature poetry and the attempt to record and represent Australian scenery is apparent in much early settler poetry. The Australian-born Charles Harpur, son of convict parents, writes of his admiration for William Wordsworth as a poet responding to nature, and also of the difficulty of speaking for his new environment. Harpur felt that his mission was to become a poet of and for the country of his birth, writing how the Muse of the forest encouraged him to

> Be then the Bard of thy Country! O rather
> Should such be thy choice than a monarchy wide!
> Lo, 'tis the land of the grave of thy father!
> 'Tis the cradle of liberty! – Think, and decide.[18]

And these lines from 'To the Lyre of Australia' might be read as a response to the Marcus Clarke passage printed above:

> Lyre of my Country, first it falls to me
> From the charm-muttering Savage's rude-beating hand
> To snatch thee, that so thy wild numbers may be
> No longer but writ on the winds of this land.[19]

While Harpur admired Wordsworth as one who responds directly to nature and to a sense of the sublime, like Walt Whitman he found Alfred, Lord Tennyson far too 'gentlemanly' to provide a model for Australian or American poets, commenting:

[H]e is an old-world 'towney' – a dresser of parterres, and a peeper into parks. I am a man of the woods and mountains – a wielder of the axe, and mainly conversant with aboriginal nature; a man made stern and self-reliant, and thence plain and even fierce, by nearness (if I may so speak) to the *Incunabula mundi*. Hence poetry, with him, should be nice and dainty, rather than wise and hearty: while to affect my admiration, it must be free, bold and open, even at the risk of being rude.[20]

Harpur voices here the issues that will recur into the twenty-first century in discussions of the appropriate imagery, forms, attitudes, diction and style which should define a distinctively Australian literature. It is above all Australia's natural scenery, rather than its history or developing urban culture, which makes and marks the Australian poet. In poems such as 'A Mid-Summer Noon in the Australian Forest', one notes the precision of detail, the close observation of small minutiae like the dragonfly whose 'drowsy humming' and vivid colouring both disrupt and blend with the 'the mighty stillness', the heat haze, of a summer day in the bush. His more ambitious and Wordsworthian narrative poem, 'The Creek of the Four Graves', foreshadows the narrative in White's *Voss,* telling of four explorers who are murdered by Aborigines, 'Wild men whose wild speech had no word for *mercy!*'. Their deaths and their graves become part of an oral, and now a written, history which interweaves their story with the Australian landscape and thus lays claim to it. It is fitting that the tribute of a later poet, Henry Kendall, should link the site of Harpur's grave with his claim to belong to and speak for Australia:

> Where Harpur lies, the rainy streams,
> And wet hill-heads, and hollows weeping.
> Are swift with wind, and white with gleams,
> And hoarse with sounds of storms unsleeping.
>
> Fit grave it is for one whose song
> Was tuned by tones he caught from torrents,
> And filled with mountain-breaths, and strong
> Wild notes of falling forest-currents.[21]

Harpur might well have found Kendall's tribute, as well as much of his best-known poetry, too Tennysonian for his taste. But Kendall also sought to give voice to Australian nature, as the title of his second volume *Leaves from Australian Forests* (1869), announces. A contemporary reviewer, George Oakley, represents the contemporary critical opinion that Kendall had surpassed Harpur in the technique of his versification, his passion and his nationalistic quality:

Harpur might perhaps be a stronger, haply even more original, thinker; but he lacked the grace which Kendall infused by a more cultivated attention to metrical laws. Harpur's verse was always rude and lawless. . . His love knows nothing of chastity or purity, it is a wild foaming passion, libidinous in thought, and preying solely upon physical beauty. . . Kendall . . . has thus become the first poet in whom, it may be said, Australia speaks.[22]

This view of Kendall has been prevalent for a century or more, though it has been questioned by Wright, and by nationalists of the *Bulletin* tradition who preferred the ballads and commemorations of bush men enduring a bleaker and more barren version of nature than Kendall's lyrical and often lush poetry depicts. In the often anthologized and recited 'Bell-Birds' and 'September in Australia', the music of alliterative sound and regular metre delight the ear, but the actual depiction of the wildlife and vegetation is generalized, and, except for the actual mention of bell-birds and the fact that September is associated with spring rather than autumn, could just as well be located in any idealized European setting mediated by Algernon Swinburne or Tennyson. Thus, not unlike Yeats's 'The Lake Isle of Innisfree' written some twenty years later, the first and last stanzas of 'Bell-Birds' invoke a romanticized natural world which calls up the innocence of childhood and contrasts nature with an urban experience:

By channels of coolness the echoes are calling,
And down the dim gorges I hear the creek falling:
It lives in the mountain where moss and the sedges
Touch with their beauty the banks and the ledges.
Through breaks of the cedar and sycamore bowers
Struggles the light that is love to the flowers;
And, softer than slumber, and sweeter than singing,
The notes of the bell-birds are running and ringing.
. . .
Often I sit, looking back to a childhood,
Mixt with the sights and the sounds of the wildwood,
Longing for power and the sweetness to fashion,
Lyrics with beats like the heart-beats of Passion; –
Songs interwoven of lights and of laughters
Borrowed from bell-birds in far forest-rafters;
So I might keep in the city and alleys
The beauty and strength of the deep mountain valleys;
Charming to slumber the pain of my losses
With glimpses of creeks and a vision of mosses.[23]

Such lines, so often presented to Australian schoolchildren as the epitome of Australian nature poetry (alongside ballads like 'The Man from Snowy River' as the epitome of the Australian character) lead Wright to express her preference for Harpur's vision (in all senses of the word) of Australia and to declare, 'Kendall, in fact, is not, as his admirers tell us, the "first Australian poet"; looked at hard and honestly, he is scarcely to be called an interpreter of Australia at all. He is, however, something quite as important, the poet of his own desperate struggle and final self-mastery.'[24]

While Harpur and Kendall sought to express themselves as Australian poets through their response to its 'pure' natural environment, later writers acknowledged the presence and culture of Australia's aboriginal inhabitants. For those seeking to construct an Australian literature uncontaminated by European traditions and influences, aboriginal culture, so closely linked to the land, seemed to provide a means and an exemplar. Influenced by his reading of an anthropological study of the Arunta people in Central Australia,[25] the poet Rex Ingamells published in 1938 the first of several *Jindyworobak Anthologies* with the following explanation:

> 'Jindyworobak' is an aboriginal word meaning 'to annex, to join', and I propose to coin it for a particular use. The Jindyworobaks, I say, are those individuals who are endeavouring to free Australian art from whatever alien influences trammel it, that is, bring it into proper contact with its material. They are the few who seriously realize that an Australian culture depends on the fulfilment and sublimation of certain definite conditions, namely:
>
> 1. A clear recognition of environmental values.
> 2. The debunking of much nonsense.
> 3. An understanding of Australia's history and traditions, primaeval, colonial and modern.[26]

If the second condition perhaps recalls Ezra Pound's iconoclastic manifestos, and refers to the elimination of nineteenth-century poeticisms as exemplified in Kendall's lyrics, the first and third suggest a more distinctively Australian concern to relate to what was then understood as a primeval landscape and a primeval culture.

Not all Ingamells's poems conform to this manifesto, but poems such as 'Australia' illustrate his deployment of aboriginal words and references to portray the land, its geology and contours, and his avoidance of the comparatively bountiful coastal forest environment and wildlife celebrated by Harpur and Kendall:[27]

> This is the oldest land
> wisest, most stoic,
> where rock-hearted ranges stand
> Archeozoic.

Around raves the ocean . . .
above stream the stars,
wed to earth's motion
with her tjurungas.

Moons of her dream-time,
guardian still,
rove over scrub, climb
cliff-scarp and hill.

Ruthless the sun spites
skeletal mallee,
and, fierce in the blue, smites
legended valley.

Day bleeds on shingle
and billabong,
while solitudes tingle
to shrill parrot song.

Where ghostly the tribes go,
dwindled and few,
Alcheringa dusks know
didgeridoo.

In gunyah and windbreak,
by desert and sea,
the lubra sings heart-ache
for birrahlee.[28]

As Brian Elliott points out, the Jindyworobaks were not interested in rewriting Australian history or campaigning for aboriginal rights; their work was directed to white Australians, 'Our Race that should stride / on a sun-facing ridge', and rested on the assumption that 'tribesmen must grieve / and campfires depart'.[29] What inspired them imaginatively was the concept of 'dreamtime', as they interpreted it, the spirit of the land, eternal presences which united man to place and to totemic native animals. And for Ingamells, 'it was a white Dreamtime really, that sustained that faith most of the time. The Aboriginal Dreamtime excited him. But it was the Australian one – the Great Australian Uniqueness – that he most deeply believed in.'[30]

One should note here that for Ingamells, 'Australian' appears to exclude the Aborigines, despite his insistence that their relationship to the land and their communal, nonmaterialist culture demonstrated values that white Australians would do well to share. At a time when Aborigines were considered a dying race, when the general policy was to encourage racial and cultural assimilation into white Australia, when Aborigines were denied the right to vote, and segregation was the norm, such attitudes were rarely questioned. Contemporary critics are more likely to judge the limitations of the Jindyworobak movement in its use of aboriginal myth and culture, but it has nevertheless had considerable influence, and also focuses trends in Australian literature that preceded it. Katherine Susannah Pritchard's fifth novel, *Coonardoo* (1929), could be seen as a precursor to the movement in its endeavour to express an indigenous and non-European relationship to the land. Thus the opening paragraph of *Coonardoo* seeks to represent an aboriginal response to a particular landscape:

> Coonardoo was singing. Sitting under dark bushes overhung with curdy white blossom, she clicked two small sticks together, singing:
> 'Iowera chinima poodinya,
> Iowera jinner mulbeena . . .'
> Over and over again, in a thin reedy voice, away at the back of her head, the melody flowed like water running over smooth pebbles in a dry creek bed.[31]

The song, the language, the voice all blend into and become one with the character and the land, the melody like water, the words rattling together like the smooth pebbles and the sticks. Throughout the novel, the analogy between Coonardoo and the land is insistent, and Coonardoo is also the embodiment of her people. It is tempting to read this novel as an allegory of white settlement, moving from the mystical and communal world of the aboriginal people living in harmony with the land, to a feudal structure brought by the first white settlers and exemplified in the person of Mrs Bessie, mother/father to the Aborigines who cheerfully serve her. But her son's reluctance to acknowledge his affection for and attraction to Coonardo and his wife's determination to maintain class distinctions destroy that feudal relationship; in consequence, both Coonardoo and the land are degraded and ruined. Coonardoo (named after the deep well near which she was born) is also linked throughout to female sexuality and fertility, and to a feminine principle which is ascribed to the Aborigines and the land generally. In contrast, Mrs Bessie's son, Hugh (referred to always by the Aborigines as 'You' and thus always 'Other') clings to European ideals of masculinity nourished by his reading of Homer and the values of his boarding school. The mixed-race son of Hugh and Coonardoo, we are told, 'looked at her with the eyes of his aboriginal intuition, instinctive wisdom, his white man's intelligence, reasoning.'[32]

Despite her acknowledgement of aboriginal understanding of and respect for the land, Pritchard's portrayal of the Aborigines as an essentially feminine race, instinctive and intuitive in their closeness to nature, is highly questionable. Even more difficult to accept is her constant emphasis on Coonardoo's devotion to Mrs Bessie and Hugh, despite their exploitation of her. Nor do the other Aborigines on the station question the sovereignty of the white man or woman. As we have seen in the previous chapter, Sally Morgan's autobiographical *My Place* (1987), set in the same region as *Coonardoo*, powerfully challenges this perception of the relationship between white settler and the indigenous peoples they dispossess. She allows her aboriginal spokesmen and women to give expression to the Aborigines' suffering, anger, amazement and contempt for those white settlers who usurped their land while claiming to care for them.

Pritchard sought a reconciliation of European and aboriginal values; as a member of the communist party in Australia, she endorsed communalism and rejected capitalist exploitation of human and environmental resources. In this respect she may be seen as a predecessor to Wright, but Wright in her later years was much more active in the cause of 'doing something to redress the old wrongs',[33] as she put it. Wright was a member, with the aboriginal writers Kath Walker (Oodgeroo) and Kevin Gilbert, of the Aboriginal Treaty Committee (1978–83), and wrote the book *We Call for a Treaty* (1985). From the 1970s until her death in 2000, she was also an active campaigner on environmental issues, a concern expressed in much of her poetry written during this period. But even her earliest poems articulate a consciousness of a landscape resonant with a history of conquest and dispossession, and of an aboriginal culture which had formed and given meaning to aspects of that landscape. Of her childhood and ancestral home she writes:

> A bora ring and sacred way survived not far from my grandmother's home, and the paddock was named the Bora Paddock – I wrote 'Bora Ring' about that. I am told the ring area has now been ploughed; and a very old carved tree near the woolshed on Wallamumbi where I was brought up has disappeared too. They were some of the last signs of an occupation stretching many thousands of years into the past, but they were not thought worth preserving.[34]

Published in 1946, her poem 'The Bora Ring' eloquently and movingly evokes that consciousness of a landscape which carries a history of dispossession, a site which though now ploughed over survives in Wright's poem:

> The song is gone; the dance
> Is secret with the dancers in the earth,
> the ritual useless, and the tribal story
> lost in an alien tale.
>
> Only the grass stands up
> to mark the dancing-ring; the apple-gums

posture and mime a past corroboree,
murmur a broken chant.

The hunter is gone; the spear
is splintered underground; the painted bodies
a dream the world breathed sleeping and forgot.
The nomad feet are still.

Only the rider's heart
halts at a sightless shadow, an unsaid word
that fastens in the blood the ancient curse,
the fear as old as Cain.[35]

Another early poem, 'Nigger's Leap, New England', commemorates the terrible story of an aboriginal group, suspected of killing cattle, being driven by settlers over a high cliff to fall to their deaths. Here again, the consciousness of the intersection between the land and a violent history of dispossession, indeed the land as a cause for that violent dispossession, is recorded and made permanent, not only in the lines below but also in the juxtaposed names of the title:

Did we not know their blood channelled our rivers,
and the black dust our crops ate was their dust?
O all men are one man at last. We should have known
the night that tidied up the cliffs and hid them
had the same question on its tongue for us.
And there they lie that were ourselves writ strange.
Never from earth again the coolamon
or thin black children dancing like the shadow
of saplings in the wind. Night lips the harsh
scarp of the tableland and cools its granite.
Night floods us suddenly as history
that has sunk many islands in its good time.[36]

Wright frequently invokes the presence of the past in geographic sites of aboriginal life and death, but for her the Australian landscape is also made meaningful through its history of settlement. In the land she finds traces of the lives of pioneers like the farmer in 'Soldier's Farm', the singer in 'The Blind Man', the old woman in 'Hawthorn Hedge', the solitary bullock-driver commemorated in 'Bullocky':

Grass is across the wagon-tracks,
and plough strikes bone beneath the grass,
and vineyards cover all the slopes
where the dead teams were used to pass.[37]

But it is not only the history of others but her own lived history, her own body, and the stories she has heard others tell, that the New England landscape evokes in poems such as 'South of My Days':

> South of my day's circle, part of my blood's country,
> rises that tableland, high delicate outline
> of bony slopes wincing under the winter,
> low trees blue-leaved and olive, outcropping granite –
> clean, lean, hungry country.[38]

The critic and poet Vivian Smith has compared Wright to the artists Sidney Nolan and Arthur Boyd in her ability to take a situation or image (and, I would add, a landscape or scene) which sums up 'a whole phase of the Australian past, and by new vision lifted them to a higher level'.[39] Like these artists, she actually involves us in the process of mythologizing and transforming the Australian scene. That gift for telling detail and involvement in the process of mythologizing and so 'forging the conscience' of her readers as participants in their natural environment is also evident in a later series of poems which focus not so much on the contours of the land and the traces of past inhabitants as on the present flora and fauna. A volume entitled *Birds* (1962) is dedicated to her daughter Meredith and brings to each bird a keenly observed, witty and often deceptively naive point of view, perhaps reminiscent of William Blake. Such poems make animals and birds specific to Australia both uncanny and yet less strange by anthropomorphizing them. 'Currawong' provides a fine example of that process of vivid painterly description combined with subjective memory and meaning which transforms both the poet's and the reader's perception of this particular Australian bird:

> The currawong has shallow eyes –
> bold shallow buttons of yellow glass
> that see all round his sleek black skull.
> Small birds sit quiet when he flies;
> mothers of nestlings cry *Alas!*
> He is a gangster, his wife's a moll.
>
> But I remember long ago
> (a child beside the seldom sea)
> the currawongs as wild as night
> quarrelling, talking, crying so,
> in the scarlet-tufted coral-tree;
> and past them that blue stretch of light,

the ocean with its dangerous song.
Robber then and robber still,
he cries now with the same strange word
(*currawong – currawong)*
that from those coxcomb trees I heard.
Take my bread and eat your fill,
bold, cruel and melodious bird.[40]

Although belonging to a later generation, Les Murray shares many of Wright's concerns as a poet and admires her work. He lists as his avocational interests '[g]eography, regional studies, landscape, farming, mythology, animals, plants, fine machinery, tall tales, driving through beautiful country'.[41] The critic Neil Corcoran has compared Murray to Heaney, describing his poems as 'immensely rich in their ability to convey a country felt, as it were, along the arteries.'[42] Like Wright, Murray has sought to write Australia's birds and animals into poetry, and in 1992 published 'Presence: Translations from the Natural World', a long sequence in which the different poems give voice to such creatures as the echidna, bats, molluscs, foxes, and also to trees and plants such as the fig and the sunflower. But whereas Wright might be seen to be allegorizing the animals and plants, or writing about a human, subjective response to each one, Murray is interested in their nonhuman, or suprahuman, qualities, and seeks to express the inner or essential nature of each subject. This difference between the two poets in their response to Australian wildlife is evident when one compares the poems each has written about lyrebirds, shy and elusive birds distinguished by their lyre-shaped tails and their extraordinary gift for mimicking an enormous range of sounds. (Lyrebirds feature as one of Australia's symbols, for example on the twenty-cent coin.) Wright moves from an outer, 'objective' reference to these birds and their habitat ('Over the west side of this mountain, / that's lyrebird country'), to conceiving of them in terms of a metaphor ('I'll never see the lyrebirds – / the few, the shy, the fabulous, / the dying poets'), and concludes that like the wellsprings of poetry, it is better to leave them as imagined rather than actual presences, inhabiting 'nowhere but the reverence of the heart'.[43]

In contrast, Murray's poem mimics the mimickers, linking sight and sound in the first lines, and emulating the bravura performance of these birds whose sounds remain unheard and even unimagined by Wright:

Liar made of leaf-litter, quivering ribby in shim,
hen-sized under froufrou, chinks in a quiff display him
or her, dancing in mating time, or out. And in any order,
Tailed mimic aeon-sent to intrigue the next recorder,

> I mew catbird, I saw crosscut, I howl she-dingo, I kink
> forest hush distinct with bellbirds, warble magpie garble, link
> cattle-bell with kettle-boil; I rank duck's cranky presidium
> or simulate a triller like a rill mirrored lyrical to a rim.
> I ring dim. I alter nothing. Real to real only I sing,
> Gahn the crane to Gun the chainsaw, urban thing to being,
> Screaming woman owl and human talk; eedieAi and uddyunnunoan.
> The miming is all of I. Silent, they are a function
> of wet forest, cometary lyrebirds. Their flight lifts them barely a
>   semitone.[44]

Whereas Wright takes nature as an occasion for meditation on the interrelationships between the natural and the human, for the intertwining of the land, its history, its creatures and plants within the consciousness of her fellow Australians, Murray tends to emphasize what an earlier Catholic poet, Gerald Manley Hopkins, might have termed the 'inscape' of the things that inspire him; he celebrates their uniqueness. He also celebrates their plenitude and variety, which in turn provide the stimulus for Murray's marvellous inventiveness and variety in his use of language and form. But he also seeks to capture their strangeness, their indifference to human categories, language and norms. Thus in a poem such as 'The Cows on Killing Day' it is not the human being who speaks about or to the cows, but the cow whose consciousness is translated for us:

> All me ate standing on feed. The sky is shining.
> All me have just been milked. Teats are tingling still
> from that dry toothless sucking by the chilly mouths
> that gasp loudly in in in, and never breathe out.[45]

This characteristic of Murray's 'Translations from the Natural World' compares with an aspect of aboriginal culture and poetry, which often seeks to express and incarnate the spirits of animals and birds. Thus, in the 'Song Cycle of the Moon-Bone', composed by the Wonguri-Mandjigai people of northeastern Arnhem land, as translated by R. M. Berndt in 1948, dancers and singers imitate and in some sense become or express the cockatoos flying in search of food, the male and female rat, the duck who announces, the words echoing her quacking sound, 'I carried these eggs from a long way off, from inland to Arnhem Bay . . . / Eggs, eggs, eggs; eggs she is carrying, swimming along.'[46]

Indeed, this particular Song Cycle provided the acknowledged model for Murray's 'Buladelah-Taree Holiday Song' (1977), like the Moon-Bone Cycle composed in thirteen sections. Murray's Song Cycle celebrates the annual holiday ritual in which Australian families leave the city to return to their more recent origins in rural Australia, a ritual in which he perceives these families as 'going back to their ancestral places in a kind of unacknowledged spiritual walkabout, . . . – looking for their country in order to draw sustenance from it. Or newcomers looking for the real Australia.' Reflecting on the significance of aboriginal cultures to Australian consciousness and identity, and his composition of the Song Cycle, Murray went on to say:

> As I thought about it, I realised it would be necessary to incorporate in it elements from all three main Australian cultures, Aboriginal, rural and urban. But I would arrange them in their order of distinctiveness, with the senior culture setting the tone and controlling the movement of the poem. What I was after was an enactment of a longed-for fusion of all three cultures . . . The poem would necessarily celebrate my own spirit country.[47]

The celebration of his 'own spirit country' has dominated Murray's poetic output, but he has also written of urban landscapes in poems such as 'The Sydney Highrise Variations', 'An Absolutely Ordinary Rainbow', '1980, In a Street of Federation Houses' and 'Mirror Glass Skyscrapers'. Murray acknowledges the influence of the Jindyworabaks in drawing attention to the importance of aboriginal culture for the creation of an Australian consciousness and identity, but believes that their view of aboriginal culture was a romanticized one based on limited and incomplete sources. In turn, Murray has been criticized for claiming for his Scottish ancestors and settlers an equal history of dispossession and rural culture with aboriginal people, and has been seen as glossing over the injustices and differences in the treatment of Aborigines and poor white settlers.[48] While Murray celebrates the plenitude of the natural world, he also appreciates cultural variety, buildings and machines that are manmade, and indeed varieties of cultures, European as well as Australian. He is, like Heaney, Derek Walcott and Wright, both an international and a parochial poet, and like them demonstrates that there is no conflict in these designations.

African, Australian, Indian and Irish poets have often sought to wed the landscapes of their countries to the consciousness of its inhabitants through historical or developing cultural associations. In contrast, the West Indian poet Walcott has contended that a Caribbean consciousness can best be created through circumventing the past, eschewing a 'history of recrimination', in order to name and locate oneself in the 'new world'. The Caribbean poet's task, he claims, should be to start afresh, like Adam, and name his world. Walcott's long autobiographical poem, *Another Life* (1982), maps his native St Lucia, and in so doing also charts his progress towards visualizing and describing it. Critics such as Paula Burnett and Patricia Ismond praise Walcott's originality in using 'the island's natural phenomena' to create fresh metaphors.[49] For Walcott, the figure of Robinson Crusoe provides a persona which allows him to approach the problem of abandoning dead metaphors and engaging with elemental nature.

> Godlike, annihilating godhead, art
> And self. I abandon
> Dead metaphors: the almond's leaf-like heart,
> The ripe brain rotting like a yellow nut
> Hatching
> Its babel of sea-lice, sandfly, and maggot,
>
> That green wine bottle's gospel choked with sand,
> Labelled, a wrecked ship,
> Clenched sea-wood nailed and white as a man's hand.[50]

While still using the comparison with Crusoe, Walcott has described the process of renaming and possessing the landscape more positively in the speech he gave when awarded the Nobel Prize for Literature in 2003:

> Deprived of their original language, the captured and indentured tribes create their own, accreting and secreting fragments of an old, an epic vocabulary, from Asia and from Africa, but to an ancestral, an ecstatic rhythm in the blood that cannot be subdued by slavery or indenture, while nouns are renamed and the given names of places accepted like Felicity village or Choiseul. The original language dissolves from the exhaustion of distance like fog trying to cross an ocean, but this process of renaming, of finding new metaphors, is the same process that the poet faces every morning of his working day, making his own tools like Crusoe, assembling nouns from necessity, from Felicity, even renaming himself. The stripped man is driven back to that self-astonishing, elemental force, his mind. That is the basis of the Antillean experience, this shipwreck of fragments, these echoes, these shards of a huge tribal vocabulary, these partially remembered customs, and they are not decayed but strong. They survived the Middle Passage and the *Fatel Rozack*, the ship that carried the first indentured Indians from the port of Madras to the cane fields of Felicity, that carried the chained Cromwellian convict and the Sephardic Jew, the Chinese grocer and the Lebanese merchant selling cloth samples on his bicycle.[51]

And in the poem 'Names', he dramatizes the process whereby succeeding generations reject 'dead metaphors', and begin to see the island not through ironic comparisons with European places and cities, but through metaphors and similes which derive from a distinctively Caribbean context and environment.

Speaking in the voice of a weary schoolmaster teaching children the dialect words alongside the standard English names, seeking to encourage them to accept their natural world as having as much beauty as, or more than, the famed European monuments, defining their world by what it is not, he suddenly finds that the children have already gone beyond him to see and describe their world in fresh metaphors:

> Listen, my children, say:
> *moubain*: the hogplum,
> *cerise*: the wild cherry,
> *baie-la*: the bay,
> with the fresh green voices
> they were once themselves
> in the way the wind bends
> our natural inflections.
> These palms are greater than Versailles,
> for no man made them,
> their fallen columns greater than Castille,
> no man unmade them
> except the worm who has no helmet,
> but was always the emperor,
>
> and children look at these stars
> over Valencia's forest!
>
> Not Orion,
> not Betelgeuse,
> tell me. what do they look like?
> Answer, you damned little Arabs!
> Sir, fireflies caught in molasses.[52]

The differences between Yeats and Heaney, Harpur, Kendall, Wright and Murray, earlier Caribbean poets and Walcott, relate not only to the differences in generations as they tackle the problem of creating or recreating a literary tradition that is, in a popular Irish nationalist idiom, 'racy of the soil', but also to differences in class and ancestral origin. Yeats identified with the Anglo-Irish settler Ascendancy, Heaney with the Catholic Celtic peasantry; Harpur's parents were transported as convicts to imprisonment in Australia, Wright's grandparents were voluntary settlers and belonged to a relatively wealthy and entrenched landowning class; Murray's parents, on the other hand, were part of that Scottish diaspora forced into exile by land clearances and economic necessity. Thus, while Wright may acknowledge the role of her forefathers in dispossessing the Aborigines who had occupied the land they took and farmed,

Murray sees a shared kinship with the dispossessed; his family, too, were among the rural poor alongside the Aborigines who lived on the outskirts of small rural towns in northern New South Wales. That view is expressed in his essays, as well as poems such as 'Thinking About Aboriginal Land Rights, I Visit the Farm I will Not Inherit', or the defiantly titled volume *Subhuman Redneck Poems* (1996). Nevertheless, the convergence between indigenous and imported cultures that Murray (and before him the Jindyworabaks) affirm is a matter of choice, a willed marriage, rather than the 'natural' intermingling to which Morgan (and to some extent Heaney) lay claim.

In a recent essay addressing Irish literature, Thomas Docherty asks whether 'in an age of globalisation, poetry can serve the functions that it used to when it was firmly and clearly located, tied to a local habitation and a name'.[53] The question applies also to drama and prose such as Synge's and Friel's, and relates also to debates about the different trajectories of poets such as Murray and John Tranter in Australia, or Kamau Brathwaite and Walcott in the Caribbean. Docherty sees the necessity of acknowledging the fractures in time and space brought by modernity and globalization, so that 'belonging' is not limited to one place and one nation, and arguably such an acknowledgement of belongings (and cosmopolitan identity) is inherent in Walcott's *Omeros* (1990) as well as Joyce's *Ulysses*. Nevertheless, we need also to acknowledge the difference between the role of poetry of place for Indian, Irish or West African poets, whose ancestral past and culture is deeply rooted in their places of habitation, so that the need is not so much to dig in as to spread out, and the poetics of place in settler or immigrant countries such as Australia, Canada, the Caribbean and New Zealand, where belongings are already double (at least), and place has to be worked into the consciousness of its new inhabitants.

Chapter 6

Appropriating the word: language and voice

To speak means to be in a position to use a certain syntax, to grasp the morphology of this or that language, but it means above all to assume a culture, to support the weight of a civilization . . . The Negro of the Antilles will be proportionately whiter – that is he will become closer to being a real human being – in direct relation to his mastery of the French language . . .

Every colonized people . . . finds itself face to face with the language of the civilizing nation; that is, with the culture of the mother country.[1]

– The language in which we are speaking is his before it is mine. How different are the words *home, Christ, ale, master,* on his lips and mine! I cannot speak or write these words without unrest of spirit. His language, so familiar and so foreign, will always be for me an acquired speech. I have not made or accepted its words. My voice holds them at bay. My soul frets in the shadow of his language.[2]

Language, for the individual consciousness, lies on the borderline between oneself and the other. The word in language is half someone else's. It becomes 'one's own' only when the speaker populates it with his own intention, his own accent, when he appropriates the word, adapting it to his own semantic and expressive intention. Prior to this moment of appropriation, the word does not exist in a neutral and impersonal language (it is not, after all, out of a dictionary that the speaker gets his words!), but rather it exists in other peoples' mouths, in other people's contexts, serving other people's intentions: it is from there that one must take the word and make it one's own.

(Mikhail Bakhtin, 'Discourse in the Novel')[3]

The issue of language is one of the most hotly debated topics among postcolonial writers, critics and readers. In some nations the debate has to do with the question of whether to use an imposed colonial language – in this case English, or whether writers should use their native language or mother tongue. In other areas, such as Australia, Canada, or the Caribbean the debate is more to do with the *kind* of English or French that writers should use, standard English as

97

spoken in the metropolitan country or the English spoken by those who live in the new nation. The three quotations above suggest some of the issues and consequences involved in the deployment of the colonial language, and a variety of attitudes towards the difficulties and possibilities which that deployment may entail.

To take the first question: whether to write in a colonial (European) language or in the writer's native language. The painter, sculptor or musician may confront many of the same ideological issues as the postcolonial writer with regard to his or choice of subject and approach, but the medium chosen – the paint or stone or music – is not so intrinsically problematic. But artists who use language are using a medium which is in itself meaningful, and if they choose the language of their colonizer they are working with words and syntax which express the perception and characteristic modes of thinking of a culture which scorned their own. As the African American writer LeRoi Jones (Amiri Baraka) declared, 'European language carries the bias of its inventors and users. You *must* be anti-black, speaking in their language, except by violent effort.'[4]

Languages not only carry sets of associations related to particular words, such as 'tribe', 'fetish', 'black' and 'white', but also particular ways of thinking and perceiving. Even within the context of different European languages, we could notice the lack of a variety of nuanced words for love or relationships in English compared with French; or the difference in attitude implied in the word '*belle-mère*' rather than 'mother-in-law'! Structuralists and poststructuralists such as Roland Barthes, Jacques Derrida and Michel Foucault have argued that we are enclosed in the language we inherit; we cannot think outside of it, and therefore it cannot express a different way of thinking and perceiving. Thus some writers from Africa, the Indian subcontinent and Ireland have argued that literatures in European languages cannot be defined as African or Indian or Irish literature, but merely as minor appendices to European literature.

There is also an argument that while the English language brought by the colonizer can convey intellectual concepts and denotative references, only the mother tongue spoken in childhood and in the home carries the emotional weight and connotations that are important to poetry and prose. A Nigerian critic, Obianjunwa Wali, claims that for this reason writing by Africans in European languages must be sterile and derivative.[5] Moreover, he claimed, the use of a European language limited the writer's audience to a tiny elite of Westernized college graduates. He attacked the choice of Wole Soyinka's *A Dance of the Forests* (1960) for staging during Nigeria's independence celebrations, claiming that it was accessible to less than 1 per cent of the Nigerian people and that it was 'tagged on to the idiom and traditions of a foreign culture'.[6] A similar argument is made by the Kenyan writer Ngugi wa Thiong'o, who decided after writing five novels and two plays in English to use only his mother tongue, Gikuyu. Ngugi's later novels *The Devil on the Cross* (1980; English translation 1982) and *Matigari* (1986; English translation 1989) are written in Gikuyu, and also draw on oral forms such as ballads and folktales. He categorizes works by African writers using the English language as 'Afro-Saxon literature'.[7]

For Ngugi, the choice of language is also related to the choice of audience. In his essay 'Return to the Roots', he quotes Frantz Fanon:

> 'To choose a language is to choose a world', once said a West Indian thinker, and although I do not share the assumed primacy of language over the world, the choice of a language already pre-determines the answer to the most important question for producers of imaginative literature: For whom do I write? Who is my audience? . . . If a Kenyan writer writes in English – no matter how radical the content of that literature – he cannot possibly directly talk to the peasants and workers of Kenya. If a Kenyan acts a play in English, he cannot possibly be assuming a truly Kenyan audience.[8]

Ngugi also believes that it is the African writer's duty to his culture to nourish the languages and cultures that exist there. He goes on to say that 'Kenyan national literature should mostly be produced in the languages of the various nationalities that make up modern Kenya. Kenyan national literature can only get its stamina and blood by utilizing the rich national traditions of culture and history carried by the languages of all the Kenyan nationalities.'[9] As writers create in indigenous languages, they will keep them alive and growing. Without this there is the likelihood that English will take over completely and the local languages, with all that belongs to them, will die out.

As we have seen, the issue of language is central to Brian Friel's play *Translations* (1980), and was also central to the nationalist movement in Ireland for at least a century. In his 1892 speech on 'The Necessity of De-Anglicising Ireland', Douglas Hyde urged the revival of the Gaelic language as a means of healing the schizophrenic mentality developed by opposing English domination while embracing her language and culture. Hyde was to become president of the Gaelic League, one of whose chief aims was the revival of Gaelic as the national tongue, and himself wrote both poetry and drama in Gaelic. Forty years later, Daniel Corkery argued that Irish literature must be defined first of all as literature written in the Irish language. Yet in response to Hyde, W. B. Yeats argued that it was possible to 'build up a *national* tradition, a national literature which [would] be none the less Irish in spirit for being English in language'.[10] Citing the examples of Bret Harte, Henry Thoreau, and Walt Whitman and their formation of a specifically American literature, Yeats argued that Irish subjects, rhythms and attitudes could produce a distinctive and distinguished Irish literature, declaring that 'when we remember the majesty of Cuchulain and the beauty of sorrowing Deidre, we should not forget that it is that majesty and that beauty which is immortal, and not the perishing tongue which first told them'.[11]

Yeats's attitude was in part a pragmatic one – he could not speak or read Irish. But he also believed that it was necessary to reach both a national and an international audience to convince the world that Ireland was not 'the home of buffoonery and easy sentiment, as it has been represented, but the home of an ancient idealism'.[12] By writing in the English language, Irish authors would not exclude that wider audience. In Africa and India, writers such as Chinua Achebe and Salman Rushdie have argued that writing in English allows them to reach a national audience, and so to break down the barriers between different ethnic groups within the nation. In India English is the common language that might bring together Bengali, Hindi, Gujerati, Oriya, Parsi, Tamil and Urdu speakers. Likewise in Nigeria, English is the official national language which enables Hausa, Igbo and Yoruba peoples to communicate with each other and with the central government. In response to Wali, Achebe argues that there is plenty of evidence that English-language works by African writers from the eighteenth century to the present such as John (Pepper Clark) Bekederomo, Olaudah Equiano, Casely Hayford and Christopher Okigbo, are far from sterile. Their double inheritance equips them to question the language and its assumptions even as they deploy it. Indeed, all of Achebe's novels to some degree make the use of the English language an issue. *Things Fall Apart* (1958) calls to the reader's attention the existence of the Igbo language and its inclusion of non-European concepts, such as *agbala, chi* and *ndichie,* which English can never quite encompass. In this and many other ways, the issue of language is foregrounded in the novel, so that the English language is seen not only to be inadequate, but at times to deny Igbo (and African) perceptions and dignity. Thus the missionary Mr Smith, who succeeds the more tolerant – and appropriately named – Mr Brown, 'saw things as black and white. And black was evil. He saw the world as a battleground in which the children of light were locked in mortal conflict with the sons of darkness. He spoke in his sermons about sheep and goats and about wheat and tares. He believed in slaying the prophets of Baal.'[13] Not only the connotations of black and white, but also the Manichean world view which insists on absolute distinctions between 'children of light' and 'sons of darkness' are anathema to members of an Igbo community that, according to Achebe, affirms the values of tolerance and the belief that 'wherever something stands, something else also stands'.[14]

Distinguishing between ethnic and national literatures, and acknowledging that Nigeria is a nation created by the British, who imposed their language as the national language, Achebe declared that as a *national* writer he had no choice but to write in English, and argued that this tongue could be used to create an African song. In 'The African Writer and the English Language', he cited James Baldwin's comments on the English language:

> My quarrel with the English language has been that the language reflected none of my experience. But now I begin to see the matter another way . . . Perhaps the language was not my own because I had never attempted to use it, had only learned to imitate it. If this were so, then it might be made to bear the burden of my experience if I could find the stamina to challenge it, and me, to such a test.

Achebe went on to say that while recognizing that Baldwin's problem was not exactly the same as his, he felt 'that the English language will be able to carry the weight of my African experience. But it will have to be a new English, still in full communion with its ancestral home but altered to suit its new African surroundings.'[15] In the same essay he gave an example of how a short passage from his own novel, *Arrow of God* (1964), might read if it were written from the perspective of an Englishman. In this novel the Chief Priest, Ezeulu, tells his youngest son why he wants him to attend the Christian missionary school:

> I want one of my sons to join these people and be my eyes there. If there is nothing in it you will come back. But if there is something there you will bring home my share. The world is like a Mask dancing. If you want to see it well, you do not stand in one place. My spirit tells me that those who do not befriend the white man today will be saying *had we known* tomorrow.

Now supposing I had put it another way. Like this for instance:

> I am sending you as my representative among these people – just to be on the safe side in case the new religion develops. One has to move with the times or else one is left behind. I have a hunch that those who fail to come to terms with the white man may well regret their lack of foresight.

> The material is the same. But the form of the one is *in character* and the other is not. It is largely a matter of instinct, but judgement comes into it too.[16]

One might feel that Achebe has stacked the cards here, or rather that he has ensured there are no aces in his English-English example, but the general point is clear.

In later years, however, Achebe's view on English as the only national language for Nigerians has changed, and he has written poetry in Igbo. More recently, he has written of Nigerian literature in English as 'only one of the branches of a growing tree' and does not see writings in other languages such as Hausa or Yoruba as any less national.[17] In this attitude he differs from Rushdie, who not only insisted on English as the appropriate national literary language for India, but provoked controversy when he declared that there was no worthwhile Indian writing that was not originally in English. He maintained:

> the prose writing – both fiction and non-fiction – created in this period [the fifty years following Indian independence] by Indian writers *working in English*, is proving to be a stronger and more important body of work than most of what has been produced in the 16 'official languages' during the same time; and indeed, this new, and still burgeoning, 'Indo-Anglian' literature represents the most valuable contribution India has yet made to the world of books.[18]

Out of their selection of thirty-two works, Rushdie and Elizabeth West included in their 1997 anthology *The Vintage Book of Indian Writing, 1947–1997* just one that had been translated into English, S. H. Manto's short story 'Toba Sekh Singh', originally composed in Urdu. Their claim regarding the inferiority of vernacular works – or at least the translations of these works – has been angrily contested, and has been seen as yet another example of the unfortunate influence of British and North American academics such as Fredric Jameson who assume that the only worthwhile literature is that which is accessible to them.[19] However, Rushdie would agree and demonstrates in his own writing that 'Indo-Anglian' writing takes much of its energy and distinctiveness from its contact with other languages in India and the speech rhythms, idioms and cultural contexts that they bring to English. As Rushdie notes, 'Indian English, sometimes unattractively called "Hinglish", is not "English" English, to be sure, any more than Irish or American or Caribbean English is. And it is part of the achievement of the writers in this volume to have found literary voices as distinctively Indian, and also as suitable for any and all the purposes of art, as those other Englishes forged in Ireland, Africa, the West Indies, and the United States.'[20]

As Achebe acknowledges, but Rushdie glosses over, Baldwin's problem with the English language was not identical with his. Whereas Africans or Indians or Sri Lankans who write in English are in daily contact with other ethnic languages which embody alternative world views, African American and African Caribbean writers must have recourse to some form of English. And while those who belong to the African diaspora can draw on a distinctive form of English influenced by African idioms, formations and borrowings, white Australians and Canadians and many Anglo-Irish writers do not even have these distinctive resources with which to construct a national literature.

In the Caribbean, as in Ireland, the choice of a distinctively local form of English as the medium for writing has to confront a history of mimicry and mockery by metropolitan writers. Through the traditions of 'stage Irish' and minstrel shows, the forms of English or 'dialect' spoken by Irishmen or West Indians had become so strongly associated with the stereotypes established by colonialist writers that their use tended not only to connote but to reinforce such stereotypes. The comments that the American critic William Dean Howells made on the poems of the African American poet Paul Laurence Dunbar illustrate the attitudes which Irish and West Indian writers also met with when they wrote in the English spoken by their compatriots:

> Yet it appeared to me then, as it appears to me now, that there is a precious difference in temperament between the two races which it would be a great pity ever to lose, and that this is best preserved and most charmingly suggested by Mr. Dunbar in those pieces where he studies the moods and traits of his race in his own accent of our English. We call such pieces dialect pieces for want of some closer phrase, but they are really not dialect so much as delightful personal attempts and failures for the written and spoken language.[21]

In contrasting the language of Dunbar's poems with 'true dialect', Howells indicates that it is in fact merely 'a broken tongue' rather than simply another way of speaking, a viable alternative as American English is to Standard English, or Yorkshire to Scottish. Rather, he sees it as a 'failure' to meet a norm implicitly accepted by the speakers themselves, and therefore to be linked with malapropisms, Irish bulls, the misuse of polysyllabic words, mispronunciations and childish babble. As failures to meet a norm accepted by both speaker and listener, 'dialect' verses and speeches are viewed as charming, amusing or cute, not as products or expressions of men and women who have the dignity and authority to run their own lives and societies. Fanon makes a similar point with regard to the use of 'pidgin-nigger' when French men address black people, seeking to keep them 'in their place': 'A white man addressing a Negro behaves exactly like an adult with a child and starts smirking, whispering, patronizing, cozening ... To make him talk pidgin is to fasten him to the effigy of him, to snare him, to imprison him, the eternal victim of an essence, of an appearance for which he is not responsible.'[22]

This link between the form of language and racial stereotype is also evident in the English critic Walter Jekyll's Preface to the Jamaican poet Claude McKay's first collection:

What Italian is to Latin, that in regard to English is what is the Negro
variant thereof. It shortens, softens, rejects the harder sound alike of
consonants and vowels; I might almost say, refines. In its soft tones we
have an expression of the langorous sweetness of the South; it is a
feminine version of masculine English; pre-eminently a language of love,
as all will feel who, setting prejudice aside, will allow the charmingly
naive love-songs of this volume to make their due impression on
them . . .

As a broad general direction, let it be observed that the vowels have
rather the continental than the English sounds, while in the manner of
the consonants the variation from the English is of the nature of a pretty
lisp.[23]

However favourable Jekyll supposed his Preface to be, it nevertheless maintains
a firm hierarchy in relation to Standard English and Jamaican English, a hierarchy which rests on a masculine/feminine dichotomy, as in Matthew Arnold's
view of the Celtic as opposed to the Germanic races. And here again the 'dialect'
works are regarded, like Dunbar's, as 'charmingly naive', and the language as a
failure to meet an accepted norm, but instead 'pretty lisping'. It is interesting
to note that these early verses are dedicated to Sir Sidney Olivier, the British
Governor of Jamaica who 'by his sympathy with the black race has won the
love and admiration of all Jamaicans'. Such a gesture would seem impossible
in the later McKay, author of the fierce and proud sonnet 'If We Must Die', a
sonnet which employs the form and language of Standard English.

In his Preface to his 1921 and 1931 editions of *The Book of American Negro
Poetry,* the African American poet and critic James Weldon Johnson points
out the limitations which he had come to believe were inherent in the use
of dialect. It had become associated with the stereotype of the black man as
happy-go-lucky, singing, shuffling and childishly unaware of his own psychology ('charmingly naive'), an image based on minstrel traditions, 'traditions
that had but slight relation – often no relation at all – to actual Negro life, or
are permeated with artificial sentiment'. And, Johnson continued, 'it is now
realized both by the poets and their public that as an instrument for poetry the
dialect has only two main stops, humor and pathos'.[24] In his 1921 Preface, he
proposed imitation of the Irish playwright J. M. Synge in the attempt to find a
form of language expressive of African American life:

What the colored poet in the United States needs to do is something like
what Synge did for the Irish; he needs to find a form which will express
the racial spirit by symbols from within rather than by symbols from
without, such as the mere mutilation of English spelling and
pronunciation. He needs a form that is freer and larger than dialect, but

which will still hold the racial flavor; a form expressing the imagery, the idioms, the peculiar turns of thought, and the humor and pathos too, of the Negro, but which will also be capable of voicing the deepest and highest emotions and aspirations, and allow of the widest range of subjects and the widest scope of treatment.[25]

Johnson demonstrated that freer and more expressive form in his collection of poems *God's Trombones* (1927), which imitate in verse the form and language of African American sermons. In so doing he foregrounds the language itself, rather than the content. Similarly in Synge's plays, and especially *The Playboy of the Western World* (1907), the language is often the centre of attention. Such a focusing on the means of expression not only celebrates and draws attention to the possibilities of that particular form of language, but also disintegrates the standard associations between the native form of the language and certain stock characters. The mechanics of this change seem to be analogous to those described by the Russian critic Viktor Schlovsky, who sees the poet's drawing attention to the words themselves and their 'laying bare the poetic device' as a means of 'disautomatization', a freeing of the word or image from the stock response associated with it.[26]

Works by Kamau Brathwaite, Lorna Goodison, Langston Hughes, Johnson, Una Marson and other African American and African Caribbean poets also refer to other artistic modes as a means of giving the language validity. In particular, they refer to blues, spirituals, reggae and jazz in their compositions – forms recognized by audiences nationally and internationally as valid and culturally distinct forms of music in their own right. Moreover, the choice of that form of language and form signifies a choice of audience, and that, too, is part of the message of the poem or prose, for it thus affirms its validity in the face of those who cannot or will not accept those forms of speech as viable poetic or communicative alternatives to their own. Thus the dual celebration and rejection inherent in the choice of a form of language implies a rejection of the absolute standards of the colonizer and asserts that the people with whom the poem identifies are not only fit subjects for poetic expression but also the source of a poetic language. That double celebration of the people and their language is made explicit in Synge's Preface to *The Playboy of the Western World*:

> In countries where the imagination of the people, and the language they use, is rich and living, it is possible for a writer to be rich and copious in his words, and at the same time to give the reality, which is the root of all poetry, in a comprehensive and natural form . . . In Ireland, for a few years more, we have a popular imagination that is fiery, and magnificent, and tender; so that those of us who wish to write start with a chance that

> is not given to writers where the springtime of the local life has been
> forgotten, and the harvest is a memory only, and the straw has been
> turned into bricks.[27]

Synge's use of 'Hiberno English' and his influence on Derek Walcott have been
noted in chapter 2 on drama. Walcott's poetry also at times draws on the
language and 'folk imagination' of St Lucians and Trinidadians in poems such
as 'Pocomania' and 'Parang'. But the language and form of Walcott's poetry,
as distinct from his plays, generally compares more closely with Yeats than
with the language of Synge's drama in his choice of a sinuous Standard English
syntax and vocabulary modulated by local inflections and idioms. Other West
Indian poets and prose writers have more consistently advocated and employed
variations of local patois, creating and enriching a characteristic West Indian
tradition.

One of the most influential advocates of the use of Creole or Caribbean
English rather than Standard English has been Brathwaite, Barbadian poet and
historian. Brathwaite coined the term 'nation language' which he defines as 'the
kind of English spoken by the people who were brought to the Caribbean, not
the official English now, but the language of slaves and labourers, the servants
who were brought in by the conquistadors'.[28] Thus 'nation language' refers to
culturally specific ways of speaking in the Caribbean – i.e., those aspects which
are distinctively Caribbean in terms of vocabulary, syntax, intonation and pronunciation. Of course, the use of Creole is not confined to the Caribbean. In
Nigeria, Ken Saro-Wiwa used a mixture of linguistic registers, including pidgin, which draws on a variety of indigenous languages in combination with
English, and Standard English to create his novel, *Sozaboy: A Novel in Rotten
English* (1985). In a short story recently published in *Kunapipi*, David Mavia
illustrates the use of 'Sheng', a combination of Swahili and English in which
Swahili is the base language, and goes on to discuss the ways in which contemporary Kenyans may use and switch between several different languages and
personae depending on the context in which they are speaking, and including
an indigenous language, Swahili, Sheng and Engsh (a combination of English
and Swahili in which English forms the base language). Mavia points out the
influence of contemporary popular music, radio and television in the development of Sheng and Engsh as language media.[29] In these examples the syntax
as well as the vocabulary is often inflected by two or more languages. Another
slightly different example of combined languages is Hinglish, where speakers
(or writers) switch back and forth from one language vocabulary to another, in
this case Hindi and English. Different kinds of examples of the use of Hinglish
in writing can be seen in Sujatta Bhatt's poem, 'Search for My Tongue' and
G. V. Desani's novel *All About H. Hatterr* (1948).[30]

However, whereas Nigerian pidgin or Sheng or Hinglish are formed by two or more languages which continue to coexist and interact, Caribbean nation language as defined by Brathwaite is the result of an underground or suppressed language influencing the English that slaves were forced to speak. Brathwaite believes that Caribbean English carries with it a suppressed African identity which surfaces and continues in particular words and forms, for example 'nam' for 'to eat'; 'I and i' for 'we'; 'What it mean?' for 'What does it mean?' The underground African language also surfaces in the sound of the language, and particular characteristics of voice. Brathwaite dismisses terms such as 'dialect' because they reiterate the hierarchy between metropolitan Standard English and suggest that the language as it is spoken by Caribbean people is marginal or inferior.

He also argues that the rhythm most prevalent in English poetry from Chaucer to the present day, the iambic pentameter, is inappropriate to the cadences of Caribbean speech and the natural environment of the West Indies. The pentameter, Brathwaite declares, 'carries with it a certain kind of experience, which is not the experience of the hurricane. The hurricane does not roar in pentameters.'[31] Moreover, the pentameter is linked to metropolitan English speech and musical forms, while Caribbean poetry needs to be connected to 'native musical forms and the native language. That music is, in fact, the surest threshold to the language which comes out of it.'[32] Together, the local music and local speech form a major part of the oral tradition which has sustained and developed a distinctive Caribbean culture. One example is calypso, which employs dactyls rather than the pentameter and is, in Brathwaite's view, more suited to Caribbean speech rhythms and intonations.

Brathwaite stresses the importance of orality, the significance of sound, for 'the noise that it makes is part of the meaning . . . When it is written, you lose the sound or the noise, and therefore you lose part of the meaning.'[33] But the oral tradition also demands a community, a listening and responding audience, whereas reading is an isolated and isolating mode. For Brathwaite, and for many other postcolonial writers, orality is linked to authenticity, for it does not rely on technology, or artificial modes of preservation. The performer and his audience together create 'a continuum where meaning truly resides':

> And this *total expression* comes about because people be in the open air, because people live in conditions of poverty ('unhouselled'), because they come from a historical experience where they had to rely on their very *breath* rather than on paraphernalia like books and museums and machines. They had to depend on *immanence,* the power within themselves, rather than the technology outside themselves.   (italics in original)[34]

Contrasting McKay's sonnets with his early 'dialect' poems, and lamenting the fact that he 'forsook his nation language' in order to be 'universal', Brathwaite suggests that performance poets such as Louise Bennett (whose work is discussed below) and calypso poets such as Mighty Sparrow provide more useful models for contemporary Caribbean writers. But he also acknowledges the influence of T. S. Eliot on 'mainstream poets' moving from Standard English to nation language, claiming that 'what T. S. Eliot did for Caribbean poetry and Caribbean literature was to introduce the notion of the speaking voice, the conversational tone. That is what really attracted us to Eliot.'[35]

Brathwaite's first major work, the trilogy *The Arrivants* (1973), compares interestingly with Eliot's *The Waste Land* (1922). Not only does it seek to express the quest of a whole society for spiritual healing through the deployment of a variety of voices, invoking past and present memories and loss, it also invokes continuing imagery of desert and water, sterility and fertility, within that quest. Like Eliot, at times in *The Arrivants* Brathwaite makes present the yearned-for water, or healing spring, through the invocation of its absence, and in each case it is the *sound* of the words which creates the illusion of presence. Compare this passage from Part V of *The Waste Land* with certain passages in the opening Prelude to the first volume of *The Arrivants*:

> If there were water
> And no rock
> If there were rock
> And also water
> A spring
> A pool among the rock
> If there were the sound of water only
> Not the cicada
> And dry grass singing
> But sound of water over rock
> Where the hermit-thrush sings in the pine trees
> Drip drop drip drop drop drop drop
> But there is no water.[36]

An equivalent section, evoking presence through sound, from Brathwaite's work reads:

> Soon
> rock
> elephant-
> hided boulders
> dragged in now

dry river
beds, death's
valleys.
Here clay
cool coal clings
to glass, creates
clinks, silica glitters,
children of stars.
Here cool
dew falls
in the evening
black
birds blink
on the tree
stump ravished
with fire
ruined with its
gold.[37]

Eliot's use of musical forms and speech cadences is also developed by Brathwaite in new and distinctively Caribbean modes. Whereas the musical genres of the prelude, operatic overture and quartet are explicit structures for Eliot's poetry, Brathwaite draws on blues, calypso, jazz and reggae rhythms. Thus in 'The Wings of the Dove' he draws on a reggae rhythm to convey the voice of a Rastafarian speaker:

Down down
white
man, con
man, brown
man, down
down full
man, frown-
ing fat
man, that
white black
man that
lives in
the town.

Rise rise
locks-
man, Solo-
man wise

man, rise
rise rise
leh we
laugh
dem, mock
dem, stop
dem, kill
dem an' go
back back
to the black
man lan'
back back
to Af-
rica.[38]

With regard to a 'West Indian tradition' and language, however, a distinction
needs to be made between poets like Brathwaite who use a modified form of
local patois, accessible to a wide audience throughout as well as outside the
Caribbean, and draw on a variety of West Indian voices, including Barbadian,
Jamaican and Trinidadian, and those like Bennett and Mikey (Michael) Smith
who draw on the patois of one island, in their case Jamaica. Brathwaite's project
can be seen in the context of the Caribbean Artists Movement (CAM), which
in the late 1960s brought together artists residing in London but originating
from Barbados, Guyana, Jamaica and Trinidad and seeking to create distinctively Caribbean literature and art forms. These artists also looked to African
American models and ideologies as a source of inspiration, and believed in
the potency of a united Caribbean political and cultural movement, involving
hispanophone as well as francophone countries such as Cuba and Martinique.

While Brathwaite is read and heard internationally, in Europe, North America and the United Kingdom, as well as the West Indian islands including
his native Barbados, Bennett is best known in her native Jamaica, where she
drew enormous audiences for her dramatic performances of her poems. Jahan
Ramazani describes her as 'an outstanding example of the poet as public figure
in the postcolonial situation. Though little known among poetry enthusiasts
outside the West Indies, Jamaica's national poet is arguably one of the most
significant English-language world poets in the middle decades of the twentieth century.'[39] Bennett began publishing her poems in the *Gleaner*, Jamaica's
national newspaper, in the 1940s, poems which were read by and to local audiences, who delighted in her ironic and humorous debunking of self-important
politicians and characters. Her work embodies a celebration of folk humour and
language, and foregrounds its capacity for mockery and self-mockery. Drawing on Jamaica's traditional folk stories, proverbs, myths and songs, preserved

primarily through oral retellings, Bennett performed and wrote in the native Jamaican English dialect, which is known variously as Creole, 'Jamaica talk', West Indian English, Jamaican dialect or patois. Regarding her choice of language, Bennett said, 'One reason I persisted writing in dialect was because . . . there was such rich material in the dialect that I wanted to put on paper some of the wonderful things that people say in dialect. You could never say "look here" as vividly as "kuyah".'[40] Through this use of language, and through her playful ironizing of 'the emergent nation state and its symbols, nationalists and anti-nationalist, the poor and the wealthy', Bennett builds what Ramazani has nicely termed an 'amiable community' of Jamaicans.[41] Often the issue of language is foregrounded, as in the following stanzas from 'Noh Lickle Twang':

> Bwoy, yuh no shame? Is so yuh come?
> After yuh tan so lang!
> Not even lickle language, bwoy?
> Not even lickle twang?
> . . .
> An yuh sister what work ongle
> One week wid Merican
> She talk so nice now dat we have
> De jooce fi understan?[42]

Here Bennett makes fun of a mother who is embarrassed because her son, after six months in the United States, has returned without a trace of accent; hence he cannot be exhibited to the neighbours as a 'sophisticated' traveller. His sister, on the other hand, after one week with American visitors has acquired an American accent so broad that her parents, to their delight, can no longer understand her.

Using the Jamaican patois, Bennett's humour is directed against those who are shamed by their own use of it. Similarly, she draws on the resources of patois to satirize those who believe their colour makes them inferior, punning on the various meanings of 'passing' in the poem 'Pass Fe White':

> Miss Jane jus hear from 'merica,
> her daughta proudly write
> fe sey she fail her exam, but
> She passin' dere fe wite!
> . . .
> Jane get bex, sey she sen de gal
> Fe learn bout edication,
> It look like sey de gal gawn weh
> Gawn work pon her complexion.
> . . .

> her fambily is nayga, but
> Dem pedigree is right,
> She hope de gal noh gawn an tun
> No boogooyagga wite.[43]

Unlike the mother in 'Noh Lickle Twang' who desires her son to sound less Jamaican, this mother takes pride in her ancestry, and uses the forceful and specifically Jamaican word 'boogooyagga' (good for nothing) to express her fear that her daughter assumes that skin colour, or acquired whiteness, makes it unnecessary for her to achieve anything worth while.

Bennett's poems comment ironically on local politics and politicians, on the foibles of mothers, sons and daughters, on issues of unemployment, war and emigration. Often the irony is double- or triple-edged – directed towards the colonizers and the colonized, the persona of the poem as well as her audience, as in 'Colonization in Reverse'. Here she observes the phenomenon of the 1950s rush by Jamaicans to emigrate to Britain (the Windrush generation), and wonders how the British who colonized Jamaica in previous centuries will respond to this new reversal which led to some 200,00 Jamaicans arriving in Britain in the decade after 1948. But the unrealistic dreams of those who emigrate (and then behave as the colonizers did – living off the labour of others) are also mocked.

> Wat a joyful news, Miss Mattie,
> I feel like me heart gwine burs'
> Jamaica people colonizin
> Englan in Reverse
>
> By de hundred, by de t'ousan
> From country and from town,
> By de ship-load, by de plane-load
> Jamaica is Englan boun.
>
> Dem a-pour out o' Jamaica,
> Everybody future plan
> Is fe get a big-time job
> An settle in de mother lan.
>
> What an islan! What a people!
> Man an woman, old an young
> Jusa pack dem bag an baggage
> An turn history upside dung!
>
> [. . .]
> An week by week dem shippin off

Dem countryman like fire,
Fe immigrate an populate
De seat o' de Empire.

[. . .]
Jane says de dole is not too bad
Because dey payin' she
Two pounds a week fe seek a job
Dat suit her dignity.

Me say Jane will never find work
At the rate how she dah-look,
For all day she stay pon Aunt Fan couch
An read love-story book.

Wat a devilment a Englan!
Dem face war an brave de worse,
But me wonderin' how dem gwine stan'
Colonizin in reverse.[44]

In this poem, as in many others, one can see Bennett's affiliation with a specifically Jamaican genre of oral performance, the mento, a forerunner of ska and reggae, and sometimes fused (and confused) with calypso, with whose satiric and self-ironizing humour it has much in common. Mentos were songs performed in dance halls and at rural gatherings in Jamaica, and can be traced back to the mid-nineteenth century. Topics included politics, daily life and personal relationships; in the 1950s the difficulties and troubles encountered by Jamaicans migrating to England were the subject of many mentos.[45] Moreover, the figure of Miss Mattie, as a representative Jamaican audience, invoked in 'Colonization in Reverse' and other poems by Bennett, also frequently recurs in mento songs. In some of her performances, Bennett interspersed her dramatic renditions of her verses with mento songs.[46] Bennett's affiliation with the mento tradition allows her to define her audience and her role as performer, and in so doing to speak to specific expectations and conventions which her audience will recognize. It also allows her to affirm Jamaican culture and language. But she expands and renews the tradition, which had generally been confined to male performers. As a female performer, Bennett challenges the conventions, and her male and female personalities and her use of stock characters like Miss Mattie take on an altered dimension when they are recreated and performed by a woman.

Her use of Jamaican patois and popular traditions, indeed her very popularity, for a long time encouraged academics and critics to dismiss Bennett as not a poet to be taken seriously. In a 1968 interview she complained:

'I have been set apart by other creative writers a long time ago because of the language I speak and work in. From the beginning nobody ever recognized me as a writer. 'Well, she is doing dialect'; it wasn't even writing you know. Up to now a lot of people don't even think I write. They say 'Oh, you just stand up and say these things.'[47]

Since the 1970s, however, Bennett has been recognized as an important influence. The Jamaican poet and prose writer Olive Senior commented in a 1994 interview, 'all of us, I think, have been influenced by Louise Bennett, who was a pioneer in writing Creole and speaking it – because it was something revolutionary'.[48] Influential West Indian academics such as Rex Nettleford and Mervyn Morris have written Introductions to her collected poems, giving them serious attention[49] As Denise deCaires Narain puts it, 'Louise Bennett's poetry . . . is often cited as marking the birth of an "authentic" West Indian poetry, the moment when the region *finds its voice* . . . in her exclusive use of Creole, her work is seen as redefining and *indigenizing* the contours of the "poetic"' (italics in original).[50]

In 'finding a voice' for the region, Bennett also finds and defines an audience. Whereas West Indian poets such as Brathwaite, Martin Carter, Lorna Goodison and Walcott have more often drawn on forms of language readily accessible to West Indian and other audiences outside of Jamaica, Bennett's poetic performances, in their use of patois and reference to local characters and events, explicitly acknowledge Jamaicans at home and abroad as her chosen primary audience. Her ironic treatment of Jamaican characters and events, and of the personae she performs, her assumption that her audiences will understand and respond to such ironic treatment of their own foibles and failings, allows her to avoid the danger of sounding patronizing; between performer and audience there is a mutual respect.

Bennett's use of patois has been significant not only in performance, but also in writing. As Susanne Mühleisen comments, 'her first poetry collection in print, published in 1942, must be seen as a milestone in the transformation between oral and written Creole form'.[51] The very act of inscribing Creole on the page affirmed its status on an equal footing with Standard English publications, and provided a model for successor poets such as Jean Binta Breeze and Senior. Bennett drew on a system of orthography which is more accessible to those already literate in Standard English. However, some critics and writers have argued that such a choice decreases the authenticity and status of Creole as a nation language, whereas a system of transliteration which is more closely phonetic makes the Creole more autonomous and also more consistent in its language formations.[52]

Bennett's approach and her use of patois in performed poetry has been taken up by younger Jamaican poets such as Valerie Bloom and Binta Breeze, both of whom now live in Britain and are sought after as performers there. Male poets have also continued the tradition she has made famous: in Britain James Berry, who emigrated from Jamaica in the 1950s, wrote in a modified Jamaican patois a series called *Lucy's Letters* (1982). Perhaps the most compelling author to use Jamaican patois in performance poetry was Mikey Smith, whose highly rhetorical denunciations of abuses of power employ a grimmer and more cutting kind of irony than Bennett's. As deCaires Narain points out, Smith's 'Me Cyaan Believe It' alludes to the opening lines of Bennett's poem 'Is Me' ('Is who dat a-sey, "who dat"?'). But Smith's characterization of politicians, and the failure of ordinary Jamaicans to reject them, lacks Bennett's humour. That humour, together with the conventional rhythms and rhymes of Bennett's verse, diffuses some of the political bite, and perhaps encourages a resigned response to their failures, and those of other Jamaicans. In contrast, Smith's use of repetition and staccato broken lines, as well as stanzas which produce a call-and-response effect, generates a more disquieting feeling, which emphasizes 'the paranoia, madness, and hardship of life in Jamaica'.[53] The following stanzas from the middle section of the poem illustrate his technique and use of voices:

> Sittin on de corner wid me frien
> talkin bout tings an time
> me hear one voice seh
> 'Who dat?'
> Me seh 'A who dat?'
> 'A who a seh who dat
> when me a seh who dat?'
>
> When yuh teck a stock
> dem lick we dung flat
> teet start fly
> an big man start cry
> me seh me cyaan believe it
>
> me seh me cyaan believe it
> De odder day
> me a pass one yard pon de hill
> When me teck a stock me hear
> 'Hey bwoy!'
> 'Yes, mam?'
> 'Hey, bwoy!'
> 'Yes, Mam!'
> 'Yuh clean up de dawg shit?'
> 'Yes, mam.'

An me cyaan believe it
me seh me cyaan believe it

Doris is modder of four
get a wuk as a domestic
Boss man move een
and bap si kaisico she pregnant again
an me cyaan believe it
me seh me cyaan believe it
Deh a yard de odder night
when me hear 'Fire! Fire!'
Who dead? You dead!
Who dead? Me Dead!
Who dead? Harry Dead!
Who dead? Eleven dead!
Woeeeeeee
Orange Street fire
deh pon me head
an me cyaan believe it
me seh me cyaan believe it

Lawd
me see some blackbud
livin inna one buildin
but no rent no pay
so dem cyaan stay
Lawd
de opress and de dispossess
cyaan get no res
Wha nex?[54]

In an interview with Morris, two years before he was assassinated in 1983, Smith acknowledged that his poetry had a political purpose, although not linked to partisan politics:

> So when I write now I just want them fi understand wha I a deal with: describe the condition which them live in but also to say, 'Boy, don't submerge yourself under the pressure. You can do better, and if you organise yourself and make demands on who there is to make demands on, then you will achieve your objective. And just break up the little dependency attitude that is so characteristic of J. A.'[55]

Lines such as those quoted from 'Me Cyaan Believe It' exemplify Smith's attempt to involve his audience in an understanding and rejection of the politics, including gender politics, which leave so many Jamaicans among 'de opress and de dispossess'.

The populations of the islands of Barbados and Jamaica are predominantly of African descent, so it is understandable that Brathwaite should emphasize the significance of African languages and cultures in the formation of nation language and West Indian folk traditions. But this emphasis can also exclude other important sections of the population, such as those whose ancestors came from the Indian subcontinent and who form nearly half of the populations of Guyana and Trinidad. Thus David Dabydeen from Guyana and V. S. Naipaul and Samuel Selvon from Trinidad draw on the idioms, vocabulary and linguistic formations of an English inflected by a variety of Indian languages. Dabydeen's *Slave Song* (1984) draws on a Guyanese Creole which combines African and Indian formations of English far removed from Standard English. But, in a manner reminiscent of Maria Edgeworth's Irish novel *Castle Rackrent* (1800), Dabydeen includes an almost parodic critical apparatus, whose glossary and translations reveal the distinctiveness and untranslatability of the Creole words and phrases. In this manner Dabydeen performs his own duality, as a descendent of the coolie workers and also an Oxford graduate, problematizing the relationship which is at the core of Caribbean writing: that between the articulate writer and the supposedly voiceless workers and peasants. That awareness of this relationship is also articulated in Brathwaite's 'The Wings of the Dove' in which the introductory section is voiced in Standard English, and in which the Rasta man voices his own distrust of 'them clean-face browns', whom he compares to vultures or crows that 'na / feet feel firm / pun de firm stones'.

Discussions of language and diction in postcolonial writing have tended to set up an opposition between 'literary' language, seen as tied to Standard English and the imported book, and 'voice', connected to the speech of 'the folk' and oral traditions. In this paradigm, as Brathwaite's argument makes explicit, voice and orality are seen as more 'authentic' than written language. As Irish cultural nationalists sought to create a literature that was 'racy of the soil' and drew on the culture and language of rural Ireland, and the more rural the more authentic it was held to be, so George Lamming affirmed those Caribbean novelists who had related 'Caribbean experience from the inside', for 'it is the West Indian novel that has restored the West Indian peasant to his true and original status of personality'.[56] But in practice Lamming, like Brathwaite and Walcott, draws on a whole range of registers. His writing acknowledges the value of a flexible approach to and appreciation of the potential to be found in the linguistic diversity of the Caribbean. As the poet Marlene Nourbese Philip remarks:

To say that the experience can only be expressed in standard English (if there is any such thing) or only in the Caribbean demotic (there is a such a thing) is, in fact, to limit the experience of the African artists working in the Caribbean demotic. It is in the *continuum of expression* from standard to Caribbean English that the veracity of the experience lies. (italics in original)[57]

Chapter 7

Narrating the nation: form and genre

The emphasis on voice and oral traditions discussed in the previous chapter relates not only to language but also to the form and structure of literary works. We have seen how Chinua Achebe contrasts oral history and narrative with the written history planned by the British District Commissioner, not only in terms of content but also in terms of a form which is attentive to its immediate audience and which develops organically rather than according to a rigidly conceived structure. However, a comparison between Louise Bennett's and Mikey Smith's performed poetry also shows that works which rely on oral performance can vary from the conventional ballad form used by Bennett to the more 'natural' and flexible verse stanzas employed by Smith, even though both poets rely on formulas and conventions which will be recognized by their audiences. And like Achebe, Kamau Brathwaite, Les Murray and Raja Rao, both poets create hybrid forms, which draw on literary as well as oral traditions.

Just as postcolonial writers and critics have argued passionately about whether or not their worlds and experiences can be articulated adequately in the language of the colonizer, and the extent to which a hybrid or Creole language has the resources to express a full and nuanced range of feeling and thought, so, too, they have disputed, though perhaps less passionately, whether forms created within the English literary tradition are appropriate to postcolonial societies. Among those who have most forcefully rejected the conventions of the English novel and called for a new kind of fiction with a new set of expectations is Wilson Harris, whose own novels exemplify that rejection. In 'Tradition and the West Indian Novel', an influential lecture given in 1964 to the London West Indian Students' Union, Harris contended that most novelists who work in the twentieth century within the framework of the nineteenth century novel are preoccupied with 'the consolidation of character'.[1] Harris relates the rise of the conventional realist novel in Europe to the historical context of European societies concerned with 'consolidating their class and other vested interests', with the result that

'character' in the novel rests more or less on the self-sufficient
individual – on elements of 'persuasion' . . . rather than 'dialogue' or
'dialectic' . . . The novel of persuasion rests on grounds of apparent
common sense: a certain 'selection' is made by the writer, the selection
of items, manners, uniform conversation, historical situations, etc., all
lending themselves to build and present an individual span of life which
yields self-conscious and fashionable moralities. The tension which
emerges is the tension of individuals – great or small – on an accepted
plane of society we are persuaded has an inevitable existence.[2]

V. S. Naipaul's novel *A House for Mr Biswas* (1961) exemplifies for Harris the limitations of the conventional novel, the novel of 'persuasion', in the
Caribbean context. While admiring Naipaul's gifts as a comic writer, his careful
and 'scrupulous' style, his achievement in mingling comedy and 'memorable
pathos' in his depiction of the central character, Mr Biswas, Harris regrets
Naipaul's willingness to confirm 'one's preconception of humanity, the comedy of pathos and the pathos of comedy', to rest his work on this 'common
picture of humanity'. For Harris, the Caribbean novel should seek to raise 'revolutionary or alien question[s] of spirit', opening rather than restricting the
ground for choice, and pushing beyond the boundaries of epic and tragedy. It
should respond to societies in formation, to the fragmented histories of those
who inhabit the Caribbean and Latin America, to encourage 'plural forms of
profound identity' rather than 'a persuasion of singular and pathetic enlightenment'.[3]

Many critics would disagree with Harris's evaluation of Naipaul's novel –
some have seen *A House for Mr Biswas* as Naipaul's best work and place it
among the most significant works of fiction to come from the Caribbean.
In his afterword to Harris's critical essays, the radical critic and philosopher
C. L. R. James refers to *A House for Mr Biswas* as 'in literature the finest study
ever produced in the West Indies (or anywhere that I know) of a minority and
the herculean obstacles in the way of its achieving a room in the national
building'.[4] Naipaul himself acknowledges the influence of Charles Dickens
on his creation of this and earlier novels, and so to some extent confirms
Harris's perception of this work as belonging to a nineteenth-century English
literary tradition, disagreeing with Harris's rejection of that tradition. However,
Naipaul moved away from that realist tradition in his subsequent fiction. Later
novels such as *The Mimic Men* (1967), *In a Free State* (1971), *Guerrillas* (1975)
and *A Bend in the River* (1979), employ modernist forms and techniques to
question constructions of identity and character in colonial and postcolonial
societies. *The Enigma of Arrival* (1987), referred to by the Swedish Academy as
his masterpiece when he was awarded the Nobel Prize for Literature in 2001,

also questions the construction of identity and place within English society, and moves far from the conventional novel in its mingling of genres which include autobiography, travel writing and fiction.

Whereas Dickens provided an early model for Naipaul, Joseph Conrad has been a stronger influence on his later work. *A Bend in the River* is set in the same area as Conrad's *Heart of Darkness* (1902) and alludes to its imagery and metaphors, as well as exploring recurring themes in Conrad's fiction of marginality, corrupt power and displacement. Naipaul's travels in India are recorded under the title *An Area of Darkness* (1964), alluding to Conrad's novel, and in his Nobel Prize acceptance speech he referred to having grown up in 'one of the dark spots' of the world. Despite his negative response to Naipaul, Harris is also an admirer of Conrad, and has written about him sympathetically. His early novels share with some of Conrad's that interaction of place and allegory which creates a metaphysical landscape, and his interest in mapping and navigating territory (Harris worked as a land surveyor in the Guyanese interior, and his early novels draw on that experience). Moreover, Harris sees *Heart of Darkness* as a 'frontier novel', one which is aware of the need for a changing vision of the world and its peoples in relation to one another, but is unable to move beyond the categories enforced by the acceptance of a realist mode. Harris comments that *Heart of Darkness* 'stands upon a threshold of capacity to which Conrad pointed though he never attained that capacity himself. Nevertheless, it was a stroke of genius on his part to visualize an original necessity for distortions in the stases of appearance that seem sacred and that cultures take for granted as models of timeless dignity.'[5]

Elleke Boehmer reads Harris's first novel the *Palace of the Peacock* (1960) as 'a rewriting of *Heart of Darkness*'.[6] *Palace of the Peacock* follows a diverse crew on its phantasmic journey upriver into the heart of British Guyana and far from the coastal city of Georgetown. But the central narrator is no 'commonsense' navigator like Conrad's Marlow; in this voyage the narrative interweaves past and present, tales and echoes of conquest with the stories of the conquered, the quest for land with the quest for a legendary woman called Mariella. Dream and 'reality' become inseparable, and characters are fluid, changing from one persona to another. Thus the dreaming first person narrator has an alter ego named Donne, a figure of the archetypal imperialist and conqueror, while also alluding to the metaphysical poet. The mixed crew includes some of the many strands that make up the Guyanese population – African, Amerindian, English, German, Indian, Portuguese – and the novel culminates in a vision which fuses Amerindian and Christian symbols. In some ways one might see Harris drawing on the magic realism which has been characteristic of Latin American fiction in the latter half of the twentieth century, and is exemplified so powerfully in

Gabriel García Márquez's *Cien anos de soledad* (1967; *One Hundred Years of Solitude*, 1970). However, Harris's style differs from that of Márquez and other magic realist writers, and the transformations of people and place are more reminiscent of dreaming (the narrator is said to be dreaming) than the uses of myth, legend and folk belief by Márquez or Isabel Allende, for example.

Harris's dismissive attitude to realist or romantic novels and their conventions as appropriate modes for societies which need to remake themselves is shared by many other postcolonial writers, including Ama Ata Aidoo, Kojo Laing, Ben Okri, Salman Rushdie, and before them, Joseph Furphy, James Joyce, and Christina Stead. Tom Collins, the narrator in Furphy's long rambling novel *Such is Life* (1903), declares that the demand for a plot, especially a romantic plot, in the novel is contrary to the reality of life. Its laconic title is taken from the supposed last words of Ned Kelly, an Australian bushranger executed in 1880, but it is also an assertion of the novel's aim to depict life as it is. Thus Furphy rejects the conventions of the nineteenth-century realist novel or gothic romance in the name of a greater 'truth to life', especially Australian life, but the novel itself also constantly raises questions as to the nature of reality, and the ways in which writing or talking about events, people and places determine how we perceive them.

When he sent his novel to the editor of the *Bulletin*, a nationalist Australian journal, Furphy defined the novel succinctly in one sentence: 'I have just finished writing a full-sized novel, title, *Such is Life*, scene, Riverina and Northern Vic; temper democratic, bias offensively Australian.'[7] Written in the form of random selections from the diary of Tom Collins, the fictional narrator, whose name refers to a colloquial phrase in Australia for a purveyor of rumours,[8] the novel is also described by Furphy as a 'loosely federated' assembly of seven chapters. That description suggests a correlation between the structure of his novel and the structure of the newly established Australian federation in 1901 of seven colonies (six states plus the Northern Territory), a constitutional change celebrated by most Australians as the birth of the new nation. The form, style and content of this novel also eschew the fictions which were seen as typically Australian in the past and which appealed to European audiences. There is a scene towards the end of the novel where Collins is eagerly questioned by two travellers from Germany, seeking the Australia they have read about, with its 'inevitable brush with outlaw or savage [and] the no less inevitable golden reef'.[9] After their departure 'towards the land of Disillusionment', Collins reflects: 'As big fools as ever! Between asleep and awake, I pondered on the quantity and quality of Australian-novel lore which had found utterance there. The outlawed bushrangers; the lurking blackfellows; the squatter's lovely Diana-daughter, awaiting the well-bred greenhorn (for even she had cropped up in conversation) – how these things recalled my reading!'[10] Such fictions are replaced by a series of tales and anecdotes told by the bullock team drivers (bullockies), tramps, itinerant workers and others that Collins encounters as he surveys the land (he is a state government official, 'a Deputy-Assistant-Sub-Inspector'). Questions of ownership, and rights to the resources of the land, are a continuing issue, as the bullock drivers seek grass and water for their teams, and itinerant workers seek a place to rest. Throughout the novel, it is the stories of the poor and dispossessed that are heard most fully, though Collins himself, like his creator, is widely read in literature and philosophy.

Furphy rejects what Harris termed 'the novel of persuasion' and many of the conventions of nineteenth-century British and Australian novels in order to create a kind of fiction that is democratic, open-ended and expressive of 'the common man', envisioning in the person of young Mary O'Halloran, child of dispossessed Protestant and Catholic Irish immigrants, 'the coming Australian'. His fiction is comparable to Walt Whitman's poetry, particularly *A Song of Myself* (1855), or to Herman Melville's *Moby Dick* (1851), in its narrative technique and structure. But Furphy also relies on many of the strategies of the nineteenth-century novel: coincidence plays a large part in the stories, there is a lost child, and her death is full of pathos. However, in its form and conception it has more in common with eighteenth-century novels such as Laurence Sterne's *Tristram Shandy* (1759–69), and it is novels such as these that will also influence later postcolonial writers like Salman Rushdie. *Such is Life*, in its rejection of conventional plot and narrative, and its desire to give expression to the stories and voices of 'the common man' in a specifically national context, stories interwoven and contrasted with the thoughts and commentary of a more literate protagonist, can also be compared to James Joyce's *Ulysses* (1922). There are important differences, however, between Furphy and Joyce, or other modernist writers, for, as John Barnes points out:

> Furphy was striking out on his own in *Such Is Life*, but the attempts to represent him as a 'modern' writer, to be compared with James or Joyce or Woolf, all miss the fundamental point that Furphy was not an explorer of the human consciousness . . . His experiment, if *Such Is Life* can be properly so-called, was not with the stream of consciousness or the interior life of human beings, or indeed with point of view, but with the traditional method of narrative.[11]

Furphy's belief that fiction which is to be 'Australian' and 'democratic' must eschew established conventions of plot and character was shared by other writers published in the *Bulletin*. Typically, the short stories which appeared in this journal were episodic and anecdotal in form and style, presented as sketches of Australian life and character. Henry Lawson, viewed by many Australian critics as the founder of an authentically Australian literary tradition, wrote, like Furphy, about the men who struggled to make a bare living from the land, seeing heroism in that day-to-day struggle, and crafting a language and form which suggested the voice and idiom of such men. In that identification of national identity with the rural worker and peasant, and their shaping of an appropriate language, Furphy and Lawson have some affinities with J. M. Synge in his representation of the Aran Islanders and the poor tenants and farmers of Co. Wicklow and the west coast of Ireland. But while Synge generally focused on a community which has ancestral links to the landscape it inhabits, Furphy's and Lawson's characters are typically lone men who are suspicious or resentful of communal or family ties. The landscape they inhabit is not only hostile and barren, but alien. And perhaps most strikingly different from African, Indian or Irish nationalist writing is the absence of the past (and of fathers) in Australian literature of this period. Very rarely do we find a family history for Lawson's characters; they come into being and exist in an unchanging present, and what-ever changes they do experience occur in space, in change of location – which is nevertheless almost always a similar location – rather than in time. This is a world in which community is yet to be created, out of isolated individuals, not a world where community is to be restored and where there is a nostalgia for a precolonial past. Hence the ingredients of romantic nationalism – myth, legend, history – are absent from the works of the most influential Australian writers of the 1890s and early decades of the twentieth century. Their project is Whitmanesque, though less optimistic, and their characters and the anecdotes they narrate are metonymic rather than symbolic.

Joyce, too, rejected the romantic nationalism, the nostalgia for a precolonial community, which characterized much Irish nationalist writing, but unlike African, Australian, Caribbean and Indian nationalist writers, he also rejected the notion that it was the peasant or rural worker who should be celebrated as the carrier of national identity. All of his fiction is set in Dublin, and when his autobiographical protagonist Stephen Dedalus determines, at the end of *A Portrait of the Artist as a Young Man* (1916), to go forth 'to forge the uncreated conscience of [his] race', it is an urban consciousness that is to be created. (Here Joyce uses the word 'conscience' in the French sense of 'consciousness' as well as moral conscience.) But Joyce does share with Furphy and Lawson the distrust of conventional plots and fictional forms, and the concern to affirm the unheroic heroism of the ordinary man. His collection of stories, *Dubliners* (1914), features children, layabouts, laundry workers, office workers, fallen priests and elderly spinsters, as well as would-be politicians and writers. Disdaining rhetoric and written, in Joyce's own words, with 'a scrupulous meanness', it seeks to 'hold a mirror up to Dubliners', whom in one story he describes as 'the gratefully oppressed', while Dublin is viewed as 'the centre of paralysis'.

Although Joyce went on to reject the realist mode of *Dubliners*, and to construct a new kind of epic in *Ulysses* (1922), he remained firm in his resolution that the ordinary Dubliner should be at the centre of his creation, a heroic ordinariness deliberately emphasized by the overarching title and reference to Homer's epic account of the journeys and trials of Odysseus (translated by the Romans as Ulysses). As Declan Kiberd writes, 'In this book, the very ordinariness of the modern Ulysses, Mr Leopold Bloom, becomes a standing reproach to the myth of ancient military heroism. Man's littleness is seen, finally, to be the inevitable condition of his greatness. What one man does in a single day is infinitesimal, but it is nonetheless infinitely important that he do it.'[12]

Joyce, like Synge, rejected the formation of a national literature which found recourse to an aristocratic and military ideal, to an 'unmodern, ideal breezy [*sic*], springdayish, Cuchulanoid national Theatre'.[13] At the age of twenty-one he had attacked what he termed the 'vulgar nationalism' espoused by Lady Gregory, Patrick Pearse and W. B. Yeats, seeing their celebration of military and aristocratic heroes such as Cuchulain as a mimicry of colonialist culture.

Like Furphy (and Harris in a later era), Joyce saw that the construction of a novel which was to be democratic in temper, and was also to reject the forms, assumptions and structures of the existing colonial Irish society, demanded a radical break from the conventions of the nineteenth-century novel. Rather than moulding his fiction to the exigencies of a conventional plot or storyline, he used two main kinds of structure, myth and anatomy. Like Furphy and Harris, he created a nomadic fiction, an odyssey, a quest for understanding and affirmation, a homecoming, one which would take not twenty years, or several years, or even several centuries, but twenty-four hours. It was to be a minutely detailed exploration of the physical and mental events and sensations experienced in one day (16 June 1904), and perhaps daily – a daily odyssey. But it was also to be an anatomy, in both a literal and metaphysical sense. In the more literal sense of anatomy, the book is structured so that almost every episode is keyed to an organ or feature of the body; more potently, it portrays, as no previous novel had done, the sensations and functions of the body, the world and the self as physically experienced. As Kiberd comments with regard to the scandalized contemporary response to *Ulysses*, Joyce, like D. H. Lawrence, 'wanted to afford the body a recognition equal to that given the mind, but to a post-Victorian generation which had lost this just balance, both men *appeared* to elevate the body above all else'.[14]

In the metaphysical or literary sense of anatomy, *Ulysses* is a detailed exam-
ination, an analysis of Irish culture and consciousness in 1904, as formed by a
history of colonialism, anticolonialism and Catholicism, of oral and literary traditions, and economic demand. The opening three episodes focus on the consciousness of Stephen Dedalus, an intellectual and would-be writer, besieged
by poverty, guilt and irritation caused by the Englishman who occupies his
home, and the ready acquiescence of his erstwhile friend, Buck Mulligan, to
this occupation. Stephen's cast of mind constantly turns material objects into
symbols – the 'wine-dark / snot-green sea' is a reminder of Homer and mater-
nity, the tower is a navel, the eggs they have for breakfast evoke the Trinity, the
old woman who brings milk is an image of Cathleen ni Houlihan or the Shan
Van Vocht, the old woman who symbolizes Ireland. In episode 4 we see how
Stephen's consciousness is contrasted with that of Leopold Bloom, who savours
the smell and taste of the kidney he is cooking, the feel and sound of the cat,
and appreciates the sensations of his body, including the relief of defecation.
By expressing Stephen's consciousness, as well as Bloom's and his wife Molly's,
and his innovative use of a stream-of-consciousness technique, Joyce not only
demonstrates the differences in modes of perceiving the world, and the fluid
intercourse between self, body and surroundings, but also acknowledges the
desirability of their coexistence.

Through his variety of narrative techniques and perspectives, and his
adaptation of Homer's *Odyssey*, Joyce creates a radical break from preceding narrative methods. The frequent reminders of Homeric parallels are often
double in their effect; they are, as Kiberd says, 'both ironic and playful'.[15] For
the parallels suggest that history is not, as the colonizers would claim or as Mr
Deasy declares, a linear narrative of progress towards 'one great goal, the manifestation of God',[16] but repetition: both a recurring nightmare and a recurring
affirmation of human endurance. The patterns traced by Homer, Ovid, Dante
and Shakespeare, the quest for 'home', reappear again and again in different
forms, century after century, but also day after day. Joyce's choice of central
protagonist, an Irish Jew of Hungarian descent, is also a radical one, particularly in the context of his cultural nationalist project to 'forge the uncreated
conscience of [his] race'. Through Bloom he foregrounds the issue of national
identity as well as the issue of resistance to colonialism, for Bloom is a pacifist,
and is derided for his lack of manliness by those who affirm an essentialist Irish
racial identity and endlessly recount and celebrate deeds of violent resistance
through memories of the legendary warrior hero Cuchulain, the 1798 insur-
rection (dramatized in Yeats's *Cathleen ni Houlihan* (1902)), the attempted
rebellion led by Robert Emmet in 1803, the Fenians, and the assassination
of Chief-Secretary Burke and Under-Secretary Cavendish in Phoenix Park in
1882. Episode 12, 'Cyclops', will be discussed in greater detail in chapter 11 of

this book, but here one may point out that Bloom's quiet citizenship (he is busy trying to ensure that a recent widow has an adequate income) is set against 'the Citizen', the representative of the Gaelic League, and his noisy proclamations of allegiance and manliness. Moreover, Bloom's hesitant definition of a nation as 'the same people living in the same place', and assertion that he, too, is Irish, for he was born in Ireland,[17] in opposition to the Citizen's essentialist racial definition of Irishness, is affirmed not only by Joyce's choice of Bloom as his protagonist, but also by the frequent reference to Anglo-Irish, Italian and Spanish residents, and other Irish men and women not of Celtic origin, including Joseph Patrick Nanetti, who was to become in real life Mayor of Dublin from 1906 to 1907.

Moreover, *Ulysses* is a novel that constantly tests and makes manifest the limits of language. It imitates the sensuousness and cadences of musical form in the (Sirens) episode, the immediacy of visual forms in the 'Wandering Rocks' episode, the use of montage in cinema, the surreal transformations of dream and nightmare; it tests demotic speech, heroic literature, the whole register of the English literary tradition from Anglo-Saxon through to minstrel theatre, all of which show both the possibilities but also the inadequacies of the English language (or any other language) to express the fullness of experience. Many critics have suggested that Joyce's intention is to exhaust or explode the English literary tradition so that a new beginning must be made. Joyce's insistence that the reader be aware of the ways in which meaning and perception are intrinsically bound up with the media through which they are expressed is common to modernist art in Europe and the United States, but arguably his extreme (and sometimes laboured) insistence on the limitations of the English language and literary traditions also has much in common with other postcolonial writers who wrestle with the English language and literary formations.

The use of myth as a structural device is found in the works of many postcolonial writers. Yeats drew on Celtic myth and legend, but also frequently on Greek myth, as, for example, in his 'Leda and the Swan', which reinvents the sonnet tradition to comment on history and violence. Wole Soyinka draws not only on Yoruba myth to give structure and resonance to many of his plays and his novels, but also on the Greek myth of Orpheus and Eurydice to inform his post-civil war novel *Season of Anomie* (1973). R. K. Narayan from the Indian subcontinent alludes to traditional legends and oral forms found in the *Ramayana* to add a deeper dimension to his novels about the fictional village of Malgudi, and we have already noted in chapter 3 how Raja Rao adapts the form of the traditional *harikatha* in *Kanthapura* (1938), while a tale from the *Mahabarata* provides the structure for his second novel, *The Serpent and the Rope* (1960). Rushdie drew on a medieval Persian poem, Farid ud-Din 'Attar's

Conference of the Birds, as the basis for his first novel, *Grimus* (1975), and, like Soyinka, found the Orpheus and Eurydice story an appropriate structure for a later novel, *The Ground Beneath Her Feet* (1999).

Derek Walcott's epic poem *Omeros* (1990) refers, like *Ulysses*, directly to Homer and *The Odyssey* (as well as *The Iliad*), and like Joyce's novel is an affirmation of the heroism of ordinary men and women in their daily struggle for physical and psychic survival. Indeed, Walcott's epic includes a section where the poet-narrator visits Ireland and envisions Joyce as his guide. In an earlier prose version of his autobiographical poem, *Another Life* (1973), Walcott had mimicked Joyce and mocked his own aspiration to be the James Joyce of the Caribbean: 'Reading Joyce, you have, of course. Even Stephen, Son of a pastiche. Some article I read by whathisnamenow, in a Life and Letters yes, predicting that some day a new Ulysses will come forth out of these emerald, ethnic isles, and sure that he had put his finger on me. Imitation, imitation, when will I be me?'[18]

Omeros seeks to revisit and recreate the world of Walcott's native St Lucia and its inhabitants. Like Joyce's *Ulysses*, it draws on a foundational and canonical epic both to question an epic tradition linked to imperial values *and*, by insisting on the heroism of 'ordinary' men and women in their day-to-day lives, to revalue those who have been marginalized or ignored by that tradition. And like Joyce he presents the writer autobiographically as one of the central figures in his narrative. Like Joyce also, Walcott rejects nostalgia for the precolonial past in order to affirm the possibility of shaping a new beginning. Just as *Ulysses* ends with Molly Bloom's thrice-repeated 'yes', and the sense of a move towards reconciliation, *Omeros* begins and ends with the affirmation of the possibility of a revisioning and reshaping of Walcott's native island.

However, Walcott's deployment of Homer differs from Joyce's in that he draws on both *The Iliad*, a narrative of war, martial heroism and conquest, and *The Odyssey*, a narrative of wandering and homecoming. Two of Walcott's central characters, Achilles and Helen, feature most prominently in *The Iliad*. Helen, rather than Penelope, becomes the central female figure in Walcott's poem. The cast also includes a Hector and a Philoctetes. In using these names Walcott is not being merely whimsical, for it was the custom of slaveowners to give their slaves classical names, such as Socrates, Cassius (Cassius Clay was the given name of the champion boxer who renamed himself Muhammad Ali) and Jupiter (the name of the slave in Edgar Allan Poe's story 'The Gold Bug'). While these names may have been assigned by slave owners in mockery, Walcott seeks to restore their dignity, and to give them a new resonance and meaning.

Also, more explicitly and urgently than Joyce, Walcott confronts the double bind involved in drawing on canonical works from the European tradition in order to express a New World experience, a strategy which runs the danger of simply assimilating Caribbean history and consciousness into European paradigms. Tobias Döring in his fine discussion of *Omeros* notes that the figure of the English soldier Plunkett is introduced 'in order to dramatize the characteristic problems of colonial discourse'.[19] Seeking to give St Lucia 'its true place in history,'[20] Plunkett compares his St Lucian servant, named Helen, to her Greek namesake, an action preceded by and implicitly compared with that servant's acquisition of Maud Plunkett's dress, which Helen claimed her mistress gave her, but Maud said was stolen: 'but that dress / Had an empire's tag on it, mistress to slave. / The Price was envy and cunning.'[21] Plunkett, in many ways like Walcott or the narrator-poet himself, is trapped in the parameters of such metaphors, reinscribing the Caribbean in European points of comparison.

Walcott insistently confronts this issue, for example in the following lines:

> All that Greek manure under the green bananas,
> under the indigo hills, the rain-rutted road,
> the galvanized village, the myth of rustic manners,
>
> glazed by the transparent page of what I had read.
> What I had read and rewritten till literature
> was guilty as History. When would the sails drop
>
> from my eyes, when would I not hear the Trojan War
> in two fishermen cursing in Ma Kilman's shop?
> When would my head shake off its echoes like a horse
>
> shaking off a wreath of flies? When would it stop,
> the echo in the throat, insisting, 'Omeros';
> when would I enter that light beyond metaphor?[22]

One strategy to avoid producing a reverse mirror image of the Greek epics is Walcott's avoidance of a linear narrative; as John Figueroa points out, the structure of *Omeros* is mosaic, a series of complicated patterns; and juxtapositions, rather than straight-line development.[23] Another tactic is the frequent intervention of the narrator, who merges at times with Walcott himself, or with other characters such as Plunkett, in order to comment on and raise the problem of drawing on classical epic analogies. For example, as Döring remarks, the scene in chapter 57, near the end of the poem, where the poet accompanies Homer/Omeros to the rim of the volcano on Soufriere mountain, 'combines a self-dramatization of this anxiety of epic influence with a self-critical castigation for the rhetoric of simile and classical figuration'.[24] Here, in a replication of Dante's descent into the Seventh Circle of Hell (in Canto XVII of the *Divine*

Comedy) to be shown the punishment of those who have done violence to art, the poet sees other poets who took pride in metaphors and analogies:

> In one pit were the poets. Selfish phantoms with eyes
> who wrote with them only, saw only surfaces
> in nature and men, and smiled at their similes,
>
> condemned in their pit to weep at their own pages.
> And that was where I had come from. Proud in my craft.
> Elevating myself. I slid, and kept falling
>
> towards the shit they stewed in;[25]

One of the most important metaphorical figures in this poem is Philoctetes.[26] Like the character in Homer's *Odyssey* who is abandoned on an island because of the festering and foul-smelling wound on his ankle, Walcott's Philoctetes, a native of St Lucia and the poem's opening speaker/narrator, shows his scar to visiting tourists, 'who try taking / his soul with their cameras':[27]

> For some extra money, under a sea-almond,
> he shows them a scar made by a rusted anchor,
> rolling one trouser leg up with the rising moan
> of a conch. It has puckered like the corolla
> of a sea urchin. He does not explain its cure.
> 'It have some things' – he smiles – 'worth more than a dollar.'[28]

Philoctetes' scar becomes a metaphor for the physical and psychic trauma of history, the suffering of slavery and exploitation experienced not only by those who were transported from Africa, but also the Amerindians who were massacred or driven off the islands of the Caribbean, and the Indians brought from the subcontinent to work on the plantations. Philoctetes, like writers that Walcott has criticized elsewhere for indulging in recrimination and the status of victims, gains an audience by showing his scar, a record of past suffering. But Philoctetes' wound has been healed; it does not continue to fester, and the healing is implicit in yet another metaphor (or in this case a simile), for the scar is likened to 'the corolla of a sea urchin'. In fact, this is a metaphor within a metaphor, for the corolla is a 'little crown', the circle surrounding the seeds and in turn surrounded by the petals of a flower. So the scar is transformed into something not festering or stagnating, but natural and fertile, an image associated with the life of the island and the seashore.

Yeats declared, 'We make out of our quarrel with others, rhetoric, but of the quarrel with ourselves, poetry.'[29] Like Yeats's later poetry, Walcott's poems, including this long epic, should be read not as a statement, but as the poet's 'quarrel with himself', a process which records the experience of a divided self and desire, the acknowledgement of a wound for which a cure must be sought, yet the scar cannot ever be forgotten. As he sees Philoctetes waving to him on the beach, the poet observes, 'and I waved back; / we share the same wound, the same cure'.[30] That acknowledgement of sharing with Philoctetes and the other inhabitants of St Lucia a mutual history, a double inheritance (African and European), and a common home, of being like them an islander ever aware of the surrounding sea, is intrinsic to the 'cure'. In those aspects the movement towards a rapprochement between poetic persona and his native island seems comparable to Makak's recovery of his name and identity in *Dream on Monkey Mountain* (1970). But *Omeros* has a more ambiguous ending; in the poet's and the reader's mind, but not in her own, Helen remains evocative of Helen of Troy. In the following lines her innocence of her name's resonances, the enumeration of what she is not aware of, brings into being the analogies that Walcott and his reader cannot escape:

> She waits for your order and you lower your eyes
> away from hers that have never carried the spoil
>
> of Troy, that never betrayed Menelaus
> or netted Agamemnon in their irises.
> But the name Helen has gripped my wrist in its vise
>
> to plunge it into the foaming page. For three years,
> phantom hearer, I kept wandering to a voice
> hoarse as a winter's echo in the throat of a vase!
>
> Like Philoctetes' wound, this language carries its cure,
> its radiant affliction; reluctantly now,
> like Achille's. My craft slips the chain of its anchor,
>
> moored to a cross as I leave it; its nodding prow
> lettered as simply, ribbed in our native timber,
> riding these last worried lines; its rhythm agrees
>
> that all it forgot a swift made it remember
> since that green sunrise of axes and laurel-trees,
> till the sunset chars it, slowly, to an ember.[31]

These lines come from the final chapter and penultimate section of *Omeros*. Rather as Joyce gives the final section and words of his novel to Molly Bloom, whose consciousness is relatively unshaped by literary traditions, Walcott allocates the last section of his epic poem to Achilles, his world, and his perception of the world, a perception which is distinguished by its decidedly unheroic, but nevertheless vivid and evocative, use of metaphor and simile in the closing lines of the whole poem:

> He liked the odours
>
> of the sea in him. Night was fanning its coalpot
> from one catching star. The No Pain lit its doors
> in the village. Achille put the wedge of dolphin
>
> that he's saved for Helen in Hector's rusty tin.
> A full moon shone like a slice of raw onion.
> When he left the beach the sea was still going on.[32]

Both Walcott and Rushdie have acknowledged their admiration for Joyce, and Rushdie's *Midnight's Children* (1981) has often been compared to *Ulysses* with regard to its inventiveness and formal experimentation, as well as its ambition to encapsulate the life of a nation in formation. When asked, in an interview with Una Chaudhuri, what influences lay behind the creation of *Midnight's Children*, Rushdie mentioned Sterne's *Tristram Shandy*, Günter Grass's *The Tin Drum* (1959), and Márquez's *One Hundred Years of Solitude*, and went on to say, 'As for other influences, well, there's Joyce for a start. And Swift. And Sterne . . . So yes, I would have thought the eighteenth-century novel has something to do with mine. And Joyce, because Joyce shows you that you can do anything if you do it properly.'[33]

In that *Midnight's Children* encompasses the history of a nation, its coming into being and development, and in that it seeks to create what Benedict Anderson has termed 'an imagined community',[34] Rushdie's novel might be described, like *Ulysses* and *Omeros*, and like Homer's works before them, as belonging to the genre of national epic. But whereas Joyce's Leopold and Molly Bloom, and Walcott's St Lucian fishermen, provide a solid grounding for their works, contrasted with the more abstract and solemn musings of the autobiographical narrators, Rushdie's use of magic realism eliminates the boundaries between fantasy and 'reality'. Speaking of his choice of the magic realist mode, and the influence of writers such as Márquez, Rushdie refers to 'the inability of classical writing to encompass the nature of contemporary experience'. However, he goes on to say, 'fantasy is not interesting when you separate it from actuality and it's only interesting as a mode of dealing with actuality'.[35] For Rushdie, this conjunction of fantasy and actuality, as well as the structure of his novel, is akin to 'stories that are not written', the stories told by his father and mother. 'The book', Rushdie says, 'is a stylization of all [oral] narrative. It's obviously not a narrative because it's written to be read but it uses something of the structure and circumlocution and digression of all narrative which is where Padma came from.'[36]

Among other things, the character of Padma represents an audience which is acquainted with and responds to India's great epics, the *Ramayana* and the *Mahabharata*, and the fables of the *Panchatantra*. For Rushdie, these ancient narratives and tales offer a new starting point, a means of escaping the confines of the English novel tradition. They also provide a structure which is in Rushdie's view more appropriate to India. In an interview with Kumkum Sangari, he explains why he believes this:

> India is very much a plural culture, and if you are dealing with a country in which there is, and always has been, a mixed tradition, then you have to find a plural form. The oral epic tradition is the most flexible form that's ever been discovered. It gives a great freedom, allows for interpolations and digressions and circularities. I used it in *Midnight's Children* because I wanted to communicate a sense of fertility and fecundity, and to do this I had to very consciously waste material. That idea of unfinished stories, I thought, would be the only way of giving the sense of infinite possibility, of the narrator taking a path, not as the inevitable but as one of several possible paths.[37]

But as Rushdie also acknowledges, the narrative voice of his protagonist Saleem Sinai speaks for a fragmented individual consciousness, often alienated, and often at odds with his audience. Whereas the autobiographical heroes or heroines of many modernist novels or poems in the European tradition (and here one might include Joyce and Walcott) both desire to speak for their community and yet are aware of their separation from it, Saleem is at first presented as the embodiment of the new nation, containing in his consciousness a thousand different voices, the children born at the moment of the nation's birth at midnight, on 14 August 1947. But Saleem gradually learns that he cannot embody the nation or contain all its voices, so he himself fragments and dies.[38]

The variety of voices, the questioning of memory and the reliability of the narrator, the 'unfinished stories', the fantasy elements in *Midnight's Children*, have led some critics to label Rushdie as a postmodernist writer, but this is a label Rushdie rejects. According to Rushdie, postmodernism assumes that literature is not referential, does not relate to actuality, but is self-contained within the text. On the other hand, he does see himself as a modernist, by which he means that he is a writer who cannot take the ways things have been described, and the means of describing them, for granted. Like Harris, Rushdie rejects realism as a mode of writing because it depends for its validity upon a consensus between writer and reader about the nature of reality. But once that consensus ceases to exist, 'the description of the world becomes something you want to argue with, and you therefore resist its presentation as objective'.[39]

Among the things that Rushdie's novel argues with are the official histories of India, from both the colonial and the national perspectives. Presented as Saleem's autobiography, written at the age of thirty and in the face of his own disintegration, it is an account of the ways in which Saleem's life, like that of the poet Nadir Khan, 'has been transmuted into grotesquery by the irruption into it of history'.[40] Or, as he describes it elsewhere, his is a life 'mysteriously handcuffed to history, [his] destinies indissolubly chained to [his] country'.[41] Among the historical and fictional colonial narratives challenged are the versions of the Amritsar massacre which took place in 1919,[42] and E. M. Forster's *A Passage to India* (1924), which is set at the same time as the massacre but avoids reference to it (or rather transmutes it into a threatening but ultimately harmless riot). Forster's central Indian character is Dr Aziz, and a Dr Aziz becomes Saleem's grandfather, who is caught up in caring for those wounded in the Amritsar shootings described in Rushdie's novel 'from the inside' and capturing the terror and chaos which results as the soldiers fire 'a total of one thousand six hundred and fifty rounds into the unarmed crowd. Of these, one thousand five hundred and sixteen have found their mark, killing or wounding some person.'[43] Although much emphasis is placed on Jawaharlal Nehru's speech at the moment of independence, and his invocation of a united and secular India, there is only a passing mention of Mahatma Ghandi and his movement, which features so prominently in most official histories of India's progress towards nationhood. Saleem's account gives much greater importance to his Muslim ancestors and their colleagues who formed the 'free Islam League' and sought to play their part in a united and independent Indian nation.

In many ways *Midnight's Children* appears to have the ingredients of a conventional historical novel, covering the history of the Indian subcontinent from one seemingly trivial moment in 1915 when Saleem's grandfather 'hit his nose against a frost-hardened tussock of earth while attempting to pray', through the achievement of independence in 1947, the Partition of the subcontinent, and later of Bengal, the 1958 military coup in Pakistan, the war between India and Pakistan in 1971, Indira Gandhi's suspension of civil rights during the 1975–7 State of Emergency, and the sterilization campaign led by Sanjay Gandhi. But it also includes sometimes deliberately unreliable references to actual historical events, as for example the narrator's misremembering the date of Gandhi's assassination, and this should alert the reader to some of the many ways in which Rushdie questions conventional historical narrative and the truth of memory.

However, it is the form of Rushdie's novel which offers the most considerable challenge to conventional historical narratives. Many critics have noted its hybrid nature, its marriage of traditional Indian oral traditions and European literary traditions. Like Joyce, but to a much greater extent, Rushdie draws on cinematic techniques, in his case the thriving traditions of Bollywood film, and the novel includes as one of its more significant characters a film director, Homi Catrack. But, as Michael Gorra explains in his lucid analysis of this novel, it is above all the 'literalization of metaphor' which distinguishes Rushdie from other more realist or modernist writers in the English tradition, and makes him more comparable to Eastern European writers like Gogol (especially the Gogol of 'The Nose'), Grass and Franz Kafka, whose characters are metamorphized or 'deformed into grotesquery by the tyranny of the bureaucracy within which they work'.[44] In these works, as in Rushdie's, characters are no longer examples of psychological change and development within a specific and well-defined social environment, but carry a symbolic weight. As Gorra remarks, 'So in Rushdie we never lose our awareness of the protagonist's emblematic value, for Saleem stands himself as the site of that struggle [between different cultural, political, or religious beliefs]; he is always and explicitly as much the embodiment of the "polyglot frenzy . . . [and] the flooding multitudes" inside him as he is an individual.'[45] Both his birth at midnight and his enormous nose mark Saleem as emblematic, on the one hand of India's postcolonial citizens, and on the other of India's folkloric heritage, for his nose links him with Ganesh, the elephant-headed god who is also the god of writers who broke off his tusk to write down the *Mahabharata*. As a character, he is also in contest with Prime Minister Indira Ghandhi, who strives to make herself emblematic, a symbol of India, with the political slogan 'Indira is India, India is Indira', and is in turn metamorphized into a grotesque witch by Saleem/Rushdie. Both attempts to embody the nation are shown to fail, but Saleem reluctantly acknowledges that failure, while Indira Gandhi is shown to destroy the lives of others in her refusal to acknowledge the error and impossibility of defining the nation as indistinguishable from herself (or her family).

Saleem is further emblematic not so much of the Indian nation, but of the Indian nation's ambition to be all-inclusive, as in Nehru's dream of a secular nation without religious or caste discrimination. Here, too, the form of the novel is fashioned to be all-encompassing, with its episodic and digressive nature, its variety of characters and cultures and localities (including Bengal, Bombay, Delhi and Kashmir), its dialogue (however weighted) between Padma and Saleem, themselves also on the one hand emblems of female sceptical pragmatism grounded in Hindu tradition and, on the other, male political and intellectual aspiration influenced by European cultural traditions. Saleem's 'biography' also offers a challenge to conventional historiography and fiction. Having been offered a geneaology leading from Aadam Aziz to his birth and childhood in a wealthy Muslim family, the reader suddenly learns that Saleem may in fact have been the illegitimate child of an Englishman, William Methwold, whose house his family inhabits, and Vanita, the wife of a poor Hindu street musician. As in so many eighteenth- and nineteenth-century novels and comic operas, the children are swapped, and their identities changed. Perhaps. But whereas in these earlier novels the 'true' identity of the child is discovered and he is restored to his rightful place in society, this does not happen in Rushdie's novel. We are never certain whether it is the aggressive gang and military leader Shiva or the storyteller Saleem who should be the recipient of Nehru's letter to a child who was born at the stroke of midnight on 15 August 1947, and whose role is to mirror the development of the nation. So the validity of Saleem's history is put in question, as is the issue as to who should be foregrounded in the narration of a national history.

At the end of the novel, Saleem is working in a chutney factory, and he compares his narrative to the process of pickling. The sections of the novel are likened to jars of pickles, and his attempt to record the past is described as the 'chutnification of history'. Not only are the ingredients the events of history chopped up and intermingled, but the very process of preservation involves a distortion, the introduction of new flavours with the spices, mixed according to the preserver's personal preference. But they are also presented to the taster, the consumer, with the desire to please the palate and at the same time convey the 'authentic taste' of the fruit, vegetable or fish that has been pickled. Thus Rushdie seeks to remind his readers of the democratic ideals and hopes which accompanied the founding of the nation, as well as the betrayals of those ideals, not least by his own class, the wealthy and educated families whom Methwold has chosen to inhabit his abandoned mansion on the hill above the slums of Bombay.[46] Rushdie's novel sets out to provide both intellectual sustenance and aesthetic enjoyment in the consumption of his colourful, spicy and artistically arranged jars of chutney.

Chapter 8

Rewriting her story: nation and gender

The first chapter of *Midnight's Children* (1981) is entitled 'The Perforated Sheet', referring to the sheet with its small circular hole through which Dr Aziz was expected to diagnose, treat, and then court Saleem's grandmother, Naseem, while she remained in purdah. Gradually, we are told, 'Doctor Aziz came to have a picture of Naseem in his mind, a badly-fitting collage of her severally-inspected parts. This phantasm of a partitioned woman began to haunt him, and not only in his dreams. Glued together by his imagination, . . . she moved into the front room of his mind.'[1] The image of 'a partitioned woman', a figure 'glued together by the imagination' becomes a metaphor for the imagined Indian subcontinent as a whole, made up of many disparate cultures, languages and faiths, and partitioned in 1947, remaining even now bitterly divided over Kashmir, where Naseem and Aadam Aziz first meet. As a female figure who dominates the imagination, Naseem will be supplanted later in the novel by Indira Gandhi, who seeks to create an identification between India and herself ('Indira is India, India is Indira'), and also by Padma, an intermediary for the writer's imagined audience. Rushdie's later novel *The Moor's Last Sigh* (1995) makes frequent reference to the image of 'Mother India' and to the famous 1957 film with that title, replacing the devout peasant mother featured in the film with, as he describes his protagonist Aurora, his 'own sort of Mother India . . . metropolitan, sophisticated, noisy, angry and different'.[2]

All these important woman characters in Rushdie's novel in varying ways suggest an identification between the feminine and the national, an identification which recurs in the nationalist rhetoric during India's struggle for freedom, when as Ranjana Ash says, '*Bharatmata*, Mother India, bound in chains waiting for her children to free her, became a popular figure in the literature, music, and art of the period.'[3] The Indian nationalist Sri Aurobindo drew on already established mythography when he invoked the image of his country as mother and called on Indian men to come to free her from colonialist oppression: 'I know my country as Mother. I offer her my devotions, my worship. If a monster sits upon her breast and prepares to suck her blood, what does her child do? Does he quietly sit down to his meal . . . or rush to her rescue?'[4] For

Aurobindo, the liberation of the mother country would also involve the recovery of the mother tongue, in his case Bengali, and the rejection of English. But the Indian scholar Ashis Nandy notes that Aurobindo's devotion to Mother India bore little relation to his attitudes to real women. His wife, Mrinalini Devi, was neglected by him and she died 'lonely, heart-broken, and perhaps unlamented' after seventeen years of marriage.[5] And in other nations, as Elleke Boehmer notes, 'Figures of mothers of the nation are everywhere emblazoned but the presence of women in the nation is officially marginalised and generally ignored.'[6] Thus Helen becomes an image of the island of St Lucia in Derek Walcott's *Omeros* (1990); Wilson Harris's *Palace of the Peacock* (1960) conflates the quest for Mariella with the ghostly crew's journey through inland Guyana; Cathleen ni Houlihan appears in Irish poetry, drama and fiction as a symbol of Ireland; and there is frequent appeal to 'Mother Africa' in works by writers such as Kofi Awoonor, Camara Laye, Léopold Senghor, and Wole Soyinka. Some women writers have endorsed such identification between woman and nation: Buchi Emecheta, the London-based Nigerian novelist, declares that 'the white female intellectual may still have to come to the womb of Mother Africa to re-learn how to be a woman'.[7] Maud Gonne, the Irish nationalist leader and founder of the Daughters of Erin, appeared on stage in the title role in W. B. Yeats's *Cathleen ni Houlihan* (1902) and identified herself with Erin. The Indian poet and politician Sarojini Naidu wrote of 'Mother India lying in darkness, until she could be led into the dawn of progress by her sons and daughters'.[8]

Of course, the identification of the nation with a female iconic figure is not limited to colonized or postcolonial countries – Britain and France are most frequently allegorized in female form, while patriotic citizens and colonial subjects were exhorted to fight for 'Mother England'. Moreover, colonialist writing frequently depicted both the country and its inhabitants as feminine. Thus Joseph Conrad in *Heart of Darkness* (1902) contrasts Kurtz's two mistresses, one white and one black, as symbolizing European and African worlds respectively, and in contrast with Kurtz's frail and idealistic 'Intended', the African mistress epitomizes what Europeans conceived of as a dark, mysterious and barbaric continent:

> She was savage and superb, wild-eyed and magnificent; there was something ominous and stately in her magnificent progress. And in the hush that had fallen suddenly upon the whole sorrowful land, the immense wilderness, the colossal body of the fecund and mysterious life seemed to look at her, pensive, as though it had been looking at its own tenderous and passionate soul.[9]

British visual portrayals of India and Ireland tend to depict them as frail and girlish, depending on a portly John Bull or a robust Mother England (or Queen Victoria) for protection from fierce and brutal male nationalists.[10] But the allegorical figure of the nation in need of protection often overlaps with depictions of 'native' women who need to be rescued from allegedly barbarous customs inflicted by native men. As Gayatri Chakravorty Spivak has phrased it, the justification for imperial rule is often articulated in terms of 'white men saving brown women from brown men'.[11] Paradoxically, colonial writing also depicted, African, Indian and Irish men as effeminate. In his 1865 series of lectures advocating the establishment of Celtic Studies at Oxford University, Matthew Arnold counterposed a childlike and feminine image of the Celt to a mature and masculine Anglo-Saxon character. The Gael, he claimed, was marked by sensitivity, irrationality ('always ready to react against the despotism of fact') and sentimentality, while the Germanic element in the English race brought honesty, industry, rationality and a sense of order. The Celtic nature, Arnold declared, has something feminine in it, and the Celt is thus 'peculiarly disposed to feel the spell of the feminine idiosyncrasy'.[12] Similarly, as Boehmer notes, Indians, and especially Bengalis, 'were typically characterized as passive, soft, seductive, languid, and generally effeminate when compared to the robustly male personae of the colonisers', and she cites James Mill's *History of India* (1818) and John Ruskin's *The Two Paths* (1859) for their insistence on a dichotomy between a 'febrile, decorative, delicate, all too feminine' Hindu culture and a masculine Englishness.[13] Edward Said's *Orientalism* (1978) documents and decries similar European portrayals of all peoples and cultures in Asia, the Indian subcontinent and the Middle East.

Such racial characterizations helped to justify colonial missions, whether religious, commercial or military. If Indians and the Irish were perceived to be like women and the English claimed to possess all the most worthy male attributes, in a nineteenth-century context it could be argued that these feminine nations needed benevolent (but firm) male governance, just as English law enforced the belief that wives should be subject to their husbands, should not participate in politics, and should not possess property of their own. Despite his advocacy of academic study of Celtic literature, it is not surprising that Arnold strongly opposed granting Home Rule to Ireland when a bill was brought before parliament in 1886, arguing that the Irish were not capable of ruling themselves and were generally 'insubordinate, idle, and improvident'.[14]

In an anticolonial context, the gendered rhetoric of the relationship between the country and its indigenous peoples is often more intense and more complex, while the paradigm of a family (now a Western family model) of mother and sons, father and children, husband and wife, is reinforced. Thus one finds the passionate calls by nationalists such as Aurobindo to the sons of the colonized country to come to the rescue of the motherland. Frequently also the drama or poetry or prose which calls for national liberation is structured as a kind of

Oedipal or family romance in which the sons of the nation seek to usurp the imperial father-figures who have laid claim to the mother/wife. In this contest also, the sons seek to affirm their manhood in the face of colonialist disparagement and in the process of redeeming the mother country and restoring her to her youthful beauty, as we have seen in the Irish nationalist drama *Cathleen ni Houlihan*. Meanwhile, the leaders of the struggle, and later the presidents of the new nation, such as Jomo Kenyatta and Nelson Mandela, become designated 'Fathers' of the nation.

Nandy draws on the experience of India to argue that colonial and anti-colonial discourses generally tended to narrow concepts of sexuality and gender roles, setting up a sharp dichotomy between an aggressive warrior masculinity and a submissive, passive femininity as the norms for male and female behaviour, a dichotomy which Mahatma Gandhi's nonviolent movement sought to subvert.[15] Gandhi also to some extent tried to make 'a new equation between womanliness and political potency, denying in the process the Western association between maleness and control over public affairs and statecraft'.[16] But in India and other postcolonial nations, the dichotomy between public activity defined as male, and feminine roles defined as private and domestic, have prevailed. Boehmer succinctly summarizes the general points made by Partha Chatterjee, Anne McClintock and other theorists regarding the formation of gender roles in colonial and postcolonial discourse and practice wherein 'the historical formation of gender was ... succesfully recast as women's externalised, static, and a-historic relationship to power. If men occupied the dimension of time – linear, future-directed, associated with change and progress – women presided over the static dimension of space – the past, tradition, nature.'[17] Or, as she has put it elsewhere, 'Typically ... the male role in the nationalist scenario may be characterised as metonymic ... The "female", in contrast, puts in an appearance chiefly in a metaphoric or symbolic role.'[18]

This identification of the nation as woman, and of men as her saviours, frequently influences the portrayal of women in anticolonial and postcolonial literature. The Ghanaian novelists Ayi Kwei Armah and Awoonor, the Kenyan writer Ngugi wa Thiong'o and the Nigerian writer Soyinka all centre their fiction, and the activities of their male characters, around a woman whose story and significance parallel that of their people and land. Ngugi's Mumbi and Wanja, in *A Grain of Wheat* (1967) and *Petals of Blood* (1977) respectively, Awoonor's Dede in *This Earth, My Brother* (1971), Soyinka's Iriyesi in *Season of Anomie* (1973), and Armah's Jessawa in *The Healers* (1978), are all to some degree allegorized as the nation, which has suffered, has been betrayed, and awaits or seeks a true and devoted male partner to rescue her. Often these novels give considerable space to elaborating this central woman's role as the repository or carrier of traditional culture. In all these novels the redemption of this central female figure depends on her partner taking on his manly responsibilities, and that also involves an acknowledgement of and reconciliation with the woman's complicity in betrayal.

In Indian and Irish literature there is often a similar overloading of central women characters so that they become in some sense signifiers of the nation. The mothers in Sean O'Casey's plays are examples, even though he is sceptical of particular manifestations of Irish nationalism (as promulgated by Padraic Pearse) and also makes an ironic contrast between the gendered rhetoric of nationalists and their neglect of or dependency on their actual wives and mothers. Thus in *The Plough and the Stars* (1928) Clitheroe and Brennan, members of the Irish Citizen Army (led by James Connolly), and Langdon, a member of the Irish Volunteers (led by Padraic Pearse), incite each other to go out and fight in the name of Ireland, declared to be 'greater than a mother' and 'greater than a wife'. Several characters in J. M. Synge's plays, for example Maurya in *Riders to the Sea* (1902), Nora in *Shadow of the Glen* (1904) and Pegeen in *The Playboy of the Western World* (1907) were perceived by audiences not only as 'figures of Irish womanhood' but also as in some sense representing the race as a whole in its suffering and its yearning for redemption. In *A Portrait of the Artist as a Young Man* (1916) and *Ulysses* (1922), James Joyce presents with some irony Stephen Dedalus's identification of Emma Clery and the serving woman with 'her race', and his sense of betrayal that they listen to others, especially priests and Englishmen, rather than to him. Molly Bloom has been seen as connoting a faithless Mother Earth/Mother Ireland and, as in the African novels, the central protagonists must come to terms with that history of betrayal before there can be reconciliation and hope. As we have demonstrated earlier in this chapter, Rushdie's central women characters in *Midnight's Children* and *The Moor's Last Sigh* both compete with and evoke Mother India, while Aurora in the latter novel is suspected of multiple infidelities.

For postcolonial women authors, this tradition of portraying the nation as a woman and their female characters as to some degree symbolic of the nation and its precolonial culture is problematic. In 'Mother Ireland' the Irish poet Eavan Boland portrays that relationship ironically: 'At first / I was land / . . . / I did not see. / I was seen, / Night and day / words fell on me.' But, the narrator goes on:

> From one of them
> I learned my name.
> I rose up. I remembered it.
> Now I could tell my story.
> It was different
> from the story told about me.[19]

Boland has written of her need to combat 'the association of the feminine and the national – and the consequent simplification of both'.[20] Referring to her alienation from the rhetoric and imagery of much Irish nationalist poetry, and yet its appeal to her, she went on to say:

> I had tribal ambivalences and doubts, and even then I had an uneasy sense of the conflict which awaited me. On the one hand I knew that as a poet, I could not easily do without the idea of a nation. Poetry in every time draws on that reserve. On the other hand, I could not as a woman accept the nation formulated for me by Irish poetry and its traditions. At one point it even looked to me as if the whole thing might be made up of irreconcilable differences. At the very least, it seemed to me that I was likely to remain an outsider in my own national literature, cut off from its archive, at a distance from its energy. Unless, that is, I could repossess it.[21]

In a sequence of poems entitled 'Outside History' (1990), like the essay from which the above quotation is taken, Boland challenges earlier depictions of Irish women. The first poem in the sequence, 'The Achill Woman', portrays a woman whom Stephen Dedalus or actual male writers might have seen as emblematic of Ireland, the Shan Van Vocht or Cathleen ni Houlihan, a woman who is poor and old. But Boland resists any impulse on the part of the reader to turn this woman into a symbol, and thus deprive her of her own subjectivity, by providing a very detailed and specific description of the woman and the place that insists on both her ordinariness and her distinctiveness:

> She came up the hill carrying water.
> She wore a half-buttoned, wool cardigan,
> a tea-towel round her waist.
>
> She pushed the hair out of her eyes with
> her free hand and put the bucket down.[22]

The subject, the plainness of the diction, the subtle half-rhymes in later stanzas and the understated metre all contrast with the poems the student poet was reading at the time, poems by John Davies, Walter Raleigh and Philip Sidney, who were among the English colonizers of Ireland in the sixteenth century, and who brought an English literary tradition to Ireland. Boland tells how at the time she

> failed to comprehend
> the harmonies of servitude
> the grace music gives to flattery
> and language borrows from ambition – [23]

African women writers have also taken exception to the conflation of the feminine and the national by African male writers. The Senegalese novelist Mariama Ba forcefully dismissed a tradition associated with the *négritude* school of francophone African writers headed by Léopold Senghor. She declared:

> The nostalgic songs dedicated to African mothers which express the anxieties of men concerning Mother Africa are no longer enough for us. The Black woman in African literature must be given the dimension that her role in the liberation struggles next to men has proven to be hers, the dimension which coincides with her proven contribution to the economic development of the country.[24]

Anglophone male writers such as Chinua Achebe, Ezekiel Mphalele and Wole Soyinka have also expressed scepticism about *négritude*'s idealization of the precolonial past, and in *A Man of the People* (1966) Achebe provides a clever parody of those 'nostalgic songs' in a poem purportedly written by the would-be national leader Cool Max. The poem is called 'Dance-Offering to the Earth-Mother' and begins:

> I will return home to her – many centuries have I wandered –
> And I will make my offering at the feet of my lovely mother:
> I will rebuild her house, the holy places they have raped and plundered,
> And I will make it fine with black wood, bronzes and terra-cotta.[25]

Nevertheless, the plot of *A Man of the People* involves the courtship by rival politicians of three different kinds of women (an older rural woman, a younger sophisticated and fickle urbanite and an even younger village girl), each of whom can be read as standing for different groups of voters, and all of whom await the advent of a sincere male leader to champion them. As I mentioned earlier, 'the anxieties of men concerning Mother Africa' are also demonstrated in the novels of the Ghanaian writers Armah and Awoonor. Awoonor's hero in *This Earth, My Brother* is haunted by the memory of his dead girl cousin, Dede, whom the imagery of the novel links to the mythical Mammy Water, and who is also a symbol of the Ghanaian nation. In Armah's fifth novel, *The Healers*, Araba Jessiwa, the main woman character, receives therapy from the male healer and guru Damfo, allowing her at last to find her 'true' fulfilment as a mother. When she is almost destroyed physically and psychologically by her son's murderers, she becomes a symbol of fragmented Africa, whom the men must carry around, becoming both their burden and their hope for salvation.

Armah's compatriot and fellow author Ama Ata Aidoo is scathing about his depiction of women:

He is like any of the male African writers. They can only portray women
the way they perceive them . . . Armah's female characters are very much
out there to act as foils to his male heroes. For me, the quintessential
female character is this old woman in *The Healers*. She is so articulate
and clear, but what does he do? He encases her in this orthopaedic
contraption which symbolically and literally immobilises her
completely. For me that is very symbolic. If they are up and about, they
are servicing men; if they are clear, they are lying prone.[26]

In response to such portrayals in which women become passive symbols
rather than active, individual characters, women writers such as Aidoo and
the Nigerian writer Flora Nwapa have created fiction and drama that give
women voices and agency. Aidoo's first play, *The Dilemma of a Ghost* (1965)
contrasts a young African American woman's idealization of Mother Africa
with the 'real' mothers and mother-in-law she encounters in Africa, and also
dramatizes different attitudes to motherhood and the roles expected of women.
As we have seen in chapter 2, her second play *Anowa* (1970) features a heroine
who resists traditional roles, becomes a trader, and rejects a way of life which
accepts slavery and collaborates with the colonial culture. Aidoo's short stories
collected in *No Sweetness Here* (1971) present a variety of women, rural and
urban, mothers and daughters and friends, who are remarkable for their spirit,
humour and resilience. They include teachers, doctors and market women, all
of whom are given distinctive voices, often as the main narrators and com-
mentators. The title of the opening story, 'Everything Counts', is indicative of
Aidoo's firm belief that the personal and the political are interrelated. As she
has said in an interview, 'Even in terms of the relationship between a man and
a woman, the factors that affect the relationship are very often outside of themselves; they have to do with social structure, with economics, with political
reality.'[27] In 'Everything Counts', as in several of her other stories, the narrative voice is that of a young Western-educated Ghanaian whose adherence to
the more exterior aspects of African identity is tested by her encounter with
Ghanaians of a different generation, class or background. Here the teacher-
narrator becomes nauseated as she observes that every young woman student
in her class wears a wig, and that the winner of the Miss Ghana beauty contest is
the most light-skinned of all the contestants. One of the many levels of irony in
the story relates to her earlier insistence in arguments in the United States with
her African American and African friends (including her fiancé) that her own
wig-wearing was a mere convenience, that appearance was irrelevant, that it was
economics and nation-building they should concentrate on. The reader accepts
this argument to some extent, but also becomes aware that the wearing of wigs
by Ghanaian women, and the beauty contest, are all aspects of a mentally and

economically colonized society in which European goods and fashions, even if they are secondhand, are judged superior to African products; and where women are also seen as commodities, valued chiefly for their appearance and their approximation to European standards of attractiveness. What begins in the story as a simple dilemma – whether or not to wear a wig – opens out into a much wider and deeper problem for those who might seek not to choose between tradition and modernity, viewed all too often as a choice between Africa and the West, but to put their knowledge gained in the West to the benefit of an African society, while still retaining its fundamental identity and dignity.

This opening story is followed by and paired with one of the few stories to feature a male narrator, 'For Whom Things Do Not Change', in which a young idealistic Ghanaian administrator in a rural village gradually realizes that gender roles are associated with power rather than sexuality. His male cook insists on preparing 'English' food for him, since such cooking is a 'job' which does not threaten his identity as a male; African food must be prepared by his wife. But the narrator also hears the husband and wife comment acutely on the corruption of those in power, both British and Ghanaian, and on the lack of any material change for those, like them, who are the workers and servants. And throughout the story we hear the contrasting voices of the young educated administrator, Kobina, whose voice and thoughts are narrated in Standard English, and his cook, Zirigu, who speaks in broken pidgin English to his master, just as he serves an imitation of English cuisine. Zirigu literally and metaphorically seeks to wake the sleeping Kobina, as he urgently and repeatedly knocks on his door. But the real awakening comes when Kobina visits Zirigu's home and hears him talking with his wife (in the local language presented now through Standard English) about the economic and sexual exploitation of the poor in their community.

These two opening stories, the title story 'No Sweetness Here' and the final story in the collection all foreground young Western-educated Ghanaians, whose changing consciousness is expressed mainly through interior monologue or memories – memories which, significantly, record other voices and allow the reader to question the narrator's point of view. In this sense they are relatively 'literary' in style, and self-consciously so; they are, despite the idealistic ambitions of the protagonists to serve their communities and contribute to the new nation, self-absorbed and self-reflective, and there is little sense of an audience beyond themselves. Each story ends with the beginning of a rupture in that self-absorption, though it is left to the reader to move beyond those beginnings.

These narratives contrast with stories like 'The Message', 'In the Cutting of a Drink', and 'Something to Talk About on the Way to the Funeral', which consist almost entirely of dialogue, and relate more closely to oral and dramatic forms of performance. Indeed, many of these stories were written for performance on radio, thus deploying a Western import to continue and develop African oral storytelling traditions, and illustrating how such technology can be put to the service of African culture rather than replacing or subduing it. Aidoo has spoken of her desire to draw on oral storytelling techniques and traditions, which have in her view a dynamism lacking in European literature:[28] 'One doesn't have to be so patronizing about oral literature . . . The art of the speaking voice can be brought back so easily . . . We don't have to write for readers, we can write for listeners'[29] Thus the opening lines of 'The Message' plunge the reader/listener into the midst of a lively discussion by group of anonymous women speakers and listeners, of whom we become a part:

> 'Look here my sister, it should not be said but they say they opened her up.'
> 'They opened her up?'
> 'Yes, opened her up.'
> 'And the baby removed?'
> 'Yes, the baby removed.'
> 'I say . . . '
> 'They do not say, my sister.'
> 'Have you heard it?'
> 'What?'
> 'This and this and that . . . '
> 'A-a-ah! That is it . . . '
> '*Meewuo!*"
> They don't say *Meewuo* . . .'
> 'And how is she?'
> 'Am I not here with you? Do I know the highway which leads to Cape Coast?'
> 'Hmmm . . .'[30]

As Ketu Katrak comments, here and in other stories in this collection, Aidoo 'creatively transmutes several characteristics of orality – conversing with the listeners, audience participation, communal voices as chorus, dramatic dialogue, repetition – into written, "heard" texts, her own dynamic form of oral textuality'.[31]

But the deployment of oral traditions and techniques has additional significance in a context where women writers have been marginalized, where it has been considered important to educate boys but not girls (though Aidoo's father was an exception and was strongly in support of education for women), and where as a consequence oral storytelling and traditional songs and tales remain *de facto* the most readily available means of artistic expression for women. Additionally, the concentration on dialogue rather than exterior description places the emphasis on women's subjectivity, their emotions, thoughts and motives, rather than their appearance, so these 'heard' texts also provide a telling contrast with the opening story which focuses on appearance, on how women are seen as bodies and judged to be desirable.

Nwapa uses a similar technique in her first two novels, *Efuru* (1966) and *Idu* (1970). Like Aidoo, she regarded Achebe's work as inspirational, but like Aidoo also she seeks to place her women characters in the foreground rather than the background. Her novels are set in rural Igbo communities similar to those that Achebe recreates, but, as Boehmer notes, 'Women press into Nwapa's narrative as speakers, actors, decision-makers, brokers of opinion and market prices and unofficial jurors in their communities.' Boehmer also remarks on Nwapa's distinctive use of 'choric language to enable and empower her representation'.[32] The effect, as in Aidoo's stories, is to disperse portrayals of mothers as symbols of the nation or tradition and replace them with women who are active participants in and makers of community life; no longer seen as metaphoric, they take on metonymic roles, specific and contiguous. Nevertheless, Nwapa also includes mythic female figures. Thus Efuru, in the novel named for her (and it is in itself a statement of women's importance that her name gives the novel its title, as Aidoo titles her play for its 'heroine' Anowa) devotes herself to the goddess Uhamiri, a dedication which gives her status in the community and counteracts the 'shame' of being childless. Uhamiri brings wealth and beauty to compensate for childlessness, but she also suggests the contradictory desires and ambitions which women experience in traditional rural villages and urban environments alike, for motherhood on the one hand and for beauty and independence on the other. However, Uhamiri is not only a feminine presence, as is the Earth Goddess in *Things Fall Apart* (1958), but a *woman's* goddess, providing meaning and status for particular women in the community.

In comparison with Achebe, Armah and Soyinka, Aidoo and Nwapa have received relatively little acclaim from critics in their own countries, or elsewhere. Nwapa's work was dismissed as lacking plot (meaning the kind of heroic struggle and political activity in which Achebe's male characters were involved), and purveying mere gossip. Unable to find a publisher for her later works, Nwapa set up her own publishing companies, Tana Press and Flora Nwapa Books, and distributed her own works. Aidoo's stories and plays were not reprinted after their first appearance in the 1970s and were unavailable in Ghana and the United States until the 1990s. During the early decades of the historically postcolonial period, after independence, critical studies by male Africanists tended to ignore or disparage African women writers.[33] Aidoo herself has commented on the lack of visibility of African women writers in a 1986 interview:

> The question of the woman writer's voice being muted has to do with the position of women in society generally. Women writers are just receiving the writer's version of the general neglect and disregard that woman in the larger society receives ... [T]he assessment of a writer's work is in the hands of critics who put people on pedestals or sweep them under the carpet, or put them in a cupboard, lock the door and throw the key away. I feel that, wittingly or unwittingly, people may be doing this to African women writers.[34]

In southern Africa white women authors such as Nadine Gordimer and Doris Lessing, and before them Olive Schreiner, have become canonical in studies of South African or postcolonial writing. Meanwhile, the mixed-race writer Bessie Head died neglected in her adopted homeland, Botswana, where she had lived in exile from her native South Africa, despite the fact that her powerful and disturbing 1973 novel, *A Question of Power*, had been adopted as a central text in North American and British Women's Studies courses focusing on writing by women of colour or on women's experience of marginalization, disorientation and 'madness' (as diagnosed by male doctors or partners). In the latter courses she was read alongside Margaret Atwood (*Surfacing* (1972)), Janet Frame (*Faces in the Water* (1961)), Keri Hulme (*The Bone People* (1984)) and Jean Rhys (*Wide Sargasso Sea* (1966)), all written in postcolonial contexts and published between 1960 and 1985, as well as earlier works by Charlotte Perkins Gilman (*The Yellow Wallpaper* (1899)) and Virginia Woolf (*Mrs Dalloway* (1925)).

It was the British Women's Press and New York Feminist Press which first published *Nervous Conditions* (1988 and 1989 respectively) by the Zimbabwean novelist Tsitsi Dangarembga, a novel which, by ignoring the armed struggle, comments obliquely on a preceding series of novels and stories addressing the Zimbawean struggle for self-government against the British and then the Ian Smith regime. Authors such as Wilson Katiyo, Charles Mungoshi and Stanlake Samkange had dealt with the armed confrontation with the colonialists and the economic and psychological consequences of colonialism in historical novels. In his novellas and short stories collected in *House of Hunger* (1979) and *Black Sunlight* (1980), Dangarembga's near contemporary Dambudzo Marechera (deploying a style and structure much more intense and surreal than that of his predecessors) also wrote of memories of violent confrontation; the guerrilla warfare in which many of his fellow students were involved; and the squalor, poverty, drinking and drugs which had become a feature of the urban slums.

His story of the nation is not one of heroic struggle, but a nightmare from which no one can awake.

One of the stories in *House of Hunger* is called 'Black Skin What Mask', a clear allusion to Frantz Fanon's first book, and a satiric portrayal of a black man who desperately scrubs himself three times a day and tries to get rid of his accent: 'He tried to purge his tongue too, by improving his English and getting rid of any accent from the speaking of it. It was painful to listen to him, as it was painful to watch him trying to scrub the blackness out of his skin.' This man, the narrator tells us, 'finally slashed his wrists' and 'is now in a lunatic asylum'.[35]

The title of Dangarembga's novel also alludes to Fanon, quoting from Jean-Paul Sartre's Introduction to Fanon's *The Wretched of the Earth* (1965), where Sartre writes, 'The condition of native is a nervous condition.' But whereas Fanon (and Sartre), and after them Marechera, generalize with reference to the condition of male 'natives', Dangarembga produces a gendered study of the psychological consequences of colonialism. Moreover, although set during the period of nationalist military activity, the novel makes almost no mention of that armed struggle, and foregrounds the effects of mental colonization on Zimbabwean women, both directly through education and European influence, and indirectly, through the impact of mental and economic colonization on the male characters. In a colonial society where economic and social status is associated with Western acculturation and the ability to impersonate a white male, the black female is doubly disadvantaged. In the opening pages of the novel, the narrator, Tambu, finds that the money she has earned for her own education is to be used to send her brother to the mission school where her uncle, Babamukuru, with his degree earned in England, is headmaster. Only when her brother dies can Tambu take his place, becoming a surrogate son, and in the process of that education she gradually becomes aware of the costs in terms of her alienation from her rural background (and her parents); her English-educated cousin Nyasha's despair at her loss of her native Shona language and culture, expressed in her increasing emaciation and anorexia; her aunt's suppressed bitterness at the waste of her own education and talents because she must perform the role of submissive wife; and her uncle's determination to be a traditional patriarch, caring for and governing his whole extended family, while also performing his role as head of the mission school. Dangarembga's novel announces its agenda aggressively in its opening paragraph, and uses the terms relating to rebellion and lack of freedom, associated with nationalist rhetoric, to describe the situation of women and their responses to it:

> I was not sorry when my brother died. Nor am I apologising for my
> callousness, as you may define it, my lack of feeling . . . For though
> the event of my brother's passing and the events of my story cannot
> be separated, my story is not after all about death, but about my
> escape and Lucia's; about my mother's and Maiguru's entrapment; and
> about Nyasha's rebellion – Nyasha, far-minded and isolated, my
> uncle's daughter, whose rebellion may not in the end have been
> successful.[36]

As Boehmer has pointed out, this pairing of female characters (Tambu and
her aunt Lucia, Tambu and her cousin Nyasha, her mother and Maiguru) is a
recurring device in novels by African women, and she persuasively argues that
these pairings, particularly that of Tambu and Nyasha, may sometimes be read
in terms of the paradigm of same-sex love, an awareness and understanding of
each other's bodies, a relationship in which 'the cousins' mutual discovery and
exploration is specifically realized through their bodily proximity and mutual
bodily awareness, as well as in their striving, as in Vera [Yvonne Vera, *But-
terfly Burning* (2000)], for a not-yet-defined beyond'.[37] From the beginning,
Tambu is aware that it is her gender, her female body, which determines that
her brother will continue his education while she will be kept at home, and
her cousin Nyasha enacts her rebellion against her father's insistence that she
enact his notion of femaleness by starving her body. But these pairings are also
a means of establishing women's roles as metonymic rather than symbolic; as
'split selves' Tambu and Nyasha (and Tambu and Lucia) indicate the variety
of roles and choices each woman may or may not seek to follow. There is no
clear solution to the dilemmas and circumstances in which many of the women
are caught, but there is a sense in which Lucia, Nyasha and Tambu might be
seen as seeking an independence through an amalgamation of African and
Western traditions, a mixed menu, which mirrors the new nation's choices as
it moves towards independence. Such paralleling with the nation's uncertain
progress towards autonomy and its own hybrid culture has in the past tended
to foreground male protagonists – 'G' and Trumper in George Lamming's
In the Castle of My Skin (1953), Odili in Achebe's *A Man of the People*, 'the Man'
in Armah's *The Beautyful Ones Are Not Yet Born* (1968), Leopold Bloom in
Joyce's *Ulysses*, Mr Biswas in V. S. Naipaul's *A House for Mr Biswas* (1961), Rama
in Raja Rao's *The Serpent and the Rope* (1960). Dangarembga makes women
central to the future directions the nation's citizens must choose, though fully
aware of how difficult and complex those choices are. Asked, in an interview
with her publisher about the novel, what direction African women should take,
and whether Tambu, the narrator, is 'headed in the right direction', Dangarembga replied, 'People make individual choices. I think mapping the ground helps

in making the choices. Such maps, written in an engaging way, are part of what I perceive my responsibility as a novelist to be.'[38] But she is also concerned that her maps should reveal the complex situations in which her characters are caught, for 'one can hold a person responsible for reacting to a situation in a certain way, but the situation that exerted the pressure to behave in that way must also be addressed'.[39]

'The pressure to behave' in certain ways, to perform certain roles, is exerted on male and female characters alike in *Nervous Conditions,* but for the female characters in this novel it is specifically linked to the consumption of food and its refusal. The effects of colonialism and neocolonialism are expressed in terms of an assault on the body, a condition which is internalized and becomes indistinguishable from the daily cycle of consumption, digestion and evacuation. In this novel the double colonization to which women are subjected is also experienced as a rejection of the female body by men. Thus Tambu's mission-educated brother not only insists on speaking English but hates riding on the bus because he claims 'the women smelt of unhealthy reproductive odours, the children were inclined to relieve their upset bowels on the floor, and the men gave off strong aromas of productive labour'.[40] (The echoing of 'reproductive' and 'productive' here links women also to a 'labouring' class – in the double sense of that adjective.) Nyasha rejects the roles of assimilated 'native' (the 'native' who has thoroughly digested a colonial diet) and docile daughter (one who serves food for others to consume) through vomiting up the food she is forced to eat, or through refusal of any food. In the scene of her final breakdown, she tears up her school history book with her teeth, chews and spits it out. These two images of consuming food and consuming books are also linked when Tambu's father pours scorn on the idea of her desire to continue with her education: 'My father thought I should not mind. "Is that anything to worry about? Ha-a-a, it's nothing," he reassured me, with his usual ability to jump whichever way was easiest. "Can you cook books and feed them to your husband? Stay at home with your mother. Learn to cook and clean. Grow vegetables."'[41]

As we have seen, food and its cultural significance in terms of gender roles is a recurring trope in Aidoo's stories and plays. In her first novel, *Our Sister Killjoy* (1977), Aidoo's protagonist Sissie and her friends are plied with rich and enticing foods when they are in Germany, contrasting with the second-rate imported tinned foods served to her at the German Embassy in Ghana. Sissie's visit to Europe makes her aware of her body as 'black' in contrast to the pink Europeans who surround her, and also makes her aware of her body as consuming and consumable. The long section entitled 'Plums', which recounts this visit, is replete with imagery of food, eating and temptation. In a scene which alludes to the biblical story of Eve's being tempted to eat the apple in the Garden of Eden, Sissie is offered plums by her German friend Marija: 'So she sat, Our Sister, her tongue caressing the plump berries with skin colour almost like her own, while Marija told her how she had selected them especially for her, off the single tree in the garden.'[42]

For Sissie and her compatriots, the attraction of Europe has much to do with the abundance of consumer goods, epitomized in the delectable foods they offer for the appreciative 'Third World' user, and the resulting wellbeing. Here Sissie becomes what she consumes, 'her tongue caressing the plump berries with skin colour almost like her own'. The 'almost' is significant, however; Marija offers Sissie a flattering and lovable self-image, but Sissie realizes that she herself is in danger of being consumed, and rejects Marija's advances. Yet in her rejection of Marija there is also complexity and blurring of motives, for as Caroline Rooney points out, Sissie refuses in the end to perform the role of the absent husband, supplying love and sensual satisfaction, but her very refusal reduplicates that of the white male, and she feels a certain pleasure in the power that role gives her.[43]

Such blurring and questioning of gender roles is a persistent feature of this novel (and other writing by Aidoo); here distinctions between male and female, white and black, consumers and consumed, moral and immoral, are repeatedly constructed and deconstructed. The heroine's selves are multiple, and are cast in different perspectives depending on the context and the audience to which she responds. This sense of a shifting and problematic identity is linked to Aidoo's awareness of the English language as an inadequate medium which obscures personal and political relationships and interrelationships. But as Rooney suggests, Sissie's ability to question and draw back from performing the role of either a white man or a white woman may relate on the one hand to a perhaps healthy narcissism, the very act of realizing that she is desirable in the eyes of others, and on the other to her different relationship to the concept of Mother Africa. Whereas 'sons' of Africa are cast into an Oedipal relationship, rivalling the white male colonizer, 'daughters' may identify with Africa as a mother figure. Rooney draws on Slavoj Žižek's view that identification with an ideal ego entails 'identification with the image in which we appear likeable to ourselves' to read both the savouring of the plums episode quoted above, and the final lines of the novel, as endorsing the recovery of a 'healthy narcissism', which is 'perhaps paradoxically, both self-affirming and altruistic', and which also allows a healthier and more satisfying identification with Africa ('She was back in Africa. And that felt like fresh honey on the tongue').[44]

We began this chapter by discussing the recurring trope of Mother India in Indian subcontinental politics and fiction, and the ways in which it was used by Indira Gandhi to add to her authority and aura, and by Rushdie to give added resonance to woman characters in his novels. Women writers in the Indian subcontinent have dealt with this gendered image of the nation and narratives of its history in different ways. Thus in *Ice-Candy-Man* (1988) (published in North America as *Cracking India*) Bapsi Sidhwa, who was born in Pakistan of Parsi parents, portrays the traumatic events of Partition through the eyes of an eight-year-old Parsi girl, Lenny, living in Lahore. Critics have compared her narrative technique to Rushdie's use of Saleem as a child narrator in *Midnight's Children*, but Sidhwa's technique is very different in style and effect from Rushdie's self-conscious magic realist and modernist approach. For Lenny does not from the very beginning announce herself as emblematic or 'special'; nor does she have any supernatural access to or knowledge of the national community. Indeed, it is Lenny's naivety and limited understanding that make the unfolding story so powerful and painful for readers who see beyond those limitations and at the same time understand the pain that Lenny, as a vulnerable child, will continue to experience. Speaking of her choice of narrator, Sidhwa says:

> In *Ice-Candy-Man,* it was very useful to use the device of a Parsi child narrator, because it does bring about an objectivity here. Your own emotions are not so . . . or at least your participation in events is not so involved. You are more free to record them, not being an actor immediately involved . . . When you put yourself in the persona of a child, in a way you remove all those blurred images – other people's opinions, expectations about what life is teaching you and the stereotypes which come in. Everything is a little fresher and refreshing, I think, from a child's point of view – more direct.[45]

Lenny's triple difference – she is a Parsi in a predominantly Muslim and Hindu community, she is a girl, and she is crippled by polio – all make her an outsider in the community, but as a child she is protected by it, and does not possess the prejudices that will later destroy that community. Her innocence and unquestioning acceptance of Muslims and Hindus alike, her devotion to her Hindu ayah and her affection for her ayah's Muslim suitor, the Ice-Candy-Man of the title, establish the possibility of a harmonious and undivided community, a possibility brutally disrupted by the events of Partition. Moreover, she is able to identify with two older female figures, and surrogate mothers, her Parsi godmother who is portrayed as a strong, wise and independent woman, and her ayah, who is beautiful and vivacious. But she also witnesses the ways in which the politics of nationalism and partition reduce people to tokens rather than complex human beings:

> Gandhi, Jinnah, Nehru, Iqbal, Tara Singh, Mountbatten are names I
> hear. And I become aware of religious differences.
>   It is sudden. One day everybody is themselves – and the next day they
> are Hindu, Muslim, Sikh, Christian. People shrink, dwindling into
> symbols. Ayah is no longer just my all-encompassing Ayah – she is also a
> token. A Hindu. Carried away by a renewed devotional fervour she
> expends a small fortune in joss-sticks, flowers and sweets on the gods
> and goddesses in the temples.[46]

But Sidhwa also shows how the gendering of the nation, and the emphasis on
a manhood which involves protecting the nation and its (or 'their') women, has
terrible consequences for actual women. In different ways Ayah becomes, for
the Muslim and Hindu male characters in the novel who fight to possess her *and*
for the reader, symbolic of India itself. During the riots which accompany Partition, Ayah is abducted and raped by a group of Muslim men, led by Ice-Candy-
Man, who then carries her off to Hira Mandi, the district of Lahore associated
with dancing girls and prostitutes, marries her and renames her Mumtaz. Ayah,
who feels herself disgraced and destroyed, is rescued by Lenny's godmother
and sent to a camp for fallen women before finally being sent to India. Sidhwa
makes clear the relationship between the heightened religious nationalism that
accompanied Partition and the treatment of women as pawns in the contest
for a piece of the subcontinent. At the same time the reader associates Ayah
with the Indian subcontinent itself, ravaged, divided and fought over. And like
Pakistan, she loses her original identity as a member of a multicultural community, to be given a name which resonates with the history of Muslims in
India, for Mumtaz was the beloved wife of the Moghul Emperor Shah Jehan,
who built the Taj Mahal in her honour. (Mumtaz is also a significant character
in Rushdie's *Midnight's Children*, as the dutiful second daughter of Aadam Aziz
and wife to the poet in hiding, Nadir Khan).

Through Lenny's voice Sidhwa also critiques the development of Islamic
fundamentalism in Pakistan and its increasing intolerance of other beliefs and
cultures. Ayah in her bright sari, midriff showing, laughing in a circle of Hindus, Sikhs and Muslims is replaced by another nursemaid, Hamida, who is a
Muslim:

> The garden scene had depressingly altered. Muslim families, who added
> colour when scattered among the Hindus and Sikhs, now monopolise
> the garden, depriving it of colour. Even the children, covered in brocades
> and satins, cannot alleviate the austerity of the black burkas and white
> *chuddars* that shroud the women. It is astonishing. The absence of the
> brown skin that showed through the fine veils of Hindu and Sikh
> women, and beneath the dhoties and shorts of the men, had changed the

complexion of the queenless garden. There are fewer women.
More men.

Hamida, her head and torso modestly covered by her coarse *chuddar,*
holding her lank limbs close, sits self-consciously on the grass by herself.
There is little comfort in laying my head on her rigid lap.[47]

With the loss of Ayah, a mother figure who has come to represent the possibility of a whole and multicultural Indian subcontinent, Lenny's world becomes
'queenless'; there is no longer a Mother India character with whom she can
bond. Earlier, Lenny has rejected various father figures, including Gandhi,
whom the child sees as merely human and rather ludicrous in his dhoti, obsessed
with dieting and bad-tempered, an 'improbable toss-up between a clown and a
demon'.[48] But the child also experiences his considerable charisma, his sympathy for women – and lame children. Her demystification of Gandhi compares
with Rushdie's virtual ignoring of him, and like Rushdie, in her historical narrative she gives much greater space to the role of the Muslim nationalists. Unlike
him, however, she seeks to restore Jinnah as a dignified and principled father
figure who shared the dream of a tolerant multicultural nation. Lenny is not
born on the eve of independence, but she celebrates her eight birthday as Jinnah
makes an inaugural address to the new Constituent Assembly:

> Cousin returns with brown paper bags and a dented cardboard cake box.
> I blow out the candles and cut the squashed cake. And then we sit
> around the radio listening to the celebrations of the new Nation.
> Jinnah's voice, inaugurating the constituent Assembly sessions on 11
> August, says: 'You are free. You are free to go to your temples. You are
> free to go to your mosques or any other place of worship in the State of
> Pakistan. You may belong to any religion or caste or creed, that has
> nothing to do with the business of State . . . etc., etc., etc. *Pakistan
> Zindabad!*'[49]

The revisioning and retelling of India's history from a woman's point of view
has been undertaken by other writers from the subcontinent, among them
Manju Kapur, Githa Hariharan, Anita Desai and Nayantara Sahgal. Kapur's
first novel, *Difficult Daughters* (1998), parallels the broken relationships and
disillusionment involved in the nation's move towards independence with its
heroine Virmita's struggle for autonomy, her battle to achieve an education,
her partial fulfilment as a teacher and her disastrous marriage as a second
wife to 'the Professor' she idolizes. Her story is told sympathetically by her
unmarried and less restricted daughter, and is also contrasted with the stories
of other women who joined in the independence movement and retained some
autonomy and control over their lives. Hariharan's *A Thousand Faces of Night*

(1992) and *When Dreams Travel* (1999) both allude to Scheherazade as well as other portrayals of women in Indian myth (such as Devi and Sita, for whom two of the main women characters are named in *A Thousand Faces of Night*) to suggest the ways in which representations of women in the past can act to subdue or inspire women.[50]

Desai's *Clear Light of Day* (1980) also has as its central character a woman teacher, significantly a history teacher, Bim, who with her married sister Tara remembers their childhood and the changes which took place in their domestic world in the period leading up to 1947. The novel recounts the saga of the Das family, a Hindu clan from Old Delhi, and is set in the family house, now shabby and desolate, where Bim lives with Baba, her autistic younger brother. It is a house haunted by memories of her alcoholic aunt Mira and the youthful excitement of Bim's and her brother Raja's shared enthusiasm for English Romantic poetry and Urdu culture. As in Dangarembga's novel, the history of the period is told obliquely, and the ambivalent privilege of a colonial education is a central issue. Here, too, the focus is on the lives of women in a patriarchal society at a period of transition. Among the recurring images in this richly textured novel are those of a cow, brought to the house by the widowed Mira, and the white horse proudly ridden by their Muslim neighbour, Hyder Ali. The cow drowns in the well at the back of the garden and becomes a recurring metaphor and memory of stagnation, linked also to the fates of Bim and Mira, trapped in the decaying house in Old Delhi. Bim's and Tara's parents were also bypassed by history, ignoring the events leading up to independence and Partition, totally immersed in a mimic Britishness, as they play bridge endlessly at the Club and ignore their children, who have been consigned to the care of their Aunt Mira. In contrast, their son Raja is entranced by the image of Hyder Ali on his white horse, and idealizes Muslim culture and Urdu poetry, which they encourage him to compose. Raja becomes involved with defending Muslims when the riots which lead up to Partition begin, and when Hyder Ali and his family leave for Hyderabad he joins them; he eventually marries their daughter and becomes a wealthy landlord. Tara meanwhile has married a diplomat and mainly lives abroad, spending much of her time trying to appease her arrogant husband and demanding daughters.

The novel is by no means an allegory, nor are the characters symbolic, but the analogies with Indian history are suggested at various points in the novel. Thus when Tara speaks warmly of her need to return from time to time and not lose touch, Bim bitterly likens Delhi to a cemetery, which never changes, only decays, and goes on to claim:

> 'Whatever happened, happened long ago – in the time of the Tughlaqs, the Khiljis, the Sultanate, the Moghuls – that lot.' She snapped her fingers in time to her words, smartly. 'And then the British built New Delhi and moved everything out. Here we are left rocking on the backwaters, getting duller and greyer, I suppose. Anyone who isn't dull and grey goes away – to New Delhi, to England, to Canada, the Middle East. They don't come back.'[51]

Bim's character is a complex one; she is portrayed with sympathy as the elder daughter who cannot abandon her parents or her autistic younger brother. She is sharp and intelligent, and also deeply appreciative of poetry (both English and Urdu) and music (Western and Indian). She has forged a career for herself, gaining a degree and becoming a rather eccentric but devoted teacher of history in a girl's college. But she is also trapped by her commitment to caring for her helpless young brother, and like him is caught in the 1940s, from which era he endlessly replays the English and American songs popular in that period – 'Smoke Gets in Your Eyes', 'I'm Dreaming of a White Christmas', 'Don't Fence Me In'. (The titles are all too ironic.) But perhaps what confines her spirit most of all is her inability to forgive Raja for not becoming the poet and hero she encouraged him to be, and for his lack of sensitivity in patronizing her as a poor tenant of the house he has inherited but abandoned. Having devoted herself to him, lived through him as a young girl, she cannot accept his abandoning of their shared ideals for the sake of money and status. Thus Desai comments obliquely and more subtly than Rushdie on her central character's disillusion with her imaginary homeland, the failed hope for a renewal of Indian culture in the newly independent nation. Yet there is a glimpse of renewal at the end of the novel, when Bim listens to a performance by a Hindu singer of words by the great Urdu poet Iqbal, and acknowledges him as part of her world (not just her brother's former one). It is a line from T. S. Eliot that helps her to see the significance of this acceptance: 'Time the destroyer is time the preserver.' And:

> With her inner eye she saw how her own house and its particular history linked and contained her as well as her whole family with all their separate histories and experiences – not binding them with some dead and airless cell but giving them the soil in which to send down their roots, and food to make them grow and spread, reach out to new experiences and new lives, but always drawing from the same soil, the same secret darkness. That soil contained all time, past and future, in it. It was dark with time, rich with time. It was where her deepest self lived, and the deepest selves of her sisters and brothers and all those who shared that time with her.[52]

The structure of Desai's novel emphasizes the inextricable relationship between past and present, for as we explore the memories of the two sisters, we learn not only how they construct the past differently, how one forgets or gives different significance to what the other remembers, but also how past traditions may continue to inflect or constrict the lives of others, especially women. Bim and Mira have both been caught in the traditional expectations that women should be at the service of their families, and should always place the desires and careers of parents and brothers above their own. That role has been made bearable by a certain amount of self-deception and self-importance on Bim's part, as she realizes when she admits that she might not be as central to everyone's lives, even Baba's, as she had told herself: 'All these years she had felt herself to be the centre – she had watched them all circling in the air, then returning, landing like birds, folding up their wings and letting down their legs until they touched solid ground. Solid ground. That was what the house had been – the lawn, the rose walk, the guava trees, the verandah: Bim's domain.'[53]

Bim had believed herself central to and inseparable from the pattern of their lives. 'But the pattern was now very old.' It is faded, and she has become a mere 'brown fleck in a faded pattern'. Yet there is a day-by-day heroism in Bim's commitment to looking after her younger brother and alcoholic aunt, as well as her dedication as a teacher, and even in her obstinate clinging to a belief in the promise that Raja (and perhaps India) have, in her eyes, betrayed. There are no easy solutions, no glowing futures, in this novel, and it is clear that all movements forward must in some ways involve compromise. And perhaps, too, they involve an acceptance of hybridity, the intermingling of India's various heritages, bringing together Iqbal, Hindu music and T. S. Eliot, the meaning of each transformed in a changing pattern through time, not separated and static, or fixed in the past.

Sahgal's novel *Rich Like Us* (1985) also foregrounds an Indian tradition of female self-sacrifice in its exploration of changing India, and also has as one of its main women characters a historian, Sonali. But whereas Bim had used history as an escape from the present, immersing herself in the time of the Moghul emperors, for Sonali the historical research is a means of understanding the present, and how India has become a place of corruption. Sahgal is the niece of Jawarhalal Nehru and the daughter of two politicians deeply involved in the freedom movement, and like Rushdie she laments the loss of the Nehruvian ideals announced at the birth of the nation, deploring in particular the consequences of his daughter (and her cousin) Indira Gandhi's rule. Speaking of her fiction and its preoccupations, Sahgal said in a lecture given in 1989:

. . . I prefer to think of my fiction as having a sense of history, in a country where race, religion or caste can decide the course of a love affair, where it can take as much raw courage to choose a husband or to leave him, as to face a firing squad . . .

Then, societies that have lived long under foreign domination bring their own behaviour characteristics into play. Passivity can become an active choice, a strength, among people where invasion and re-conquest have been the pattern, because it's one's best chance of remaining whole. Sycophancy, too, is the hallmark of the survivor and all cultures have sycophants. But when I wonder why *we* produce them in such abundance – and this struck me strongly during the 1975–77 dictatorship known as the Emergency – then I have to ask, as I did in my novel *Rich Like Us*, whether Hinduism inclines a whole society to the status quo. Does it put out the fires of rebellion? Does it incline women to victimization, to individual and mass acts of horrifying self-sacrifice? Has the cult of virtue (female) and honour (male) been so ferocious and merciless in any other society that prides itself on its humane values? How do we explain this aspect of ourselves? I have been much preoccupied with the effects of Hinduism on character in my novels.[54]

Sonali, who is the first person narrator in the novel and comes from a similar background to Sahgal, is dismissed from the Indian Civil Service during the period of the Emergency introduced by Indira Gandhi, and begins to investigate stories of women who have chosen or been forced to commit *sati*. The novel sets side by side the stories of several women, past and present, British and Indian, and explores the ways in which Hindu traditions are abused and exploited by some of the male characters often for material ends, and the acquisition of Western goods and business. A central section in the novel is a manuscript by Sonali's grandfather describing his mother's forced self-immolation, or *sati*, on her husband's funeral pyre. This episode links with his grandson's first wife's attempted self-immolation after he marries an Englishwoman, Rose. And Rose herself is murdered by her stepson, Dev, because she discovers that he is forging his father's signature and siphoning off large sums of money. Through the family's history, from the sensitive and idealistic Keshav who is haunted by his mother's cruel death in 1905, and rejects Hinduism, but finds the British administration unready to act forcefully to put an end to the practice of *sati*, to the marriage of his son Ram to two women, the first Indian, the second British, and finally to the callous and corrupt son Dev, who typifies his class and its culture during Indira Gandhi's regime, we read a particular history of the Indian nation. It is a narrative which raises questions about the long-term consequences of British colonization, about the divided allegiances of Indians to Indian and British traditions and values (suggested by Ram's two wives), as well as divisions of class, race and gender (Rose comes from a working-class background but can be accepted as a member of the elite in India, and ultimately forms an alliance with Mona, Ram's first wife, and Sonali). Like *Clear Light of Day*, it also questions the demands of family loyalty and the privileging of sons, both in Indira Gandhi's determination to establish a family dynasty, and through the envisioning of the nation as a family, homogenous in terms of caste and ethnicity.

Chapter 9

Rewriting the nation: acknowledging economic and cultural diversity

Early nationalist and anticolonial authors often countered essentialist depictions of the colonized peoples with rather monolithic portrayals of their communities and cultures, deploying what may have been a necessary 'strategic essentialism', as Gayatri Chakravorty Spivak suggests in her essay 'Can the Subaltern Speak?'[1] As Frantz Fanon remarks with regard to African writers, and specifically the *négritude* movement, the colonial defamation of the 'Negro', of Africans as a 'race', does not make discriminations between Angolans and Nigerians – 'colonialism's condemnation is continental in scope'.[2] In response, the culture which is affirmed by writers from countries such as Ghana, Kenya or Senegal, or from the African diaspora, is often 'African Culture', rather than a specific national or regional culture, and it is defined in racial terms, as we have seen in the brief discussion of *négritude* in chapter 1. We have also seen how later anglophone writers expressed their scepticism of the *négritude* school of writing and its emphasis on a glorious precolonial past. Nevertheless, many would now agree with Fanon that this recovery and affirmation of African achievements in the past was a historical necessity. But in Fanon's view, '[t]his historical necessity in which the men of African culture find themselves to racialize their claims and to speak more of African culture than of national culture will tend to lead them up a blind alley'.[3]

Early nationalist fiction and drama by writers such as Chinua Achebe, Ngugi Wa Thiong'o and Wole Soyinka, who seek to affirm or validate their own cultures, and 'show that Africans did not hear of civilization for the first time from Europeans',[4] avoid the pan-African racialization found in the writings of Kwame Nkrumah or Léopold Senghor (with reference to 'the African personality'). Instead, they locate their fiction and drama in very specific communities – Igbo, or Gikuyu, or Yoruba. Rather than affirming essential characteristics, their works bear witness to the workings of a culture within a community in the process of encountering change. But the Igbo or Gikuyu or Yoruba community portrayed is also presented as a metonym for the nation as a whole, for Nigeria or Kenya, and indeed, is often *read* as a metonym for the peoples of the African continent as a whole. Similarly, Raja Rao's *Kanthapura*

(1938) and *The Serpent and the Rope* (1960), and R. K. Narayan's novels set in a fictional Malgudi, represent small village communities and/or Hindu culture as metonymic of India. In Australia, Canada and Ireland the very affinities between the metropolitan and colonial populations in terms of colour, culture and language often led to an even more determined emphasis on a homogenized or essential difference, opposing the rural Celt or 'democratic' bush worker to an urban English colonizer. And in almost all these early nationalist works, the focus is on agrarian and self-contained communities or individuals, closely connected to the land.

Despite their focus on specific local communities, these works succeeded in speaking to and for a concept of national identity, and quickly became established as canonical works not only in the national educational curriculum, but also in Commonwealth and postcolonial literature curricula in the West. The very existence of African, Caribbean and Indian writing of such distinction became in itself a source of national and racial pride, and the works of Achebe, Ngugi and Soyinka were also of considerable significance in the formation of Black (or African American) Studies programmes in the United States.

But as ethnic and class tensions became more apparent in the newly independent nations, these same writers and their successors began to portray a greater ethnic diversity and to respond to issues of inequality. In the earlier discussion of *Ulysses* (1922) in chapter 7, we noted how James Joyce reacts to the monolithic Celtic identity endorsed by the Gaelic League and the Celtic Revival by foregrounding a Jewish Irishman of Hungarian descent as his central protagonist, and including also Italian and Anglo-Irish characters and an array of European and American references. In so doing he moves away from the Catholic Irish focus of his earlier fiction. Similarly, Achebe's fourth and fifth novels, *A Man of the People* (1966) and *Anthills of the Savannah* (1987), include not only Igbo characters and communities but also Hausa and Yoruba people. In particular *Anthills of the Savannah* stresses the ways in which Nigeria is divided by inequalities of class and education, and by religious and ethnic differences, all exacerbated by a corrupt and power-hungry leadership. Moreover, this novel explicitly addresses the role of the writer, and the need to create fiction which responds to and enters into dialogue with a wider national audience. The novel ends with a scene which provides a microcosmic model for a better Nigeria, as two women, Beatrice and Elewa, become the centre of a group including Captain Abdul, a Muslim from the North, Braimoh, a taxi driver, Emmanuel, a student leader, and Agatha, Beatrice's evangelist Christian servant. It is the women who lead the union of different groups and cultures in an ecumenical dance which brings together Christian, Igbo and Muslim traditions, a dance which is also a symbol of a new but as yet unrealized and utopian Nigeria.

Between 1964 and 1968 novels and plays by Ngugi made the encounter between his own Gikuyu community and British missionaries and military forces their main focus. These novels and plays seek to narrate the history of that encounter from a Gikuyu point of view, and draw on Gikuyu myths and traditions, as well as a hybrid Christian/Gikuyu culture. His best-known novel, *A Grain of Wheat* (1967), ends on a note of reconciliation within the Gikuyu village where it is set, but also indicates the imminent betrayal of the promise of independence by politicians who grab the land for which the villagers fought. Ten years later, Ngugi published *Petals of Blood*, which, like Achebe's last two novels, emphasizes a neocolonial elite's betrayal of the hopes that accompanied independence. Influenced by the political arguments of Fanon and Karl Marx, *Petals of Blood* presents a powerful illustration and denunciation of the ways in which multinational companies, with the collaboration of politicians, businessmen and educational and religious institutions, have replaced colonial administrations to control the economies of newly independent nation states. Like *Anthills of the Savannah* (which includes a not very veiled critique of Ngugi's avowedly Marxist stance), Ngugi's last novel in English creates in the fictional village of Ilmorog a microcosm of the nation, with characters of varied ethnic and educational backgrounds – including Arab, Gikuyu, Indian and Masai. And like *Anthills of the Savannah* also it places a strong woman at the centre of the novel, though Ngugi's heroine Wanja differs from Beatrice in that she is not a member of the elite but has been a prostitute and figures as a symbol of the exploited and abused nation, in which the selling of one's body for sex represents the quintessence of a wage-labour capitalist system and the commodification of the body. Furthermore, both novels are more self-consciously 'literary' than earlier works of fiction by these two authors, raising questions about the role of literature and storytelling in the education of the nation (in terms of both educational curricula and a wider readership), and also referring back to a developing African literary canon. Munira, the village schoolteacher in Ngugi's novel, has a small library which includes 'torn school editions' of *Things Fall Apart* (1958) and *Song of Lawino* (by the Ugandan poet Okot p'Bitek (1966)). Moreover, the first three major sections in *Petals of Blood* are headed by phrases ('Walking', 'Towards Bethlehem', 'To Be Born') which allude to the same W. B. Yeats poem, 'The Second Coming', that Achebe drew on for the title of his first novel.

Petals of Blood, like Achebe's two last novels, focuses on neocolonialism and the collaboration of the nation's leaders with multinational companies and foreign governments, their betrayal of those who fought for independence and voted for them. Similarly, the Ghanaian writer Ayi Kwei Armah's novels are bleak and scathing depictions of the corruption which has blighted the hopes of ordinary Ghanaians. His first novel *The Beautyful Ones Are Not Yet Born* (1968), published eleven years after Ghana became the first African colony to achieve independence and when Nkrumah's presidency and socialist ideals had become exemplary for Africans throughout the continent, is teeming with images of pollution, decay and defecation. What has polluted the early vision of an African socialist state, of a new and shining future once the injustices and inequalities of colonial rule had been removed, is consumer capitalism. The novel is narrated through the consciousness of 'the Man', an intellectual who remains an anonymous railway clerk, despised by his wife and acquaintances because of his refusal to join in the widespread practice of accepting or giving bribes. In the modern Ghana portrayed by Armah, nothing is produced; there is only consumption and waste. Critics such as Derek Wright and Neil Lazarus have drawn attention to the influence of Fanon, especially his chapter entitled 'The Pitfalls of National Consciousness' in *The Wretched of the Earth* (1965), on Armah's portrayal of Ghana's elite, the new leaders who merely ape the colonizers, and thus betray the masses.[5]

Elsewhere, the betrayal of socialist ideals by the leaders of newly independent states in the Caribbean is portrayed by V. S. Naipaul in *The Mimic Men* (1967), where the protagonist Ralph Singh meditates on how the politicians desperately cling to the trappings of power and status, as they had been signified by the colonial rulers, through the use of bribery, election-rigging and the manipulation of the people through political rhetoric. Unlike Naipaul's earlier novels, *The Mimic Men* foregrounds a more diverse Caribbean society ethnically, for although Singh, like Naipaul himself and most of his protagonists, is of Indian descent, we are made aware of the significant part played in the Caribbean by those of African and Chinese descent, and the prejudices and class and cultural differences associated with them. One might compare Naipaul's novel with that of another Trinidadian novelist, Earl Lovelace – his *Salt* (1996) focuses on a schoolteacher who has become a politician and storyteller who refuses 'unfreedom'. In this novel, as in his earlier *The Dragon Can't Dance* (1979), the main characters are African Caribbean, but it acknowledges and celebrates the diversity of Trinidad's population, which includes French Creole and Indian Caribbean communities.

Achebe, Armah, Naipaul and Ngugi implicitly or explicitly suggest that the corruptions of power and money, and the discord between different ethnic groups, are a consequence of colonialism and neocolonialism. Indeed, their works illustrate not only the collaboration between members of the new ruling classes and multinational companies or foreign governments, but also the ways in which politicians manipulate fear and suspicion among different ethnic groups in order to bolster their own support, and to turn attention away from their disreputable financial dealings. Those ethnic divisions have often been at least partially created by the policies of the colonial administration, for example in their differing treatment of Igbo Christian and Muslim Hausa groups in Nigeria, or of indentured Indian workers and indigenous Africans in Kenya and Uganda, or of Hindus and Muslims in the Indian subcontinent. But while many postcolonial writers acknowledge and deplore these ethnic divisions and gesture towards a more inclusive society, the basic culture and point of view presented and endorsed in their fiction remains Igbo, Asante, Hindu or Gikuyu.

In this respect one can note a difference between, for example, Armah's novels focusing on the Asante, or the Asante in dire conflict with Arab invaders over the centuries, and the short stories of Ama Ata Aidoo, in which she portrays a variety of ethnic groups, cultures and religious beliefs as making up a Ghanaian amalgam. Similarly, one might contrast the Hindu-oriented fiction of R. K. Narayan and Raja Rao with the multicultural worlds given presence and validity by later writers such as, Anita Desai, Arundathi Roy, Salman Rushdie and Bapsi Sidhwa. And whereas early works by Achebe, Narayan, Ngugi and Rao often focus on a self-contained rural village, and perhaps its encounter with and opposition to British colonial power and culture, later postcolonial fiction is frequently set in an urban context, where different peoples and cultures mingle and interact. In these later novels, typically, the narrator or central character is a member of a minority or marginalized group, not identified with the majority – a Parsi child in Lahore (*Ice-Candy-Man* (1988)), a Jewish/Muslim mother and son in Bombay (*The Moor's Last Sigh* (1995)), a Syrian Christian family in Kerala (*The God of Small Things* (1997)).

In his fourth novel, *Paradise* (1994), the British Tanzanian writer Abdulrazak Gurnah offers a different perspective from many other African novelists who write in English. This novel, like *Things Fall Apart*, is set during the period when Europeans (in this case Germans) first begin to colonize that area of Africa. But the Africa the Europeans come to in Gurnah's fiction is a complex one, already shaped by centuries of interaction with and partial control by various groups of traders and immigrants. The narrative centres on Yusuf, a twelve-year-old boy from a Muslim Swahili family, whose world consists of many cultural distinctions and hierarchies:

> His father did not like him to play far from home. 'We are surrounded by savages,' he said. 'Washenzi,[6] who have no faith in God and who worship spirits and demons which live in trees and rocks. They like nothing better than to kidnap little children and make use of them as they wish. Or you'll go with those other ones who have no care, those loafers and children of loafers, and they'll neglect you and let the wild

dogs eat you. Stay here where it's safe, so someone can keep an eye on you.' Yusuf's father preferred him to play with the children of the Indian storekeeper who lived in the neighbourhood, except that the Indian children threw sand and jeered at him when he tried to get near them. 'Golo, golo,' they chanted at him, spitting in his direction. Sometimes he sat with the groups of older boys who lounged under shades of trees or lees of houses. He liked being with the boys because they were always telling jokes and laughing. Their parents worked as vibarua,[7] labouring for the Germans on the line-construction gangs, doing piece-work at the railhead, or portering for travellers and traders. They were only ever paid for the work they did, and at times there was no work. Yusuf had heard the boys say that the Germans hanged people if they did not work hard enough . . .

The vibarua who were their parents came from all over, from the Usumbara highlands north of Kawa, from the fabulous lakes to the west of the highlands, from the war-torn savannahs to the south, and many from the coast. They laughed about their parents, mocking their work-songs and comparing stories of the disgusting and sour smells they brought home. They made up names for the places their parents came from, funny and unpleasant names which they used to abuse and mock each other.[8]

Yusuf's story is in part a *Bildungsroman*, in which he moves from the restricted and prejudiced vision expressed by his father, and the teasing contempt for their elders articulated by the boys he plays with, to encounters with different peoples and cultures and a series of journeys into and beyond that almost mythical world their parents come from. His story also alludes to and combines the versions in the Bible and the Koran of the story of Joseph/Yusuf, a handsome boy who is sold by his brothers into bondage to an Egyptian merchant named (in the Koranic version) Aziz. There he becomes the servant of Aziz (in the biblical version Potiphar), and is put in charge of his goods. But his master's wife is attracted by his beauty, and attempts to seduce him. In the biblical version she is simply referred to as Potiphar's wife, and there are numerous artistic depictions of her (by Rembrandt, for example); in the Koranic narrative she is named Zulaykha. Yusuf resists her advances, and when she attempts to clasp him to her he tears himself away, leaving behind a torn shirt, whereupon she accuses him of attempted seduction. He is imprisoned, but in the Koranic version witnesses prove him innocent. In both the Judaic and Islamic narratives, Joseph/Yusuf also becomes known for his ability to interpret dreams.

Within Islamic culture the story of Yusuf is well known and frequently retold and commented upon. Some commentaries claim that when asked for a story that did not contain commandments and prohibitions, a story that would soothe the heart, the Prophet Muhammad said that he would recite to them 'the best story', and that was the story of Yusuf.[9] According to Gayane Karen Merguerian and Afsaneh Najmabadi, the 'sura Yusuf' is not only the subject of many commentaries, but is also

> referred to in literary and historical texts of various genres, including books of advice, mirrors of princes, and tales of the prophets . . . It has inspired erotic/mystical love poetry in Persian, Turkish, and Arabic; it constitutes one of the most narrated popular tales of the oral tradition. It continues to the present day to be a centrally important narrative in Islamic cultures, in particular as it contributes to the construction of the category 'woman,' with 'guile' viewed as an essential female characteristic.[10]

Paradise focuses more on the construction of Yusuf, his experiences and inner resistance as a disempowered subject, than on the 'construction of the category 'woman', though it also becomes a love story in which the women who love Yusuf and are loved by him are portrayed with great compassion. While one can read the novel without being aware of the Koranic and biblical stories it relates to and still be moved profoundly by the account of Yusuf's experience, knowledge of those stories provides an extra resonance, and places greater emphasis on the moral issues. Moreover, within the novel characters make specific comparisons between Yusuf and his namesake. Indeed, the language and imagery of the opening paragraph may also alert readers to the novel's resonance with those older stories embedded in religious texts:

> The boy first. His name was Yusuf, and he left his home suddenly during his twelfth year. He remembered it was the season of drought, when every day was the same as the last. Unexpected flowers bloomed and died. Strange insects scuttled from under rocks and writhed to their deaths in the burning light. The sun made distant trees tremble in the air and made the houses shudder and heave for breath. Clouds of dust puffed up at every tramping footfall and a hard-edged stillness lay over the daylight hours. Precise moments like that came back of the season.[11]

Here the use of a series of simple statements, the references to 'the season of drought' and 'the 'unexpected flowers' which bloom and dry, elemental and natural images, seem reminiscent of biblical language and parable, including the narrative of the seven years of famine which afflicted Egypt and the land of K'nan (Canaan) foretold by Yusuf. And of course, these resonances are also present in the title and central image of the novel, the paradise which recalls the Garden of Eden, the dream of an innocent and harmonious world, and also the Arabic word for a walled garden such as the one which surrounds Aziz's house and from which Yusuf is finally excluded.

It is interesting to compare this opening paragraph with that of Achebe's *Things Fall Apart*. Achebe's novel also conveys the feeling of a legendary tale, told and retold, and indeed later in the novel there is an unobtrusive parallel between the fate of Ikemefuna and the biblical story of Abraham and Isaac. But whereas Achebe's novel draws attention to its fictional status as oral narrative, and to the dialogue between written English and Igbo orality, Gurnah's novel gives the impression of taking its world for granted. And Yusuf's consciousness, which becomes the narrative point of view in the paragraphs from pages 6 and 7 quoted above, provides a seamless continuum with the more distanced and general perspective of the preceding introductory pages. But throughout the novel, the biblical and Koranic parallel allows a reader to see Yusuf within a wider cultural matrix and share his perspective, while also creating a slight distance as one steps back to compare his experiences with those of his namesake. In particular, the ending of the novel, leaving Yusuf 'choosing' servitude to the German army, contrasts poignantly with the triumphant success of the original Yusuf/Joseph, who becomes a powerful man in Egypt and is able to redeem his family. Discussing Gurnah's technique in depicting a world inhabited by many different languages and cultures, none of which is European, Robert Fraser writes:

> Over this swarming canvas the alien English language hovers, distancing itself by intermittencies, silences, tiny discretions of taste, which contrive to make the action perfect and yet somehow alien, both plangent and remote. To read *Paradise* is like peering through exceptionally clear water to shapes dimly discerned beneath its surface, shapes of objects languishing on a river bed, whose depth is impossible to determine. The society described is indeed multilinguistic, and energetically so. Yet this is a multiglossia in which the language of the narrative itself – English and aloof – never dares participate.[12]

Yusuf and his family speak Swahili but see themselves as also part of a larger Islamic culture, and so 'related' to the Arabic-speaking merchant 'Uncle' Aziz to whom Yusuf is pawned by his family in payment for the debts his father has incurred. Once taken to Aziz's coastal home, he finds a mentor in an older youth, Khalil, also (with his sister) a bondsman to Aziz and whose Swahili is strongly inflected by his native Arabic, much to the amusement of the Swahili community in the small town where Aziz has his store. Dispatched by Aziz to work with another of his store managers further into the interior, Yusuf must then learn Arabic and attend Koranic school. But while living with Hamid, he also becomes acquainted with Kalasinga, a Sikh driver and mechanic, listens to his debates with Hamid about religion, and hears his versions of Indian legends and myths. Khalil, Hamid and Kalasinga create a fabulous world, inhabited by wolfmen, jinns, giants, demons and imprisoned princesses, a world in which the borders between the mythical and the real often become blurred, not only in the tales told about Europeans (particularly the Germans), and other ethnic groups, but also in interpreting their own experience. Thus we read the recounting of the story of a princess imprisoned by a cruel jinn who turns the woodcutter with whom she has fallen in love into an ape, and remember this story when Yusuf and Amina, Aziz's second wife and Khalil's sister, fall in love. When Aziz returns from a journey and discovers that Yusuf has visited both Zulekha and Amina, Yusuf wonders what Aziz will say and do: 'Would he turn him into an ape and send him to the summit of a barren mountain as the jinn had treated the woodcutter?'[13]

While it is a mixture of Arabic, Islamic and Swahili cultures that makes up Yusuf's consciousness and therefore the perspective on which the main narrative is based, it is shadowed by a different kind of narrative from the English literary tradition, Joseph Conrad's *Heart of Darkness* (1902). Like Conrad's novel, *Paradise* has at its centre a journey into the African interior, an interior unknown and mysterious, leading to an encounter with a brutality which Aziz and his henchmen recognize as commensurate with their own. They are rescued by a contingent of Germans whom Aziz's servants acknowledge as yet another group, like themselves, seeking ivory and gold, and perhaps slaves. And at the end of the novel, the German commander who comes to conscript men from their area is described in terms which recall the reader's first glimpse of Kurtz, whom Marlow depicts as 'a bony head that nodded with grotesque jerks', rather like 'an animated image of death carved out of old ivory'.[14] In Gurnah's novel Yusuf perceives the German officer as a kind of death's head:

> The skin on his face was stretched tight and smooth, as if he had suffered burning or a disease. His smile was a fixed grimace of deformity. His teeth were exposed, as if the tightly stretched flesh on his face had already begun to rot and slough off around his mouth. It was the face of a cadaver, and Yusuf was shocked by its ugliness and its look of cruelty.[15]

Gurnah's novel tells the story of that journey into the interior, a story also told by other Westerners like Stanley (in search of Livingstone), and Richard Burton and John Speke (in search of the source of the River Nile). In the expeditions recounted by Conrad, Stanley, and Burton and Speke, the Arabic and indigenous peoples form a shadowy background, or are demonized as slave traders or cannibals; it is the European who is the subject and hero of the narration. But *Paradise*, which retraces much of the territory traversed by Burton and Speke, makes Aziz, Yusuf and his companions the protagonists; it is their adventure, and the land and the people they encounter, including the Europeans, are seen from their point of view. However, Gurnah is interested not only in countering the European version of their intervention in East Africa as a 'benign deliverance of Africans from the Arab slavers'; nor does he seek to provide an unambiguous countertext to Conrad's *Heart of Darkness*, in terms of its representation of Africa and Africans as a metaphor for the darkness within a European psyche.[16] With regard to the relationship between Conrad's novel and *Paradise*, Gurnah comments that his novel is not an attempt to rewrite *Heart of Darkness*, but that Conrad's 'ironical view of the whole enterprise of imperialism is useful to resonate against. This activity that Conrad saw as destructive to the European mind also destroyed the African mind and landscape.'[17]

As Susheila Nasta points out, *Paradise* is concerned not simply with countering the standard European narrative of 'benign' colonial missions in East Africa (white men rescuing black men and women from brown men), but rather seeks to examine 'how such histories came to be constructed, by exposing parallel ways of seeing the past that existed simultaneously with it',[18] and, in Gurnah's words, 'showing the [full] complexity of what went on before – without *forgiving* it'.[19] Nasta goes on to quote Gurnah's statement that when he began writing, he 'understood that history, far from being a rational discourse, is successively rewritten and fought over to support a particular argument, and that, in order to write, you had to find a way through this competing babble'.[20] However, it is the competing constructions (rather than the way through them) that *Paradise* brings to life, as we see how Yusuf, Khalil, Aziz, Kalasinga and Chatu (the wealthy Sultan who seizes Aziz's goods in the interior) all seek to compose and impose versions of their past and present realities. And as Elizabeth Maslen remarks, the stories and observations made by the different characters in this novel often construct personality and culture in terms of 'otherness', as a means of defining the self.[21] Such oppositional constructions are seen in the passage quoted earlier in this chapter, where Yusuf's father presents him with a world made up of the 'savage' and the 'civilized' (in this case the 'Washenzi' and Swahili peoples), the lazy and the hardworking. While his father sees the Indians as more like his own people, the Indian children reject Yusuf as belonging to a different group. And the children of the railway workers also reject their parents and each other as coming from elsewhere.

This same passage also opens up another theme in the novel which resonates against the insistent mapping and naming of territory by European explorers and settlers, and before them by Arabic traders. We have seen in chapters 2 and 5 the importance placed on charting and naming the territories occupied by colonizers and reclaimed in a postcolonial context. In this introductory section of *Paradise*, the boys foreshadow the ways in which European settlers will 'make up names for the places their parents come from', and although theirs is a relatively harmless game, it is nevertheless a means of establishing hierarchies. Renaming becomes a means of empowerment and disempowerment.

In contrast, the narrator in this novel refrains from naming a great deal of the territory traversed in the journeys and expeditions undertaken by Yusuf. As a consequence, 'the lakes to the west of the highlands' remain in some sense 'fabulous', their geographical identity is blurred even as we may identify them by their later names, 'Lake Tanganyika' and 'Lake Victoria'. Part of the achievement of *Paradise* is its ability to retrieve the territories of East Africa and the interior from those later imposed maps, and allow us to experience the wonder and 'terror' (to use Yusuf's word) of seeing it for the first time, and from the perspective of his consciousness nourished on a particular cultural matrix of anecdotes, stories and beliefs. For Yusuf, that journey of discovery (like the voyages of Christopher Columbus) are experienced in the context of what he has already heard about this unknown world, for him and his companions also an area of darkness. In response to Yufuf's asking why the light to the west is green, the shopkeeper Hussein tells him:

> 'When you get as far as the lakes in your travels you'll see the world is ringed with mountains which give the green tint to the sky. Those mountains on the other side of the lake are the edge of the world we know. Beyond them, the air has the colour of plague and pestilence, and the creatures who live in it are known only to God. The east and the north are known to us, as far as the land of China in the farthest east and to the ramparts of Gog and Magog in the north. But the west is the land of darkness, the land of jinns and monsters. God sent the other Yusuf as a prophet to the land of jinns and savages. Perhaps he'll send you to them too.'[22]

As David Punter notes, 'the west' has a double reference for the reader, who reads it not only as the territory inland from the East African coastal regions, but also as 'that further "west" from which come the Europeans, with their meaningless armies, their false accusations, their violent redrawings of boundaries'.[23] (One might add to this list, as witnessed in the novel, their arbitrary 'justice', their exploitative labour practices.) For Europeans and for Yusuf and his companions, the interior is the unknown, the nightmare – or perhaps the dream paradise – beyond their reality. Like Marlow, Yusuf narrates the details of his journey at night-time to his companion, but the difference between Marlow's account of a journey through fog and confusion and Yusuf's description of the terrain is striking, and essential to our revisioning of that part of Africa. Moreover, Yusuf's reference to the green light on the mountain revises and reminds us of Hussein's account given earlier in the novel and quoted above:

> 'The light on the mountain is green', [Yusuf] said. 'Like no light I've ever imagined. And the air is as if it has been washed clean. In the morning, when the sun strikes the peak of snow, it feels like eternity, like a moment which will never change. And in late afternoon near water, the sound of a voice rises deeply to the skies. One evening, on a journey up the mountain, we stopped by a waterfall. It was beautiful, as if everything was complete. I have never seen anything as beautiful as that. You could hear God breathing. But a man came and tried to chase us away. Night and day, everywhere throbbed and shook with noise. One afternoon near a lake I saw two fish eagles calmly roosting on a branch of a gum tree. Then suddenly both of them whooped with great energy, two or three fierce yells with neck bent back and the open beak pointing at the sky, wings pumping and body stretched taut. After a moment, a faint reply came back across the lake. A few minutes later, a white feather detached itself from the male bird, and in that great silence it drifted slowly to the ground.'[24]

Yusuf's description conveys eloquently, one might say magically, the wonder and sense of the sublime experienced by a dweller on the coastal regions when he first experiences mountain heights and landscapes. Furthermore, it reveals the change in Yusuf himself, referred to half-teasingly by Khalil until now as a feeble 'kifa urongo' (meaning living death – a kind of zombie). In the past it was Yusuf who constantly asked questions, and Khalil who gave the answers; now their roles are reversed. Now also Yusuf is confident enough to make his own judgements, which are often more compassionate and even-handed than those of Khalil and others. Thus when Khalil gloats about the savage beating that Chatu had given Abdalla, the expedition's overseer notorious for his harsh treatment of the porters and other members of the team, Yusuf refuses to join in or to discuss his reputation for sexually assaulting the men in his power, and simply reports that Abdalla had treated him kindly. Nor, remembering his desire for Chatu's daughter (and perhaps his own plight as a boy sold to Aziz, whose trade is not precisely 'innocent'), does he join in the demonizing of Chatu and his people 'as savages and thieves who rob innocent traders and sell their own brothers for trinkets'.[25]

Yusuf is also confident enough to fall in love with Amina, Aziz's youthful second wife, and to defy Khalil's warnings when he enters the walled garden in order to see her. He dreams of defiance, of persuading Amina to leave the walled garden and house which others see as paradise, and which she has described as a 'Hell on earth', of building their own walled garden. But ultimately he recognizes that he cannot challenge Aziz, nor overcome his status as one who has been committed to servitude, sold by his own parents; he cannot 'escape the oppressive claims everything made on him', for 'he knew that a hard lump of loneliness had long ago formed in his displaced heart, that wherever he went it would be with him, to diminish and disperse any plot he could hatch for small fulfilment'. Asked about his family and his ancestors, about where he had come from, and 'what he had brought and what he hoped to take away', he could give only 'evasive answers', for:

> [T]he seyyid could travel deep into strange lands in a cloud of perfume, armed only with a bag of trinkets and a sure knowledge of his superiority. The white man in the forest feared nothing as he sat under his flag ringed by armed soldiers. But Yusuf had neither a flag nor righteous knowledge with which to claim superior honour, and he thought he understood that the small world he knew was the only one available to him.[26]

Yusuf's 'decision' to join the regiment recruited by the Germans led by the officer with 'the face of a cadaver' is the consequence of this bitter self-knowledge, his inability to see himself as a hero, who can claim 'superior honour.' The novel's ending contrasts sombrely with the biblical and Koranic stories of Yusuf, who becomes a prophet with honour in his own land. Nor can he speak with the authority of Burton or Marlow or Stanley, whose versions of expeditions into the African interior have, for the European reader, effaced or ignored the alternative narratives of Aziz, Chatu and Yusuf, and the ways in which imperialism and earlier mercantile enterprises 'also destroyed the African mind and landscape'. There is a sense in which this restoration of parallel histories, and the portrayal of the psychic damage done to Amina, Khalil, and Yusuf, so betrayed by those whose economic and social status gave power over them, destroys any glimmer of national redemption; there is little suggestion of an imagined community which might have existed in the past or which might come into being in the future. In this respect the title and narrative of *Paradise* seems almost entirely ironic, and this novel differs from other postcolonial fiction which depicts the betrayal or abuse of those early hopes that accompanied independence, such as *The Beautiful Ones Are Not Yet Born*, *Our Sister Killjoy* (1977), *Petals of Blood*, *Clear Light of Day* (1980), and *Anthills of the Savannah*, whose endings point to a possibility of reconciliation or homecoming, and the formation of a more harmonious community. But if there is no possibility of achieving Paradise in the novel of that name, those who long for it and are denied it are not scorned; the humanity of Amina, Khalil and Yusuf is fully realized; they retain a certain integrity and attain self-understanding even through the constant humiliations they experience, so that we realize not only how much they have been damaged but also how much is lost through their powerlessness to fulfil their potential.

In its concern to acknowledge the presence and humanity of marginalized groups within the postcolonial nations, *Paradise* might be compared with other postcolonial fiction published since 1970, though in many settler postcolonies there continues to be a need to give voices and space to 'first nation' people, the aboriginal inhabitants who preceded the British, and other European immigrants. In New Zealand writers such as Patricia Grace, Keri Hulme and Witi Ihimaera have achieved considerable prominence for the skill and power with which they have brought to life the history and culture of Maori characters, as well as other Pacific islanders who have settled in that country.[27] The Samoan novelist Albert Wendt articulates the ways in which his project and that of Maori writers differs from that of settler writers when he takes a Samoan tatoo as a metaphor for the 'post-colonial body':

> By giving it a Samoan tatau, what am I doing, saying? I'm saying it is a body coming out of the Pacific. Not a body being imposed on the Pacific. It is a blend, a new development, which I consider to be in heart, spirit, and muscle, Pacific; a blend in which influences from outside (even the English language) have been indigenised, absorbed in the language of local and national, and in turn have altered the local and national.[28]

In Canada, Rudy Wiebe's *Blue Mountains of China* (1970) focuses on the history of Mennonite communities exiled from Russia and seeking to hold to their beliefs and customs in a changing Canada, while Joy Kogawa's *Obasan* (1981) traces the history of three generations of Japanese families, the first of which settled in Canada towards the end of the nineteenth century and the third of which suffered internment in their chosen homeland during World War II. Michael Ondaatje's *In the Skin of the Lion* (1987), acknowledges the multiple stories of the various immigrant communities which contributed to the building of Toronto. More recently, the stories of Canada's 'first nation' peoples are being published and discussed, and one might see their project in similar terms to those expressed by Wendt, giving space to bodies coming out of Canada, not imposed on that territory. Robert McGill's novel *The Mysteries* (2004) focuses on a small-town community in Ontario, which is in some ways a microcosm of Canada, with its various names which point to a diversity of origins (Daniel Barrie, Robert DeWitt, Stoddart Fremlin, Alice Pederson, Cam Usher), and suppressed and multilayered histories. Those histories are signified in the contested attempt by Usher to build on top of a 'first nation' burial site.[29]

These Canadian and New Zealand fictions give prominence to previously marginalized lives within the nation, and recreate varied ethnic and changing cultural histories and communities. In South Africa, where race and colour have been crucial signifiers of identity, involving political and economic inclusion or exclusion, the affirmation of racial identity and diversity has been important not only as a response to apartheid, but also in the formation of a new nation which seeks to dismantle racial barriers. Thus Alex La Guma's *In the Fog of the Season's End* (1972) brings together Asian, coloured and Zulu resistance fighters, who work collectively to defeat the apartheid system. Through the use of flashbacks, La Guma reveals the poverty and despair which are the source of the political movement, and also the traditions (especially Zulu narratives and visions in the case of the hero Elias) which inspire and strengthen them in their resistance.

While racial difference and diversity constitute both the oppressive past and a more positive future for the imagined community in much African fiction, it is religious difference which must be acknowledged and accommodated in literature from the Indian subcontinent. But recent Indian fiction offers little optimism. Rushdie's *The Moor's Last Sigh* ends with disintegration and death, in a kind of postmodern filmic scenario which denies the glimmer of imagined community and tolerance suggested by the allusions to medieval Spain, or the earlier existence of a multicultural community in Bombay. Roy's *The God of Small Things* also introduces a diverse society in Kerala, and focuses on the children of a mother of Syrian Christian ancestry married to a Bengali Hindu. But the novel ends in desolation, after retracing the deaths of the twin's Anglo-Indian cousin and the murder of their mother's lover because he belongs to the wrong caste; only those who are almost the same (the twins) can communicate with one another. As in Rushdie's *Midnight's Children* (1981), one of the central metaphors in Roy's novel is a pickle factory, started as a local kitchen enterprise by the children's grandmother Mammachi, and it is difficult not to read Roy's use of this trope as a commentary on Rushdie's earlier use of this metaphor. But whereas the metaphor of pickles as signifying the preservation and mingling of diverse histories and memories, 'the chutneyfication of history', works relatively positively and playfully in Rushdie's novel, Mammachi's independent pickling shop is taken over, turned into a factory and renamed by her son as 'Paradise Pickles & Preserves'. Here. as in Gurnah's novel, paradise connotes an ideal that has become corrupted. By the end of the novel, the factory has been abandoned and Mammachi's son has emigrated to Canada. And the dilapidated house is ruled not by a grandmother or mother figure, but by the children's aunt, Baby

Kochyma, single-minded in her prejudices, largely responsible for the ruin of their mother, spending her days dreaming of romance with the Christian priest Father Mulligan, and filling in coupons which might win her unneeded goods from those who advertise them. In Roy's novel, as in *Ice-Candy-Man*, *Clear Light of Day*, *Paradise* and *The Moor's Last Sigh*, we are shown both the desirability of coexistence between diverse peoples and cultures, and at the same time the difficulty of sustaining a community which accommodates difference.

Chapter 10

Transnational and black British writing: colonizing in reverse

The previous chapter considered some of the ways in which postcolonial writers have revisited concepts of nationality and community by attending to the diverse histories and cultures of the areas they grew up in, histories which precede and accompany European colonization. Many of those writers, including Abdulrazak Gurnah, Wilson Harris, Michael Ondaatje and Salman Rushdie, had emigrated to Britain or Canada, and to some extent their attention to those early multicultural communities is influenced by their location in the more recent immigrant communities which have become a feature of those countries since World War II. Australia, Britain and Canada had all encouraged large-scale immigration to rebuild their postwar economies and supplement diminished labour forces. In Australia the immigrants came mostly from Britain and Europe, and until the 1970s non-European peoples were turned away under the White Australia Policy; Britain, on the other hand, actively recruited workers from the West Indies and the Indian subcontinent to service transport systems, the new National Health hospitals, and the steel and cotton factories. Consequently, although all three still have predominantly white populations of Anglo-Saxon and Celtic origin, Australia, Britain and Canada provide different contexts for the development of multicultural societies. Moreover, as the primary colonizing power, seen and seeing itself as the metropolitan centre, or as the 'mother country', Britain also differs significantly from Australia and Canada as a symbolic and actual site for those who had formerly been her imperial subjects.

Although there had been a trickle of immigrants and visitors to Britain from her Crown Colonies for a good two hundred years prior to World War II, there is a significant change in numbers and reasons for emigration after 1948, when the first boatload of people from the West Indies arrived on HMS *Windrush*. During the next three decades, the percentage of people in Britain of African or Indian descent increased from less than 1 per cent to more than 6 per cent, of whom nearly half settled in London. Additionally, during the postwar decades many Irish immigrants sought work in London, Liverpool, Glasgow and other major cities, joining the large Irish communities already established there since the famine of 1845–9 and the depression that had been a feature of the Irish economy until the 1980s.

The majority of those who came to Britain assumed they would find work; they sought money to send back to and feed and house their families in the Caribbean, Ireland, India or Pakistan, and most of them expected to return to those families and houses after a few years. For many, there was also a sense of adventure and glamour in the possibility of living in England, and becoming acquainted with the scenes and the culture which had formed the substance of their education. Some, like Kamau Brathwaite, Buchi Emecheta and her husband, and V. S. Naipaul, came as students; others, like George Lamming and Samuel Selvon, wanted to be writers, and in 1950 it was difficult to be accepted as a writer (either by others or in one's own mind), unless one had the imprint of British publication. In a 1960 essay entitled 'The Journey to an Expectation', Lamming writes:

> It is now ten years since that morning in mid-March when Sam Selvon and I left for England. I have tried to chart, through my own experience, some of the events of that period, for it is also the decade in which the West Indian acquired recognition as a writer, first outside and later within his own society. The order of acceptance was logical since a native commodity of any kind must always achieve imperial sanction before it is received back in its own soil . . . England lay before us, not a place, or a people, but as a promise and an expectation. Sam and I had left home for the same reasons. We had come to England to be writers.[1]

Another writer, James Berry from Jamaica, expresses in 'Migrant in London' the mingled feelings of achievement and apprehension, of nostalgia for the world left behind and excitement at being in the 'worl' centre' and recognizing a city and its landmarks already known through a shared culture. Here he is both culturally at home, and physically homeless.

> Sand under we feet long time.
> Sea divided for we, you know,
> how we turned stragglers to Mecca.
>
> An' in mi hangin' drape style
> I cross worl' centre street, man.
> An' busy traffic hoot horns.
>
> I see Big Ben strike
> the mark of my king town.
> Pigeons come perch on mi shoulder,
> roun' great Nelson feet.

I stan' in the roar, man,
in a dream of wheels
a-vibrate shadows.
I feel how wheels hurry in wheels.
I whisper, man you mek it.
You arrive.
Then sudden, like, quite loud I say,
'Then whey you goin' sleep tenight?'[2]

Both the imagery and the language of the poem convey that paradoxical double experience of familiarity and strangeness. The sensation of sand underfoot and the sound of the sea in the speaker's island homeland is contrasted with the streets of the city and the noise and confusion of traffic. As the memories of the past are supplanted by the sights and sounds of his present setting, his sense of self, and his ambivalence are marked by the variations of language from Jamaican English to Standard English. And the speaker's reference to London as Mecca not only suggests the central symbolic significance of London for West Indians, as a place where one can and must pay homage, but also a place to be visited rather than lived in. (A later collection of short stories by Farrukh Dhondy, *Come to the Mecca* (1978), also indicates the ways in which British imperial culture has appropriated 'exotic' place names such as Mecca for more commercial ends. One could compare the use of 'Araby' in the story of that title by James Joyce.)

Among those who came to write, study and work in Britain in the first two decades following World War II and then remained there were the poet Dom Moraes from Bombay; the novelist and short story writer Attia Hosain from Lucknow; the novelist Kamala Markandaya from Bangalore; the poet Ketaki Kushari Dyson from Bengal; the historian and travel writer Nirad Chaudhuri from Bengal; the novelist and journalist Farrukh Dhondy from Poona; the novelist Salman Rushdie from Bombay; the fiction and travel writers V. S. Naipaul and his younger brother Shiva Naipaul from Trinidad; the novelist Selvon also from Trinidad; the poets James Berry and Andrew Salkey, who was also a novelist, from Jamaica; the novelists Wilson Harris and Edgar Mittleholzer from Guyana; the poets and critics Peter Porter and Clive James; the novelists Christina Stead and Randolph Stow from Australia; the poet Fleur Adcock from New Zealand; the novelist and poet Elizabeth Smart from Canada; the novelist and short story writer William Trevor from Ireland; and the novelists Buchi Emecheta from Nigeria, Lauretta Ngcobo from South Africa, and Abdulrazak Gurnah from Zanzibar. Gurnah and Ngcobo came to England as political refugees, as did many writers of Asian descent from East Africa in the late 1960s. The list is by no means exhaustive, but rather is indicative of the multifarious places and cultures from which these writers came.

Both the size and the diversity of this influx of writers and other workers produced a significant shift in British writing and perspectives on Britain. White novelists like Doris Lessing and Stead from settler colonies took either the world they had left behind or a changing postwar English society as their subject, offering sharply observed critiques. In 1952, according to Ann Blake, Stead had applied for a grant to write a novel of the 'New Australia', provisionally called 'Migrants'.[3] The grant was unsuccessful, so instead she wrote several stories about migrants in England, including 'Days of the Roomers', which portrays a European landlord who has emigrated to London rejecting 'dark-skinned foreign students'.[4] Her 1965 novel, *Cotters' England* (originally published as *Dark Places of the Heart*, perhaps suggesting a reference to Joseph Conrad's *Heart of Darkness* (1902)) analyses the material and psychological poverty of working-class Britain through a study of the Cotter family in Newcastle and three generations of working-class activists. Both this novel and *Miss Herbert: Suburban Wife* (1976) depict a bleak postwar England, in which neither the working class nor liberal intellectuals like Miss Herbert can escape from the dead hand of traditional attitudes. In contrast to Australia, whose lack of a feudal past made possible, in Stead's view, 'a Labour Commonwealth', postwar England seemed little changed from the England she knew in the 1930s, when she wrote to one of her brothers:

> I detest and despise the London Englishman who runs the Empire; they are the smuggest, bootlickingest, most class-saturated, most conceited and ignorant people I ever met. This only goes for the middle and Eton classes, too, the clerks and counter-jumpers and the white collar brigades of London. The underdog is smart, comical and lively, in London. But the 'intelligentzia' – woe is me.[5]

Whereas white authors from the Commonwealth presented a jaundiced view of England for an English audience and readers back 'home', writers from the Caribbean, and later from Sri Lanka and the Indian subcontinent, increasingly spoke of and to a black and South Asian community *within* Britain; moreover, this new group of immigrant authors was often seeking to *create* a community here and now in Britain. It is in this role as a creator of community that Selvon's writing is particularly innovative and significant. *The Lonely Londoners*, published in 1956,[6] assembles a cast of African and West Indian men seeking companionship and support in the face of a bleak, impoverished and unfriendly white London. Through their stories (or 'ballads') and through the voice of the narrator, Moses, this diverse group of Africans, Jamaicans and Trinidadians comes into being as a gathering of people who find their identity less through their different places of origin than through their mutual presence in London. This new group identity is expressed through the ambivalent sense of longing for 'home' and belonging in London, as well as the language of the narrator, a subtle blend of Trinidadian and other West Indian idioms and inflections with Standard English which we find in passages such as this one towards the end of *The Lonely Londoners* where Moses reflects on his position and that of his fellow immigrants, remembering and hearing in his head the voices of other speakers:

> Why don't you go back to Trinidad.
> What happening man, what happening.
> If I give you this ballad! Las night –
> You went to see the Christmas tree in Trafalgar Square?
> Harris giving a dance in Brixton next Saturday – you going?

> A fellar asking the Home Secretary in the House of Commons: 'Are you aware there are more than 40,000 West Indians living in Great Britain?' 'You know who I see in Piccadilly last night? Gomes! He must be come up for talks of federation.'
> One night of any night, liming on the Embankment near to Chelsea, he stand up on the bank of the river, watching the lights of the buildings reflected in the water, thinking what he must do, if he should save up money and go back home, if he should try to make it by next year before he change his mind again.
> The old Moses, standing on the banks of the Thames. Sometimes he think he see some sort of profound realisation in his life, as if all that happen to him was experience that make him a better man, as if now he could draw apart from any hustling and just sit down and watch other people fight to live. Under the kiff-kiff laughter, behind the ballad and the episode, the what-happening, the summer-is-hearts, he could see a great aimlessness, a great restless, swaying movement that leaving you all standing in the same spot. As if a forlorn shadow of doom fall on all the spades in the country. As if he could see the black faces bobbing up and down in the millions of white, strained faces, everybody hustling along the Strand, the spades jostling in the crowd, bewildered, hopeless. As if, on the surface, things don't look so bad, but when you go down a little, you bounce up a kind of misery and pathos and a frightening – what? he don't know the right word, but he have the right feeling in his heart. As if the boys laughing, but they only laughing because they fraid to cry, they only laughing because to think so much about everything would be a big calamity – like how he here now, the thoughts so heavy like he unable to move his body.

> Still, it had a greatness and a vastness in the way he was feeling
> tonight, like it was something solid after feeling everything else give way,
> and though he aint getting no happiness out of the cogitations he still
> pondering, for is the first time he ever find himself thinking like that.
>   Daniel was telling him how over in France all kinds of fellars writing
> books what turning out to be best-sellers. Taxi-driver, porter,
> road-sweeper – it didn't matter . . .
>   He watch a tugboat on the Thames, wondering if he could ever write a
> book like that, what everybody would buy.[7]

In this passage Moses gropes for the words which might express the strangely
ambivalent feelings he recognizes in himself and the other West Indians who
have become 'Londoners'. And out of his desire to express and make some
sense of his and their experience he contemplates becoming a writer, a possibility made real for someone like him by the publications of African, African-
American and Caribbean immigrants to France such as James Baldwin, Aimé
Césaire, Léon Damas, Sembene Ousmane and Richard Wright. And, of course,
the book he contemplates writing is the book we have just read, *The Lonely
Londoners*.[8] That impulse to write out of the experience of dislocation or
estrangement is one shared by many immigrant writers, and is expressed
cogently by Gurnah in a BBC programme broadcast in 2001:

> To write in the bosom of my culture and my history was not a possibility,
> and perhaps is not a possibility for any writer in any profound sense. I
> know I came to writing in England in estrangement and I realize now
> that it is this condition of being from one place and living in another
> that has been my subject over the years, not as a unique experience
> which I have undergone, but as one of the stories of our times.[9]

The presence of a black and Asian community in the metropolitan centre
also helped to create a new sense of community and shared aims between
representatives of the colonial cultures in Britain and 'back home'. Moreover,
immigrants from Africa, the Caribbean, the Indian subcontinent and Ireland
were confronted with prejudice fuelled by years of imperial rule and contemporary caricatures in the British media responding dismissively to the freedom
struggles of African and Caribbean nations seeking independence. This was the
era when British troops were being sent to confront the so-called Mau-Mau
fighters in Kenya, and the British media portrayal of the stark division between
the two sides in terms of bestial Kikuyu 'terrorists' opposed to civilized Britons
is presented ironically in this line from a poem published by Derek Walcott in
1962: 'The gorilla wrestles with the superman.'[10] Those who came from the
Indian subcontinent faced different attitudes, which mingled prejudice against

darker-skinned people who did not speak the English language or adhere to the Christian religion with an interest in the 'exotic' and a certain glamour attached to India as a realm of Indian princes and palaces, metaphorically as well as actually providing 'the jewel in the crown'. Those attitudes, in relation to the popular films and television series *Gandhi* (1982), *A Passage to India* (1984), *The Far Pavilions* (1984) and *The Jewel in the Crown* (1984) were incisively critiqued by Rushdie in his 1984 essay 'Outside the Whale'.[11]

Among the increasing numbers of temporary and permanent immigrants from all parts of what was now named 'the British Commonwealth' were many students and professional writers such as Kamau Brathwaite and George Lamming from Barbados, Ngugi wa Thiong'o from Kenya, and John (Pepper Clark) Bekederemo and Wole Soyinka from Nigeria. It was in Britain that writers such as Ngugi encountered writings by the francophone Caribbean author Frantz Fanon, as well as Lamming's powerful and innovative novel *In the Castle of my Skin* (1953)[12] and his eloquent and influential essays on cultural politics, *The Pleasures of Exile* (1960),[13] all of which were to have a profound influence on Ngugi's career as an educator and writer.

Lamming was one of the key speakers at the first two Caribbean Artists Movement (CAM) Conferences, held at the University of Kent in Canterbury in 1967 and 1968. The conferences grew out of a series of smaller group meetings which began in January 1967, and featured monthly readings and discussions of work by African, African American and Caribbean writers and artists. Brathwaite was a regular participant, as were the poet and publisher John LaRose, the novelist and sociologist Orlando Patterson, and the poet and novelist Andrew Salkey. Others who frequently attended or spoke at the meetings and conferences included Berry, Harris, C. L. R. James and Kenneth Ramchand.[14]

Both the interaction between artists from different Caribbean islands, and the discussions and formulations concerning the objectives of a meaningful Caribbean art, were to have a continuing influence on art and cultural politics produced in the Caribbean itself once writers such as Brathwaite and Lamming had returned there. In Britain and in the Caribbean, it had the consequence of questioning the centrality of the English canon, and of creating alternative foci and lines of communication and response. Journals such as *The West Indian Gazette*, edited by Claudia Jones, and the CAM Newsletter and its successor in the Caribbean, *Savacou*, became important outlets for the publication of black British and Caribbean writers. Publishing houses such as LaRose's New Beacon Press and Eric and Jessica Huntley's Bogle L'Ouverture Press came into existence and have continued to publish important new works and collections by black British and Caribbean writers.

The CAM group debated and sought to redefine the language, forms and content of a black British and Caribbean writing appropriate to a community which had also redefined its audience. In Britain CAM writers and artists were becoming aware of innovative fiction and poetry drawing on oral and folk traditions, jazz structures and spoken idioms, published by African and African American writers such as Chinua Achebe, Ralph Ellison and Langston Hughes as well as Hispanic and francophone Caribbean writers such as Césaire, Damas and Nicolas Guillén. Encouraged by their creative brilliance and success, Brathwaite, Lamming, Selvon and others fashioned a language which recalled the voices and idioms and rhythms of everyday Caribbean life and culture. For Brathwaite, as was discussed in chapter 6, this involved specifically rejecting in his poetry the iambic pentameter line characteristic of the English poetic tradition; and instead drawing on calypso, blues, and African drum rhythms. Berry, Brathwaite and Selvon also drew on oral and folk traditions, as had Louise Bennett and Una Marson earlier, to make Caribbean voices heard within the English literary tradition. Berry's series of 'Lucy' poems, in the form of letters from a Jamaican woman settled in London and writing back to a friend in her former home, and reminiscent of Bennett's use of Jamaican women speakers, vividly evoke the contrasts in place and culture through the voice of a Jamaican Londoner.[15] These poems, like Brathwaite's, were most effective when performed by the poet and heard by audiences – first at CAM meetings and later much more widely throughout England. Such poems, and works by a subsequent generation of poets such as John Agard and Grace Nichols from Guyana, and Linton Kwesi Johnson from Jamaica, both celebrated and authenticated the presence of Caribbean-inflected voices, and hence bodies, in Britain. Through the performance of their poetry to multicultural audiences within the United Kingdom, these poets created and reinforced a sense of communal identity and established a hybrid oral/literary tradition different from but affiliated to the preexisting English literary tradition. Or rather, in their speaking directly to and of groups rather than individuals, one might see their work as giving new life and new directions to an older oral/literary tradition characterized by Chaucer's *Canterbury Tales* and the drama of Shakespeare.

The aims and aesthetics embraced by some members of CAM did not appeal to all writers who had emigrated from Africa, the Indian subcontinent or the West Indies. Naipaul was never a member of CAM, and his fiction, unlike Selvon's, maintained a clear distinction between the Standard English of the narrative persona, and the Trinidadian voices of his characters. As Susanne Mühleisen contends, Naipaul uses Creole speech in his early fiction to symbolize and satirize what he described and dismissed as the 'half-bakedness' of colonial society.[16] Despite the sympathetic fictionalizing of his father's story in the most

Dickensian of his novels, *A House for Mr Biswas* (1961), West Indian critics such as Harris and Lamming saw Naipaul's early fiction as cruelly mocking and disdainful of the Caribbean community, while Harris argued that Naipaul's adherence to what Harris saw as the traditional genre of the 'novel of manners' reinforced static and unchanging views of a people and a society desperately in need of growth and change, particularly as the new West Indian nation states came into independent being.[17] Although reservations have frequently been expressed by Caribbean and other 'Third World' writers and critics, such as Achebe, Naipaul's reputation within Britain has continued to grow, resulting in the award of the Booker Prize in 1971, a knighthood in 1990, the David Cohen Prize recognizing 'a lifetime's achievement by a living British writer' in 1992, and the Nobel Prize for Literature in 2001.

Notwithstanding their differences and disagreements, Naipaul in his early fiction shares with other immigrant writers a preoccupation with the search for accommodation in both the literal and the metaphorical sense. That search is suggested by the title of *A House for Mr Biswas*, in which at one point the protagonist expresses a kind of existential terror at the thought of remaining alone, isolated and unaccommodated. *The Mimic Men* (1967) regards with disdain and sharp scrutiny the disjunction between European architectural, political and cultural structures and traditions, and those of the newly independent peoples and places in the Caribbean. Its narrator, an exiled political leader, traces his life and search for order through a series of bleak lodgings and hotel rooms in London, as well as ramshackle or pretentious villas in the Caribbean, finally affirming his existence as a permanent lodger or guest, a man without rootedness. For Naipaul's narrator, this discontinuity between his past and his present allows him to reinvent himself, sometimes in terms of the fantasies of British people, so that, for example, he can become 'the exotic dandy'. Selvon's characters, on the other hand, cling to an identity which links them to their Caribbean past and continues ways of speaking and narrating ('it have a ballad'), so that they also identify with one another rather than with white Londoners. Thus there is a difference, and not only in class, between Naipaul's inhabitants of isolated attic rooms and Selvon's narrator and friends who come together in the basement rented by Moses. But, as Susheila Nasta has pointed out, there is also an affinity in their sense of transience, the discovery that the myth of finding a home and motherland, a tradition to which they could lay claim, was a barren one. For Naipaul's protagonist, Ralph Singh, the magic of the past is powerless, the city remains colourless and two-dimensional.[18] Moses and his black London compatriots invoke with a certain awe legendary names such as Piccadilly Circus and Trafalgar Square, but even after many years, London remains both theirs and not-theirs.

The Irish author William Trevor, who moved to England from Cork in 1953, is one of the few white writers of the period who consistently acknowledge the presence of African and West Indian immigrants. Like Naipaul and Selvon, and later Caryl Phillips (in *The Final Passage* (1985)), he sets his fiction in lonely boarding houses, lodgings and hospitals. Combining compassion and irony, his novels, whether set in London or Ireland, portray the lives of those who are lonely and alienated. In a comment which compares interestingly with Achebe's remarks about the benefits of being a Christian outsider in Nigeria, Trevor said of his childhood in Ireland, 'What is now apparent to me is that being a Protestant in Ireland was a *help*, because it began the process of being an outsider – which I think all writers have to be.'[19] The *Boarding-House* (1965) has a cast of nine diverse characters, including a Nigerian, Mr Obd, who continues courting an Englishwoman long after she has stopped acknowledging him – an analogy perhaps with England's unwillingness to respond supportively to the African, Irish and West Indian immigrants who had seen England as an admired mother country. The novel's ending, in which Mr Obd, finally realizing his rejection, sets the boarding house on fire, might also be seen as analogous to the burnings of Anglo-Irish 'Big Houses' during the Irish Civil War, acts which accompanied the end of empire in Ireland and which also feature in some of Trevor's later fiction (as well as Jean Rhys's *Wide Sargasso Sea* (1966)). *Miss Gomez and the Brethren* (1971) has as its central protagonist a Jamaican woman who has been orphaned by fire. In London she has worked as a stripper and a prostitute before becoming an ardent member of the Brethren of the Way and a cleaner at a decaying English pub, 'The Thistle Arms'. Her newfound faith allows her to act as a mainstay of compassion and intuitive understanding for the other (English) characters. She discovers on returning to Jamaica that the leader of the Brethren is a fraud, but nevertheless is able to sustain her faith. Despite the comedy that is a feature of Trevor's novel, and despite the illusions which arise out of deep psychological need and border on insanity, Miss Gomez is portrayed as a redemptive figure who clears up the physical and psychological mess that is postimperial England.[20]

The generation of writers who came to England in the 1950s and 1960s were typically male and single, and often believed themselves to be transient. Twenty years later, a new generation of authors, male and female, write out of the experience of being located in Britain, many of them either born in the United Kingdom or arriving as young children. Their fiction often focuses on the attempt to make a home in Britain, and frequently the protagonists are women, seeking to hold their families together and establish some sense of permanence. Emecheta's *Second Class Citizen* (1974), David Simon's *Railton Blues* (1983), Phillips's *The Final Passage*, Ravinda Randhawa's *A Wicked Old Woman*

(1987), Gurnah's *Dottie* (1990) and Farhana Sheikh's *The Red Box* (1991) all explore with varying degrees of complexity and ambivalence the meaning and consequences for young African, Asian and Caribbean women, their husbands, siblings and children, of living in a British community which is reluctant to accommodate them. The 1980s also saw the emergence of many women writers and supportive groups such as the Asian Women Writers Collective (to which Rukhsana Ahmad and Randhawa belonged), and the Caribbean Women Writers group. Much of their early work was featured in anthologies specifically devoted to writing by Asian and/or black women, and often reinforcing a rather homogenized sense of the situation and writing of immigrant women in Britain. Such collective identities were useful in establishing the presence of Asian and black women writers in Britain, expressing a sense of empowerment through collaboration, and often addressing specific grievances against their male counterparts. Many of the women anthologized in those early years have gone on to create powerfully individual visions and, indeed, to influence male writers to give greater attention to women characters.

Writers such as Gurnah, Phillips, Randhawa, Rushdie and, more recently on film and television as well as in fiction, Hanif Kureishi and Meera Syal, also play mockingly and ironically with the stereotyped identities within and against which those of Asian and African descent in Britain find themselves living. Agard, who arrived in England from Guyana in 1977, performs his sardonic poem 'Stereotype' with straw hat, beach shirt and accompanying trappings denoting popular images of the Caribbean. Such texts and performances reiterate the understanding that race and ethnicity are constructed identities, which may be performed differently within different contexts and for different audiences.

Kureishi's novel *The Buddha of Suburbia* (1990), later translated to film, wittily satirizes both the English liberals and the immigrant Asians who trade in ethnicity. The child of an Indian father and English mother, Kureishi questions and subverts notions of fixed racial or sexual identity (his main protagonist, Karim, is bisexual), and writes from the perspective of someone who grew up in London in the 1960s. The novel begins:

> My name is Karim Amir, and I am an Englishman born and bred, almost. I am often considered to be a funny kind of Englishman, a new breed as it were, having emerged from two old histories. But I don't care – Englishman I am (though not proud of it), from the South London Suburbs and going somewhere. Perhaps it is the odd mixture of continents and blood, or here and there, of belonging and not, that makes me restless and easily bored.[21]

That opening line recalls Homi Bhabha's description of the ways in which educated Indians were seen as 'white but not quite',[22] but here it is the protagonist who identifies himself, partly in acknowledgement of how he is perceived by others, as 'an Englishman born and bred, almost'. But if his mixed race and sexuality fix certain parameters and contexts for his identity, they also allow him to construct and perform changing selves. Above all, they allow him (and the author) to cast a sardonic eye on the ways in which his father, Haroon, and others cater to and profit from certain stereotypes. Thus Haroon presents himself as an Indian guru, teaching the 'Path' to enlightenment. And although Karim expostulates that 'Dad couldn't even find his way to Beckenham',[23] his performance as a guru is eagerly accepted by his white liberal mistress, Eva Kay, and her friends. Meanwhile, Karim and Eva's son Charlie are equally seduced by white working-class culture and each other. As Ruvana Ranasinha comments, *The Buddha of Suburbia*

> illustrates two defining features of Kureishi's work. First it exemplifies
> the liminality of Kureishi's position as an 'in-between' or
> insider/outsider, which relates to the ironic distance that characterizes
> the novel, and is linked to Kureishi's specular function. From this
> position as an 'in-between', Kureishi (via his deeply autobiographical
> Karim) holds up a self-ironizing and satirical mirror to the white and
> minority communities that he moves between . . . This pervasive
> ironizing is linked to the second characteristic: the subversive, anarchic
> streak in Karim/Kureishi that resists all forms of authority.
> Karim/Kureishi is not simply positioned against the dominant culture,
> he takes that form of resistance as given: he questions all forms of
> subcultures, affiliations, and collectivities.[24]

Ravinda Randhawa also takes as her subject the temptation to appropriate and perform stereotyped roles, but in contrast to Kureishi her 1987 novel *A Wicked Old Woman* suggests, in the end, the need for 'affiliations, and collectivities'. The central character, Kulwant, is culturally, if not racially, hybrid, having grown up in England, the daughter of immigrant parents from India. The motif of multiple identities, a series of exterior layers which hide inner selves, is introduced in the novel's opening childhood memory, where Kulwant remembers her attempt to transform a Russian doll into an Indian one that has a *bindi*, a red mark on its forehead. As a schoolgirl, Kulwant has responded to a reflected image of herself as an oriental princess, an exotic and mysterious maiden who is the focus of desire for the blond English Michael. This image gives her status in her all-white school, and also provides an escape from her embarrassingly un-English parents. But when Michael seeks marriage, Kulwant retreats in confusion from assimilation into an English family and goes to the other extreme, seeking to become 'the complete Indian woman'. From accepting an identity defined as 'the other', she turns to an identity which asserts her belonging within the Indian community, and demands an arranged marriage. Inevitably, her attempt to conform to that stereotype is doomed to failure, for it is based on fear, resentment and self-denial. Only later, after her husband has sought a more fulfilling relationship elsewhere, does Kulwant begin to understand the paradox that in her attempt to reject assimilation into Englishness, she took as the signifier of Indianness that special feature emphasized by Europeans as the mark of cultural difference, the arranged marriage.

Kulwant's third assumed identity, which corresponds to Western media images of India in the 1970s and 1980s, is that of the Third World Victim, the needy recipient of Oxfam and welfare state handouts. If she cannot become 'English' or 'Indian' in more acceptable terms, then she will become the monster they have created, as the title of this episode, 'Frankly Frankenstein', implies. As such, she need no longer take responsibility for her failures, for her family, or for her community. Her only project is to retreat, and perform her role as a helpless and poverty-stricken old woman, from whom nothing can be expected. She envisions her future as one of the unaccommodated, so marginalized that she will be able to take refuge as 'a smelly old hag whose address would be a patch under Charing Cross Bridge'.[25] As in *The Lonely Londoners, The Mimic Men,* Emecheta's *Second Class Citizen* and Phillips's *The Final Passage,* the motif of accommodation as a metaphor of belonging, or not belonging, in the larger society becomes significant. But as in these other novels, the problem of finding a home is not just metaphorical; there are numerous images of rejection and homelessness, or fear of homelessness. Randhawa's novel also contains the story of Rani, who runs away from home, denies any Indian identity, assumes the name of Rosalind, and finds meagre shelter in hostels, empty houses and squats. Most horrific are Kulwant's memories of the Indian family burned to death in their house by racist arsonists, an event which recalls other actual arson attacks in the 1970s and 1980s, such as the fire which caused the deaths of Mrs Abdul Karim and her children,[26] and the burning to death of thirteen young black people at a party in New Cross Road, London, in January 1981.

Although characters like Ammi and her daughters, who place community commitment above personal fulfilment, are presented positively, Randhawa is by no means uncritical of the artificiality of some aspects of Indian community in England. For Kulwant, the Asian Centre is a 'simulation Sub-Continent patched together with a flotsam of travel posters, batik work, examples of traditional embroidery, cow bells and last but not least woven baskets that you knew were from Oxfam'.[27] She wonders if centres like these provide work merely for 'professional coolies', 'making a profession of their nationality'. Randhawa is also sceptical of writers and media workers who seek to write 'ethnic novels' or to present the community on stage and screen, and there is mingled sympathy and satire for Maya, who has embarked on research for a television programme on 'Madness in the Indian Community'. Randhawa's ambivalent portrayal of Maya's project is a precursor to the ambitious Indian women media presenters who are major characters in Atima Srivastava's novel *Transmissions* (1992) and Meera Syal's novel (subsequently a television series), *Life Isn't All Ha Ha Hee Hee* (1999).

Nevertheless, Randhawa's novel suggests that it is through community and storytelling that healing and some sense of wholeness can be found, and in this aspect it reflects Randhawa's own involvement in the Asian Women Writers Collective. Kulwant sheds her isolation and her chosen identity as a helpless cripple when she joins Maya, West Indian Angie and others in a marathon of storytelling which gradually pulls Rani back from semi-consciousness and the abyss of madness. Storytelling can heal the individual whose mind has been nearly destroyed by the seeming contradictions of being Asian, British and female. Communication can in turn create community and heal divisions within it. But collective political action is also required in the face of the vicious hatred displayed by white Englishmen who are unwilling to hear the stories. As a novel by a writer who explores the alternatives for immigrants of assimilation and/or reinvention as opposed to adherence to an ancestral identity, *A Wicked Old Woman* compares interestingly with Rushdie's *The Satanic Verses* (1988), though Rushdie focuses on male immigrants rather than female ones.

Along with the many writers who explore a new sense and consequence of location and identity in Britain, these and others also continue the tradition of travel writing which was such a feature of colonialist writing, and still represents an important genre in contemporary British writing. While Anglo-English works emphasize the 'otherness' of the regions they explore and the people they encounter, postcolonial British writers often revisit and revision those places depicted by metropolitan travellers, or focus their travel writing on Britain and Europe. Here V. S. Naipaul is perhaps the preeminent example of a writer who alternates writing about his encounters with other cultures and places with the search for location within England and Englishness, culminating most powerfully and complexly in *The Enigma of Arrival* (1987). Naipaul described his return to and turn away from the Caribbean in *The Middle Passage* (1962), contentiously (and in contrast to C. L. R. James) pronouncing that

'History is built around achievement and creation; and nothing was created in the Caribbean.'[28] The incisive detail of Naipaul's descriptions led reviewers to compare him to D. H. Lawrence as a travel writer, and encouraged commissions for later works, such as *An Area of Darkness* (1964), which traverses India and finds there a static and sterile culture, *A Congo Diary* (1980), and *Among the Believers: An Islamic Journey* (1981). Naipaul's later novels often incorporate and build on the places and cultures described in the travel books, and simultaneously allude to earlier novelists and travellers such as Joseph Conrad. Thus *A Bend in the River* (1979) draws on his earlier 'Congo Diary' and essay on Conrad to create a contemporary version of Conrad's *Heart of Darkness* (1902), while *Guerrillas* (1975) fictionalizes his series of essays on Michael X while also alluding to both *Jane Eyre* (1847) and *Wuthering Heights* (1847). One of the main protagonists, a South African journalist, is named Roche, while the Michael X figure sees himself as a kind of Heathcliff.

Whereas earlier British novels have tended to separate the genres of adventure/travel/quest and domestic/romance fiction, one of the distinctive and intriguing features of these novels by Naipaul is the creation of a hybrid fiction combining the quest and the domestic genres. Naipaul has generally focused on contemporary settings, but a later generation of black and Asian British novelists has begun to combine the exploration of place with the exploration and revisioning of history, resulting in a remapping and revisioning of both. Thus Phillips has published trenchant travel writing, most notably *The European Tribe* (1987), where he echoes, in his description of himself as both of and not of Europe, James's more optimistic vision of a new generation of black Britons. But his fiction also moves across time and location. Set in the late eighteenth century, *Cambridge* (1991) alludes to both Equiano and the Brontës through its linguistic mimicry and its two main protagonists. One is a deeply religious slave named sequentially Olumide, David Henderson and Cambridge; the other is Emily Cartwright, whose diaries express a romanticized and evasive picture of the Caribbean plantation she visits and the slaves who work on it. In this novel Phillips also alludes to yet another predecessor, the white Caribbean novelist Jean Rhys, and her response to *Jane Eyre* in *Wide Sargasso Sea*. The name and character of Cambridge's common law wife, Christiana, echoes the name of the formidable black servant and supposed 'obeah woman', Christophine, in Rhys's novel. In his 1989 novel *Higher Ground*, Phillips links the story of an eighteenth-century African with those of a twentieth-century African American prisoner and a Jewish woman whose family died in the concentration camps in Poland. *The Nature of Blood* (1997) revisits and revisions the Venice of Shakespeare's Othello and Shylock.

Like Naipaul, the novelists David Dabydeen and Gurnah have also drawn on Conrad's *Heart of Darkness* as a textual background and map against which to ground a new vision of African or black identities and terrains. *Paradise* was discussed in the previous chapter. Dabydeen's *The Intended* (1991) provides a sharp and witty rereading of Conrad through its relocation and 'filming' of the novel in the heart of London by a group of schoolboys of African, Asian and Caribbean descent. Like Phillips, Dabydeen has also turned to the eighteenth-century and the history of slavery as a means of bringing to life a suppressed history. *Slave Song* (1984), *Coolie Odyssey* (1988) and *Turner* (1994) are long poems or poetic sequences giving voice, sometimes in the Creolized and vivid language of Guyanese 'coolies' and slaves, to the experience of plantation life and immigration from India to Britain and Guyana. *Turner* takes as its starting point J. M. W. Turner's painting *Slavers Throwing Overboard the Dead and Dying*, with both the picture and the poem recreating the 1783 HMS *Zong* case, in which the captain of a slave ship was tried for throwing more than a hundred slaves overboard in order to collect insurance for this 'property', a crime which the ex-slave and abolitionist Olaudah Equiano had been instrumental in publicizing and contesting. In almost all his works, Dabydeen sets up a linguistic and aesthetic struggle between the cultural traditions and experiences framed by the Western canon, and histories and experiences which he as the descendant of a Guyanan plantation worker seeks to express.

The *Zong* case is also taken as the inspiration for Fred D'Aguiar's novel *Feeding the Ghosts* (1997), which writes back to Dabydeen, Turner, and the early slave narrators in its recreation of the consciousness and voice of an imagined survivor, Mintah, an enslaved woman. Mintah's memories, dreams and visions as she floats in the sea encapsulate the struggle between a destructive history and the potentially redemptive powers of imagination. As members of that younger generation who were educated in Britain in the 1970s, both Dabydeen and D'Aguiar offer in their poetry and fiction a confident response not only to a specifically canonical English literary tradition, but also to a tradition of black and Asian writing within and without Britain. For Dabydeen and D'Aguiar that tradition includes a distinctively Guyanan one, featuring the powerful visionary and antirealist fiction of Harris, and later Pauline Melville, as well as other poets such as Agard and Nichols.

This later generation of writers (including Gurnah, Phillips and Rushdie) responds implicitly or explicitly to the experience of living in a Britain which heard outbursts of racist and anti-immigration rhetoric from Enoch Powell, Margaret Thatcher and other prominent members of the establishment. It also witnessed riots in many British cities, and a concerned response to these by liberal institutions and members of the public. Schools and some universities in Britain in the late 1970s and 1980s sought to revise the literary curriculums to include works by African, African American, Asian and black British writers such as Achebe, Agard, Anita Desai, Dhondy, Ellison and Toni Morrison. Organizations such as the Inner London Education Authority (ILEA) and the Association for Teaching Caribbean and African Literature (ATCAL) brought together teachers and writers from educational institutions and community organizations throughout the country to discuss texts and curriculums, and to disseminate information about Asian and black writing. ATCAL was responsible for inaugurating in 1984 the still flourishing journal of Caribbean, African, Asian and Associated literatures, *Wasafiri*. Under Susheila Nasta's editorship *Wasafiri* has continued to fulfil its original aim of creating an accessible forum for multicultural debates and to promote and give space to new creative writing. As a focus for postcolonial writing both inside and outside Britain, *Wasafiri* remains unique, though its presence has had a considerable influence on other journals and publishers in encouraging them to include within their briefs anglophone writing from a wider spectrum of writers and cultural traditions. But perhaps most importantly for this discussion, it has helped to reinforce that sense of a wider cultural community, a multicultural audience, which is responsive to black and Asian British writers.

Such a sense of a diverse and multicultural audience has in turn encouraged a greater diversity of writing which paradoxically often rests upon a feeling of solidarity among black and Asian Britons in the face of the 'little England' mentality expressed by Mrs Thatcher, some members of her cabinet, and some newspapers. In the 1980s Rushdie celebrated the 'hybridity' of his culture and identity, and 'hybridity' has become a term proclaimed by many later writers and critics, including preeminently Homi Bhabha. In a 1995 manifesto, 'Re-Inventing Britain', Bhabha advocated a move away from 'the multi-culturalist thinking of the eighties', which in his view 'sought to revise the homogenous notion of national culture by emphasizing the multiple identities of race/class/gender' and thus reinforced the notion of national or ethnic identities as given. For Bhabha, multiculturalist thinking obscures 'the hybrid cosmopolitanism of contemporary metropolitan life', a hybridity which is constantly in process and transformation.[29] Like Rushdie, he draws attention to the transformational powers of a cosmopolitan migrant culture, for not only do migrants reimagine their 'homelands', their places of ancestral origin, they also 'impose their needs on their new earth, bringing their own coherence to the new-found land, imagining it afresh'.[30] Commenting on Bhabha's manifesto, Stuart Hall perhaps reflects his experience as a Jamaican who came to England in the 1950s, and his academic grounding as an eminent sociologist, when he expresses some scepticism about the view that globalization 'has completely evaporated the space of national culture'.[31] Indeed, he sees in many cases a hardening of cultural nationalism in the face of dislocation and globalization, though he, too, has also advocated a move away from fixed identities to an acceptance of the 'positionality' of identity, a sense of self which foregrounds different aspects (race, history, gender, family, location, work, cultural affiliations, etc.), according to the context in which one is speaking or acting.[32]

Rushdie's own fiction is perhaps the most widely recognized example of writing which reinvents histories and identities and celebrates hybridity, in terms of not only cultures but also genres. Variously described by critics as magic realist, postmodern and postcolonial, his novels draw on traditional Indian oral and written narrative forms, and popular Indian film and theatre, as well as shifting and often disconcerting perspectives embraced by writers such as Gabriel García Márquez. Remarkable for their energy, linguistic playfulness and exuberance, his novels are also sharply satiric regarding the politics of India, Pakistan, and contemporary Britain. *Midnight's Children* (1981), discussed in chapter 6, won the Booker Prize in 1981 and was subsequently named the 'Best of the Bookers' in the twenty-five years of the award. Paradoxically *The Satanic Verses* (1988), the only one of Rushdie's novels which is mainly set (if not grounded) in Britain, is also the one which has received the most virulent attacks from abroad, and resulted in a death sentence (*fatwa*) by Iran's Ayatollah Khomeini, as well as bannings, book-burnings and death threats elsewhere.

Sharply critical of conservative British nationalism (as well as other nationalisms), *The Satanic Verses* revisits British history and migrancy through the scenes set in the Hot Wax Club, an alternative version to that established by the iconic figures in Madame Tussaud's. Here the wax figures include the eighteenth-century black British writer Ignatius Sancho, Mary Seacole 'who did as much in the Crimea as another magic-lamping Lady, but, being dark, could scarce be seen for the flame of Florence's candle',[33] Abdul Karim, Grace Jones, Septimus Severus (a black slave brought to Britain by the Romans), and the eighteenth-century African antislavery campaigner Ukawsaw Gronniosaw. Its episodic structure, its linguistic and generic transformations, and its character as a kind of *Bildungsroman* also recall G. V. Desani's *All About H. Hatterr* (1948), whose influence Rushdie has acknowledged. But as Leela Gandhi points out, the historical icons of an immigrant history in Britain are deployed by the Hot Wax Club's DJ, Pinkawalla, to 'lay claims to the nation's present'.[34] And, in a mode reminiscent of the poet Linton Kwesi Johnson (the novel also playfully refers to a character named Hanif Johnson, presumably an amalgamated allusion to Kureishi and Johnson), the DJ chants: '*Now-mi-feel-indignation-when-dem-talk-immigration-when-dem-make-insinuation-we-no-part-o-de-nation-an-mi-make-proclamation-a-de-true-situation-how-*

we-make-contribution-since-de-Rome-occupation.'[35] Pinkawalla is described as
a remarkably hybrid character, 'a seven-foot albino, his hair the palest rose, the
whites of his eyes likewise, his features unmistakably Indian, the haughty nose,
long thin lips, a face from *Hamza-nama* cloth. An Indian who has never seen
India, East-India-man from the West Indies, white black man. A star.'[36] As an
albino Indian and a singer, Pinkawalla recalls the albino child in 'The Feast of
Lights', a story written almost a century earlier by another immigrant from
India, Cornelia Sorabji,[37] but the difference between the child's shrill mimicry
of Englishness and Pinkawalla's confidently hybrid mingling of cultures
and linguistic forms marks the historical change that has taken place in the
movement from a bicultural identity, opposing two established traditions and
homelands, to the fluidly communal and immigrant inflected cosmopolitan
culture that Rushdie celebrates.[38]

In the 1990s and the first years of the twenty-first century, new realist fiction and drama continues to make an impact, for instance in the prizewinning
White Teeth (2000) by Zadie Smith, which gives voice to Anglo-Saxon, Asian
and West Indian families in a grounded London setting, or the 'yardie' novels of Courttia Newland, or the historical revisiting of the eighteenth-century
black British community in S. I. Martin's *Incomparable World* (1996), or the
Bildungsromans by Andrea Levy of young West Indian women rediscovering
their family histories.[39] But the last decade of the century also produced some
striking experimental fiction and poetry, which sidesteps the powerful models
provided by Rushdie by drawing on African and Amerindian traditions which
in turn transform canonical English and European literary icons. Ben Okri's
The Famished Road, awarded the Booker Prize in 1991, takes the traditional
Yoruba (and Igbo) figure of the *abiku* (a child returned from the dead) to portray a hauntingly surreal picture of urban Nigeria, and its thoroughly hybrid
culture. Pauline Melville links Dante, Amerindian legend and clever mimicry of
Claude Lévi-Strauss and Evelyn Waugh to revisit Guyana in *The Ventriloquist's
Tale* (1997). Bernardine Evaristo's *Lara* (1997) combines verse and prose in a
richly evocative traversing of Brazilian, British/Irish and Nigerian traditions
and communities. Evaristo is also a witty and unusual poet, whose second
verse novel, *The Emperor's Babe* (2001), recreates the world of a young girl
of Sudanese parentage who grows up in Roman London 1800 years ago. In
her autobiographical *The Adoption Papers* (1991), a set of poems which inter-
weave the voices of a natural and an adoptive mother with that of their Scottish
Nigerian child, Jackie Kay draws on the distinctively Scottish female tradition
exemplified by Liz Lochhead. Kay's novel *Trumpet* (1998) tells the story of the
love between a Scottish woman, a black trumpeter who 'passes' as a man, and
their adopted mixed-race son. *Trumpet* allows the reader to understand the

extent to which individual selves as well as visions of Britain may be continu-
ally invented and reinvented. Her writing, like Evaristo's, Phillips's and Syal's,
is also a reminder that London is not the only locale for black and Asian British
writing; within Britain the voices and accents of writers from the postcolonies
have become multiple in their inflections, locations and hybrid cultures, transforming concepts of Britishness.[40]

Chapter 11

Citizens of the world: reading postcolonial literature

Over the past forty years, writing by postcolonial writers in Britain and the former British colonies has attracted numerous prestigious literary prizes. The Nobel Prize for Literature has been awarded to the Australian novelist Patrick White, the Nigerian playwright, poet and novelist Wole Soyinka, the St Lucian poet Derek Walcott, the Trinidadian author V. S. Naipaul, the South African novelist Nadine Gordimer and the Irish poet Seamus Heaney (and earlier in the century to the Irish writers W. B. Yeats and Samuel Beckett). Since its inception in 1969, nearly half of the winners of Britain's most prestigious literary award, the Man Booker Prize for fiction, have been writers from former colonies, including Salman Rushdie (whose 1981 *Midnight's Children* was also named 'Best of the Bookers' J. M. Coetzee (twice), Peter Carey (twice), V. S. Naipaul, Michael Ondaatje, Margaret Atwood, Ben Okri, Keri Hulme, Nadine Gordimer, Thomas Keneally, J. G. Farrell, Roddy Doyle, John Banville, Arundhati Roy, and Ruth Prawer Jhabvala. Many of these writers have also appeared several times on the shortlist, as have other postcolonial authors such as William Trevor, Abdulrazak Gurnah, Rohinton Mistry, Carol Shields, Doris Lessing, Anita Desai, and André Brink.

As journalists and critics have been quick to point out, literary prizes provide welcome publicity not only for their sponsors but also for the publishers of these authors, and the Man Booker Prize is conducted in such a way as to maximize publicity and book sales through advertising the shortlisted writers and encouraging speculation and participation by readers before the televised announcement of the winner. Many critics, including myself, would agree with Richard Todd's argument that the Booker Prize awards have encouraged a greater awareness of Britain as a pluralist society,[1] and welcome its recognition of writers from 'the Commonwealth'. However, the very success of postcolonial writers in these and other awards has given rise to cynicism, a suspicion among certain critics that the metropolitan centre has appropriated postcolonial writing for its own ends, and has sought to control which ones should be given the seal of approval. Thus some African and African American critics claimed that the award of the Nobel Prize for Literature to Wole Soyinka and

Derek Walcott (and also Toni Morrison) indicated that their writing was more European and 'elitist' than 'authentically' African or Caribbean. The fact that the Booker McConnell company had originally been based in Guyana, and had derived its income from the Demerara sugar plantations, and that one of the criteria for the award is that the book must have been published in Britain, added to the suspicion that its sponsorship of the literary awards was another form of neocolonialism.

Indeed, the whole institutionalization of postcolonial literary studies has been declared suspect by critics such as Aijaz Ahmad, who sees both the emphasis on literature in English and an embrace of poststructuralist theory as antipathetic to the development of indigenous literatures and societies.[2] And while welcoming the growing interest in postcolonial literatures, many teachers and critics have also been concerned about the biases that may be built into our understanding of these literatures by the rapid establishment of a postcolonial literary canon, and a (related) reliance on particular publishers and anthologies to make the literature available to students. Moreover, certain values and concepts such as 'authenticity', 'otherness' and 'hybridity' have become embedded in discussions of postcolonial writing, so that the texts that seem to foreground these qualities receive continuing attention. This book might well be seen as an example of such foregrounding, though it also seeks to encourage the questioning of canon formation and certain postcolonial critical paradigms. Graham Huggan has analysed and critiqued the institutionalising and marketing of postcolonial literatures for their emphasis on and commodification of 'the exotic', an emphasis arising in part from the predominance of values such as 'otherness' and 'authenticity' in postcolonial theory. He argues that works by Hanif Kureishi, Naipaul and Rushdie exemplify a 'staged marginality' – 'the dramatisation of their "subordinate status" for the imagined benefit of a majority audience'.[3] While acknowledging that in the case of these writers this 'staged marginality' has a subversive intent, and seeks to challenge majority stereotypes and exoticizing of the other, Huggan points out that nevertheless the works are *marketed* and often read in terms of that perceived marginality or 'otherness'. This is a process defined by Huggan as the creation of the 'postcolonial exotic', that is, a process of domesticating the other, or, as he puts it, 'a mode of aesthetic perception which domesticates the other even as it makes it strange'.[4]

Huggan cites Pierre Bourdieu's concept of centrally and hierarchically owned cultural capital, 'negotiated through the interactions between the producers and consumers of goods', which involves the power to confer legitimacy on the writers and kinds of writers, through prizes, favourable reviews, etc. – and, one might add, the power to include particular writers in academic curriculums and textbooks. *The Postcolonial Exotic* (2001) seeks to question what Huggan sees as 'the neo-imperialist implications of a postcolonial literary/critical industry centred on, and largely catering to, the West', an industry mainly articulated in English, depending on publishing houses in London and New York, offering 'translated' products for metropolitan consumers, and privileging 'a handful of famous writers (Achebe, Naipaul, Rushdie)' and 'its three celebrity critics (Bhabha, Said, Spivak)'.[5]

The questions Huggan raises are important ones, and anyone reading post-colonial writers needs to take them into account, though in my view he gives too much importance to 'Western readers', who, in any case, are a far more diverse group than this term or his arguments suggest. Publishing data for Chinua Achebe's books, for example, demonstrates that the majority of his readers are in Africa rather than Europe or North America. Scholars such as Karin Barber and Stephanie Newell have shown the significance of indigenous publishing and marketing networks within Nigeria,[6] while Ahmad and others have pointed to thriving writing and publishing in the Indian subcontinent in a number of languages (of which English is merely one), and assuming a local audience.

Yet it is also the case that many anticolonial and postcolonial works of literature have been banned and so made unavailable in their own countries. James Joyce's *Ulysses* (1922) was banned in Ireland (and some other countries, such as Australia and the United States) because it was considered obscene, and hence was unavailable to Irish readers unless they were able to obtain copies from abroad. Rushdie's *The Satanic Verses* (1988) was banned in India, Pakistan and many other countries on religious grounds, because some authorities denounced it as blasphemous and offensive to Muslims. In Britain and the United States, copies of the book were burned by indignant Muslim protesters, and many bookshops were unwilling or afraid to have copies of *The Satanic Verses* or other works by Rushdie available for sale. Indeed, Iran's Ayatollah Khomeini declared a *fatwa*, or sentence of death, on Rushdie, so that he was forced to live in hiding for almost a decade. In South Africa many authors have had their works banned because they were considered subversive on moral or political grounds; these authors included such well-known and internationally esteemed writers as Peter Abrahams, Brink, Gordimer, Alex La Guma, and Lauretta Ngcobo. South Africans were also forbidden to read thousands of texts by outside writers such as Ayi Kwei Armah, Leonard Cohen, Langston Hughes, Martin Luther King, Stephen King, Ngugi wa Thiong'o – and Woody Allen! Ernest Hemingway's *Across the River and Into the Trees* (1950) was banned in both South Africa and Ireland. Such restrictions meant that many voices were suppressed, and that the lives and cultures of black and coloured people in South Africa were either not represented at all or represented in limited and distorted ways. For those who were able to have access to the works, one effect of such bans was to foreground the political, religious and racial themes in fiction and poetry which might otherwise be read in more complex ways.

This chapter goes on to raise questions about the experience of reading postcolonial texts where they are available, and to suggest some of the ways in which this experience differs between readers who belong to the author's community and those who do not. The underlying assumption here is that the reading of an anticolonial or postcolonial text is a process in which readers may assume a number of positions or identities, and become aware of the relationships, including power relationships, between those positions. I will explore the role of implicit readers within the texts of *Ulysses* (1922), and other anticolonial and postcolonial works, and speculate on how these roles may shape the responses of actual readers in different locations and times.

My discussions of the texts in the preceding chapters have tended to focus on the writer and his or her context, and less on the reader's context. Indeed, most critical analyses of postcolonial writing implicitly or explicitly presume that the reader is either a member of the writer's nation, as in Benedict Anderson's *Imagined Communities* (1983), or, more frequently, a generalized cosmopolitan Westerner. In Huggan's *The Postcolonial Exotic* or Timothy Brennan's *At Home in This World* (1997), it is taken for granted that the reader is American or European, and there is little differentiation between kinds of Western readers. As a result, there is an implicit assumption that the texts may be read in one way, that there is a manner of homogeneous or universal reading. Thus Huggan declares that Achebe's *Things Fall Apart* (1958) 'implicitly address[es] a Western model reader who is constructed as an outsider to the text and to the cultural environment(s) it represents'.[7] Where there is diversity or ambiguity of meaning, many critics assume it to be a property of the text rather than a consequence of diverse readerships. Moreover, those diverse reader responses may exist to varying degrees in the same person, and I will argue that the construction of a multiple or hybrid reader is one of the properties of many postcolonial texts, whether they originate in Africa, the Indian subcontinent or Ireland.

There are clearly many questions arising from the complexities surrounding the readers of postcolonial texts, and the varieties of readings and responses that may then emerge. Many postcolonial writers and critics have celebrated their double status as insiders and outsiders, but we can go on to ask how an 'inside reader's' response to a text might differ from that of an 'outside reader'? That is, how might an Igbo or a Nigerian reading of *Things Fall Apart* differ from a Danish or English or North American one? How does a British reader's response to Les Murray's poetry differ from mine, as an Australian with a similar rural and urban background to Murray's? Or how might readings of Joyce's *Ulysses* differ between that of his contemporary Irish audience and that of present-day Englishmen and women? And even given readers with similar national or ethnic identities, how does the context in which the book is published and read alter their responses? To some extent, one could give sociological answers to these questions by carrying out multiple surveys and checking reviews, and work has begun on the history of 'the postcolonial book', its modes of publication and responses to it.[8] However, this chapter will concentrate on problems and issues rather than seeking to provide a survey and give statistical data.

My argument is that many anticolonialist and postcolonial writers differ from American, English and European modernist and postmodernist writers in their sense of a *double* audience, one existing as an immediate community within or identified with the colonized people, the other an outside or metropolitan readership, often connected with the colonizer. For the immediate community, reading might be largely an act of *recognition* and bonding; naming of people and places or allusions to them, and specific idioms (or the use of 'nation language', in Kamau Brathwaite's term) become an assertion and (re)creation of this intimate inside community. Hence the small group of people who originally received copies of W. B. Yeats's 'Easter 1916' from its privately printed run of twenty-five copies did not need to be told the names; they knew who was being referred to by 'That woman who rode to harriers', 'This man who kept a school', 'This other his helper', 'This other who seemed a drunken vainglorious lout'. Among the ways in which the participants in the Easter Rising have 'changed, changed utterly' is that they become not only members of an inside community but *also* members of an outside community, for which they become *merely* the names invoked at the end of the poem. (One might note that women remain barred from that outside community; 'That woman', though she is the first to be described, is not named in the final stanza along with 'MacDonagh and MacBride / And Connolly and Pearse.') Thus 'Easter 1916' in part commemorates the changing status of Ireland from colonized and marginalized community to the status of nation that speaks its own history and names its own heroes.

Although Joyce's *Ulysses* makes a more oblique response to the 1916 Easter Rising and its aftermath, it nevertheless presupposes an inner audience, acquainted with the cultures and personas involved, and responding to Joyce's parodic version differently from readers less inward with those events. As W. J. McCormack has pointed out, *Ulysses* is a historical novel, and its Irish readers would have been particularly aware of the gap between the Ireland of 1904, when the novel is set, and the Ireland of 1922, when it was published.[9] The

'Cyclops' episode in particular is likely to create an awareness for its Irish readers of the differences between then and now. The cultural and political world represented in 1904 by 'Citizen' Michael Cusack, the Gaelic League, and the Gaelic Athletic Association had now been overlaid by the fearful bloodshed of World War I, the Easter Rising and subsequent executions, the elections that brought Sinn Féin to power in Ireland, the declaration of Irish independence, and the fierce fighting between Irish Republicans and the British Black and Tans. In this context the romantic and racially based nationalism espoused by the Citizen is brought into question and seen as one of the sources of the performance of the Rising and the defects of its ensuing narration.

More specifically Joyce parodies the narration of events surrounding Robert Emmet's execution, and his role as a model for twentieth-century rebels. The leader of a failed Irish rebellion in 1803, Emmet is invoked and recalled throughout *Ulysses*. Irish readers would have been quick to recognize the events and the restaging of events (there existed at the time some forty plays and numerous ballads and popular novels with Emmet as the central character).[10] He was a role model for Padraic Pearse, who spoke thus of him in relation to the ideology of St Enda's, the school Pearse founded:

> Here at St Enda's we have tried to keep before us the image of Fionn during his battles – careless and laughing, with that gesture of the head, that gallant, smiling gesture, which has been an eternal gesture in Irish history; it was most memorably made by Emmet when he mounted that scaffold in Thomas Street, smiling, he who had left so much, and most recently by those three who died at Manchester. I know that Ireland will not be happy again until she recollects that old proud gesture of hers, and that laughing gesture of a young man that is going into battle or climbing a gibbet.[11]

This particular speech about Emmet was made by Pearse in 1913, and the scenario is reiterated in other speeches around the same time. Lennox Robinson's play about Emmet, *The Dreamers* (1915), which represents the hero in a similar light, was staged in Dublin in 1915. Emmet's marriage to Sarah Curran on the eve of his execution may well have inspired one of the 1916 rebels, Joseph Plunkett, to wed his fiancée Grace Gifford the day before he was executed for his part in the Easter Rising. Joyce and his Irish readers must surely have had both the Easter Rising and the post-1904 iconography of Emmet in mind when writing or reading the parodic account of Emmet's death in the 'Cyclops' episode: 'She would never forget her hero boy who went to his death with a song on his lips as if he were but going to a hurling match in Clonturk Park . . . Oblivious of the dreadful present, they both laughed heartily, all the audience, including the venerable pastor, joining in the general merriment.'[12]

Joyce's burlesque of this sentimentalized and romantic heroism speaks to an American and European audience which has seen the deaths of thousands of young men in World War I; but it speaks more directly and intimately to an Irish audience which has witnessed the replaying of Emmet's story on the streets of Dublin, and would have recognized the Easter Rising in that context, and indeed in the wider context of a series of heroic martyrdoms and rebellions, remarked by Leopold Bloom in his dispute with the Citizen about 'the point, the brothers Sheares, and Wolfe Tone beyond on Arbour Hill and Robert Emmet and die for your country, the Tommy Moore touch about Sarah Curran and she's far from the land'.[13] Bloom's detailed consciousness of Irish history, culture and places, his consciousness of himself as an Irishman rather than an 'other', unites him with the Irish readers of *Ulysses* and the community depicted by Joyce. Writing *Ulysses* in the years between 1914 and 1921, Joyce may have wished to construct an Irish readership which would be ready to identify Bloom as one among them, and to reject an outdated and xenophobic nationalism which was unable to acknowledge Bloom as an insider. It might also be a readership growing towards the affirmation of Ireland as an independent nation, writing and reading itself into its own version of history.

However, while Joyce provides a critique (via the Citizen and others) of Irish readings of their history and culture, he also sets up a model and implicit critique of readings by outsiders, and contrasts 'outsider' readings with the responses of an 'insider' Irish community. For Joyce's Irish contemporaries, the act of reading *Ulysses* was in many ways an act of recognition, the retracing and hence the sharing and repossession of familiar places, names and persons. The novel is peopled with actual Dubliners, with familiar figures, and with passing references to familiar places, anecdotes, and events. Some are explicitly named (like Best, Eglinton, Nanetti (who was to become Mayor of Dublin) and George Russell); others like Buck Mulligan and the Citizen are given names and characteristics which disguise only to reveal.[14] *Ulysses* is a novel for which inside knowledge and authority as a reader comes from being part of a community which Joyce seeks to extend but also to define. In this novel Haines is not only a caricature of the English imperialist, with his nightmares about guns and panthers, his collecting of folklore and his amateur anthropological and philological interests, he is also a figure of the excluded or outside reader, who fails to 'get' Stephen's jokes or to understand the nuanced references in the speech and banter of the Dublin community.

The distinction being made here between Haines as 'excluded' or outside reader, and the insiders who share jokes and understanding to which he has no access, has to do with 'constructed' or fictional readers, rather than 'real' ones. The issue of Joyce's actual readership is a complicated one; nevertheless, it could be argued that Joyce sets up a tension between a number of implicit readers and his actual readers – if only in terms of engagement and disengagement. In seeing how Haines 'misreads' Mulligan, Stephen Dedalus, the old woman who brings the milk, we can perhaps become more nuanced readers ourselves. Many critics have shown the significance of the multiplicity of voices in *Ulysses*, and have commented in varying ways on the problem of locating an authoritative voice in this novel. A corollary of the multiplicity of voices and the question of the authoritative speaker is the multiplicity of listeners and the question of the authoritative reader.

Ulysses is a book noteworthy for the number of listeners who inhabit it, and for the number of scenes which draw attention to the listener hovering on the margins of conversations. In the first two episodes of the novel, Stephen suffers the chatter of Mulligan, the earnest commentary of Haines, the preaching of Deasy, the halting mistranslations and misreadings of his pupils; he himself says remarkably little, though his unspoken responses to Mulligan, Haines and Deasy suggest how we should read what they say. In the ninth episode Stephen is heard, but he also frequently overhears himself, and at certain points nudges his readers towards sceptical detachment from his autobiographical readings of Shakespeare. Indeed, this central episode in the Dublin National Library is as much about reading and misreading as it is about authorship, whether of Irish writers, Shakespeare or Percy Bysshe Shelley. The 'Aeolus' episode, set in the newspaper offices, also shows Bloom and Stephen as listeners and readers, both at times seeking to insert themselves into the community of speakers. John Nash has demonstrated the interplay and clash between modes of writing displayed in this episode, and Joyce's use of the London *Times* as a source for news which reveals here and in the Cyclops episode Joyce's awareness of London as a centre of empire.[15] But this chapter also invokes a series of readings dependent on insider knowledge which is unavailable to Londoners. Beginning with that resounding phrase, 'In the heart of the Hibernian metropolis',[16] with its playful insistence on Dublin as a centre, not only of paralysis and a mimic culture, but also of a history and 'Hibernian' counterculture of its own making, Irish metropolitan readers find themselves in an almost entirely known world, amid a familiar series of place names and a group of speakers who assume both a mastery of Greek, Latin and Judaeo-Christian oral and written cultures *and* an insider knowledge of Irish history and affairs. The references to lines from 'The Boys of Wexford', a ballad well known to Irishmen and women, to the Wild Geese, Isaac Butt, [James] Whiteside, John Philpott Curran, the mass meetings held by Daniel O'Connell, news sheets such as *Paddy Kelly's Budget* and *The*

Skibbereen Eagle invoke a specific national history and culture which has little or no meaning for readers outside Ireland. The anecdote narrated by Myles Crawford about the reporting of the Phoenix Park assassinations in coded form, whose decoding depended on access to the Irish *Freeman's Journal* and a ready knowledge of Dublin's streets and suburbs, can be seen as a paradigm for the reading of many sections of *Ulysses*, in which incidents, names, phrases signify differently for Irish and non-Irish readers. The effect is not to make those sections meaningless to those who do not share the knowledge of Irish place and history; it is rather to create an awareness among Irish readers of a shared knowledge and history, over which they have authority and mastery, and which non-Irish readers must be taught.[17]

This tactic of 'writing in' the outside reader is found in different ways in many other anticolonialist and postcolonial novels and plays. The District Commissioners in Achebe's *Things Fall Apart* and *Arrow of God* (1964) are comparable to Haines in their misreading of 'native' culture, and as with Haines their misreading depends partly on an anthropological approach to the world they observe. Ngugi wa Thiong'o's *A Grain of Wheat* (1968) recalls for Kenyan readers a particular and specific understanding of Kikuyu history and culture from which the English administrator, Thompson, is excluded. In these African novels, as in *Ulysses*, the role of the outsider as a misreader of the culture also functions to encourage the actual readers to disengage themselves from the constructed misreading allocated to the English administrators. At the same time, the use of Igbo or Gikuyu words and references, the construction of an inner audience which belongs to a specific village community and is aware of a history that often remains slightly mysterious to outsiders, gives Igbos and Kikuyus (and at a further distance, other Nigerians, Kenyans and Africans) a sense of authority and community.

As Huggan points out, the construction of the insider or insider knowledge in novels such as *Things Fall Apart* is by no means uncomplicated, for the question of who speaks for the local culture and who interprets it is clearly bound up with questions of power and production.[18] Anthropological discourse is both presented and questioned in this novel. One could argue that *Arrow of God* takes the issue of the relationships between power and knowledge, authentic histories and their interpretation, further – indeed, the question is central to the novel, to the contests between the two priests, and to the relationship between Ezeulu and Clarke and Winterbottom, all of whom claim to speak truths sanctioned by an outside and higher authority, divine or imperial. And whereas the failure of the outsider in *Things Fall Apart* lies in his arrogant dismissal of Igbo institutions as merely primitive, the failure of Clarke and Winterbottom stems additionally from their unwillingness to acknowledge or even conceive of the complex divisions and power struggles, personal and political, within that particular Igbo society, and their assumption that one model (indirect rule as applied to the North) is appropriate for all of Nigeria.

Thus one trait of outsider reader characters, whether Haines or a District Commissioner, is their generalization from particular individuals to judgements about the group as a whole. Haines views the woman who brings the milk as representative of Irish-speaking peasant folk; the District Commissioner sees Okonkwo's behaviour, regarded as aberrant by the members of his own clan, as useful for drawing conclusions about all Africans.

In this respect one might regard Fredric Jameson's much-debated essay describing Third World texts as 'national allegories' as a more contemporary example of outsider reading practice.[19] Jameson's argument that *all* Third World texts are to be read as national allegories assumes that characters and plot represent a whole nation's values and history – in other words, the native writer and his or her characters become native informants who speak for the race or society as a whole. Not only does his argument ignore the very contested nature of 'the nation' in most Third World countries (one would have thought that the civil war in Nigeria would have been caution enough against such homogenizing), it also ignores the different kinds of fiction produced within those so-called Third World countries. It is the case, of course, that some writers set out to produce allegories of the national condition and its past: Armah's *The Beautyful Ones Are Not Yet Born* (1968), Sembene Ousmane's *Xala* (1973) and Rushdie's *Shame* (1983) could be considered examples. However, as Ahmad vehemently affirms, their work is by no means typical of the majority of fiction and drama produced in Africa and the Indian subcontinent.[20] But, as Huggan suggests, the *marketing* of African fiction contributes to the construction of it as 'other', as works providing anthropological understanding which will reinforce Western preconceptions about Africa, rather than aesthetic pleasure, or sympathetic identification, or even political comprehension. Huggan takes the Heinemann African Series as the prime example of such marketing which, in his view, 'has often shown symptoms of the controlling imperial gaze', with book covers which according to Huggan emphasize their status as African and primitive.[21] To some extent, there seems to be an elision here in Huggan's own thinking between drawings which are clearly African and images which are primitive, for some of Africa's leading and most talented and sophisticated artists were employed to illustrate the covers. Nor does he take sufficiently into account the role of African writers such as Achebe, Gurnah, and Adewala Maja-Pearce as general editors for the series.[22] And although he acknowledges the enormous readership that the series gained within Africa, he still maintains that the series and the novels selected illustrate mainly the desire to reflect a Western concept of Africa back to Western readers. What Huggan seems to ignore is the cosmopolitan culture of readers *within* Africa or India, the fact that they will all have had access to European literatures, films, advertising and systems of knowledge, including those influenced by anthropology, as well as indigenous cultures and systems of knowledge. It is this cosmopolitanism or multiple consciousness which African and other postcolonial writers acknowledge, the diverse reading practices and backgrounds within each local reader, which arguably their works seek to develop in the outside reader. In other words, their texts seek to encourage outsiders to become not observers but more like insiders, and to recognize the interplay as well as the ironies which exist in such a double consciousness.

Rushdie's novels also include a wealth of reference to Indian cultures, characters and histories which will be more readily recognizable to readers from the Indian subcontinent than to American or English readers. But he differs from Achebe, Joyce and Ngugi in that an outsider reader is not given a significant role within the novels. Here might be one indication of the difference between anticolonial and postcolonial texts, for in Rushdie's novels different historical narratives are contested *within* the Indian subcontinent rather than between colonizer and colonized. Thus *Midnight's Children* foregrounds the marginalized history of Muslim participants in India's move towards independence, and almost ignores the mainstream histories placing Mahatma Gandhi at the centre (except where the narrator 'deliberately' gives an inaccurate date for Gandhi's assassination). One could argue also that the fluidity of Rushdie's characters and the manifest unreliability of their narratives (including that of the central narrator, Saleem Sinai), is one means of making it difficult for the outsider reader to make them representative spokesmen. Similarly the assumption of an informed national audience might be implicit in *Clear Light of Day* (1980), *Nervous Conditions* (1988) and *The God of Small Things* (1997), whose authors take it for granted that their readers can supply the details of an official national history barely alluded to in their novels.

How might these reflections affect the reading and teaching of postcolonial texts in Britain and the United States? One response could be to move away from an emphasis on cultural and anthropological analyses which on the one hand distance the text, and on the other encourage readers to see the worlds they encounter as static and unchanging. Rather, we need to foster an understanding of identities in process, or what Stuart Hall has called a cultural identity of 'positioning'. In a 1982 interview with Kwame Anthony Appiah, Achebe explained:

> I'm an Ibo writer because this is my basic culture; Nigerian, African and
> a writer ... no, black first, then a writer. Each of these identities does
> call for a certain kind of commitment on my part. I must see what it is to
> be black – and this means being sufficiently intelligent to know how the
> world is moving and how the black people fare in this world. This is
> what it means to be black. Or an African – what does Africa mean to the
> world? When you see an African, what does it mean to a white man?[23]

These are the multiple and shifting identities, *and the tensions between them*,
that call upon Achebe's commitment as a writer, and which emerge in that
ironic and creative interplay which make his novels so rewarding. But they are
also the multiple identities which call upon our commitments as readers and
as teachers. By opening ourselves to that creative and ironic interplay between
observer and observed, between insider and outsider, by allowing ourselves
to become hybrid readers, we can enter into dialogue with the texts and their
political implications. We can understand what it means to be both inside and
outside varied cultural contexts, and experience the different kinds of spaces
and insularities that those contexts permit. In other words, we allow ourselves
to be transformed and translated culturally, entering into dialogue with the
work, its implicit readers, and the power relationships between them.

Notes

Preface

1. The correct name is the 'Commonwealth of Nations', but this organization is frequently, though controversially, referred to as the 'British Commonwealth' – a description which for many former colonies gives too much eminence to Britain rather than including it on equal status with the other members of the Commonwealth.
2. William Shakespeare, *The Tempest*, I:2.363–4 (London: Penguin, 1968), p. 77
3. Ibid., III.2.136–9.
4. George Lamming, *The Pleasures of Exile* (London: Michael Joseph, 1960), p. 109

1 Introduction: situating the postcolonial

1. For distinctions made between the hyphenated term 'post-colonial' and the unhyphenated 'postcolonial' see the Glossary.
2. See, for example, the books by Peter Childs, Leela Gandhi, Ania Loomba, Bart Moore-Gilbert and Ato Quayson listed in the Bibliography. See also John Thieme, *Postcolonial Studies: The Essential Glossary* (London: Arnold, 2003), and the following anthologies of postcolonial theoretical essays: Patrick Williams and Laura Chrisman, eds., *Colonial Discourse and Postcolonial Theory: A Reader* (Hemel Hempstead: Harvester Wheatsheaf, 1993); Bill Ashcroft, Gareth Griffiths and Helen Tiffin, eds., *The Post-colonial Studies Reader* (London: Routledge, 1995); Gregory Castle, ed., *Postcolonial Discoures: An Anthology* (Oxford: Blackwell, 2001); and Bart Moore-Gilbert, Gareth Stanton and Willy Maley, eds., *Postcolonial Criticism* (London: Longman, 1997).
3. Nayantara Sahgal, 'The Schizophrenic Imagination', *Wasafiri: Journal of Caribbean, African, Asian and Associated Literatures and Film* 11 (Spring 1990), pp. 17–20.
4. This conference convened by Bismarck in Berlin was attended by fourteen European nations, including Belgium, Britain, France, Germany, Italy, Portugal and Spain, to determine and share control over Africa. A series of geometric lines, which paid little attention to the boundaries established by the hundreds of indigenous cultures and regions within the continent, divided Africa into fifty regions, each allocated

to one of the European powers. As H. J. de Blij and Peter O. Muller remark, 'The Berlin Conference was Africa's undoing in more ways than one. The colonial powers superimposed their domains on the African continent. By the time independence returned to Africa in 1950, the realm had acquired a legacy of political fragmentation that could neither be eliminated nor made to operate satisfactorily.' See de Blij and Muller, *Geography: Realms, Regions, and Concepts* (Chichester: John Wiley & Sons, 1997), p. 340.

5. Stuart Hall, 'When was "The Postcolonial"?: Thinking at the Limit', in Iain Chambers and Lidia Curti, eds., *The Post-Colonial Question* (London: Routledge, 1996), p. 245.

6. India and Pakistan achieved independence in 1947; Sri Lanka in 1948; Ghana in 1957; and Nigeria, Kenya, Tanganyika, Uganda, Jamaica, Trinidad and Tobago, British Guyana, Malaysia and Singapore, and many other states between 1960 and 1965.

7. The papers from the Leeds conference were published under the title *Commonwealth Literature: Unity and Diversity in a Common Culture*, ed. John Press (London: Heinemann, 1965). Courses in Commonwealth literature were taught in the 1960s and 1970s by faculty members at the universities of Kent, Leeds, Stirling and Sussex, for example. Many of these academics had taught or been taught in former British colonies.

8. See Ngugi wa Thiong'o, *Decolonising the Mind: The Politics of Language in African Literature* (London: James Currey, 1986).

9. See Paul Gilroy, *The Black Atlantic: Modernity and Double Consciousness* (Cambridge, MA: Harvard University Press, 1993).

10. Frantz Fanon, *Black Skin, White Masks*, trans. Charles Lam Markmann (New York: Grove Press, 1967), p. 10.

11. Ibid., p. 12.

12. Ibid., p. 14.

13. Léopold Senghor, *Ethiopiques* (Paris: Editions de Seuil, 1956), p. 116. See also Clive Wake and John Reed, eds., *Senghor: Prose and Poetry* (London: Oxford University Press, 1965), p. 34.

14. Jean-Paul Sartre, *Black Orpheus*, trans. Samuel Allen (Paris: Présence Africaine, 1956), pp. 50–1. Originally published as 'Orphée Noir', in L. S. Senghor, ed., *Anthologie de la nouvelle poésie négre* (Paris: Presses Universitaires de France, 1948).

15. Wole Soyinka, 'The Future of African Writing', *The Horn* (Ibadan) 4:1 (June 1960), pp. 10–16.

16. Chinua Achebe, 'The Role of the Writer in a New Nation', *Nigeria Magazine* 81 (1964) p. 157.

17. Frantz Fanon, *The Wretched of the Earth*, trans. Constance Farrington (New York: Grove Press, 1968).

18. The use of the term 'native' is problematic, since it carries so many disparaging connotations in European discourse. However, I retain its usage here as Fanon

does, with some irony, to emphasize the contrast set up and maintained between the indigenous peoples and the colonizers.

19. For example, the Oxford Professor of Modern History Sir Hugh Trevor-Roper stated, 'At present undergraduates are demanding to be taught African history, . . . [but]at present there is only the history of Europeans in Africa. The rest is largely darkness … And darkness is not a subject for history.' See Trevor-Roper, *The Rise of Christian Europe* (London: Thames & Hudson, 1965), p. 9.

20. G. W. F. Hegel, *Introduction to the Philosophy of History* (New York: Dover Publications, 1956), p. 99.

21. Edward Said, *Orientalism* (1978; rev. edn Harmondsworth: Penguin, 1991).

22. Ibid., p. 3.

23. Edward Said, *Culture and Imperialism* (London: Chatto & Windus, 1993).

24. See Gayatri Chakravorty Spivak, *In Other Worlds: Essays in Cultural Politics* (London: Methuen, 1987); *The Postcolonial Critic: Interviews, Strategies, Dialogues*, ed. Sarah Harasym (London: Routledge, 1990); *Outside in the Teaching Machine* (London: Routledge, 1993); and *A Critique of Post-Colonial Reason: Toward a History of the Vanishing Present* (Cambridge, MA, and London: Harvard University Press, 1999). See also Donna Landry and Gerald MacLean, eds., *The Spivak Reader*. (New York and London: Routledge, 1996), which includes an extensive list of publications, among them many interviews.

25. Many of Bhabha's best-known essays are collected in Bhabha, *The Location of Culture* (London: Routledge, 1994).

26. Aijaz Ahmad, *In Theory: Classes, Nations, Literatures* (London: Verso, 1992).

27. Aijaz Ahmad, *Forms/Figures/Formations* (London: Verso, 1996), and Benita Parry, *Postcolonial Studies: A Materialist Critique* (London: Routledge, 2004).

28. See, for example, 'The Novelist as Teacher' in *Morning Yet on Creation Day* (London: Heinemann, 1975). Other essays by Achebe and the influence of Fanon on African and Caribbean writers will be discussed in chapter 3.

29. Homi Bhabha, 'Foreword: Remembering Fanon: Self, Psyche, and the Colonial Condition', 'Introduction' to Frantz Fanon, *Black Skin, White Masks*, Liberation Classics (London and Sydney: Pluto, 1986), pp. vii–xxvi.

30. See especially David Lloyd, *Anomalous States: Irish writing and the Post-Colonial Moment* (Durham, NC: Duke University Press, 1993); Marjorie Howes, *Yeats's Nations: Gender, Class and Irishness* (Cambridge: Cambridge University Press, 1996); Elizabeth Butler Cullingford, *Ireland's Others: Gender and Ethnicity in Irish Literature and Popular Culture* (Notre Dame: Notre Dame Press, 2001); Glenn Hooper, ed., *Irish and Postcolonial Writing* (Basingstoke: Palgrave Macmillan, 2002); and Clare Carroll and Patricia King, eds., *Ireland and Postcolonial Theory* (Cork: Cork University Press, 2003).

31. Jahan Ramazani, *The Hybrid Muse: Postcolonial Poetry in English* (Chicago: University of Chicago Press, 2001).

32. Homi Bhabha, 'Of Mimicry and Man: The Ambivalence of Colonial Discourse', in Bhabha, *The Location of Culture* (London: Routledge, 1994), p. 92. For further discussion of Bhabha's comments on this topic, see the Glossary.

33. Charles Kingsley, *His Letters and Memories of His Life: Edited by His Wife*, 2 vols. (London: Henry S. King, 1877), II, p. 107.

34. See Howard Booth and Nigel Rigby, eds., *Modernism and Empire* (Manchester: Manchester University Press, 2000).

35. Said, *Culture and Imperialism*, pp. 265–88.

36. Wilson Harris, 'Tradition and the West Indian Novel', in Harris, *Selected Essays of Wilson Harris*, ed. Andrew Bundy (London: Routledge, 1999).

2   Postcolonial issues in performance

1. W. B. Yeats, *Autobiographies* (Dublin: Gill and Macmillan, 1955), p. 560.

2. Lady Augusta Gregory, *Our Irish Theatre* (New York: Capricorn Books, 1965), pp. 8–9.

3. Christopher Morash, *A History of Irish Theatre, 1601–2000* (Cambridge: Cambridge University Press, 2002), p. 117.

4. Stephen Gwynn, 'Modern Irish Drama', *Fortnightly Review*, December, 1902. Reprinted in, Justin McCarthy, ed., *Irish Literature*, 12 vols. (Chicago: DeBower-Elliot, 1904), X, pp. xiii–xxv.

5. For a fuller discussion of the play and the debate surrounding its first production, see Morash, *A History of Irish Theatre*, pp. 124–5. See also P. J. Mathews, *Revival: The Abbey Theatre, Sinn Fein, The Gaelic League and the Co-operative Movement* (Cork University Press/Field Day: Cork, 2003), pp. 117–45.

6. For a full description of the reaction to the first *Playboy* production, see Morash, *A History of Irish Theatre*, pp. 130–8. See also Robert Kilroy, ed., *The 'Playboy' Riots* (Dublin: Dolmen, 1971).

7. John McCallum, 'Irish Memories and Australian Hopes: William Butler Yeats and Louis Esson', *Westerly* V 34:2 (June 1989), pp. 33–40.

8. Douglas Stewart, *Ned Kelly* (Sydney: Angus & Robertson, 1943).

9. J. M. Synge, *Plays, Poems, and Prose* (London: J. M. Dent, 1949), p. 108.

10. Martin Banham (with Clive Wake), *African Theatre Today* (London: Pitman Publishers, 1976), p. 25.

11. Wole Soyinka, *A Dance of the Forests*, in *Collected Plays I* (London: Oxford University Press, 1973).

12. See, for example, Bernth Lindfors, cited in Annemarie Heywood, 'The Fox's Dance: The Staging of Soyinka's Plays', in Biodun Jeyifo, ed., *Modern African Drama* (New York: W. W. Norton, 2002), pp. 554–5.

13. Annemarie Heywood, 'The Fox's Dance', p. 555.

14. Ibid.

15. Homi Bhabha, 'Of Mimicry and Man: The Ambivalence of Colonial Discourse', in Bhabha, *The Location of Culture* (London: Routledge, 1994), pp. 85–92.

16. Ngugi wa Thiong'o, 'Preface', *The Black Hermit* (London: Heinemann, 1968), p. xii.

17. Ngugi wa Thiong'o and Micere Githae-Mugo, 'Preface', *The Trial of Dedan Kimathi* (London: Heinemann, 1976).

18. Ngugi wa Thiong'o, *Decolonising the Mind: The Politics of Language in African Literature* (London: James Currey, 1986), p. 44.

19. Ngugi wa Thiong'o, *Detained: A Writer's Prison Diary* (London: Heinemann, 1981), pp. 76–7.

20. In an interview for *Journal of Commonwealth Literature* 26:1 (1991). See also Ngugi wa Thiong'o, 'On Writing in Gikuyu', *Research in African Literatures* 16 (Summer 1985), pp. 151–6.

21. Quoted in, ed., Stewart Brown *The Art of Derek Walcott* (Bridgend: Seren Books, 1991), p. 24.

22. Derek Walcott, Interview with Edward Hirsch, *Contemporary Literature* 20:3 (1979), pp. 288–9.

23. Derek Walcott, *Dream on Monkey Mountain and other Plays*, New York: Farrar, Straus and Giroux, 1970, and Brian Friel, *Translations*, in John Harrington, ed., *Modern Irish Drama* (London and New York: W. W. Norton, 1991), pp. 340–74.

24. Walcott, *Dream on Monkey Mountain*, pp. 226–7.

25. Quoted by Bruce King in *Derek Walcott and West Indian Drama* (Oxford: Oxford University Press, 1995), p. 90.

26. Brian Friel, *Translations*, in John Harrington, ed. *Modern Irish Drama* (London/New York: W. W. Norton, 1991), pp. 340–74.

27. Edward Said, *Culture and Imperialism* (London: Chatto & Windus, 1993), pp. 271–6.

28. For a fuller description of the formation of the Field Day Company and the opening performance of the play, see Morash, *A History of Irish Theatre*, pp. 233–41.

29. Quoted by Morash in ibid., p. 238.

30. Ibid.

31. Friel, *Translations*, pp. 320–1, and Gayatri Chakravorty Spivak, 'Can the Subaltern Speak?', in Cary Nelson and Laurence Grossberg, eds., *Marxism and the Interpretation of Culture* (Basingstoke: Macmillan, 1988), pp. 271–313.

32. Friel, *Translations*, pp. 340–2.

33. Chinua Achebe, *Things Fall Apart* (London: Heinemann), p. 157.

34. Seamus Heaney, '. . . English and Irish', *Times Literary Supplement*, 24 October 1980, p. 1199. Reprinted in Harrington, *Modern Irish Drama*, pp. 557–9.

35. Ibid.

36. Friel, *Translations*, 372–3.

3 Alternative histories and writing back

1. Frantz Fanon, *The Wretched of the Earth*, trans. Constance Farrington (New York: Grove Press, 1968), p. 211.

2. Chinua Achebe, 'The Role of the Writer in a New Nation', *Nigeria Magazine* 81 (1964), p. 157.
3. Fanon, *The Wretched of the Earth*, p. 212.
4. Homi Bhabha, *The Location of Culture* (London: Routledge, 1994), pp. 1–2.
5. Raja Rao, *Kanthapura* (New York: Grove Press, 1963), p. vii.
6. Robert Fraser, *Lifting the Sentence: A Poetics of Postcolonial Fiction* (Manchester: Manchester University Press, 2000), p. 53.
7. Rao, *Kanthapura*, p. 10.
8. Ibid., p. 5.
9. Elleke Boehmer, *Colonial and Postcolonial Literature* (Oxford: Oxford University Press, 1995), p. 137.
10. Linda Hutcheon, *The Politics of Postmodernism* (London: Routledge, 1989), p. 65.
11. Linda Hutcheon, *The Canadian Postmodern* (Toronto: Oxford University Press, 1988).
12. Salman Rushdie, 'The Empire Writes Back With a Vengeance', *The Times* (London), 3 July 1982, p. 8. Rushdie's article plays with the title of the contemporary film *The Empire Strikes Back*, the sequel to *Star Wars*. See also Bill Ashcroft, Gareth Griffiths and Helen Tiffin, *The Empire Writes Back* (London: Routledge, 1989).
13. Chinua Achebe, 'An Image of Africa', in Achebe, *Hopes and Impediments: Selected Essays, 1965–87* (Oxford: Heinemann, 1975).
14. Edward Said, *Culture and Imperialism* (London: Chatto & Windus, 1993), pp. 100–16.
15. Derek Walcott, 'Pantomime' in Walcott, *Remembrance & Pantomime: Two Plays* (New York: Farrar, Straus and Giroux, 1980), pp. 90–170.
16. Karen Holst Petersen and Anna Rutherford, eds., *A Double Colonisation: Colonial and Post-Colonial Women's Writing* (Sydney and Oxford: Dangaroo Press, 1986).
17. See Roy Foster, *Paddy & Mr Punch: Connections in Irish and English History* (London: Penguin, 1995), and L. P. Curtis, *Apes and Angels: The Irishman in Victorian Caricature* (Washington, DC: Smithsonian Institution, 1996). See also C. L. Innes, *The Devil's Own Mirror: Irish and Africans in Modern Literature* (Washington, DC: Three Continents Press, 1990).
18. On 3 June 1992 the High Court of Australia gave its decision in Mabo and Others *vs* the State of Queensland, upholding the claim of the Meriam plaintiffs (from Murray Island in the Torres Strait), and in doing so held that Australia was not *terra nullius* (belonging to no one) when settled by the British in 1788. The court, in effect, recognized that Australia was occupied by aboriginal and Torres Strait Islander peoples, with their own laws and customs, whose 'native title' to lands survived the Crown's annexation.
19. Fanon, *The Wretched of the Earth*, 1963, p. 43.
20. Quoted in Philip D. Curtin, *An Image of Africa* (Madison: Wisconsin University Press, 1964), p. 281.
21. Chinua Achebe, 'The Role of the Writer In a New Nation', *Nigeria Magazine* 81 (1964), p. 157.

22. W. B. Yeats, *Yeats's Poems*, ed. and annotated A. Norman Jeffares (London: Macmillan, 1989), p. 294.

23. Chinua Achebe, *Things Fall Apart* (London: Heinemann, 1976), pp. 124–5.

24. Simon Gikandi, *Reading Chinua Achebe: Language and Ideology in Fiction* (London: James Currey; Portsmouth, NH: Heinemann, 1991), p. 4.

25. Achebe, *Things Fall Apart*, p. 3.

26. Ibid., pp. 147–8.

27. See Chinua Achebe's poem 'Misunderstanding' in his *Collected Poems* (New York: Anchor Books, 2004), pp. 43–4. See also his note on this poem, p. 82.

28. David Punter, *Postcolonial Imaginings* (Edinburgh: Edinburgh University Press, 2000), p. 17.

29. See also Achebe's poem 'An "If" of History', *Collected Poems*, p. 22. For a fuller discussion of Achebe's response to historiography, see Gikandi, *Reading Chinua Achebe*, pp. 27–31.

30. Hugh Trevor-Roper, *The Rise of Christian Europe* (London: Thames & Hudson, 1965), p. 9. The book was based on a series of lectures he had given on television. For Hegel's comments, see chapter 1, p. 8.

31. Ama Ata Aidoo, *Our Sister Killjoy: or Reflections from a Black-eyed Squint* (Harlow: Longman, 1977).

32. Ama Ata Aidoo, Interview with Sarah Chetin, *Wasafiri* 6/7 (1987), p. 25.

33. This description of *Heart of Darkness* can be and has been passionately contested by many critics, who reject Achebe's charge that it is a racist or univocal text. It is not my purpose to enter into that debate here, but to outline a reading of the novel which provides the basis for Aidoo's rewriting.

34. Philip Rogers also uses this play on the title of Conrad's novel in his essay '*No Longer at Ease*: Chinua Achebe's "Heart of Whiteness"', in, ed., Michael Parker and Roger Starkey, eds., *Postcolonial Literatures Achebe, Ngugi, Desai, Walcott* (Basingstoke: Macmillan, 1995), pp. 53–64.

35. Aidoo, *Our Sister Killjoy*, 28–9.

36. Dr Christian Barnard was a white South African surgeon who carried out the first open-heart transplant in 1967. The heart was from a black road accident victim and was given to a white patient.

37. Aidoo, *Our Sister Killjoy*, p. 112.

38. Ibid., p. 133.

39. Bessie Head, *The Collector of Treasures and Other Botswana Village Tales* (London: Heinemann, 1977).

40. Ibid., pp. 72–3.

41. Derek Walcott, 'Crusoe's Island', *Collected Poems, 1948–1984* (London: Faber and Faber, 1992), p. 69.

42. Derek, Walcott, 'Crusoe's Journal', in *Collected Poems*, p. 94.

43. Robert Hamner, ed., *Critical Perspectives on Derek Walcott* (Washington, DC: Three Continents Press, 1993), pp. 33–40.

44. V. S. Naipaul, *The Overcrowded Barracoon* (London: Andre Deutsch, 1972), pp. 203–7.

45. Boehmer, *Colonial and Postcolonial Literature*, p. 172.
46. Sandra Gilbert and Susan Gubar, *The Madwoman in the Attic: The Woman Writer and the Nineteenth-Century Literary Imagination* (New Haven: Yale University Press, 1979).
47. Fraser, *Lifting the Sentence*, p. 202.
48. For a helpful discussion of the concept of 'limited histories' in the Canadian context and with specific reference to Margaret Atwood, see Elodie Rousselot, *Re-writing Women into Canadian History: Margaret Atwood and Anne Hébert* (Canterbury: University of Kent PhD dissertation, 2004).

4   Authorizing the self: postcolonial autobiographical writing

1. See Jean-Paul Sartre, *Black Orpheus*, trans. Samuel Allen (Paris: Présence Africaine, 1956), pp. 50–1.
2. Philip Holden, 'Imagined Individuals: National Autobiography and Postcolonial Self-Fashioning', *Working Paper Series*, 13 (Asia Research Institute, National University of Singapore, 2003), p. 2. Holden discusses autobiography with specific reference to Nehru, Nkrumah and the Indonesian leader Sukarno.
3. Ibid., p. 5.
4. As Holden points out, this masculine/feminine relationship in terms of state and nation in Nkrumah's autobiography was in part constructed by his private secretary, Erica Powell, who later claimed that the narrative was made up from 'bits of a scattered mosaic, a series of interviews, and historical research which she then pieced together to give a coherent account'. See Holden, 'Imagined Individuals', p. 13, and Erica Powell, *Private Secretary (Female) Gold Coast* (New York: St Martin's Press, 1984), p. 83.
5. Gayatri Chakravorty Spivak, 'Three Women's Texts and Circumfession', in *Postcolonialism and Autobiography*, ed. Alfred Hornung and Ernstpeter Ruhe (Amsterdam: Rodopi, 1998), p. 7.
6. Ama Ata Aidoo, *Our Sister Killjoy: or Reflections from a Black-eyed Squint* (Harlow: Longman, 1977), p. 12.
7. Frantz Fanon, *Black Skin, White Masks*, trans. Charles Lam Markmann (New York: Grove Press, 1967), pp. 111–12.
8. Frantz Fanon, *The Wretched of the Earth*, trans. Constance Farrington (New York: Grove Press, 1968), p. 203.
9. W. B. Yeats, 'A Dialogue of Self and Soul', in Yeats, *Yeats's Poems*, ed. and annotated A. N. Jeffares (London and Basingstoke: Macmillan, 1989), p. 350.
10. Lady Augusta Gregory, *Our Irish Theatre* (New York: Capricorn Books, 1965), pp. 8–9.
11. W. B. Yeats, *Autobiographies* (New York: Macmillan, 1953), p. 132.
12. James Joyce, *A Portrait of the Artist as a Young Man* (New York: Viking, 1964), pp. 220–1.
13. James Olney, *Tell Me Africa* (Princeton: Princeton University Press, 1973), pp. vii–viii.

14. Quoted by Declan Kiberd, in *Inventing Ireland* (London: Jonathan Cape, 1995), p. 327.

15. Robert Fraser, *Lifting the Sentence: A Poetics of Postcolonial Fiction* (Manchester: Manchester University Press, 2000), p. 66.

16. Ibid., p. 77.

17. James Olney, *Metaphors of Self: The Meaning of Autobiography* (Princeton: Princeton University Press, 1972), p. 21.

18. Olney, *Tell Me Africa*, p. viii.

19. George Lamming, *In the Castle of My Skin* (Ann Arbor: University of Michigan Press, 1994), p. xxxix.

20. Ibid., p. xxxvii.

21. Ngugi wa Thiong'o, 'George Lamming's *In the Castle of My Skin*' in Ngugi, *Homecoming: Essays on African and Caribbean Literature, Culture and Politics* (London: Heinemann, 1972), pp. 110–26.

22. Kirsten Holst Petersen and Anna Rutherford, eds., *A Double Colonisation: Colonial and Post-Colonial Women's Writing* (Sydney and Oxford: Dangeroo Press, 1986).

23. Alison Donnell, *Twentieth Century Caribbean Literature: Critical Moments in Anglophone Literary History* (London: Routledge, 2006), p. 182.

24. Henry Lawson, 'Preface', Miles Franklin, *My Brilliant Career* (Edinburgh: Blackwoods, 1901), p. vi.

25. Quoted by Delys Bird in 'Miles Franklin', in *Dictionary of Literary Biography, Volume 230: Australian Literature, 1788–1914*, ed. Selina Samuels (Detroit: Gale Group, 2000), pp. 113–30.

26. Ian Henderson, 'Gender, Genre, and Sybylla's Performative Identity in Miles Franklin's *My Brilliant Career*', *Australian Literary Studies* 18:2 (October 1997), p. 167.

27. Fraser, *Lifting the Sentence*, p. 69.

28. Karen Blixen, *Out of Africa* (London: Jonathan Cape, 1964), p. 3.

29. Gillian Whitlock, *The Intimate Empire: Reading Women's Autobiography* (London: Cassell, 2000), p. 132.

30. Sally Morgan, *My Place* (London: Virago, 1988), p. 11.

31. Ibid., p. 12.

32. Ibid., p. 13.

33. Ibid., p. 135.

34. Ibid., p. 181.

35. Ibid., p. 233.

36. Bernardine Evaristo, *Lara* (Tunbridge Wells: Angela Roy Publishing, 1997). Evaristo's protagonist, like the author, has a Nigerian father and Irish mother; both are brought up in the same London suburbs, and both have seven brothers and sisters. Both have also made trips to Nigeria and Brazil.

37. Ibid., p. 140.

38. Neluka Silva, 'The Anxieties of Hybridity: Michael Ondaatje's *Running in the Family*', *The Journal of Commonwealth Literature* 37:2 (2002), pp. 71–84.

39. Michael Ondaatje, *Running in the Family* (London: Picador, 1982), pp. 70–1.
40. For a detailed analysis of Ondaatje's text in terms of its performativity, see S. Leigh Matthews, '"The Bright Bone of Dream": Drama, Performativity, Ritual, and Community in Michael Ondaatje's *Running in the Family*', *Biography* 23:2 (Spring 2000), pp. 352–71.
41. Tobias Döring, 'The Passage of the Eye/I: David Dabydeen, V. S. Naipaul, and the Tombstones of Parabiography,' in, eds., Alfred Hornung and Ernstpeter Ruhe *Postcolonialism and Autobiography* (Amsterdam: Rodopi, 1998), pp. 158–9.
42. Linda Anderson, *Autobiography* (London: Routledge, 2004), p. 116. Anderson is here citing Paul Gilroy, *The Black Atlantic*; *Modernity and Double Consciousness* (Cambridge, MA: Harvard University Press, 1993), p. 117.

5   Situating the self: landscape and place

1. Edward Said, 'Yeats and Decolonisation', in Terry Eagleton, Fredric Jameson and Said, *Nationalism, Colonialism, and Literature* (Minneapolis: University of Minnesota Press, 1990), p. 77.
2. Seamus Deane, *Celtic Revivals: Essays in Modern Irish Literature* (London: Faber and Faber, 1987), p. 38.
3. Daniel Corkery, *Synge and Anglo-Irish Literature* (Cork: Cork University Press, 1966), p. 14.
4. Seamus Heaney, *Opened Ground: Poems 1966–1996* (London: Faber and Faber, 1998), p. 125.
5. Declan Kiberd, *Inventing Ireland* (London: Jonathan Cape, 1995), pp. 592–3.
6. Ibid., p. 593.
7. Seamus Heaney, 'Punishment', *Opened Ground*, pp. 117–18.
8. Seamus Heaney, 'Sweeney in Flight', *Opened Ground*, p. 196. Sweeney also becomes the inspiration for Flann O'Brien's wonderfully comic and parodic novel, *At Swim-Two-Birds* (1939).
9. Wole Soyinka, 'Death at Dawn', in Gerald Moore and Ulli Beier, eds., *Modern Poetry from Africa* (Harmondsworth: Penguin, 1968), pp. 145–6.
10. Perhaps there is a suppressed reference and contrast in lines 11–14 of this poem to T. S. Eliot's *The Waste Land* (1922), and specifically Eliot's invocation of the faceless throngs that cross London Bridge in the morning fog, and his exclamation, 'I did not know that death had undone so many.'
11. Judith Wright, *Preoccupations in Australian Poetry* (Melbourne: Oxford University Press, 1966), p. xi.
12. Chinua Achebe, *Arrow of God* (London: Heinemann International, 1974), p. 29.
13. Marcus Clarke, *Stories*, ed. Michael Wilding (Sydney: Hale & Iremonger, 1983), pp. 3–4.
14. Patrick White, *Voss* (Harmondsworth: Penguin, 1980), p. 448.
15. Ibid., p. 446.

16. Barron Field, 'The Kangaroo', in Les Murray, ed., *The New Oxford Book of Australian Poetry* (Melbourne: Oxford University Press, 1986), p. 6. First published in *First Fruits* (1819).

17. *The Examiner*, 16 January 1820.

18. From 'The Dream By the Fountain', quoted by G. A. Wilkes, 'Introduction', *The Colonial Poets* (Sydney: Angus & Robertson, 1974), pp. iii–iv.

19. Charles Harpur, 'To the Lyre of Australia', quoted by Judith Wright in *Preoccupations in Australian Poetry*, p. 8. From a Harpur manuscript entitled 'Songs, Odes and Other Lyrics' (1863), Mitchell Library, Sydney, Australia.

20. From the manuscript of Harpur's unpublished book *Ago*, quoted by Judith Wright in *Preoccupations in Australian Poetry*, p. 9. Harpur's view of Tennyson as a gentleman poet and an inappropriate model for Australian poets bears interesting similarities with Walt Whitman's rejection of Tennyson as 'choked', buttoned-up and undemocratic.

21. From 'Charles Harpur', in Wilkes, ed., *The Colonial Poets*, p. 87.

22. 'Evelyn' (pseudonym for George Oakley); review in the *Colonial Monthly*, [October 1869], quoted by Ken Goodwin in 'Henry Kendall', *Dictionary of Literary Biography, Volume 230: Australian Literature, 1788–1914*, ed. Selina Samuels (Detroit: Bruccoli Clark Layman Gale Group, 2001), pp. 193–207.

23. Henry Kendall. 'Bell-Birds', in Wilkes, ed., *The Colonial Poets*, pp. 102–3.

24. Wright, *Preoccupations in Australian Poetry*, p. 46.

25. W. B. Spencer and F. J. Gillen, *The Arunta* (London: Macmillan, 1927). First published as *The Native Tribes of Central Australia* in 1899.

26. Quoted by Brian Elliott in 'Introduction', *The Jindyworobaks*, ed. Elliott (Brisbane: University of Queensland Press, 1979), p. xxvii.

27. Ingamells's 'Australia' can be contrasted with a poem of the same title by the Australian poet and Professor of Literature, A. D. Hope. Hope's 'Australia' berates Australians as 'second-rate Europeans', and he believed that a mature Australian consciousness should embrace and develop European traditions.

28. Rex Ingamells, 'Australia', in Ingamells, *The Jindyworobaks*, pp. 22–3. The aboriginal words used are here glossed by Brian Elliot according to their Jindyworobak usage, rather than 'anthropological and linguistic authority'.

> *alchera, alcheringa*: the mythical dreamtime, the eternal spirit of the dreamtime
> *birrahlee*: a small child
> *didgeridoo*: a drone pipe
> *tjurunga*: a small decorated object of wood or stone, highly sacred and secret, of personal significance and related to sacred traditions and dreamtime ancestry *(The Jindyworobaks*, p. 317)

Other words of aboriginal derivation have entered a more general Australian vocabulary and would have been familiar to white Australian readers even as they recognized the aboriginal reference. Thus 'mallee' designates a species of small and hardy eucalyptus tree, 'billabong' is the name for a stagnant pool or backwater, a 'gunyah' is a small tentlike structure constructed from bark and branches, and a 'lubra' is an aboriginal woman.

29. 'Australia', Sections III and I.
30. Brian Elliot, 'Introduction', *The Jindyworobaks*, p. xxv.
31. Katharine Susannah Pritchard, *Coonardoo* (Sydney: Angus & Robertson, 1975), p. 1.
32. Ibid., p. 133.
33. Judith Wright, *Born of the Conquerors: Selected Essays* (Canberra: Aboriginal Studies Press, 1991), p. xi.
34. Ibid., p. xi.
35. Judith Wright, 'Bora Ring', *Collected Poems 1942–1985* (Sydney: Angus & Robertson, 1994), p. 8
36. From 'Nigger's Leap, New England', *Collected Poems,* pp. 15–16.
37. From 'Bullocky', *Collected Poems*, p. 17.
38. From 'South of My Days', *Collected Poems*, p. 20.
39. Vivian Smith, *The Oxford History of Australian Literature* (Oxford: Oxford University Press, 1981), p. 393.
40. Judith Wright, 'Currawong', *Collected Poems*, p. 166.
41. Quoted in the entry for Les A. Murray, *Contemporary Authors Online* (Gale Group, 2001), p. 1.
42. Neil Corcoran, *Times Literary Supplement,* 22 August 1986, quoted in the entry for Les A. Murray, *Contemporary Authors Online*, pp. 4–5.
43. Judith Wright, 'Lyrebirds', *Collected Poems,* p. 178.
44. Les A. Murray, 'Lyrebird', *Collected Poems* (Manchester: Carcanet Press, 1998), 371.
45. From 'The Cows on Killing Day', *Collected Poems*, p. 381.
46. From 'Song Cycle of the Moon-Bone', in Les A. Murray, ed., *The New Oxford Book of Australian Poetry Verse* (Oxford University Press, 1986), p. 242.
47. Les A. Murray, 'The Human Hair-Thread', in *Persistence in Folly: Selected Prose Writings* (Sydney: Angus & Roberston, 1986), p. 24.
48. See, for example, Ashok Bery's chapter on Les Murray in *Postcolonial Poetry and Cultural Translation* (Basingstoke: Palgrave Macmillan, 2007).
49. Paula Burnett, *Derek Walcott: Politics and Poetics* (Gainesville: University of Florida Press, 2000), p. 44, and Patricia Ismond, *Abandoning Dead Metaphors: The Caribbean Phase of Derek Walcott's Poetry* (Barbados, Jamaica, Trinidad and Tobago: University of West Indies Press, 2001), chapter 3.
50. From Derek Walcott 'The Castaway', *Collected Poems, 1948–1984* (London: Faber and Faber, 1992), p. 58.
51. Derek Walcott, *Fragments from the Antilles* (London: Faber and Faber, 1993), pp. 10–11.
52. From 'Names', *Collected Poems,* pp. 307–8.
53. Thomas Docherty, 'The Place's Fault', in Ondrej Pilný and Clare Wallace, eds., *Global Ireland* (Prague: Litteraria Pragensia, 2005), p. 18.

6 Appropriating the word: language and voice

1. Frantz Fanon, *Black Skin, White Masks*, trans. C. L. Markmann (New York: Grove Press, 1967), pp. 17–18.
2. James Joyce, *A Portrait of the Artist as a Young Man* (Harmondsworth: Penguin, 1975), p. 189.
3. Mikhail Bakhtin, 'Discourse in the Novel', in Bakhtin, *The Dialogic Imagination: Four Essays*, ed. Michael Holquist, trans. Holquist and Caryl Emerson (Austin: University of Texas Press, 1981), pp. 293–4.
4. Imamu Amiri Baraka, *Raise, Race, Rays, Raze* (New York: William Morrow, 1972), p. 60.
5. Obianjunwa Wali, 'The Dead End of African Literature', *Transition 10* (1963), p. 13
6. Ibid.
7. Ngugi took a leading role in deanglicizing the school and university curriculum in Kenya. When he first became a lecturer at Makere University in Uganda, no African books were included in the literature curriculum; nor were there any in the secondary school syllabus. Here, like Achebe, he argued against the assumption that literature is 'universal', but rather saw the value of literature in its detailed and concrete depiction of a community in a particular place and a particular historical moment seeking to understand and create itself. Hence it is crucial for African students to encounter works which hold up the mirror to their own societies from an African point of view. Ngugi also introduced the study of local oral literatures into the curriculum, and believed that these should be central rather than peripheral for students of literature.
8. Ngugi wa Thiong'o *Writers in Politics* (London: Heinemann, 1981), pp. 53–4.
9. Ibid., p. 59.
10. W. B. Yeats, *Uncollected Prose*, ed. John Frayne (New York: Macmillan, 1970), p. 256.
11. Ibid., p. 257.
12. From the Irish Literary Theatre Manifesto, quoted in Lady Augusta Gregory, *Our Irish Theatre* (New York: Capricorn Books, 1965), pp. 8–9.
13. Chinua Achebe, *Things Fall Apart* (London: Heineman, 1976), p. 164.
14. Chinua Achebe, *Collected Poems* (New York: Anchor Books, 2004), pp. 43 and 82.
15. Chinua Achebe, 'The African Writer and the English Language', in Achebe, *Morning Yet on Creation Day* (London: Heinemann, 1975), p. 62.
16. Ibid., pp. 61–2.
17. Chinua Achebe, 'Modern Nigerian Literature', in Saburi O. Biobaku, ed., *The Living Culture of Nigeria* (London: Nelson, 1976), pp. 47–51.
18. Salman Rushdie 'Introduction' Rushdie and Elizabeth West, eds., *The Vintage Book of Indian Writing, 1947–1997* (London: Vintage, 1997), p. x.
19. See Fredric Jameson, 'Third World Literature and the Era of Multinational Capital', *Social Text 5* (1986), pp. 65–88. See also the response to this essay by Aijaz Ahmad, *In Theory: Classes, Nations, Literatures* (London: Verso, 1992), where Ahmad discusses the significance of vernacular works in India, and the limitations of postcolonial or

Commonwealth studies which acknowledge the existence only of English-language writing.

20. Rushdie, ed., *The Vintage Book of Indian Writing*, p. xiii.

21. William Dean Howells, 'Introduction', Paul Laurence Dunbar, *The Complete Poems of Paul Laurence Dunbar* (New York: Dodd, Mead, & Co., 1920), p. ix.

22. Fanon, *Black Skin, White Masks*, pp. 31 and 35.

23. Walter Jekyll, 'Preface', Wayne Cooper, ed., *The Dialect Poetry of Claude McKay* (New York: Harcourt, Brace & World, 1972), p. 1.

24. James Weldon Johnson, 'Preface', *The Book of American Negro Poetry* (New York: Harcourt, Brace & World, 1931), p. 1.

25. Ibid., pp. 41–2.

26. Viktor Schlovsky, 'Art as Technique', in Schlovsky, *Russian Formalist Criticism: Four Essays*, ed. and trans. Lee Lemon (Lincoln: University of Nebraska Press, 1965).

27. J. M. Synge, 'Preface', *The Playboy of the Western World* (London: Dent, 1949), p. 107.

28. Kamau Brathwaite, *History of the Voice: The Development of Nation Language in Anglophone Caribbean Poetry* (London: New Beacon Books, 1984), pp. 5–6.

29. David Mavia, 'Nyof, Nyof and Shifting Visions: Of English Language Usage in Kenya', *Kunapipi: Journal of Postcolonial Writing*, 27:1 (2005), pp. 121–9.

30. Sujatta Bhatt, *Point No Point* (Manchester: Carcanet, 1997), pp. 32–40, and G. V. Desani, *All About H. Hatterr* (London: Penguin, 1986).

31. Brathwaite, *History of the Voice*, p. 10.

32. Ibid., p. 16.

33. Ibid., p. 17.

34. Ibid., p. 19.

35. Ibid., p. 30.

36. T. S. Eliot, *Collected Poems, 1909–1935* (London: Faber and Faber, 1936), pp. 74–5.

37. (Edward) Kamau Brathwaite, *The Arrivants* (London: Oxford University Press, 1973), p. 5.

38. From 'The Wings of a Dove', Brathwaite, *The Arrivants*, p. 43.

39. Jahan Ramazani, *The Hybrid Muse: Postcolonial Poetry in English* (Chicago: University of Chicago Press, 2001), p. 106.

40. Louise Bennett, as cited by Carolyn Cooper in 'Noh Lickle Twang: An Introduction to the Poetry of Louise Bennett', *World Literature Written in English* 17 (1978), pp. 317–27.

41. Ramazani, *The Hybrid Muse*, p. 106.

42. Louise Bennett, *Jamaica Labrish* (Jamaica: Sangster's Book Stores, 1966), pp. 209–10.

43. Ibid., pp. 212–13.

44. Ibid., pp. 179–80.

45. www.mentomusic.com.

46. Eric Doumerc, 'Louise Bennett and the Mento Tradition,' *ARIEL: A Review of International English Literature* 31:4 (October 2000), p. 29.

47. Interview with Dennis Scott, quoted by Carolyn Cooper in 'Caribbean Poetry in English: 1900–1976', *World Literature Written in English* 23 (Spring, 1984), pp. 414–16.

48. Interview with Marlies Glaser, quoted by Denise deCaires Narain in *Contemporary Caribbean Women's Poetry: Making Style* (London: Routledge, 2002), p. 51.

49. Nettleford, 'Introduction', in Bennett *Jamaica Labrish*, and Mervyn Morris, 'On Reading Louise Bennett Seriously', reprinted in Alison Donnell and Sarah Lawson Welsh, eds., *The Routledge Reader in Caribbean Literature* (London: Routledge, 1996), pp. 194–7.

50. DeCaires Narain, *Contemporary Caribbean Women's Poetry*, pp. 51–2.

51. Susanne Mühleisen, *Creole Discourse: Exploring Creole Discourse and Change across Caribbean English-Lexicon Creoles* (Amsterdam and Philadelphia: John Benjamins Publishing Company, 2002), p. 191.

52. Ibid., pp. 191–8.

53. DeCaires Narain, *Contemporary Caribbean Women's Poetry*, p. 64.

54. From 'Me Cyaan Believe It', in E. A. Markham, ed., *Hinterlands: Caribbean Poetry from the West Indies and Britain* (Newcastle upon Tyne: Bloodaxe Books, 1989), pp. 286–7.

55. Michael Smith, 'Interview with Michael Smith by Mervyn Morris', in *Hinterlands*, p. 277.

56. George Lamming, *The Pleasures of Exile* (London: Michael Joseph, 1960), p. 45.

57. Marlene Nourbese Philip, *She Tries Her Tongue, Her Silence Softly Breaks* (Charlottetown, Prince Edward Island: Ragweed, 1989), p. 18.

7   Narrating the nation: form and genre

1. Wilson Harris, *Tradition, the Writer, and Society: Critical Essays* (London: New Beacon Press, 1967), p. 28–9.

2. Ibid., p. 29.

3. Ibid., pp. 39–40.

4. C. L. R. James, 'Introduction to Tradition and the West Indian Novel', in James, *Tradition, the Writer, and Society*, p. 74.

5. Wilson Harris, 'The Frontier on Which *Heart of Darkness* Stands', in Robert Kimbrough, ed., *Joseph Conrad: Heart of Darkness* (New York: Norton, 1988), pp. 263–4.

6. Elleke Boehmer, *Colonial and Postcolonial Literature* (Oxford: Oxford University Press, 1995), p. 199.

7. John Barnes, ed., *Joseph Furphy*, (St Lucia, Queensland: University of Queensland Press, 1981), p. xv.

8. Ironically, this name for a rumourmonger was replaced by another word for a rumour or false story, a 'furphy', said to have originated from the fact that Joseph Furphy's brother John manufactured water carts used during World War I, and around which soldiers gathered and gossiped.

9. *Such is Life* in *Joseph Furphy*, ed. Barnes, p. 271.

10. Ibid.

11. Barnes, ed., 'Introduction', *Joseph Furphy*, p. xvii.

12. Declan Kiberd, 'Introduction', James Joyce, *Ulysses: Annotated Student Edition* (London: Penguin, 1992), p. x.

13. J. M. Synge, *The Collected Letters*, ed. Ann Saddlemyer (Oxford: Clarendon Press, 1983), p. 76.

14. Kiberd, 'Introduction', *Ulysses*, p. xvi.

15. Ibid., p.xxx.

16. Joyce, *Ulysses: Annotated Student Edition*, p. 42.

17. Ibid., p. 430.

18. Quoted by Edward Baugh in 'The Poem as an Autobiographical Novel: Derek Walcott's "Another Life" in relation to Wordsworth's "Prelude" and Joyce's "Portrait."', in C. D. Narasimhaiah, ed., *Awakened Conscience: Studies in Commonwealth Literature* (New Delhi: Sterling, 1978), p. 230.

19. Tobias Döring, *Caribbean-English Passages: Intertextuality in a Postcolonial Tradition* (London: Routledge, 2002), p. 182.

20. Derek Walcott, *Omeros* (London: Faber and Faber, 1990), p. 64.

21. Ibid.

22. Ibid., p. 271.

23. John Figueroa, '*Omeros*', in Stewart Brown, ed., *The Art of Derek Walcott* (Bridgend: Seren Books, 1991), p. 195.

24. Döring, *Caribbean-English Passages*, p. 184.

25. Walcott, *Omeros*, p. 293.

26. The story of Philoctetes also provides the overarching analogy and title for Edmund Wilson's influential collection of critical essays, *The Wound and the Bow* (1941).

27. Walcott, *Omeros*, p. 3.

28. Ibid., p. 4.

29. W. B. Yeats, 'Anima Hominis', in *W. B. Yeats: Selected Criticism*. ed. A. Norman Jeffares (London: Macmillan, 1976), p. 170.

30. Walcott, *Omeros*, p. 295.

31. Ibid., p. 323.

32. Ibid., p. 325.

33. Salman Rushdie, *Salman Rushdie Interviews: A Sourcebook of His Ideas*, ed. Pradyumna S. Chauhan (Westport, CT.: Greenwood Press, 2001), p. 22.

34. Benedict Anderson, *Imagined Communities: Reflections on the Origin and Spread of Nationalism* (London: Verso, 1983). Anderson's book focuses mainly on the significance of newspapers and novels in the creation of a sense of belonging to a nation in Latin America and Indonesia.

35. Interview with Rani Dharker, *Salman Rushdie Interviews*, p. 52.

36. Ibid., p. 57.

37. Interview with Kumkum Sangari, *Salman Rushdie Interviews*, p. 64.

38. Ibid., p. 64.

39. Ibid., p. 69.
40. Salman Rushdie, *Midnight's Children* (London: Picador, 1982), p. 57.
41. Ibid., p. 9.
42. British estimates for the casualties which resulted when General Michael Dyer ordered his troops to fire on a group of Indian protesters who had gathered in Amritsar were 379 killed and several hundred wounded; Indian sources gave the numbers as more than 1,000 killed and more than 1,000 wounded.
43. Rushdie, *Midnight's Children*, p. 36.
44. Michael Gorra, *After Empire: Scott, Naipaul, Rushdie* (Chicago: University of Chicago Press, 1997), p. 118.
45. Ibid., p. 120.
46. For a detailed discussion of Rushdie's critique of earlier anticolonial and nationalist writers and artists, and of their search for 'authenticity', see Timothy Brennan, *Salman Rushdie and the Third World: Myths of the Nation*, (Basingstoke: Macmillan, 1989), chapter 4.

8   Rewriting her story: nation and gender

1. Salman Rushdie, *Midnight's Children* (London: Picador, 1982), p. 25.
2. Quoted by P. Balaswamy in 'A Post-Modern, Provocative, Metropolitan Mother India: Aurora Zogoiby of Rushdie's *The Moor's Last Sigh*', in Rajeshwar Mittapalli and Joel Kuortti, eds., *Salman Rushdie: New Critical Insights*, 2 vols. (New Delhi: Atlantic Publishers, 2003), II, p. 52.
3. Ranjana Ash, 'The Search for Freedom in Indian Women's Writing,' in Susheila Nasta, ed., *Motherlands: Black Women's Writing from Africa, the Caribbean and South Asia* (London: The Women's Press, 1991), p. 153.
4. Quoted by Ashis Nandy in *The Intimate Enemy: Loss and Recovery of Self Under Colonialism* (Delhi: Oxford University Press, 1983), p. 92.
5. Ibid., p. 91.
6. Elleke Boehmer, 'Stories of Women and Mothers', in Nasta, ed., *Motherlands*, p. 6.
7. Buchi Emecheta, 'Culture Conflict', *New Society*, 4 September 1984.
8. Ash, 'The Search for Freedom', p. 153.
9. Joseph Conrad, *Heart of Darkness* (London: Penguin, 1973), p. 87.
10. For images of Britain and Hibernia (Ireland), see C. L. Innes, *Women and Nation in Irish Literature and Society, 1880–1935* (Hemel Hempstead: Harvester Wheatsheaf, 1993).
11. Gayatri Chakravorty Spivak, 'Can the Subaltern Speak?' in Cary Nelson and Lawrance Grossberg, eds., *Marxism and the Interpretation of Culture* (Basingstoke: Macmillan, 1988), pp. 271–313.
12. Matthew Arnold, *On the Study of Celtic Literatures* (London: Smith, Elder, 1891), pp. 76–82. Arnold, like Yeats, was influenced by Ernest Renan's *La Poésie des races*

celtiques (1854), a work which also characterized the Celts as essentially feminine – that is, shy, delicate, sensitive and imaginative.

13. Elleke Boehmer *Colonial and Postcolonial Literature* (Oxford: Oxford University Press, 1995), p. 86.

14. Quoted in L. Perry Curtis, Jr., *Anglo-Saxons and Celts: A Study of Anti-Irish Prejudice in Victorian England* (Bridgeport, CT: Conference on British Studies, 1968), p. 45.

15. Nandy, *The Intimate Enemy*, p. 41.

16. Ibid., p. 41.

17. Elleke Boehmer, *Stories of Women: Gender and Narrative in the Postcolonial Nation* (Manchester: Manchester University Press, 2005), p. 32.

18. Boehmer, 'Stories of Women and Mothers', p. 6.

19. Eavan Boland, 'Mother Ireland', in Boland, *The Lost Land* (Manchester: Carcanet, 1998), p. 39.

20. Eavan Bolnd, 'Outside History', *PN Review* 17:1 (September/October 1990), p. 24.

21. Ibid., p. 22. Boland's argument about the dominance of a male tradition and its detrimental effects has been vigorously contested by the Northern Irish poet and academic Edna Longley in *The Living Stream: Literature and Revisionism in Ireland* (Newcastle upon Tyne: Bloodaxe Books, 1994), pp. 187–8.

22. Eavan Boland, 'The Achill Woman', in Boland, *Outside History* (Manchester: Carcanet, 1990), p. 27.

23. Ibid., p. 28.

24. Cited in Hans Zell, Carol Bundy and Virginia Coulon, eds., *A New Reader's Guide to African Literature*, in rev. edn, (New York: Holmes & Meier, 1983), p. 358.

25. Chinua Achebe, *A Man of the People* (London: Heinemann, 1966), p. 91.

26. Ama Ata Aidoo, Interview with Sarah Chetin, *Wasafiri* 6/7, (1987), p. 27.

27. 'Ama Ata Aidoo – In Conversation', Interview with Sarah Modebe, *New African* 288 (September 1991), p. 40.

28. Ketu H. Katrak, 'Afterword', Ama Ata Aidoo, *No Sweetness Here and Other Stories* (New York: Feminist Press, 1995), p. 141.

29. Ama Ata Aidoo, in Cosmo Pieterse and Dennis Duerden, eds., *African Writers Talking* (New York: Africana Publishing, 1972), pp. 23–4.

30. Ama Ata Aidoo, 'The Message', *No Sweetness Here and Other Stories*, p. 38.

31. Katrak, 'Afterword', *No Sweetness Here and Other Stories*, p. 143.

32. Boehmer 'Stories of Women and Mothers', p. 12.

33. However, it should be noted that there have been some notable exceptions to this trend by male Africanists, in particular Lloyd Brown, whose seminal *Women Writers in Black Africa* (Westport, CT.: Greenwood Press, 1981) has been influential. Chinua Achebe ensured that Flora Nwapa's work was included in the Heinemann African Writers Series, and Eldred Jones, as editor of *African Literature Today*, has included special issues on African women's writing.

34. Ama Ata Aidoo, Interview with Adeola James, in James, ed., *In Their Own Voices: African Women Writers Talk* (London: Heinemann, 1990), pp. 11–12.

35. Dambudzo Marechera, *House of Hunger* (London: Heinemann, 1978), p. 93.

36. Tsitsi Dangarembga, *Nervous Conditions* (Emeryville, CA: Seal Press, 1989), p. 1.

37. Boehmer, *Stories of Women,* p. 182.

38. 'Interview with the Author', Dangarembga, *Nervous Conditions,* p. 207.

39. Ibid., p. 206.

40. Dangarembga, *Nervous Conditions,* p. 1.

41. Ibid., p. 15.

42. Ama Ata Aidoo, *Our Sister Killjoy: Or Reflections from a Black-eyed Squint* (Harlow: Longman, 1977), p. 40.

43. C. L. Innes and Caroline Rooney, 'African Writing and Gender,' in Paul Hyland and M. H. Msiska, eds., *Writing and Africa* (London: Longman, 1997), p. 203.

44. Ibid., pp. 204–5.

45. Bapsi Sidhwa, Interview with David Montenegro, *Massachussetts Review* 31:4 (Winter 1990), pp. 513–33.

46. Bapsi Sidhwa, *Ice-Candy-Man* (London: Penguin, 1989), p. 93.

47. Ibid., pp. 236–37.

48. Ibid., p. 87.

49. Ibid., p. 147. In the interview quoted above, Sidhwa says, 'And in *Ice-Candy-Man*, I was just redressing in a small way, a very grievous wrong that had been done to Jinah [*sic*] and Pakistanis by many Indian and British writers. They've dehumanized him, made him a symbol of the sort of person who brought about the partition of India, a person who was hard-headed and obstinate. Whereas, in reality, he was the only constitutional man who didn't sway crowds just by rhetoric, and tried to do everything by the British standards of constitutional law.

    Gandhi totally Hinduized the whole partition movement. This excluded the Muslims there. He brought religion into the Congress Party. And Jinah, who was one of the founders of the party, found he had to edge away from it because it was changing into a Hindu party.'

50. In an interview with Arnab Chakladar, Hariharan comments, 'Just because *The Thousand Faces of Night* or *When Dreams Travel* address the lives of women directly, or in the second case power politics in relation to gender, this does not mean that the other novels are not informed by questions of gender. I don't think I could write a single page that would not be informed by my beliefs, or for that matter, my confusions. My work grows out of my feminism and other political beliefs. Which doesn't mean a novel I write is some kind of handmaiden to ideology.' This conversation was conducted on 12 August 12 2005, and reproduced on www.anothersubcontinent.com.

51. Anita Desai, *Clear Light of Day* (London: Vintage, 2001), p. 5.

52. Ibid., p. 182.

53. Ibid., p. 153.

54. Nayantara Sahgal, 'The Schizophrenic Imagination', *Wasafiri* 11 (Spring 1990), p. 19.

9 Rewriting the nation: acknowledging economic and cultural diversity

1. Gayatri Chakravorty Spivak, 'Can the Subaltern Speak?', in Cary Nelson and Laurence Grossberg, eds., *Marxism and the Interpretation of Culture* (Chicago: University of Illinois Press, 1988), pp. 271–313.
2. Frantz Fanon, *The Wretched of the Earth*, trans. Constance Farrington (New York: Grove Press, 1968), p. 212.
3. Ibid., p. 214.
4. Chinua Achebe, 'The Role of the Writer in the New Nation', *Nigeria Magazine* 81 (1964), p. 157.
5. See Derek Wright, *Ayi Kwei Armah's Africa* ((London: Hans Zell, 1989), pp. 90–1, and Neil Lazarus, *Resistance in Postcolonial African Fiction* (New Haven: Yale University Press, 1990), pp. 46–79.
6. *Washenzi:* plural for *mshenzi*, a native from the interior.
7. *Vibarua:* plural for Arabic *kibarua*, a casual worker.
8. Abdulrazak Gurnah, *Paradise* (London: Hamish Hamilton, 1994), pp. 6–7.
9. Gayane Karen Merguerian and Afsaneh Najmabadi, 'Zulaykha and Yusuf: Whose "Best Story"?', *Journal of Middle Eastern Studies* 29:4 (November 1997), pp. 485–508.
10. Ibid., p. 485.
11. Ibid., p. 1.
12. Robert Fraser, *Lifting the Sentence* (Manchester: Manchester University Press, 2000), p. 64.
13. Gurnah, *Paradise*, p. 239.
14. Joseph Conrad, *Heart of Darkness* (Harmondsworth: Penguin, 1973), p. 85.
15. Gurnah, *Paradise*, p. 245.
16. *Paradise* has also been read as a critique of V. S. Naipaul's Conradian novel set in the Congo, *A Bend in the River* (1979).
17. Quoted in M. Brace, 'Question Marks Over the Empire's Decision', *The Independent*, 10 September, 1994, p. 24.
18. Susheila Nasta, 'Abdulrazak Gurnah, *Paradise*', in David Johnson, ed., *The Popular and the Canonical: Debating Twentieth-Century Literature, 1940–2000*, (London: Routledge, 2005), p. 315. Nasta's essay is the fullest and, in my view the most persuasive discussion of *Paradise* published to date.
19. Abdulrazak Gurnah quoted in Maya Jaggi, 'Glimpses of a Paradise Lost', *The Guardian*, 24 September 1994, p. 31.
20. Abdulrazak Gurnah, 'An Idea of the Past', *Moving Worlds: A Journal of Transcultural Writings*, Special Issue 'Reflections', 2:2, p. 16.
21. Elizabeth Maslen, 'Stories, Constructions, and Deconstructions': Abdulrazak Gurnah's *Paradise*', *Wasafiri* 24 (1996), p. 53.
22. Gurnah, *Paradise*, p. 83.
23. David Punter, *Postcolonial Imaginings* (Edinburgh: Edinburgh University Press), p. 36.

24. Gurnah, *Paradise*, p. 180.
25. Ibid., p. 181.
26. Ibid., pp. 236–7.
27. For a comprehensive study of writing by Maori and Samoan writers in New Zealand, see Michelle Keown, *Postcolonial Pacific Writing: Representations of the Body* (London: Routledge, 2005).
28. Albert Wendt, 'Tatauing the Colonial Body', *SPAN* 42–3 (1996), p. 26. I am indebted to Michelle Keown for bringing this quotation and essay by Wendt to my attention. See her discussion of it in her book cited above.
29. Robert McGill, *The Mysteries* (Toronto: McClelland and Stewart, 2004).

10   Transnational and black British writing: colonizing in reverse

1. George Lamming, *The Pleasures of Exile* (London: Michael Joseph, 1960), pp. 211–12.
2. James Berry, 'Migrant in London', in Berry, *Fractured Circles* (London: New Beacon Books, 1976), p. 12.
3. Ann Blake, 'Christina Stead', in Ann Blake, Leila Gandhi and Sue Thomas, eds., *England Through Colonial Eyes in Twentieth-Century Fiction* (Basingstoke: Macmillan, 2001), p. 113.
4. Christina Stead, *Ocean of Story: The Uncollected Stories of Christina Stead*, ed. R. G. Geering (Melbourne: Viking, 1985), p. 94.
5. Quoted by Ann Blake in, 'Christina Stead', p. 107. From Christina Stead, *A Web of Friendship: Selected Letters 1928–1973*, ed R. G. Geering (Pymble, NSW: Angus & Robertson, 1992), p. 74.
6. Samuel Selvon, *The Lonely Londoners* (London: Longman, 1956).
7. Ibid., pp. 125–6.
8. Selvon also published a number of novels and short stories set in his native Trinidad, and in 1975 produced in *Moses Ascending* a sharply satiric sequel to *The Lonely Londoners.*
9. Abdulrazak Gurnah, 'Writing and Place' (transcript of *Strangers in a Strange Land*, BBC Radio 4, 2001), *Wasafiri* 42 (Summer 2004), p. 59.
10. Derek Walcott, 'A Far Cry from Africa', *Collected Poems* (London: Faber and Faber, 1992), p. 17.
11. Salman Rushdie, 'Outside the Whale,' in Rushdie, *Imaginary Homelands: Essays and Criticism 1981–1991* (London: Granta, 1992), pp. 87–101.
12. George Lamming, *In the Castle of My Skin* (London: Longman, 1953).
13. George Lamming, *The Pleasures of Exile* (London: Michael Joseph, 1960).
14. For a fully documented study of the Caribbean Artists Movement and its influence, see Anne Walmsley, *The Caribbean Artists Movement, 1966–72* (London: New Beacon Press, 1992).
15. James Berry, *Lucy's Letters and Loving*, London and Port of Spain: New Beacon, 1982).

16. Susanne Mühleisen, *Creole Discourse: Exploring Prestige Formation and Change across Caribbean English-Lexicon Creoles* (Amsterdam and Philadelphia: John Benjamins Publishing Company, 2002), pp. 207–10.

17. Wilson Harris, 'Tradition and the West Indian Novel', in *Tradition, the Writer, and Society: Critical Essays* (London: New Beacon Press, 1967), pp. 28–47.

18. Susheila Nasta, 'Setting Up Home in a City of Words: Sam Selvon's London Novels', in A. Robert Lee, ed., *Other Britain, Other British* (London: Pluto, 1995), pp. 51–2.

19. William Trevor, Interview with Mira Stout, 'The Art of Fiction CVIII', in *Paris Review* 110 (1989), p. 131.

20. For a fuller discussion of Trevor's early London-based novels and short stories, see Julian Gitzen, 'The Truth-Tellers of William Trevor',: *Studies in Modern Fiction Critique* 21:1 (1979), pp. 59–72.

21. Hanif Kureishi, *The Buddha of Suburbia* (London: Faber and Faber, 1990), p. 3.

22. Homi Bhabha, *The Location of Culture* (London: Routledge, 1994), p. 86. Bhabha's comments on the Derridean term *différance* in relation to colonial and postcolonial discourse is also relevant to Kureishi's novel:

    'It unsettles any simplistic polarities or binarisms in identifying the exercise of power – Self/Other – and erases the analogical dimension in the articulation of sexual difference. It is empty of that depth of verticality that creates a totemic resemblance of form and content (*Abgrund*) ceaselessly renewed and replenished by the groundspring of history . . . [It] is nothing in itself; and it is this *structure of difference* that produces the hybridity of race and sexuality in the postcolonial discourse' (*Location of Culture*, p. 53).

23. Kureishi, *The Buddha of Suburbia*, p. 13

24. Ruvani Ranasinha, *Hanif Kureishi* (London: Northcote House, 2002), p. 64. See also the discussion of Kureishi's novels and their relation to other contemporary black British fiction as *Bildungsroman* by Mark Stein in *Black British Literature: Novels of Transformation* (Columbus: Ohio State University Press, 2004), pp. 108–42.

25. Ravinda Randawha, *A Wicked Old Woman* (London: The Women's Press, 1987), p. 4.

26. Mrs Abdul Karim is also commemorated in Rushdie's *The Satanic Verses* (London: Viking, 1988), p. 292, and in his essay 'An Unimportant Fire' in *Imaginary Homelands*, pp. 139–42.

27. Randawha, *A Wicked Old Woman* p. 30.

28. V. S. Naipaul, *The Middle Passage* (Harmondsworth: Penguin, 1969), p. 29.

29. Homi Bhabha, 'Re-Inventing Britain: A Manifesto,' in *British Studies Now (Re-Inventing Britain: Identity, Transnationalism, and the Arts)*, 9 (April 1997) (London: The British Council, 1997), p. 9. Reprinted, with an interview with Homi Bhabha and comments by Stuart Hall, in *Wasafiri* 29 (Spring 1999), pp. 38–43.

30. Rushdie, *The Satanic Verses*, p. 458.

31. Bhabha, *Wasafiri* 29, p. 43.

32. Stuart Hall, 'Cultural Identity and Diaspora', in Patrick Williams and Laura Chrisman, eds. *Colonial Discourse and Postcolonial Theory: A Reader* (Hemel Hempstead: Harvester Wheatsheaf, 1993), pp. 392–403.

33. Rushdie, *The Satanic Verses*, p. 292.
34. Leela Gandhi, '"Ellowen, Deeowen": Salman Rushdie and the Migrant's Desire', in Blake, Gandhi and Thomas, eds., *England Through Colonial Eyes*, p. 160.
35. Rushdie, *The Satanic Verses*, p. 292.
36. Ibid., p. 292.
37. Cornelia Sorabji, *Love and Life Behind the Purdah* (London: Fremantle & Co., 1901).
38. For a discussion of the changing use of 'Creole' in the British context, from forms clearly identifiable as belonging to specific West Indian locations, to a more generalized West Indian form, to 'black British' mingling East London, West Indian and Asian formations, see Susanne Mühleisen, 'What Makes an Accent Funny, and Why? Black British Englishes and Humour Televised', in Susanne Reichl and Mark Stein, eds., *Cheeky Fictions: Laughter and the Postcolonial* (Amsterdam and New York: Rodopi, 2005), pp. 225–43.
39. For an excellent discussion of Andrea Levy's novels and the *Bildungsroman* genre in black British fiction, see Stein, *Black British Literature*.
40. For an extended discussion of 'the devolved cultural territory' and diasporic communities in Britain over the past fifty years, see James Procter, *Dwelling Places: Postwar Black British Writing* (Manchester: Manchester University Press, 2003).

11   Citizens of the world: reading postcolonial literature

1. Richard Todd, *Consuming Fictions* (London: Bloomsbury, 1996), p. 83.
2. Aijaz Ahmad, *In Theory: Classes, Nations, Literatures* (London: Verso, 1992), pp. 95–122.
3. Graham Huggan, *The Postcolonial Exotic: Marketing the Margins* (London: Routledge, 2001), p. xii..
4. Ibid., p. 13.
5. Ibid., p. 4.
6. See Karin Barker, ed., *Africa's Hidden Histories: Everyday Literacy and Making the Self* (Bloomington: Indiana University Press, 2006), and Stephanie Newell, *West African Literature* (Oxford: Oxford University Press, 2006), chapter 7.
7. Huggan, *The Postcolonial Exotic*, p. 46.
8. See, for example, the international conference 'The Colonial and Post-Colonial Lives of the Book 1765–2005: Reaching the Margins', which was held at the Institute of English Studies in London from 3 to 5 November 2005, and the forthcoming book by Robert Fraser on this topic.
9. W. J. McCormack, 'Nightmares of History', in McCormack and Alastair Stead, eds., *James Joyce and Modern Literature* (London: Routledge & Kegan Paul, 1982), p. 88.
10. For a description of some of these works, see Maureen S. G. Hawkins, 'The Dramatic Treatment of Robert Emmet and Sarah Curran', in S. F. Gallagher, ed., *Women in Irish Legend, Life and Literature* (Gerrards Cross: Colin Smythe, 1983), pp. 125–37.
11. Quoted by Ruth Dudley Edwards in *Patrick Pearse: The Triumph of Failure* (London: Faber and Faber, 1979), p. 177.

12. James Joyce, *Ulysses* (Harmondsworth: Penguin, 1986), p. 254.

13. Ibid., p. 251.

14. Contemporary readers would have been likely to guess from his description and portrayal that Malachi Mulligan was a thinly disguised Oliver St John Gogarty; Michael Cusack, President of the Gaelic Athletic Association, was regularly referred to by his fellow Dubliners as 'the Citizen'.

15. John Nash, '"Hanging Over the Bloody Paper": Newspapers and Imperialism in *Ulysses*', in Howard Booth and Nigel Rigby, eds., *Modernism and Empire* (Manchester: Manchester University Press: 2000), pp. 175–96.

16. Joyce, *Ulysses*, p. xxx.

17. For a fuller discussion of Joyce and Yeats in relation to their appeal to a double audience, see my essay (from which some paragraphs have been excerpted here) 'Modernism, Ireland, and Empire: Yeats, Joyce and Their Implied Audiences', in Booth and Rigby, eds., *Modernism and Empire*, pp. 137–55.

18. Huggan, *The Postcolonial Exotic*, p. 46.

19. Fredric Jameson, 'Third World Literature and the Era of Multinational Capital', *Social Text* 5 (1986), pp. 65–88. For a recent defence of Jameson's essay as a base for constructing a more sophisticated hermeneutics of postcolonial texts, see Julie McGonegal, 'Postcolonial Metacritique: Jameson, Allegory and the Always-Already-Read Third World Text', *Interventions* 7:2 (2005), pp. 251–65

20. Ahmad, *In Theory*, pp. 95–122.

21. Huggan, *The Postcolonial Exotic*, p. 52

22. Sadly, it has been announced recently that Heinemann International will no longer produce the African Writers Series, and so is lost what has been a significant outlet for new writers from the African continent.

23. Cited by Kwame Anthony Appiah, *In My Father's House* (New York: Oxford University Press, 1992), p. 73

Glossary of terms used
(compiled by Kaori Nagai)

(Terms and names which receive individual definitions in this Glossary or more extensive entries in the Biographies section are asterisked). A fuller and more detailed glossary of terms relating to postcolonial studies can be found in John Thieme's *Post-Colonial Studies: The Essential Glossary* (London: Arnold, 2003), and *Key Concepts in Post-Colonial Studies* by Bill Ashcroft, Gareth Griffiths, and Helen Tiffin (London: Routledge, 1998). For definitions of more general literary terms, see Martin Gray, *A Dictionary of Literary Terms* (Harlow: Longman, 1992) or M. H. Abrams, *A Glossary of Literary Terms* (Boston: Heinle & Heinle, 2005).

Assimilation A form of colonizing process which aims to integrate indigenous populations by the imposition of the colonizer's language and values, and sometimes through intermarriage, in order to eventually make them disappear as incongruent or opposing constituents. The term also refers to the process of integrating immigrants and other ethnocultural minority groups into a dominant culture.

Berlin Conference An international conference (15 November 1884–26 February 1885) convened in Berlin under the chairmanship of the German Chancellor Bismarck, in order to reach agreements on the European colonization of, and trade in, Africa. The conference was attended by the representatives of twelve European nations, the United States and the Ottoman Empire; no African was present to represent the interests of Africans. The conference is said to have set the stage for the Scramble for Africa by allotting 'spheres of influence' to the major European powers and by laying down the ground rules for future annexations.

Black Arts Movement An artistic and literary branch of the Black Power Movement*, which came to prominence in the 1960s. Rejecting adherence to Western models, the movement sought to develop a 'black aesthetic', which was exclusively aimed at a black audience, and placed considerable emphasis on music, dance, theatre and performance poetry, the genres considered most appropriate to express African American experiences. It was named after the Black Arts Repertory Theatre/School, founded in 1965 by LeRoi Jones (Amiri Baraka), one of the movement's leaders. Other artists belonging to this movement include Ed Bullins, Larry Neal, Sonia Sanchez and Marvin X.

Black British An umbrella term which encompasses the people of non-European origin who were born or have lived in Britain. The term gained currency in the 1970s as a political watchword calling for unity between the African, Asian and

Caribbean communities in Britain, against the common experience of racism and marginalization. More recently, the term and its agenda have shifted to include different cultural strategies, as the need to take into account the diversities and specificity of 'black' experience among these communities has become more prominent.

Black Power (Movement) A black freedom movement in the United States from the mid-1960s to the mid-1970s, which called for the rights to self-definition and self-determination of black people. The term 'Black Power' became a political slogan and rallying call for the movement, and the clenched-fist salute was also used as a symbol. The movement encompassed different strategies for black empowerment, including some militant groups such as the Black Panther Party for Self Defence.

Black Studies, also called African American Studies, is an interdisciplinary field dedicated to analysis of all aspects of black American experience, past and present, as well as the dynamics of African diaspora, and African and Caribbean cultures and histories. The movement to establish Black Studies as an academic discipline emerged during the years of the Black Power Movement*, between the late 1960s and the early 1970s. The first Black Studies programme was coordinated at San Francisco State College in 1968 by Nathan Hare, a sociologist and founding editor of *The Black Scholar*. By 1973 hundreds of Black Studies programmes had been established in predominantly white colleges and universities.

Booker Prize, Britain's most prestigious award for a contemporary work of fiction, was established in 1969. It is awarded annually to any full-length novel written in English by a citizen of the United Kingdom, the British Commonwealth* or the Republic of Ireland. Since 2002 the prize has been sponsored by the British investment company Man Group, and the award is now officially named the Man Booker Prize. Inclusion in the longlist and/or the shortlist of the prize is also considered to be highly prestigious.

Civil Rights (Movement) Civil rights are the rights of each citizen to liberty, equality, freedom of religion and speech, and equal protection under the law. In the United States the Civil Rights Movement refers to the African American struggle to abolish racial discrimination and expand black people's civil rights, and especially to the movement led by Martin Luther King, Jr. from the mid-1950s to the 1960s.

Colonialism The extension of a nation's power over territory beyond its borders by the establishment of either settler colonies* and/or administrative control through which the indigenous populations are directly or indirectly ruled or displaced. Colonizers not only take control of the resources, trade and labour in the territories they occupy, but also generally impose, to varying degrees, cultural, religious and linguistic structures on the conquered population.

The Commonwealth A voluntary association of fifty-three independent sovereign states, most of which are former territories of the British Empire. It started as the 'British Commonwealth of Nations' after World War I. After World War II, it expanded to include newly independent nations from Asia and Africa. Queen Elizabeth II is the current head of the Commonwealth.

Commonwealth Writers' Prize was founded in 1987 by the Commonwealth Foundation. Any work of prose fiction written by a citizen of the Commonwealth is eligible. Prizes are given for the Best Book and the Best First Book by writers from each of the four Commonwealth regions ('Africa', 'Eurasia' including the United Kingdom, 'the Caribbean and Canada' and 'South East Asia and the South Pacific'); from these, overall Best Book and Best First Book prizewinners are chosen.

Cosmopolitanism A term first used in the fourth century B.C. by the Greek philosopher Diogenes, who identified himself as a 'citizen of the world' or *kosmopolitês*, rather than belonging to a particular state or locality. The term was also used by Immanuel Kant to advocate a League of Nations and a sense of moral responsibility for all human beings. In his book *Cosmopolitanism: Ethics in a World of Strangers* (2006), the philosopher Kwame Anthony Appiah advocates cosmopolitanism not as a denial of different cultures, but of the boundaries between them. He calls for an acknowledgement that people, rich and poor, in different locations may be aware of and may embrace many different cultural traditions, and that all share a simple nexus of common values and humanity, including responsibility for one another.

Creole The term was originally used to designate descendants of European settlers, born and naturalized in Mauritius, South America, West Africa, the West Indies, etc., and the term has expanded to include people of mixed white and black descent in these countries. Linguistically, Creole is a language spoken by these 'Creole' people, which has developed from two or more languages. In contrast to pidgin, which is a simplified language spoken as a means of communication by people not sharing a common language, Creole has sometimes been adopted as a mother tongue of the community.

Cultural nationalism An ideology which defines, and tries to preserve, a nation as shaped by its distinctive culture, history, religions and values, traditions and language.

Diaspora Diaspora originally refers to the dispersion of Jews outside Israel and their forced exile among the Gentile nations. The term is now used more widely to describe the spreading of people from their original homeland to other countries: for example, we speak of the African Diaspora, the Irish Diaspora and the South Asian Diaspora.

Discourse/Discourse theory As used in literary and cultural studies, 'discourse' (from the Latin 'to speak at length') is a nonevaluative term referring to a body of writing or speech relating to a particular topic or discipline. Thus 'colonial discourse' may include novels, anthropological and historical publications, as well as parliamentary speeches, etc., which 'describe' the experience of colonization from the colonialists' point of view.

Epic A long verse narrative told in an elevated and grand manner, about the adventures or achievements of a heroic or legendary (and often divine) figure, whose fate is seen to embody that of a nation, a tribe or the human race. *Beowulf, The Mahabharata* and *The Odyssey* are examples of epic poems. The traditional epic poems were orally transmitted over generations before being fixed in writing, and are often distinguished from literary epics which were initially written down.

Field Day An Irish artistic and political project which began in 1980 as the Field Day Theatre Company founded in Derry (Londonderry) by Brian Friel* and the actor Stephen Rea. The project was intended as a cultural intervention in the political tensions in Northern Ireland. The company opened with the premiere of Friel's play *Translations* (1980), and grew into a larger cultural and political project when Seamus Deane, David Hammond, Seamus Heaney* and Tom Paulin joined its board of directors. Field Day published a series of pamphlets, and also published the three volumes of the *Field Day Anthology of Irish Literature* (1991) with Deane as general editor; two more volumes, which collected Irish women's writings, were added to the series in 2002.

Globalization generally means the rapid growth of worldwide networks and inter-dependence, of cross-border exchanges of people, ideas, trade and capital. Jan Aart Scholte points out that this term is also used loosely to describe a variety of concepts such as internationalisation, liberalization, universalisation, Western-isation/modernisation, and deterritorialization (*Globalisation: A Critical Introduction* (London: Palgrave, 2000),15–6).

Harlem Renaissance The African American literary and cultural revival which blossomed in the 1920s, mainly in Harlem, north Manhattan, and is noted for a dynamic outpouring of writing, music, art and social criticism. Originally known as the 'New Negro Movement', it was triggered by the flow of black American migrants from the rural South to northern cities, where a new African American identity was sought, and was redefined, through artistic expressions. The Renaissance faded during the Great Depression but it had a great impact on other black movements which followed it, such as *négritude** and the American Civil Rights Movement*. Leading writers of the Renaissance include Countee Cullen, Nella Larsen, Langston Hughes, Zora Neale Hurston, Claude McKay and W. E. B. DuBois, who edited *The Crisis*, the magazine of the NAACP (National Association for the Advancement of Colored People).

Hybridity As a biological term to denote the offspring of two different species of animals or plants, the term was used in racialist discourse to refer to those of 'mixed race'. In postcolonialism the notion has been used to refer to the processes and consequences of encounters between different peoples and cultures, and in formulating a model of identity which is not fixed and stable. The term is most associated with Homi Bhabha*, who, in his essays such as 'Signs Taken for Wonders', identifies it as a source of anxiety for the colonizer, and therefore constituting a potential site of colonial resistance.

Intertextuality A term originally coined by Julia Kristeva which refers to the multiple ways in which each text, far from being an enclosed system, is inter-twined with other texts. Concerning intertextuality, Roland Barthes writes in 'The Death of the Author' (1977): 'a text is made of multiple writings, drawn from many cultures and entering into mutual relations of dialogue, parody, contestation'. The theory of intertextuality has transformed the act of reading and writing into an important site where such interactions between texts take place.

Legend Derived from the Latin word *legenda* ('what is read'), the legend was originally a written record of saints' lives and similar stories. Unlike a myth*, the legend tells of human protagonists, thought to be real and historical, and provides a body of true and fictitious stories collected around them.

Magic realism A literary genre which freely fuses supernatural, imaginary or mythical elements with realistic representations of ordinary events. The term was used to describe the works of some Latin American writers, such as Gabriel García Márquez (Colombia) and Julio Cortázar (Argentina), and the technique is often applied to postcolonial writers such as Wilson Harris*, Ben Okri and Salman Rushdie*.

Metaphor/metaphoric A figure of speech which connects, and substitutes, one word, idea, concept, etc., with another by analogies or assumed resemblances. Metaphor has an affinity with the idea of 'translation', sharing the same etymology of 'to transfer', or 'to carry across'.

Metonymy/metonymic In metonymy, which etymologically means 'a change of name', a word, concept or thing represents (or serves as 'a name' for) something else, on the basis of shared contexts, established associations, and/or spatial and temporal contiguity. As a figure of speech which at once indicates part and whole, identity and difference, metonymy is important in Homi Bhabha's* analysis of colonial discourses, in particular in the articulation of such concepts as fetish, mimicry* and stereotype.

Mimicry A site of ambivalence in colonial discourse, identified and characterized by Homi Bhabha* in his essay 'Of Mimicry and Man' as 'almost the same, *but not quite*'. Mimicry presents a double vision of resemblance and difference, unsettling the colonial authority and its system of representation. The idea of mimicry also suggests issues of performance and authenticity, resonates with the title and subject matter of Frantz Fanon's* *Black Skin, White Masks* (1952), and is explored by V. S. Naipaul* in his *The Mimic Men* (1967), which interrogates, for instance, the alienating effects of appearing and/or seeking to be a 'mimic man'.

Modernism This term, in a narrow sense, designates the art and literary avant-garde movements (e.g., Symbolism, Futurism, Expressionism, Imagism, Dada, Cubism, Surrealism) of the first part of the twentieth century which flourished in the European metropolitan centres. Major modernist writers in the English-speaking world include T. S. Eliot, James Joyce*, Ezra Pound, Virginia Woolf and W. B. Yeats*, whose works experiment radically with literary form and language, often rejecting realism as a mode of representation and drawing attention to the media, for example language and genre, through which perceptions are filtered. Some critics argue that postcolonial writers deploy modernist techniques specific to the interaction between their home cultures and languages and those of the colonizer. See also Postmodernism*.

Multicultural A term which describes the policy or ideal of encouraging different ethnocultural groups within a society to coexist harmoniously without losing their distinctive cultural identities. Multiculturalism as a social policy was first adopted in Canada in the 1970s and quickly gained currency in other English-speaking countries.

Myth Originally derived from the Greek *muthos* (plot, story, narrative), myth is a story about gods or other supernatural beings, often featuring demigods or rulers of divine descent. A collection of myths constitutes a mythology, which illustrates and provides explanations of the origin of the world, rituals and belief systems. Recent literary and cultural criticism often uses the 'myth' to refer to the complete system of signs and structures which a society uses to express its cultural values.

Nation language A language, or a variant of a language, which is thought to best represent the national identity of a nation. The term was coined by (Edward) Kamau Brathwaite*, who, in *History of the Voice* (1984), defines the 'nation language' of the Caribbean as the spoken English of the Caribbean people, which is strongly influenced by the African heritage and its oral tradition and also by its past as the language of slaves and labourers.

Naturalism One particular form of realism*, which came to the fore as a literary movement in the late nineteenth century and the beginning of the twentieth century, especially in France. Greatly influenced by Darwinism, naturalist writers, most notably the French novelist Émile Zola (1849–1902), understood the fate of a human being to be determined by his heredity and by the effects of his environment, and aimed to present this scientifically through the graphic depiction of details. The plight and degradation of the working classes was a favourite subject of naturalist observation.

Négritude A francophone black literary movement which originated in the meetings of African and Caribbean intellectuals in Paris in the 1930s. By embracing the derisive term for black people, *nègre*, as their slogan, the participants of *négritude* firmly rejected the Western stereotypes about themselves, and affirmed African values and heritage, and a collective identity as black Africans. The movement continued until the 1960s, and its main writers include the Martiniquan poet Aimé Césaire, the French-Guyanese Léon-Gontran Damas, and Léopold Senghor from Senegal.

Neocolonialism A new form of imperialism in the postindependence era, by which major powers continue to control newly independent and/or developing nations politically, economically and culturally. The term began to be used as early as the 1950s and earlier books which analyse the new situation captured by this term include Jean-Paul Sartre's collection of essays *Colonialism and Neocolonialism* (1964), and, more extensively, Kwame Nkrumah's, *Neo-Colonialism: The Last Stage of Imperialism* (1965).

Nobel Prize for Literature One of six prizes instituted by the will of Alfred Nobel (1833–96), Swedish chemist and inventor of dynamite, the Nobel Prize for Literature is widely regarded as the world's most prestigious literary prize. The Nobel

Prize for Literature is selected by the Swedish Academy and awarded annually for 'outstanding literary achievement without regard to nationality'.

Novel of manners A realistic novel which focuses on depicting the conventions, conversations, ways of thinking and value systems of a particular social class. Jane Austen is thought to be a prime example of the novelist of manners.

Orientalism The term originally meant the study of the Orient but it was redefined by Edward Said* in his *Orientalism* (1978) as a mode of Western dominance through the production, by Orientalists and institutions, of authoritative texts concerning the Orient. It creates the Orient as an object of knowledge, which needs to be discursively and politically represented by the West, as well as constructing the Orient as the West's 'Other' and a site of dreams, myths and fantasies.

Performance poetry Oral poetry, often improvised, and performed in front of an audience, bringing together elements of music, comedy and drama. Performance poetry is a powerful medium through which many artists express their identity and heritage, sharing it with their audience, in a kind of 'orature' – an art form which combines aspects of speech, customs, rites and rituals, as well as serving as a vehicle for the transmission of collective memories. The Caribbean oral tradition is a significant influence on modern black performance poetry, which includes Louise Bennett's* Creole verses and the 'dub' poetry (spoken words with reggae music) of artists such as Mikey Smith*.

Postcolonial/Post-colonial The hyphenated and nonhyphenated terms are not always used consistently, but in general the nonhyphenated 'postcolonial' refers to the consequences of colonialism from the time of its first impact – culturally, politically, economically. Thus 'Postcolonial Studies' takes in colonial literature and history, as well as the literature and art produced after independence has been achieved. 'Post-colonial' with a hyphen tends to refer to the historical period after a nation has been officially recognized as independent and is no longer governed as a colony.

Postmodernism This term, widely debated since the 1980s, is used to articulate a rupture and/or culmination point in the paradigm of modernism and modernity and broadly to describe the period, mentality and cultural attitudes which follow 'modernism'. The definition of postmodernism therefore differs according to how one defines 'modernism' and how and when one locates the supposed rupture. Postmodernism is usually associated with concepts such as the end of grand narratives (François Lyotard), the loss of the real and meaning, cultural relativism, pastiche and multiple points of view.

Poststructuralism A term used to designate a wide range of critical approaches since the late 1960s, whose major theorists include Roland Barthes, Jacques Derrida, Michel Foucault and Jacques Lacan, though none of these formally identified themselves with the term. Whereas structuralism identified recognizable patterns and codes in language, literature and culture, poststructuralism is said to have gone beyond structuralism and to have initiated radical critiques of language and systems of signification. Main themes of poststructuralism include the decentring of the subject, the death of the author, the concept of discourse*, intertextuality* and indeterminacy of meaning.

Realism A literary mode which aims at a mimetic and 'true-to-life' representation of reality. This approach is mostly associated with nineteenth-century novels, such as those of Honorè de Balzac, Charles Dickens and George Eliot. *See also* Magic Realism* and Naturalism*.

Sati (also spelt suttee, sattee, sutee, etc.) The Hindu custom of burning widows alive on the funeral pyres of their husbands. The term literally means 'virtuous wife' and, strictly speaking, is the name for the widows who submitted themselves to this ritual. The custom was formally banned in 1829 by Lord William Bentinck, the Governor-General of the East India Company. This abolition was first imposed only in the Bengal Presidency, but was shortly after extended to other areas of India.

Settler colonies A colony which includes a relatively large and 'permanent' population of European settlers, protected by their country of origin. As *the Encyclopaedia Britannica* (1877) put it, 'A colony in the fullest sense of our usage of the term can arise only where the European colonist may look on his adopted habitation as his permanent home, where he can found a family and rear his children in robust health.' The diverse physical conditions and differing origins and circumstances of the territories in the British Empire gave rise to different forms of the settler colony, as well as different ways of ruling them.

Slave colonies are colonies built by slave labour. The West Indies and many other parts of the Americas developed as slave colonies. In the British dominion slave colonies technically ceased to exist in 1834 with the abolition of slavery.

Subaltern Studies A project which was begun in 1982 by a group of historians as an attempt to rethink Indian and South Asian colonial historiography from the perspective of the 'subaltern'. The concept of the 'subaltern' is drawn from the work of Antonio Gramsci and is used to point to those who have been excluded from the dominant national and colonial history owing to their 'inferior' position, due to, for example, their class, gender, race, ethnicity or religion. Important contributors to Subaltern Studies include Ranajit Guha, who edited the first six volumes of *Subaltern Studies: Writings on Indian History and Society* (1982–2000) and Gayatri Chakravorty Spivak*, who questioned the representability of the subaltern consciousness in her influential essay 'Can the Subaltern Speak?'

Symbol Originally derived from the Greek word meaning 'mark' and 'token', a symbol in literature is a word, phrase or image which signifies ideas or abstract concepts beyond its obvious meaning. Unlike an allegory, which makes a specific reference to what it signifies, a symbol is cryptic, and its possible implications are graspable only through interpretation. On the other hand, some objects are made conventional and public symbols, often representing religious or political ideas: for example, the Cross traditionally stands for Christianity, and 'the hammer and sickle' for communism.

Third World A term originally coined by the French demographer Alfred Sauvy in 1952 to distinguish nations which do not belong, within the context of the Cold War, to either the capitalist West (the First World) or the communist East (the Second World). The term is now used to refer to the world's poorest countries in Africa, Asia and Latin America, which are alternatively called 'the South' or 'developing nations'.

Biographies of selected postcolonial writers (compiled by Kaori Nagai)

Chinua Achebe (1930–), Nigerian novelist, was born in Ogidi, Nigeria, as the son of an Igbo Christian missionary teacher. After graduating from the University College of Ibadan, he worked for the Nigerian Broadcasting Company in Lagos, and during the Nigerian Civil War served on diplomatic missions for Biafra. From 1972 to 1977 he taught as a visiting professor in universities in the USA, and later became a Professor of Literature at the University of Nigeria, Nsukka. He was the founding editor of *OKIKE* and also of the Heinemann African Writers series. Since a serious car accident in 1990, he has lived in the USA, teaching at Bard College, New York.

BIBLIOGRAPHY *Things Fall Apart* (1958); *No Longer at Ease* (1960); *Arrow of God* (1964); *A Man of the People* (1966); *Beware, Soul-Brother* (1971); *Girls at War and Other Stories* (1972); *Morning Yet on Creation Day* (1975); *Anthills of the Savannah* (1988); *Hopes and Impediments* (1988); *Home and Exile* (2000).

Ama Ata Aidoo (1942–), Ghanaian writer, was born in the Fanti town of Abeadzi Kyiakor, in the south-central region of the Gold Coast (now Ghana), the daughter of the local chief. She was educated at the University of Ghana, and subsequently taught at various universities in Africa and the USA. After working as the Minister of Education in Ghana from 1982 to 1983, a post from which she resigned, she went into self-imposed exile in Zimbabwe and the USA, where she has carried on her writing and work in education. Her work spans a wide range of genres (plays, novels, poetry and literary criticism), many of which explore the roles of women in modern Africa.

BIBLIOGRAPHY *The Dilemma of a Ghost* (1965); *Anowa* (1970); *No Sweetness Here* (1971); *Our Sister Killjoy: or Reflections from a Black-eyed Squint* (1977); *Someone Talking to Sometime* (1985); *Changes: A Love Story* (1991); *An Angry Letter in January and Other Poems* (1992); *The Girl Who Can and Other Stories* (1997).

Ayi Kwei Armah (1939–), Ghanaian novelist, was born in Takoradi, Gold Coast (now Ghana), into a Fanti-speaking family. He was educated both in Ghana and in the USA, and obtained degrees from Harvard and Columbia universities. Before establishing himself as a writer with his debut novel *The Beautyful Ones Are Not Yet Born* (1968), he worked briefly as a translator in Algeria, as a scriptwriter for television in Ghana for three years, and in Paris as an editor and translator of

242

Jeune Afrique. He has lived and worked in different parts of Africa, mostly outside Ghana. He held visiting professorships in Dar es Salaam, Lesotho, Massachusetts and Wisconsin. He settled in Senegal in the 1980s.

BIBLIOGRAPHY *The Beautyful Ones Are Not Yet Born* (1968); *Fragments* (1970); *Why Are We So Blest?* (1971); *Two Thousand Seasons* (1973), *The Healers* (1978); *Osiris Rising: A Novel of Africa Past, Present, and Future* (1995); *KMT: In the House of Life* (2002).

Margaret Atwood (1939–), Canadian novelist, poet and critic, was born in Ottawa, Ontario. She spent much of her childhood in the backwoods of Northern Ontario and Quebec, owing to her father's research as a forest entomologist. She published her first collection of poems as an undergraduate at the University of Toronto, and undertook her graduate studies at Harvard. She is a prolific and internationally acclaimed poet and novelist, whose best-known fiction includes *The Handmaid's Tale*, which was adapted for film in 1990, and *The Blind Assassin* which won her the 2000 Booker Prize.

BIBLIOGRAPHY *Double Persephone* (1961); *The Circle Game* (1964); *The Animals in That Country* (1968); *The Edible Woman* (1969); *The Journals of Susanna Moodie* (1970); *Surfacing* (1972); *Survival: A Thematic Guide to Canadian Literature* (1972); *Life before Man* (1979); *Bodily Harm* (1981); *The Handmaid's Tale* (1985); *The Robber Bride* (1993); *Good Bones and Simple Murders* (1994); *Morning in the Burned House* (1995); *Alias Grace* (1996); *The Blind Assassin* (2000); *The Penelopiad: The Myth of Penelope and Odysseus* (2005).

Louise Bennett (1919–2006), Jamaican poet, folklorist and comedienne, is renowned for her pioneering use of Jamaican Creole in her writing and performance poetry. Bennett, also known as 'Miss Lou', was born in Kingston, Jamaica, and started performing her Creole poems publicly in her teens. In the mid-1940s she studied at RADA (the Royal Academy of Dramatic Art) in London, and worked for the BBC as a resident artist on *Caribbean Carnival* (1945–6) and *West Indian Guest Night* (1950–3). Since 1954 she has lived in Jamaica, where she has published many poems and Jamaican folktales while lecturing and performing. One of her most famous poems is 'Colonization in Reverse'.

BIBLIOGRAPHY *Dialect Verses* (1940); *Verses in Jamaican Dialect* (1942); *Jamaican Humour in Dialect* (1943); *Miss Lulu Sez* (1948); (co-author) *Anancy Stories and Dialect Verse* (1950); *Folk Stories and Verses* (1952); *Laugh With Louise: Dialect Verses, Folk-Songs, and Anancy Stories* (1961); *Jamaica Labrish* (1966); *Anancy and Miss Lou* (1979); *Aunt Roachy Seh* (1993).

Homi K. Bhabha (1949–), a critic and theorist, was born to Parsi parents in Mumbai (Bombay), India. He studied as an undergraduate at the University of Bombay, and as a postgraduate at Oxford University, and has since taught in a number of academic institutions in the UK and USA, including the University of Sussex where he taught for many years. He is currently the Anne F. Rothenberg Professor of English and American Literature at Harvard University. Many of his best-known essays are collected in *The Location of Culture* (1993).

BIBLIOGRAPHY (editor and introduction) *Nation and Narration* (1990); *The Location of Culture* (1993); *Cosmopolitanism* (ed. with Sheldon Pollock, Dipesh Chakrabarty and Carol A. Breckenridge) (2002); *Edward Said: Continuing the Conversation* (ed. with W. J. T. Mitchell) (2005).

Eavan Boland (1944–), Irish poet, was born in Dublin. She spent most of her childhood in London and New York, owing to her father's occupation as an Irish diplomat. After graduating from Trinity College, Dublin, in 1966 and briefly teaching there as an academic, she began writing full-time, much of her poetry exploring the place of women in male-dominated Irish society and broader issues of Irish history and national identity. She has taught and been a writer-in-residence at various universities in Ireland and the USA, and is currently a professor of English at Stanford University, California.

BIBLIOGRAPHY *New Territory* (1967); *The War Horse* (1975); *In Her Own Image* (1980); *Night Feed* (1982); *The Journey and Other Poems* (1987); *Outside History* (1990); *In a Time of Violence* (1994); *Object Lessons* (1995); *An Origin Like Water* (1996); *The Lost Land* (1998); *Limitations* (2000); *Against Love Poetry* (2001); *Journey with Two Maps* (2002).

(Edward) Kamau Brathwaite (1930–), Barbadian poet, historian and cultural critic, was born in Bridgetown, Barbados. He was educated in Barbados and also studied history at Cambridge University; he later obtained his PhD from the University of Sussex. From 1955 to 1962 he worked as an education officer in Ghana, and subsequently held academic positions at the University of the West Indies, Kingston, until 1991; since then he has taught in the USA. He has published many collections of poetry, including his first trilogy – *Rights of Passage* (1967), *Masks* (1968) and *Islands* (1969) – which was later published in one volume as *The Arrivants* (1973). As an academic historian, his major publication is *The Development of Creole Society in Jamaica, 1770–1820* (1971), and he is the author of *History of the Voice* (1993), in which he coined the term 'nation language' to identify aspects of the Caribbean speech. Several of his early writings were published in *BIM*, the pioneering Barbadian literary magazine, and he was also an editor of *Savacou*, the journal of the Caribbean Artists Movement (CAM).

BIBLIOGRAPHY (Poetry) *The Arrivants: A New World Trilogy* (1973, see above); his second trilogy of poems consists of *Mother Poem* (1977), *Sun Poem* (1982) and *X/Self* (1987); *Other Exiles* (1975); *Black+Blues* (1976); *Soweto* (1979); *Third World Poems* (1983); *Jah Music* (1986); *Roots* (1986); *Middle Passages* (1992); *DreamStories* (1994); *The Zoa Mexican Diary* (1994); *Words Need Love Too* (2000); *LX the Love Axe/l: Developing a Caribbean Aesthetic* (2002).

(Nonfiction) *The Development of Creole Society in Jamaica, 1770–1820* (1971); *History of the Voice* (1984).

John Maxwell Coetzee (1940–), a descendant of Dutch settlers, was born in Cape Town, South Africa. He studied mathematics and English at the University of Cape Town, and obtained a PhD in linguistics from the University of Texas, Austin, for a stylistic analysis of the works of Samuel Beckett. He taught English and literature at the State University of New York, in Buffalo, New York, in the late 1960s, and in 1971 sought permanent residence in the USA but was refused because of his involvement in protests against the war in Vietnam. He returned to South Africa and took up a post as a Professor of English Literature in Cape Town. In 2002 Coetzee moved to Adelaide, South Australia, and he became an Australian citizen in 2006. Coetzee has won the Booker Prize twice, for *The Life and Times of Michael K* in 1983, and for *Disgrace* in 1999. He was awarded the Nobel Prize for Literature in 2003.

BIBLIOGRAPHY (Novels) *Dusklands* (1974); *In the Heart of the Country* (1977); *Waiting for the Barbarians* (1980); *The Life and Times of Michael K* (1983); *Foe* (1986); *Age of Iron* (1990); *The Master of Petersburg* (1994); *Disgrace* (1999); *Elizabeth Costello* (2003); *Slow Man* (2005).

(Memoirs) *Boyhood: Scenes from Provincial Life* (1997); *Youth* (2002).

(Essay collections) *White Writing: On the Culture of Letters in South Africa* (1988); *Doubling the Point: Essays and Interviews* (1992); *Giving Offense: Essays on Censorship* (1997); *The Lives of Animals* (1999); *Stranger Shores: Literary Essays, 1986–1999* (2002); *Inner Workings: Literary Essays, 2000–2005* (2007).

David Dabydeen (1955–), British Guyanese poet, novelist, art historian and critic, was born into an Indo-Caribbean family in Berbice, Guyana, and moved to Britain in 1969. He studied at Cambridge and London universities and pursued his post-doctoral study at Oxford University. His first poetry collection, *Slave Song* (1984), won the Commonwealth Poetry Prize, and his debut novel *The Intended* (1991) received the Guyana Prize for Literature. As a scholar, he has published on the visual representations, as well as the historical presence, of black people in Britain, a theme which also runs through many of his creative works. He is currently a professor in the department of Caribbean Studies at Warwick University. He has served as Guyana's Ambassador-at-Large and was a member of the Executive Board of UNESCO.

BIBLIOGRAPHY (Poetry) *Slave Song* (1984); *Coolie Odyssey* (1988); *Turner* (1994).

(Novels) *The Intended* (1991); *Disappearance* (1993); *The Counting House* (1996); *A Harlot's Progress* (1999); *Our Lady of Demerara* (2004).

(Nonfiction) *Hogarth's Blacks: Images of Blacks in Eighteenth-Century English Art* (1985); *Hogarth, Walpole, and Commercial Britain* (1987); (co-editor with Brinsley Samaroo) *India in the Caribbean* (1987) and *Across Dark Waters* (1996).

Tsitsi Dangarembga (1959–), Zimbabwean writer, playwright and filmmaker, was born in Mutoko, Rhodesia (now Zimbabwe). She lived in England between the ages of two and six. She returned to England in 1977 to study medicine at Cambridge University, but went back to Zimbabwe in 1980 to complete a degree in psychology at the University of Harare. She is best known as the author of *Nervous Conditions* (1988), which won the Commonwealth Writers' Prize (African region) in 1989. After the book's success, she continued her education at the Deutsche Film und Fernseh Akademie in Berlin, and became the first black Zimbabwean woman to write and direct a feature film (*Everyone's Child* (1996)). She also wrote a story for the film *Neria* (1992), directed by Godwin Mawuru. She recently directed a short film, *Kare kare zvako: Mother's Day* (2005), and in 2006 published a sequel to *Nervous Conditions (The Book of Not)*.

BIBLIOGRAPHY *Nervous Conditions* (1988); *The Book of Not* (2006). She has also published a short story 'The Letter' (1985), and *She No Longer Weeps* (1987), a play.

Anita Desai (1937–), Indian novelist and short-story writer, was born in Mussoorie, India, to a Bengali father and a German mother. She studied English at Delhi University, and started her career as a novelist with the publication of *Cry, the Peacock* (1963). Her novels include *Clear Light of Day* (1980), *In Custody* (1984) and *Fasting, Feasting* (1999), each of which was shortlisted for the Booker Prize; *In Custody* was made into a film by Ismail Merchant (1993). She has written some children's stories, including *Village by the Sea: An Indian Family Story* (1982). She is a Fellow of the Royal Society of Literature in London, and currently teaches creative writing at Massachusetts Institute of Technology.

BIBLIOGRAPHY *Cry, the Peacock* (1963); *Voices in the City* (1965); *Bye-Bye, Black-bird* (1968); *Fire on the Mountain* (1977); *Games at Twilight and Other Stories* (1978); *Clear Light of Day* (1980); *In Custody* (1984); *Village by the Sea: An Indian Family Story* (1982); *Baumgartner's Bombay* (1988); *Journey to Ithaca* (1995); *Fasting, Feasting* (1999); *Diamond Dust: Stories* (2000); *The Zigzag Way* (2005).

Bernardine Evaristo (1959–), British writer, was born in London to a Nigerian father and English mother. She attended drama school, where she studied acting and began to write. She is best known as the author of two novels-in-verse: *Lara* (1997) and *The Emperor's Babe* (2001). Her latest *Soul Tourists* (2005) mingles verse, dialogue and interior monologue. She has written for radio and theatre and has taught and been a writer-in-residence at various universities in the UK and overseas.

BIBLIOGRAPHY *Island of Abraham* (1993); *Lara* (1997); *The Emperor's Babe* (2001); *Soul Tourists* (2005).

Frantz Fanon (1925–61), psychiatrist and theorist, was born in the then French colony of Martinique, in the Caribbean. He fought for the Free French Forces during WWII, and then studied psychiatry in France, during which time he wrote *Peau noire, masques blancs* (1952), before working in Blida-Joinville Psychiatric Hospital, Algeria, from 1953 to 1956, when he resigned his post and was expelled from Algeria. While there he had become involved in the FLN (Front de Libération Nationale) campaign to liberate Algeria from the French, and, in exile in Tunisia, he worked for this organization and wrote articles for its journal *El Moudjahid*. He published *L'An V de la Révolution algérienne* in 1959, and, dying of leukaemia, dictated *Les Damnés de la terre* (1961) in the last few months of his life. Many of his other writings were republished posthumously in *Pour la révolution africaine* (1964).

BIBLIOGRAPHY: *Peau noire, masques blancs* (1952; translated as *Black Skin, White Masks*); *L'An V de la Révolution algérienne* (1959; translated as *Studies in a Dying*

Colonialism (1965), republished as *A Dying Colonialism* (1967)); *Les Damnés de la terre* (1961; translated as *The Damned* (1963), republished as *The Wretched of the Earth* (1965)); *Pour la révolution africaine* (1964; translated as *Towards the African Revolution* (1967)).

(Stella) (Maria Sarah) Miles (Lampe) Franklin (1879–1954), Australian writer, was born in Talbingo, New South Wales. She made her literary debut with *My Brilliant Career* (1901), which she wrote at the age of sixteen. In 1906 she moved to the USA where she worked for the National Women's Trade Union League and co-edited its magazine, *Life and Labor*. She moved to England in 1915 and served with the Scottish Women's Hospital at Ostrovo in the Serbian campaigns of 1917–18. The novels she wrote in England include the chronicle novels *Up the Country* (1928), *Ten Creeks Run* (1930) and *Back to Bool Bool* (1931), all published under the pseudonym Brent of Bin Bin. In 1932 she went back to Australia to settle permanently. Franklin bequeathed her estate to establish the Miles Franklin Award, to be awarded annually to the best literary work 'portraying Australian life in any of its phases'.

BIBLIOGRAPHY *My Brilliant Career* (1901); *Some Everyday Folk and Dawn* (1909); *The Net of Circumstance* (1915); *Up the Country* (1928); *Ten Creeks Run* (1930); *Back to Bool Bool* (1931); *Old Blastus of Bandicoot* (1931); *Bring the Monkey* (1933); *All That Swagger* (1936); *My Career Goes Bung* (1946); *Prelude to Waking* (1950); *Cockatoos* (1954); *Gentlemen at Gyang Gyang* (1956); *Laughter, Not for a Cage* (1956); *Childhood at Brindabella* (1963).

Brian Friel (1929–), Irish dramatist and short-story writer, was born into a Catholic family outside Omagh, Co. Tyrone, Northern Ireland. He taught at various schools in Derry (Londonderry) before becoming a full-time writer in 1960. He started his literary career by writing short stories, which were collected in *The Saucer of Larks* (1962) and *The Gold in the Sea* (1966). His first international stage success came with *Philadelphia, Here I Come!* (1964). He co-founded the Field Day Theatre Company in 1980, which staged many of his plays, including the critically acclaimed *Translations* (1980). *Dancing at Lughnasa* (1990) gained him another international success; it was produced on Broadway and later adapted as a film (1998). He has also adapted plays by the Russian authors Anton Chekhov and Ivan Turgenev. His later plays include *Performances* (2003) and *The Home Place* (2004).

BIBLIOGRAPHY *The Enemy Within* (1962); *The Saucer of Larks* (1962); *Philadelphia, Here I Come!* (1964); *The Gold in the Sea* (1966); *Loves of Cass McGuire* (1966); *Lovers* (1967); *The Mundy Scheme* (1969); *The Gentle Island* (1971); *The Freedom of the City* (1973); *Volunteers* (1975); *Living Quarters* (1978); *Faith Healer* (1979); *Translations* (1980); *Making History* (1988); *Dancing at Lughnasa* (1990); *Wonderful Tennessee* (1993); *Molly Sweeney* (1994); *Afterplay* (2002); *The Yalta Game* (2002); *Performances* (2003); *The Home Place* (2004).

Joseph Furphy (1843–1912), Australian writer, was born at Yering in Victoria, the son of Protestant immigrants from Ulster. He is best remembered as the author of an Australian classic, *Such is Life* (1903). He first worked on his father's farm after finishing his schooling at the age of fourteen, briefly tried his hand at goldmining and worked as a threshing machine operator. He married in 1867 and started a new life as a farmer, in which he was unsuccessful; he subsequently worked as a labourer and as a bullock teamster. In 1884 he moved with his family to Shepparton, Victoria, to work at his brother's foundry, where he started to write. *Such is Life* was published under the pseudonym Tom Collins, and the publication of this book prompted Furphy to write two more works, *Rigby's Romance* and *The Buln-Buln and the Brolga*, which were published posthumously.

BIBLIOGRAPHY *Such is Life: Being Certain Extracts from the Diary of Tom Collins* (1903); *Poems of Joseph Furphy* (1916); *Rigby's Romance* (abridged, 1921; unabridged, 1946); *The Buln-Buln and the Brolga* (1948).

Paul Gilroy (1956–), British sociologist and cultural theorist, was born in London to Guyanese and English parents. He obtained his BA from Sussex University and his PhD from Birmingham University's Centre for Contemporary Cultural Studies, where he studied under the guidance of Stuart Hall. He was Professor of Sociology at Goldsmiths' College, University of London, where he taught until 1998. He then taught at Yale University until 2005 as the chair of Sociology and African-American Studies, and he currently holds the Anthony Giddens Professorship in Social Theory at the London School of Economics. He has written many articles and several books, including *The Black Atlantic: Modernity and Double Consciousness* (1993), which won the Before Columbus Foundation's American Book Award in 1994. As a former DJ and freelance journalist, he has written extensively on music and literature.

BIBLIOGRAPHY (co-author) *The Empire Strikes Back* (1982); *'There Ain't No Black in the Union Jack'* (1987); *The Black Atlantic* (1993); *Small Acts* (1993); (co-author) *Hendrix, Hip-Hop e l'interruzione del pensiero* (1995); (co-editor) *Without Guarantees: In Honor of Stuart Hall* (2000); *Between Camps* (2000; also published as *Against Race*); *After Empire* (2004; also published as *Postcolonial Melancholia*).

Lorna Goodison (1947–), Jamaican poet and writer, was born in Kingston, Jamaica. She started writing poems as a teenager and has published ten collections of poetry, including *I Am Becoming My Mother*, which won the 1986 Commonwealth Poetry Prize (Americas region), and two volumes of short stories. She has taught at various universities in the USA, including the University of Michigan, and at the University of Toronto.

BIBLIOGRAPHY *Tamarind Season* (1980); *I Am Becoming My Mother* (1986); *Heartease* (1988); *Baby Mother and the King of Swords* (1990); *To Us, All Flowers Are Rose* (1995); *Turn Thanks* (1999); *Travelling Mercies* (2001); *Controlling the Silver* (2005); *Fool-Fool Rose Is Leaving Labour-in-Vain Savannah* (2005).

Nadine Gordimer (1923–), South African author of novels and short stories, was born in Springs, Gauteng, near Johannesburg. Her parents were both Jewish immigrants, her father from Latvia, her mother from London. She campaigned against the apartheid system, and her works deal with the political and social tensions in multiracial South Africa, during and after apartheid. She was awarded the Booker Prize for *The Conservationist* in 1974, and the Nobel Prize for Literature in 1991. She lives in Johannesburg.

BIBLIOGRAPHY (Novels) *The Lying Days* (1953); *A World of Strangers* (1958); *Occasion for Loving* (1963); *The Late Bourgeois World* (1966); *A Guest of Honour* (1970); *The Conservationist* (1974); *Burger's Daughter* (1979); *July's People* (1981); *A Sport of Nature* (1987); *My Son's Story* (1990); *None to Accompany Me* (1994); *The House Gun* (1998); *The Pickup* (2001); *Get a Life* (2005).

(Short story collections) *Face to Face* (1949); *The Soft Voice of the Serpent* (1952); *Six Feet of the Country* (1956); *Not for Publication* (1965); *Livingstone's Companions* (1970); *Selected Stories* (1975); *No Place Like: Selected Stories* (1978); *A Soldier's Embrace* (1980); *Something Out There* (1984); *Correspondence Course and Other Stories* (1984); *The Moment Before the Gun Went Off* (1988); *Jump: And Other Stories* (1991); *Why Haven't You Written?: Selected Stories 1950–1972* (1992); *Loot: And Other Stories* (2003)

(Essays and other works) *The Black Interpreters* (1973); *Writing and Being* (1995); *On the Mines* (1973); *Lifetimes Under Apartheid* (1986); *The Essential Gesture* (1988).

Abdulrazak Gurnah (1948–), British Tanzanian novelist, was born on the island of Zanzibar. He moved to Britain in 1968 and is currently a Professor in English and Postcolonial Studies at the University of Kent. He has published seven novels, including *Paradise*, a finalist for the 1994 Booker Prize, and *By the Sea*, which was longlisted for the 2001 Booker Prize. His most recent novel is *Desertion* (2005). He is an associate editor of the journal *Wasafiri*, and is the editor of *Essays on African Writing* (2 vols 1994, 1996). His edited collection of essays on Salman Rushdie is to be published in 2007.

BIBLIOGRAPHY *Memory of Departure* (1987); *Pilgrim's Way* (1988); *Dottie* (1990); *Paradise* (1994); *Admiring Silence* (1996); *By the Sea* (2001); *Desertion* (2005).

Stuart Hall (1932–), sociologist and cultural theorist, was born in Kingston, Jamaica, into a black middle-class family. He moved to England in 1951 and studied at Oxford University, where he became involved in the New Left movement. He served as the first editor of the *New Left Review* (1961–2). In 1964 he joined the Centre for Contemporary Cultural Studies in Birmingham, and later acted as its director. In 1979 he became Professor of Sociology at the Open University. He is currently Emeritus Professor at the Open University. He has authored and edited many books, and his influential essays include 'Cultural Studies: Two Paradigms' (1980), 'New Ethnicities' (1986), 'Cultural Identity and Diaspora' (1990) and 'What is This "Black" in Black Popular Culture?' (1992).

BIBLIOGRAPHY (co-author) *The Popular Arts* (1965); (co-author) *Policing the Crisis: Mugging, the State, and Law and Order* (1978); *Reproducing Ideologies* (1987);

The Hard Road to Renewal: Thatcherism and the Crisis of the Left (1988); (co-editor) *New Times: The Changing Face of Politics in the 1990s* (1989); (co-editor) *Modernity and Its Futures* (1992); (co-editor) *Questions of Cultural Identity* (1995); (editor) *Representation: Cultural Representation and Signifying Practices* (1997); (co-editor) *Visual Culture: The Reader* (1999).

Wilson Harris (1921–) British Guyanese writer, was born in New Amsterdam, British Guiana (now Guyana), of mixed Amerindian, African and English descent. He was educated at Queen's College, Georgetown, and worked as a government surveyor from 1942 to 1958, which led him to conduct many expeditions into the interior of Guyana. He emigrated to England in 1959, where he started writing full-time. He is the author of more than twenty novels, including 'The Guyana Quartet' (*Palace of the Peacock, The Far Journey of Oudin, The Whole Armour, The Secret Ladder*), and the 'Carnival' trilogy (*Carnival, The Infinite Rehearsal,* and *The Four Banks of the River of Space*). He has twice won the Guyana National Prize for Fiction. He has lectured and has also been appointed as a writer-in-residence at many universities all over the world.

BIBLIOGRAPHY (poetry) *Fetish* (1951); *Eternity to Season* (1954). (Novels) *Palace of the Peacock* (1960); *The Far Journey of Oudin* (1961); *The Whole Armour* (1962); *The Secret Ladder* (1963); *Heartland* (1964); *The Eye of the Scarecrow* (1965); *The Waiting Room* (1967); *Tamatumari* (1968); *Ascent to Omai* (1970); *Black Marsden: A Tabula Rasa Comedy* (1972); *Companions of the Day and Night* (1975); *Da Silva da Silva's Cultivated Wilderness* [and] *Genesis of the Clowns* (1977); *The Tree of the Sun* (1978); *The Angel at the Gate* (1982); *Carnival* (1985); *The Infinite Rehearsal* (1987); *The Four Banks of the River of Space* (1990); *Resurrection at Sorrow Hill* (1993); *Jonestown* (1996); *The Dark Jester* (2001); *The Mask of the Beggar* (2003). (Critical essays) *Tradition, the Writer and Society* (1967); *Explorations* (1981); *The Womb of Space* (1983); *The Radical Imagination* (1991).

Bessie Head (1937–86), South African/Botswanan novelist, was born in a mental hospital in Pietermaritzburg, South Africa, to a white mother, who had been in an 'illicit' relationship with a black man. She was brought up by coloured foster parents until she was thirteen, then studied at an Anglican mission orphanage. She was a primary teacher for four years before working as a journalist for the African magazine *Drum*. After an unsuccessful marriage with a journalist, in 1964 she migrated with her infant son to Botswana, where she lived as a refugee for fifteen years. She was finally granted Botswanan citizenship in 1979. She is the author of three novels, *When Rain Clouds Gather* (1969), *Maru* (1971) and the widely acclaimed *A Question of Power* (1973), and is acknowledged as an eminent and original writer of short stories. She died at the age of forty-nine from hepatitis, and some of her works were published posthumously.

BIBLIOGRAPHY *When Rain Clouds Gather* (1969); *Maru* (1971); *A Question of Power* (1973); *The Collector of Treasures and Other Botswana Village Tales* (1977); *Serowe: Village of the Rain Wind* (1981); *A Bewitched Crossroad: An African Saga* (1984); *A Woman Alone: Autobiographical Writings* (1990); *Tales of*

Tenderness and Power (1990); *The Cardinals, with Meditations and Short Stories* (1993).

Seamus Heaney (1939–), Irish poet and literary critic,was born in Co. Derry, Northern Ireland. He was educated at St Columb's College and Queen's University in Belfast. He subsequently taught at St Joseph's College and Queen's University as a lecturer, publishing his first poetry collection, *Death of a Naturalist*, in 1966. He moved to the republic of Ireland in 1972 and taught at Carysfort College in Dublin until 1980. Since then he has taught part-time as a professor at Harvard and Oxford universities. He is renowned for his adaptations and translations of ancient texts, such as *Sweeney Astray* (1983), *The Midnight Verdict* (1993) and *Beowulf* (1999). He was one of the Field Day collective and was also elected as a member of Aosdána. He was awarded the Nobel Prize for Literature in 1995.

BIBLIOGRAPHY (Poetry) *Death of a Naturalist* (1966); *Door into the Dark* (1969); *Wintering Out* (1972); *North* (1975); *Field Work* (1979); *Station Island* (1984); *The Haw Lantern* (1987); *Seeing Things* (1991); *The Spirit Level* (1996); *Opened Ground* (1998); *Electric Light* (2001); *District and Circle* (2006).

(Prose) *Preoccupations* (1980); *The Government of the Tongue* (1988); *The Redress of Poetry* (1995).

(Translations and adaptation) *Sweeney Astray: A Version from the Irish* (1984); *The Cure at Troy: A Version of Sophocles' Philoctetes* (1990); *The Midnight Verdict* (1993); *Beowulf* (1999).

James Joyce (1882–1941), Irish novelist and short-story writer, was born in the Dublin suburb of Rathgar. He was taught at Jesuit schools and studied modern languages at University College, Dublin. He spent most of his life in self-imposed exile, living in European cities, including Trieste, Paris and Zurich, often working as a language teacher. In addition to a volume of short stories, a play, and a volume of poetry, he is the author of the monumental modernist texts, *Ulysses* and *Finnegan's Wake*.

BIBLIOGRAPHY *Dubliners* (1904); *Exiles* (1918; reprinted with Joyce's notes and Introduction, 1951); *Collected Poems of James Joyce*, containing *Chamber Music, Pomes Penyeach*, and *Ecce Puer*, 1936); *A Portrait of the Artist as a Young Man* (1916); *Ulysses* (1922); *Finnegan's Wake* (1939).

Jackie Kay [Jacqueline Margaret Kay] (1961–), British poet, novelist and playwright, was born in Edinburgh, Scotland, to a Nigerian father and Scottish mother. She was adopted by a white Scottish couple at birth and was brought up in Glasgow. Her experience as an adoptee provided a basis for her first poetry collection, *The Adoption Papers* (1991), which won many awards. Previously, she had explored the theme of lesbian and black identity in her plays *Chiaroscuro* (1986) and *Twice Over* (1988), and she debuted as a novelist with *Trumpet* (1998), the story of a female jazz musician who passed her life as a male. She published a collection of short stories, *Why Don't You Stop Talking?* in 2002. Her books for children include a poetry collection, *Two's Company* (1992), and the novel *Strawgirl* (2002).

BIBLIOGRAPHY *Chiaroscuro* (1986), *Twice Over* (1988); *The Adoption Papers* (1991); *That Distance Apart* (1991); *Two's Company* (1992); *Other Lovers* (1993); *Three Has Gone* (1994); *Bessie Smith* (1997); *Off Color* (1998); *Trumpet* (1998); *Why Don't You Stop Talking?* (2002); *Strawgirl* (2002); *Life Mask* (2005).

Henry Kendall (1839–82), Australian poet, was born near Milton on the south coast of New South Wales and was the grandson of a famous Anglican missionary in New Zealand. He spent his boyhood in the coastal regions of Illawarra and on the Clarence River, as well as serving two years in a whaler as a cabin boy. He began publishing his poems in Sydney journals and newspapers in 1859, and published his first book, *Poems and Songs*, in 1862. After marrying, he moved with his family to Melbourne where in 1869 he published *Leaves from Australian Forests*, which includes many of his best-known poems such as 'Araluen', 'Bell Birds', 'A Death in the Bush' and 'September in Australia'. Increasing poverty and the death of his daughter led him to alcoholism, for which he was treated during several periods in a Sydney asylum. After his recovery, he had a measure of literary success from his last volume, *Songs from the Mountains* (1880).

BIBLIOGRAPHY *Poems and Songs* (1862); *Leaves from Australian Forests* (1869); *Songs from the Mountains* (1880).

Hanif Kureishi (1954–), British novelist, playwright, essayist and screenwriter, was born in Bromley, Kent, to a Pakistani father and English mother. He began his writing career as a playwright and became internationally famous by writing the scripts for the films *My Beautiful Laundrette* (1985) and *Sammy and Rosie Get Laid* (1987). He also directed *London Kills Me* (1991), a film based on his screenplay. One of his stories was adapted as the film *My Son the Fanatic* (1997). His first novel, *The Buddha of Suburbia* (1990), won the Whitbread Book of the Year award, and since then he has published several novels, including The *Black Album* (1995) and, most recently, *My Ear at His Heart* (2004), about his father.

BIBLIOGRAPHY (Fiction and screenplays) *My Beautiful Laundrette and The Rainbow Sign* (1986); *Sammy and Rosie Get Laid: The Script and the Diary* (1988); *The Buddha of Suburbia* (1990); *The Black Album* (1995); *Intimacy* (1998); *Sleep with Me* (1999); *Gabriel's Gift* (2001); *Dreaming and Scheming* (2002); *My Ear at His Heart* (2004); *The Word and the Bomb* (2005).

(Plays) *Borderline* (1981), *Outskirts, The King and Me, and Tomorrow – Today!* (1983); *Birds of Passage* (1983).

Alex La Guma (1925–85), South African writer, was born in District Six, Cape Town. Classified as 'coloured' by the apartheid regime, he was a leader of the South African Coloured People's Organization (SAPCO), a trade union activist and a member of the South African Communist Party. He left South Africa in 1966 and spent the rest of his life in exile, much of it in Cuba. His early novels and stories were naturalistic in mode, showing the lives of poor black, white and coloured people in the cities. Later fiction, such as *In the Fog at the Season's End* (1972), mingles realism and surrealist visionary episodes. He was awarded the 1969 Lotus Prize for Literature.

BIBLIOGRAPHY *A Walk in the Night* (1962); *And a Threefold Chord* (1964); *The Stone Country* (1965); *In the Fog at the Season's End* (1972); *Time of the Butcherbird* (1979).

George Lamming (1927–), Barbadian novelist, was born in Carrington Village, Barbados. He was educated in Barbados but in 1946 travelled to Trinidad where he worked as a teacher. In 1950 he moved to England and worked briefly for the BBC and as a journalist, going on to publish his widely acclaimed first novel, *In the Castle of My Skin*, in 1953 and later three other novels. His essays on *The Tempest* and Caribbean writing in *The Pleasures of Exile* (1960) have been influential. He eventually settled back in Barbados and published two more novels, *Water with Berries* and *Natives of My Person* in 1972. He was a writer-in-residence at the University of the West Indies in Kingston, Jamaica in 1967, and since then he has taught in many universities in Australia, Tanzania, and the USA.

BIBLIOGRAPHY *In the Castle of My Skin* (1953); *The Emigrants* (1954); *Of Age and Innocence* (1958); *A Season of Adventure* (1960); *The Pleasures of Exile* (1960); *Water with Berries* (1972); *Natives of My Person* (1972).

Henry Lawson (1867–1922), Australian short-story writer and poet, best remembered for his vivid depiction of bush life, was born in the goldfields at Grenfell, New South Wales. He had a difficult and impoverished childhood, and he started losing his hearing at the age of nine. When his parents separated in 1883, he moved to Sydney with his mother, who went on to become an eminent suffragist. In 1888 he published his first short story, 'His Father's Mate', in *Bulletin*, to which he became a regular contributor. In 1896 he married Bertha Bredt and the couple taught at a Maori school in New Zealand for a year. Subsequently they moved to England, remaining there until 1902, when they returned to Sydney, separating shortly thereafter. From 1905 to 1910 Lawson was regularly in prison for failing to provide child support and alimony and for drunkenness, and he spent some periods in mental hospitals. After his recovery, he continued to write. When he died in 1922, he was the first Australian writer to be given a full state funeral.

BIBLIOGRAPHY (Poetry verses) *In the Days When the World Was Wide* (1896); *The Elder Son* (1905); *When I Was King* (1905); *The Skyline Riders* (1910); *A Coronation Ode and Retrospect* (1911); *For Australia* (1913); *My Army, O, My Army!* (1915).
   (Short story collections) *Short Stories in Prose and Verse* (1894); *While the Billy Boils* (1896); *On the Track and Over the Sliprails* (1900); *The Country I Come From* (1901); *Joe Wilson and His Mates* (1901); *Children of the Bush* (1902); *The Rising of the Court* (1910); *Mateship: A Discursive Yarn* (1911); *The Strangers' Friend* (1911); *Triangles of Life* (1913).

Sally Jane Morgan (1951–), Australian Aborigine writer and artist, was born in Perth, Western Australia. She came to know of her aboriginal heritage only when she was fifteen, and her quest for her ancestral roots inspired her early works such as *My Place: An Aborigine's Stubborn Quest for Her Truth, Heritage, and Origins* (1987) and *Wanamurraganya* (1989), a biography of her grandfather. She has also written several children's stories. Apart from her writing, she has gained international repute as an artist using aboriginal themes and styles. She is currently a professor at the School of Indigenous Studies, University of Western Australia.

BIBLIOGRAPHY *My Place* (1987), *Wanamurraganya* (1989); *Jinsu and the Magic Bird* (1990); *The Flying Emu and Other Australian Stories* (1993); *The Art of Sally Morgan* (1996); *In Your Dreams* (1997); *Just a Little Brown Dog* (1997); *Life in the Cities* (2001).

Les A. Murray (1938–), Australian poet, essayist and critic, was born in Nabiac, New South Wales, and spent his childhood on his father's dairy farm. He studied modern languages at Sydney University and worked as a translator at the Australian National University in Canberra. He became a full-time writer in 1971. Beginning with *The Ilex Tree* (1965), he has published many volumes of poetry and has also served as editor of *Poetry Australia* and *Quadrant Magazine*. He has received many literary awards, including the Petrarch Prize (1995), the prestigious T. S. Eliot Award (1996), and the Queen's Gold Medal for Poetry in 1998. His essays and poems, expressing an affiliation between aboriginal peoples and white rural Australians, have sometimes aroused controversy, but he is generally accepted as one of Australia's most eminent contemporary poets.

BIBLIOGRAPHY (Poetry) *The Ilex Tree* (1965, with Geoffrey J. Lehmann); *The Weatherboard Cathedral* (1969); *Poems against Economics* (1972); *Lunch and Counter Lunch* (1974); *Ethnic Radio* (1977): *The Peasant Mandarin* (1978); *The Boys Who Stole the Funeral* (1979); *Equanimities* (1982); *The People's Otherworld* (1983); *The Daylight Moon* (1987); *Translations from the Natural World* (1992); *A Working Forest* (1997); *Fredy Neptune* (1998); *Conscious & Verbal* (1999); *The Full Dress* (2002); *Poems the Size of Photographs* (2002).

(Essay collections) *The Persistence of Folly* (1985); *The Paperbark Tree* (1992); *A Working Forest* (1996); *The Quality of Sprawl: Selected essays about Australia* (1999).

V. S. Naipaul (1932–), British Trinidadian writer, was born in Chaguanas, Trinidad, into a Brahmin family whose ancestors had been recruited from India to work in the Caribbean sugarcane plantations. He has lived in England since 1950, having been awarded a scholarship to study in Oxford. After his graduation, he worked as a freelance broadcaster for the BBC's *Caribbean Voices*, and for the literary journal *The New Statesman*. His works of fiction include *The Mystic Masseur* (1957), *Miguel Street* (1959), *A House for Mr Biswas* (1961) and *The Mimic Men* (1967), and he won the 1971 Booker Prize for *In a Free State*. His more recent novels include the semi-autobiographical *The Enigma of Arrival* (1987) and *A Way in the World* (1994), as well as *Half a Life* (2001) and its sequel *Magic Seeds* (2004). Naipaul has also published many travel narratives, on Africa, India, Islamic countries, South Africa and the West Indies. He was knighted in 1990 and received the Nobel Prize for Literature in 2001.

BIBLIOGRAPHY (Novels) *The Mystic Masseur* (1957); *Miguel Street* (1959); *A House for Mr Biswas* (1961); *Mr. Stone and the Knights Companion* (1963); *The*

Mimic Men (1967); *In a Free State* (1971); *Guerrillas* (1975); *A Bend in the River* (1979); *The Enigma of Arrival* (1987); *A Way in the World* (1994); *Half a Life* (2001); *Magic Seeds* (2004).

(Nonfiction) *The Middle Passage* (1962); *An Area of Darkness* (1964); *The Loss of El Dorado* (1969); *India: A Wounded Civilization* (1977); *A Congo Diary* (1980); *The Return of Eva Perón with The Killings in Trinidad* (1980); *Among the Believers: An Islamic Journey* (1981); *India: A Million Mutinies Now* (1990); *Beyond Belief* (1998); *Between Father and Son* (2000); *Literary Occasions* (2003).

Ngugi wa Thiong'o (1938–), Kenyan novelist, dramatist and critic, was born in Limuru, Kenya, as James Thiong'o Ngugi. He grew up during the period of the so-called 'Mau-Mau' rebellion, attended universities in Uganda and the UK, and became a lecturer at the University of Nairobi in 1968, where he went on to become senior lecturer and chair of the literature department. His earlier works, such as *The Black Hermit* (1962), *Weep Not, Child* (1964) and *A Grain of Wheat* (1967), were published in English. After 1968, he renounced Christianity and his Christian name, James. Ngugi spent September 1975 as a guest of the Soviet Writers Union at Yalta, where he completed writing *Petals of Blood* (1977), a novel which intermingles the concern with psychological exploration found in his earlier novels with a more avowedly Marxist and Brechtian approach to fiction. The staging of his political play *Ngaahika Ndeenda* (*I Will Marry When I Want*) in an open-air theatre in 1977 provoked the Kenyan government to order his arrest, and he was imprisoned without charge for a year. Here he committed himself to writing in Gikuyu, completing *Caitaani Mutharaba-ini* (1980; translated as *Devil on the Cross*). In 1982 he and his family fled to London to avoid prosecution, and they moved to the USA in 1989. He has since taught at several universities and is currently Professor of English and Comparative Literature for Writing and Translation at the University of California, Irvine. He is also the founder and editor of the Gikuyu-language journal *Mutiiri*.

BIBLIOGRAPHY (As James Ngugi) *The Black Hermit* (1962); *Weep Not, Child* (1964); *The River Between* (1965); *A Grain of Wheat* (1967); *This Time Tomorrow* (1970). (As Ngugi wa Thiong'o) *Homecoming* (1972); *Secret Lives* (1975); *The Trial of Dedan Kimathi* (1976); *Ngaahika Ndeenda: Ithaako ria Ngerekano* (1977; translated as *I Will Marry When I Want*); *Petals of Blood* (1977); *Caitaani Mutharaba-ini* (1980; translated as *Devil on the Cross*); *Detained: A Writer's Prison Diary* (1981); *Writers in Politics* (1981); *Barrel of a Pen* (1983); *Decolonising the Mind* (1986); *Matigari ma Njiruungi* (1986; translated as *Matigari*); *Writing against Neocolonialism* (1986); *Moving the Centre* (1992); *Penpoints, Gunpoints, and Dreams* (1998); *Murogi wa Kagogo* (2006; translated as *The Wizard and the Crow*.)

Flora Nwapa (1931–93), Nigerian novelist, short-story writer and publisher, was born in Oguta, East Central State, Nigeria. She has been hailed as Nigeria's first female novelist. She obtained her BA from University College, Ibadan, and a diploma in education from the University of Edinburgh in 1958. She made her debut as a novelist with *Efuru* (1966), followed by *Idu* (1970), both of which gave a vivid picture of Igbo society from a female point of view. She established two publishing companies, Tana Press Ltd and Flora Nwapa and Co., which published the rest of her works, including three novels – *Never Again* (1975), *One Is Enough* (1982), and *Women Are Different* (1986) – as well as several books for children. All through her life she worked in both education and the civil service, and she taught at many universities in Africa and the USA. She died of pneumonia in 1993.

BIBLIOGRAPHY *Efuru* (1966); *Idu* (1970); *This Is Lagos* (1971); *Emeka, Driver's Guard* (1972); *Never Again* (1975); *Journey to Space* (1980); *One Is Enough* (1982); *The Adventures of Deke* (1982); *Women Are Different* (1986); *Wives at War* (1986); *Cassava Song and Rice Song* (1986).

Michael Ondaatje (1943–), Sri Lankan-born Canadian writer of mixed Dutch, Tamil and Sinhalese origin, was born in Colombo, Ceylon. After his parents' divorce, he moved to England with his mother and was educated at Dulwich College. In 1962 he moved to Canada and he obtained his MA in English from Queen's University in 1967. His work is innovative, often mixing poetry, prose and photographs, as in *The Collected Works of Billy the Kid: Left-handed Poems* (1970) and the autobiographical *Running in the Family* (1982). He is best known for his novel *The English Patient* (1992), which won the Canadian Governor General's Award and the 1992 Booker Prize, and was later adapted as a film (1996) that garnered nine Oscars. His recent works include *Anil's Ghost* (2000). Ondaatje is currently Professor of English at York University, Toronto.

BIBLIOGRAPHY *The Dainty Monsters* (1967); *The Man with Seven Toes* (1969); *The Collected Works of Billy the Kid: Left-handed Poems* (1970); *Coming through Slaughter* (1976); *There's a Trick with a Knife I'm Learning to Do* (1979); *Running in the Family* (1982); *In the Skin of a Lion* (1987); *Handwriting* (1998); *The English Patient* (1992); *Anil's Ghost* (2000).

Caryl Phillips (1958–), Caribbean-British novelist, essayist and playwright, was born in St Kitts, West Indies, grew up in Leeds, UK, and was educated at Queen's College, Oxford. He is the author of eight novels and several books of nonfiction, many of which deal with the theme of the African diaspora. His has received numerous awards, including the Malcolm X Prize for Literature for his first novel, *The Final Passage* (1985), and the Commonwealth Writers' Prize for Best Book for *A Distant Shore* (2003). *Crossing the River* (1993) was shortlisted for the Booker Prize. He has also written plays for radio, theatre and film. He has taught internationally at various universities and is currently a professor of English at Yale University, USA.

BIBLIOGRAPHY *The Final Passage* (1985); *A State of Independence* (1986); *The European Tribe* (1987); *Higher Ground* (1989); *Cambridge* (1991); *Crossing the River* (1993); *The Nature of Blood* (1997); *The Atlantic Sound* (2000); *A New World Order* (2001); *Distant Shore* (2003); *Dancing in the Dark* (2005).

Katherine Susannah Pritchard (1883–1969), Australian writer, communist and political activist, was born in Levuka, Fiji, where her father was a newspaper editor. Her family moved to Australia when she was three, and she spent her childhood in Tasmania and Melbourne. She made her first visit to London as a journalist in

1908 and returned there in 1912 to pursue a career as a writer. Her first novel, *The Pioneers*, was published in 1915, winning the Hodder & Stoughton All Empire Novel Competition. She returned to Australia in 1916, and lived for the rest of her life on the outskirts of Perth, West Australia. She wrote thirteen novels, including the prizewinning *Coonardoo* (1928) and her goldfields trilogy: *The Roaring Nineties* (1946), *Golden Miles* (1948) and *Winged Seeds* (1950). Her autobiography *Child of the Hurricane* was published in 1964. She was a committed communist and founded the Communist Party of Australia. She also established the Modern Women's Club in the 1930s, and was one of the founding members of the Movement against War and Fascism.

BIBLIOGRAPHY (Novels) *The Pioneers* (1915); *Windlestraws* (1916); *Black Opal* (1921); *Working Bullocks* (1926); *The Wild Oats of Han* (1928); *Coonardoo* (1928); *Haxby's Circus* (1930); *Intimate Strangers* (1937); *Moon of Desire* (1941); *The Roaring Nineties* (1946); *Golden Miles* (1948); *Winged Seeds* (1950); *Subtle Flame* (1967).

(Short story collections) *Kiss on the Lips* (1932); *Potch and Colour* (1944); *N'Goola* (1959); *On Strenuous Wings* (1965); *Happiness* (1967).

(Poetry) *Covelly Verses* (1913); *The Earthly Lover* (1932).

(Autobiography) *Child of the Hurricane* (1964).

Ravinder Randhawa (1952–) was born in India but grew up in Warwickshire. She founded the Asian Women Writers Collective in 1984 and for some years was its coordinator. The collective published two anthologies, *Right of Way* (1989) and *Flaming Spirit* (1994), which include many of her short stories. In addition to her fiction, she has published articles on Indian films, Asian women, feminism and identity, etc., in newspapers and journals. Her first novel, *A Wicked Old Woman* (1987), received considerable acclaim and was listed in the Top Twenty for the Feminist Bookfair in 1993. She received the Kathleen Burnett Award, and her short story 'Normal Times' was shortlisted for the 2001 David Wong Award. She has been a Literary Fellow at Toynbee Hall, 2000–2, and at St Mary's College, University of Surrey, 2006/7.

BIBLIOGRAPHY (Novels) *A Wicked Old Woman* (1987); *Hari-jan* (a novel for teenagers, 1992); *The Coral Strand* (2001).

Raja Rao (1909–), South Indian novelist, was born in Hassan, Mysore, into a distinguished Brahmin family. He was educated at Nizam College, Hyderabad, and went to France to study literature and history at the University of Montpellier and the Sorbonne. His first novel, *Kanthapura* (1938), was written in France and portrays the Indian independence movement from the perspective of a small village in South India. His marriage to a French woman in 1931 and its breakdown several years later provided the material for his semi-autobiographical novel *The Serpent and the Rope* (1960). After WWII, he mainly lived in France and India, and he subsequently taught Indian philosophy at the University of Texas from 1965 to 1983. In 1988 he won the prestigious Neustadt International Prize for Literature. His other works include three novels – *The Cat and Shakespeare* (1965), *Comrade Kirillov* (1976) and *The Chessmaster & His Moves* (1988) – and a biography of Mahatma Gandhi, *The Great Indian Way* (1998).

BIBLIOGRAPHY *Kanthapura* (1938); *The Cow of the Barricades and Other Stories* (1947); *The Serpent and the Rope* (1960); *The Cat and Shakespeare: A Tale of India* (1965); *Comrade Kirillov* (1976); *The Policeman and the Rose: Stories* (1978); *The Chessmaster & His Moves* (1988); *On the Ganga Ghat* (1989); *The Meaning of India* (1996); *The Great Indian Way: A Life of Mahatma Gandhi* (1998).

Jean Rhys (1890–1979), originally Ella Gwendolen Rees Williams, was born in Dominica (a formerly British island in the Caribbean) to a Welsh father and Scottish mother. She moved to England at the age of sixteen, where she worked as a chorus girl before travelling to Europe. In Paris she met other writers, including Ford Madox Ford, who published and promoted her short stories. After World War II, she lived in England. Her 1966 novel *Wide Sargasso Sea*, a prequel to Charlotte Brontë's *Jane Eyre*, won the 1967 WH Smith Literary Award and brought her back to the attention of a wider reading public.

BIBLIOGRAPHY *The Left Bank and Other Stories* (1927); *Postures* (1928) (released as *Quartet* in 1929); *After Leaving Mr Mackenzie* (1931); *Voyage in the Dark* (1934); *Good Morning, Midnight* (1939); *Wide Sargasso Sea* (1966); *Tigers Are Better-Looking: With a Selection from 'The Left Bank'* (1968); *My Day: Three Pieces* (1975); *Sleep It Off Lady* (1976); *Smile Please: An Unfinished Autobiography* (1979); *Jean Rhys Letters 1931–1966* (1984); *The Collected Short Stories* (1987).

Salman Rushdie (1947–), Indian novelist and short-story writer, was born in Mumbai (Bombay), where he spent his childhood, before moving to England to attend Rugby School at the age of thirteen. He graduated from King's College, Cambridge, in 1968. His first novel, *Grimus*, was published in 1975, though it was his second novel, *Midnight's Children* (1981) which was to gain him international recognition, as well as several awards, including the Booker Prize in 1981, and the 'Booker of Bookers' in 1993. His fourth novel, *The Satanic Verses* (1988), sparked heated controversy over what were deemed by some to be blasphemous references to the prophet Muhammad and the Koran, culminating in the issuing of a *fatwa* by the Iranian Ayatollah Khomeini that called for the assassination of Rushdie and his publishers and forced him into hiding. The Iranian government issued a 'pardon' in 1995, and since then Rushdie has enjoyed somewhat greater, though not unrestricted, freedom of movement. In addition to his considerable body of fiction, Rushdie has also published a great deal of nonfiction, including literary and film criticism.

BIBLIOGRAPHY *Grimus* (1975); *Midnight's Children* (1981); *Shame* (1983); *The Satanic Verses* (1988); *Haroun and the Sea of Stories* (1990); *Imaginary Homelands* (1991); *East, West* (1994); *The Moor's Last Sigh* (1995); *The Ground Beneath Her Feet* (1999); *Fury* (2001); *Step Across This Line* (2002); *Shalimar the Clown* (2005).

Nayantara (Pandit) Sahgal (1927–), Indian novelist and freelance political journalist, was born into one of the most politically eminent families in India: she is a niece of Jawaharlal Nehru, the daughter of India's first ambassador to the United Nations, and a first cousin of Indira Gandhi. She has written nine novels and several works of nonfiction, all of which foreground political events and affluent political elites in India. Her nonfiction includes a biography of her cousin, *Indira Gandhi's Emergence and Style* (1978), in which Sahgal gives her personal insight into Gandhi's declaration of a State of Emergency during the political unrest in 1975; the emergency is also a topic of her novel *Rich like Us* (1983). Her other novels include *A Time to Be Happy* (1958), set during the first days of India's independence, and *Storm in Chandigarh* (1969), about the partition of the Punjab.

BIBLIOGRAPHY (Nonfiction) *Prison and Chocolate Cake* (1954); *From Fear Set Free* (1962); *The Freedom Movement in India* (1970); *A Voice for Freedom* (1977); *Indira Gandhi's Emergence and Style* (1978); *Point of View: A Personal Response to Life, Literature, and Politics* (1997).

(Novels) *A Time to Be Happy* (1958); *This Time of Morning* (1965); *Storm in Chandigarh* (1969); *The Day in Shadow* (1971); *A Situation in New Delhi* (1977); *Plans for Departure* (1985); *Rich Like Us* (1985); *Mistaken Identity* (1988); *Lesser Breeds* (2003).

Edward W. Said (1935–2003), Palestinian American scholar, theorist and activist, was born in Jerusalem, Palestine. He attended Western schools in Jerusalem and in Cairo, before moving to the USA in 1951. He studied at Princeton University and gained his PhD from Harvard University for his doctoral thesis on Joseph Conrad. From 1963 until his death, he taught at Columbia University, New York, where he served as a professor of English and Comparative Literature. He is best known as the author of *Orientalism: Western Conceptions of the Orient* (1978), which became a foundational text in the field of postcolonial studies. He was a vocal pro-Palestine activist, and was a member of the Palestinian National Council from 1977 to 1991. His books on Palestinian issues include *The Question of Palestine* (1979), *The Politics of Dispossession* (1994) and *The End of the Peace Process* (2000). He also wrote about music, and with the Israeli conductor and pianist Daniel Barenboim founded the East-West orchestra, bringing together young musicians from Israeli and Arabic backgrounds. He died of leukaemia in 2003.

BIBLIOGRAPHY *Joseph Conrad and the Fiction of Autobiography* (1966); *Beginnings* (1975); *Orientalism* (1978); *The Question of Palestine* (1979); *Covering Islam* (1981); *The World, the Text, and the Critic* (1983); *After the Last Sky* (1986); *Musical Elaborations* (1991); *Culture and Imperialism* (1993); *The Politics of Dispossession* (1994); *Representations of the Intellectual* (1994); *Out of Place: A Memoir* (1999); *Reflections on Exile and Other Literary and Cultural Essays* (2000); *The End of the Peace Process* (2000); *Humanism and Democratic Criticism* (2004).

Samuel Selvon (1923–94), Trinidad-born British-Canadian novelist and short-story writer, was born to an Indian father and Indian-Scottish mother. He began writing while serving as a wireless operator for the Royal Navy Reserve during WWII. After working as fiction editor of the *Trinidad Guardian*, he moved to England in 1950, on the same ship as George Lamming. He subsequently settled in Canada in 1978. He is best known for his novel *The Lonely Londoners* (1956), which depicts the life of Caribbean and African male immigrants in post-WWII

London, and his vivid portrayal of Indo-Caribbean life in Trinidad, in works such as *A Brighter Sun* (1952), *An Island is a World* (1955), *I Hear Thunder* (1962), *Moses Migrating* (1983) and the short-story collection *Ways of Sunlight* (1957). He also wrote many plays for radio and television.

BIBLIOGRAPHY *A Brighter Sun* (1952); *An Island is a World* (1955); *The Lonely Londoners* (1956); *Ways of Sunlight* (1957); *Turn Again Tiger* (1958); *I Hear Thunder* (1962); *The Housing Lark* (1965); *The Plains of Caroni* (1970); *Those Who Eat the Cascadura* (1972); *Moses Ascending* (1975); *Moses Migrating* (1983); *El Dorado West One* (1988); *Foreday Morning* (1989); *Highway in the Sun and Other Plays* (1991).

Bapsi Sidhwa (1938–), Pakistani novelist of Parsi descent, was born in Karachi, Pakistan, and grew up in Lahore. She was educated at Kinnaird College for Women, Lahore, and started writing in her twenties. She moved to the USA in 1983 and now lives in Houston, Texas. She has published four novels, including *Ice-Candy-Man* (1988), which was adapted into a film by director Deepa Mehta as *Earth* (1999). In 1991 she received the Sitara-e-Imtiaz, Pakistan's highest national honour in the arts. She has been a vocal proponent of Asian women's rights and was appointed to the Advisory Committee on Women's Development set up by Pakistan's Prime Minister Benazir Bhutto. She has taught at many universities in the UK and the USA.

BIBLIOGRAPHY *The Crow Eaters* (1978); *The Bride* (1982); *Ice-Candy-Man* (1988; republished as *Cracking India* (1991)); *An American Brat* (1993); *City of Sin and Splendour: Writings on Lahore* (2006); *Water: A Novel* (2006).

Michael ('Mikey') Smith (1954–83), Jamaican 'dub' poet, was born in Jones Town, Jamaica, to a working-class family. He studied at various schools, including the Jamaican School of Drama, which he attended on a scholarship. He represented Jamaica at the World Festival of Youth in Venezuela and also performed in Barbados during Carifesta (the Caribbean Festival of Arts) in 1981. He was introduced to the British public through the UK-based Jamaican dub poet Linton Kwesi Johnson, and he performed at the International Book Fair of Radical Blacks and the Third World Book Fair in London in 1982. His career was cut short when he was stoned to death by followers of the ruling Jamaica Labour Party (JLP) on Stony Hill on 17 August 1983, the day after he had 'heckled' the Minister of Education, Mavis Gilmour, at a political meeting, and 'had given her a hard time'.

BIBLIOGRAPHY *Mi Cyaan Believe It* (1982); *It a Come* (1986).

Wole Soyinka (1934–), Nigerian playwright, poet, novelist and political activist, was born in Isara, Nigeria, into a Christian Yoruba family. He studied at Ibadan and Leeds universities, and worked briefly as a play reader at the Royal Court Theatre in London before returning to Nigeria in 1960. He established two theatre companies, the 1960 Masks and the Orisun Theatre; his plays, which draw on Yoruba dramatic and cultural traditions, include *A Dance of the Forests*, commissioned as part of Nigeria's independence celebrations in 1960, and *The Road*, staged in London at the World Theatre Festival in 1965. During the Nigerian Civil War, he was imprisoned for his attempt to mediate between the two sides and was left mostly in solitary confinement; his account of this experience was later published in *The Man Died* (1972). He taught drama and literature at Ibadan and Lagos universities, and was a professor of Comparative Literature and Dramatic Arts at the University of Ife from 1976 to 1985. During the dictatorship of General Sani Abacha (1993–8), he left Nigeria and launched an international campaign against the regime. He is currently the Elias Ghanem Professor of Creative Writing at the English department of the University of Nevada, Las Vegas. He has also published two novels and several volumes of poetry. In 1986 he was awarded the Nobel Prize for Literature, the first black African to receive it.

BIBLIOGRAPHY (Plays) *A Dance of the* Forests (1960); *The Swamp Dwellers* (1958); *The Lion and the Jewel* (1959); *The Trials of Brother Jero* (1960); *The Road* (1965); *Collected Plays* (1973–4); *Death and the King's Horseman* (1975); *Six Plays* (1984).

(Poetry) *Idanre and Other Poems* (1967); *Poems from Prison* (1969: republished as *A Shuttle in the Crypt* (1972)); *Ogun Abibiman* (1976); *Mandela's Earth and Other Poems* (1988); *Early Poems* (1997).

(Novels) *The Interpreters* (1965); *Season of Anomie* (1973).

(Nonfiction) *The Man Died: Prison Notes of Wole Soyinka* (1972); *Myth, Literature and the African World* (1976); *Ake: The Years of Childhood* (1981); *Art, Dialogue, and Outrage* (1988); *Ìsarà: A Voyage around Essay* (1989); *Ibadan: The Penkelemes Years: A Memoir, 1946–65* (1994); *You Must Set Forth at Dawn* (2007).

Gayatri Chakravorty Spivak (1942–), critic, theorist and translator, was born in Calcutta into a Bengali Brahmin family. She graduated from the University of Calcutta in 1959 and gained her PhD from Cornell University. She has taught in many institutions and is currently the Avalon Foundation Professor in the Humanities at Columbia University, New York. She is also a member of the Subaltern Studies Collective. In addition to her published books, she has contributed to many anthologies and journals.

BIBLIOGRAPHY *In Other Worlds* (1987); *Selected Subaltern Studies* (ed. with Ranajit Guha) (1988); *The Post-Colonial Critic* (ed. Sarah Harasym) (1990); *Outside in the Teaching Machine* (1993); *The Spivak Reader* (ed. Donna Landry and George McLean) (1995); *A Critique of Post-Colonial Reason* (1999); *Death of a Discipline* (2003).

(Translations) Jacques Derrida, *Of Grammatology* (1976); Jamelie Hassan, *Inscription* (1990); Mahasweta Devi, *Imaginary Maps* (1995); *Breast Stories* (1997); *Old Women* (1999); Nirode Mazumdar, *Song for Kali* (2000) and *Chotti Munda and His Arrow* (2002).

John Millington Synge (1871–1909), Irish playwright and poet, and key contributor to the Irish Literary Renaissance, was born in Rathfarnham, Co. Dublin, into an upper-class Protestant family. After graduating from Trinity College, Dublin, he spent several years studying in Germany, Italy and France; he first aspired to be a musician, but subsequently changed his subject to literature. In 1896 he met W. B. Yeats in Paris, and on his advice Synge spent four summers on the Aran Islands, off the west coast of Ireland, from 1898 to 1902. This experience not only resulted in his prose work *The Aran Islands* (1907), but also inspired his plays by bringing him in touch with Irish language and the ways of life of rural inhabitants. In 1905 he was made a director of the Abbey Theatre, where his plays, including *The Shadow of the Glen* (1903) and *The Well of the Saints* (1905) were performed, and his best-known play, *The Playboy of the Western World* (1907), prompted a riot among the audience in 1907. Synge also wrote poems, and his poetry collection *Poems and Translations* (1909) was published posthumously.

BIBLIOGRAPHY *When the Moon has Set* (1901); *The Shadow of the Glen* (1903); *Riders to the Sea* (1904); *The Well of the Saints* (1905); *The Playboy of the Western World* (1907); *The Aran Islands* (1907); *Poems and Translations* (1909); *The Tinker's Wedding* (1909); *Deirdre of the Sorrows* (1910).

William Trevor [Cox] (1928–), short story writer, novelist and playwright, was born into a Protestant family in Mitchelstown, Co. Cork, Ireland. He obtained a BA in history from Trinity College, Dublin, and worked as a teacher in Northern Ireland and England, while also pursuing his career as a sculptor. He published his first novel, *A Standard of Behaviour*, in 1958 and became a full-time writer in 1965. His stories are mainly set in England and Ireland; in the 1980s he wrote about Ireland's difficult past, in, for instance, the novel *Fools of Fortune* (1983), and the collections of stories *Beyond the Pale* (1981) and *The News from Ireland* (1986). *Felicia's Journey* was adapted as a film by Atom Egoyan in 1999, and *The Story of Lucy Gault* (2002) was shortlisted for the Booker Prize. His latest book is a collection of stories, *A Bit On the Side* (2004). In 2002 he was knighted for his services to literature.

BIBLIOGRAPHY *A Standard of Behavior* (1958); *The Old Boys* (1964); *The Boarding-House* (1965); *The Love Department* (1966); *The Day We Got Drunk on Cake* (1968); *Mrs Eckdorf in O'Neill's Hotel* (1969); *Miss Gomez and the Brethren* (1971); *The Ballroom of Romance* (1972); *Angels at the Ritz* (1975); *The Children of Dynmouth* (1976); *Beyond the Pale* (1981); *Fools of Fortune* (1983); *The News from Ireland* (1986); *Felicia's Journey* (1994); *After Rain* (1996); *The Hill Bachelors* (2000); *The Story of Lucy Gault* (2002); *A Bit On the Side* (2004).

Derek Walcott (1930–) St Lucian poet and playwright, was born in Castries, St Lucia, West Indies. After receiving a colonial education at St Mary's College on St Lucia, he studied at the University of the West Indies, Jamaica, from 1950 to 1954. He subsequently settled in Trinidad, where he founded a theatre company, the Trinidad Theatre Workshop, in 1959. One of his best-known works is his epic poem *Omeros* (1990). In addition to his poetry, he has written more than forty plays, including *Dream on Monkey Mountain* (1969), and a collection of essays, *What the Twilight Says* (1998). In 1981 he was appointed Professor of Creative Writing at Boston University. He was awarded the Nobel Prize for Literature in 1992.

BIBLIOGRAPHY (Poetry) *In a Green Night* (1962); *The Castaway* (1965); *The Gulf* (1969); *Another Life* (1973); *Sea Grapes* (1976); *The Star-Apple Kingdom*

(1979); *The Fortunate Traveller* (1981); *Midsummer* (1984); *The Arkansas Testament* (1987); *Omeros* (1990); *The Bounty* (1997); *Tiepolo's Hound* (2000); *The Prodigal* (2004).

(Plays) *Dream on Monkey Mountain and Other Plays* (1970); *The Joker of Seville and O Babylon!* (1978); *The Odyssey* (1993); *Remembrance & Pantomime* (1980); *Three Plays* (1986); *The Haitian Trilogy* (2002); *Walker and The Ghost Dance* (2002).

Patrick White (1912–90), Australian novelist, was born in London, England, and grew up in Sydney, Australia. At the age of thirteen, he was sent to England to attend Cheltenham College, and he subsequently studied modern languages at King's College, Cambridge. After leaving university, he lived in London, aspiring to be a writer, and his first novel, *Happy Valley*, was published in 1939. During WWII, he joined the RAF and served as an intelligence officer in Egypt, Palestine and Greece. After the war, he returned to Sydney. He published twelve novels, including *Voss* (1957) and *Riders in the Chariot* (1962), which won him two Miles Franklin Awards. His other works include *The Ploughman and Other Poems*, the play *Night on Bald Mountain* (1964), the short story collection *The Burnt Ones* (1964), and his autobiography *Flaws in the Glass* (1981). White was awarded the Nobel Prize for Literature in 1973, and he used the prize money to establish the Patrick White Literary Award.

BIBLIOGRAPHY *The Ploughman and Other Poems* (1935); *Happy Valley* (1939); *The Living and the Dead* (1941); *The Aunt's Story* (1948); *The Tree of Man* (1955); *Voss* (1957); *Riders in the Chariot* (1961); *The Burnt Ones* (1964); *Four Plays* (1965); *The Solid Mandala* (1966); *The Vivisector* (1970); *The Eye of the Storm* (1973); *A Fringe of Leaves* (1976); *The Twyborn Affair* (1980); *Flaws in the Glass* (1981); *Memoirs of Many in One* (1986).

Judith Arundell Wright (1915–2000), Australian poet, writer and activist, was born in Armidale, New South Wales, into a leading, and wealthy, pastoral family. She attended the University of Sydney and, after briefly travelling to Britain and Europe, settled in Sydney to write. She made her debut as a poet with the publication of *The Moving Image* (1946), which was followed by many further volumes of poetry, such as *Woman to Man* (1949) and *The Other Half* (1966). She was active in championing aboriginal rights and environmental issues, and these concerns permeate her work. In addition to her poetry, her works include the narration of her family's history in *The Generations of Men* (1959) and its sequel *The Cry for the Dead* (1981), and her autobiography *Half a Lifetime* (1999). She won many literary awards and honours, including the 1992 Queen's Gold Medal for Poetry, which she was the first Australian to receive.

BIBLIOGRAPHY *Woman to Man* (1949); *The Gateway* (1953); *The Two Fires* (1955); *The Generations of Men* (1959), *Birds* (1962); *Five Senses* (1963); *City Sunrise* (1964); *Preoccupations in Australian Poetry* (1965); *The Other Half* (1966); *Alive* (1973); *Fourth Quarter* (1976); *The Coral Battleground* (1977); *The Cry for the Dead* (1981); *Phantom Dwelling* (1985); *A Human Pattern* (1990); *Half a Lifetime* (1999).

William Butler Yeats (1865–1939), Irish poet and playwright, was born in Dublin into a Protestant family. He attended schools in London, while spending summer holidays in Co. Sligo, where he fostered his love for Irish mythology and folklore. He also took a deep interest in Hindu philosophy, theosophy and occultism, which led him to join the Hermetic Order of the Golden Dawn in 1890. He was a propelling force in the Irish Literary Revival, and was a co-founder of, and playwright for, the Irish Literary Theatre, which was relaunched as the Abbey Theatre in 1904. He won the Nobel Prize for Literature in 1923, and also served as a member of the Irish Senate from 1922 to 1928 after the establishment of the Irish Free State.

BIBLIOGRAPHY (Poetry) *Mosada* (1886); *The Wanderings of Oisin and Other Poems* (1889); *The Wind Among the Reeds* (1899); *In the Seven Woods* (1903); *The Green Helmet and Other Poems* (1910); *Responsibilities* (1914); *Easter 1916* (1916); *The Wild Swans at Coole* (1919); *Michael Robartes and the Dancer* (1921); *Later Poems* (1922); *The Tower* (1928); *The Winding Stair and Other Poems* (1933); *A Full Moon in March* (1935); *Last Poems and Two Plays* (1939).

(Plays) *The Countess Kathleen and Various Legends and Lyrics* (1892); *The Land of Heart's Desire* (1894); *The Shadowy Waters* (1900); *Cathleen Ní Houlihan* (with Lady Gregory, 1902); *On Baile's Strand* (1903); *The King's Threshold* (1904); *Four Plays for Dancers* (1921); *The Cat and the Moon* (1924); *Collected Plays* (1934).

(Fiction) *John Sherman and Dhoya* (1891); *The Secret Rose* (1897).

(Nonfiction) *The Celtic Twilight* (1893); *Ideas of Good and Evil* (1903); *The Cutting of an Agate* (1912); *Reveries Over Childhood and Youth* (1916); *Per Amica Silentia Lunae* (1918); *A Vision* (1925); *Autobiographies of William Butler Yeats* (1926); *On the Boiler* (1939). *Collected Works* (ed. J. Finneran & G. Mills, 14 vols., 1989–).

Brief colonial histories: Australia, the Caribbean, East Africa, India and Pakistan, Ireland, West Africa (compiled by Kaori Nagai)

Australia

Australia first became known to Europe as 'New Holland', after the Dutch visited parts of it in the seventeenth century. James Cook, who sailed along its east coast in 1770, declared it *terra nullius* (nobody's land) and claimed Britain's possession of the entire area, which he named New South Wales. Subsequently a penal colony was founded at Botany Bay (Sydney) in 1788. The British took possession of the rest of the continent in 1829. By the 1830s the introduction of the wool industry had transformed the continent from merely a depository for convicts into a pastoral colony, attracting an increasing number of immigrants. A wave of squatters penetrated into the virgin land in search of grazing ground, and, accordingly, the population of Aborigines fell sharply, many cold-bloodedly murdered, as in the case of the Myall Creek Massacre of 1838. The bush landscape became integral to the Australian identity and way of life, as well as providing hideouts for outlaws, escaped convicts and bushrangers. Tasmania, which the Dutch had named Van Diemen's Land, was first settled as a penal colony by the British in 1803 and became a separate colony in 1825. South Australia (1834), Victoria (1851) and Queensland (1859) were created as separate colonies from parts of New South Wales; along with Tasmania, they were granted limited self-government in 1855 (Queensland in 1859 and Western Australia in 1890). Gold was discovered in New South Wales and Victoria in the 1850s, and the ensuing gold rush trebled the Australian population within a decade. Many Chinese workers arrived to offer cheap labour in goldfields, which resulted in outbreaks of race hatred and violence against them. On 1 January 1901 the six colonies, which had all been given self-government, plus the area known as the Northern Territory, were federated to form the Commonwealth of Australia, as a dominion of the British Empire. It immediately implemented its 'White Australia' policy by passing a series of regulations denying citizenship and equal rights to non-Europeans, including the Immigration Restriction Bill in 1901. Australia willingly participated in the Boer War and World War I, fighting for the Empire. The Statute of Westminster of 1931 formally ended the British rule of self-governing colonies to form the British Commonwealth of Nations, which Australia ratified in 1942. After World War II, Australia began to invite large-scale immigration from Europe, and about a million British citizens emigrated there. Citizenship was granted to Aborigines after a national referendum in 1967. Legislation such as the

Aboriginal Land Rights Acts (1973) and the Native Title Act (1993) have recognized some of their ancestral rights. The White Australia policy, which had been gradually dismantled since the 1950s, effectively ended in the 1970s with reviews of the immigration law and the passing of the Racial Discrimination Act in 1975. The demography of Australia has since changed dramatically, particularly owing to the large number of Asian and other ethnic migrants. In a referendum held in 1999, the population narrowly voted against abolishing the British monarch as the head of state and establishing a republic.

The Caribbean

The colonial history of the Caribbean starts with Christopher Columbus's discovery of it as a part of the New World in 1492. It is also called the West Indies, owing to Columbus's belief that he had successfully reached the Indies (China, India, Indonesia, Japan, etc.) by sailing westward. At the time of discovery, two dominant indigenous groups populated the area; one was 'the Arawaks', whom Columbus described as a gentle and hospitable people, the other 'the Caribs', a name which gave rise to the 'Caribbean', as well as the word 'cannibal'. The Spanish and Portuguese subsequently came to the Caribbean in search of gold, and the indigenous population was reduced to near extinction by genocide, disease, slavery and mass suicide. Slaves from West Africa were introduced to replace the dwindling native populations. In the seventeenth century England, France and the Netherlands joined the struggle for supremacy over the islands, and many islands changed hands, making the Caribbean a Creole society woven out of diverse cultures and languages. The introduction of sugar plantations instigated a large-scale importation of slaves from Africa, bringing massive profits to the European countries through 'white gold' (sugar) and 'black gold' (slaves). It was not until the late eighteenth century, when Caribbean sugar lost its economic importance, that the antislavery movement gained momentum. In the British West Indies, slavery was abolished in 1834, with full emancipation coming in 1838 with the end of apprenticeship, triggering the transportation of cheap indentured labour from China and India to the Caribbean. The emancipated black population continued to suffer as a disenfranchised labouring class. The biggest and most significant black uprising during the nineteenth century was the Morant Bay Rebellion in Jamaica in 1865. The harsh punishment of the rebels meted out by Governor Edward Eyre divided British public opinion. In the late 1930s the labour movement swept across the Caribbean, seen most notably in the Labour Rebellion in Jamaica in 1938, and resulted in the formation of unions, paving the way for the independence struggles which were to come after World War II.

Jamaica, 'the Jewel in the Crown' of the Caribbean, was first colonized by the Spanish but became a British colony in 1670. Barbados, first visited by a Portuguese explorer, then ravaged by Spanish exploitation, was found to be uninhabited when Britain seized the island in 1627. Trinidad was a Spanish colony until it was taken by Britain in 1797, and was administratively combined in 1889 as a single colony with Tobago, which was ruled by the Dutch and the French before becoming British in 1814. St Lucia was colonized in 1635 by the French, who signed a treaty with the indigenous Caribs; it was later ceded to Britain in 1814. These islands and other British Caribbean islands came together to form the West Indies Federation in 1958, under the auspices of the British government, but the Federation soon disintegrated after Jamaica and Trinidad and Tobago left it and became independent in 1962. Barbados and the Bahamas followed suit, in 1966 and 1973 respectively. The rest of the colonies in the Federation, except Montserrat, have subsequently attained independence: Grenada (1974), Dominica (1978), St Lucia (1979), St Vincent (1979), Antigua and Barbuda (1981), and St Kitts and Nevis (1983). Jamaica is the home of the Rastafari movement, which originated in the 1930s and whose followers believe Haile Selassie I of Ethiopia to have been the Messiah. The movement, which rejects Western values and calls for black unity, has spread through the Carribean and beyond, following the Carribean diaspora, and through reggae music.

Guyana, though part of the South American mainland, historically and culturally constitutes part of the Caribbean. The area was colonized by the Dutch in the sixteenth century, but later changed hands between the British and the French until it finally became British Guiana in 1831. Guyana attained independence in 1966, becoming a republic in 1970, and suffers from ethnopolitical conflicts between its African and Indian communities, with the two main political parties representing each group's interests. There were serious outbreaks of violence between these communities in the 1960s, and again in 1998. French Guyana remains a department of France; the area known as Dutch Guiana is now called Surinam.

East Africa: Kenya and Tanzania

The Portuguese, after their arrival in the late fifteenth century, fought for control of the East African coast with the Arabs, and achieved this with the capture of the Omani port of Muscat in 1507. However, by 1700 the Omani Arabs had largely regained their dominance. Sayyid Said (1791–1856), Sultan of Oman, moved his court to the island of Zanzibar in 1832 and ruled most of the coastal area of the East African mainland. The island flourished as the centre of the East African slave and ivory trades, though after Said's death its influence on the mainland gradually diminished, while European explorers and missionaries were venturing further and further into East Africa's interior. Under the terms of an agreement reached in 1886, Britain and Germany partitioned East Africa along the modern boundary between Kenya (Britain) and Tanzania (Germany). This agreement also granted Zanzibar, which had become a separate sultanate in 1861, to Britain, and it was proclaimed a British protectorate in 1890. By the early twentieth century, the whole of East Africa, except Ethiopia, was divided between Britain, France, Germany, Italy and Portugal.

German colonization of present-day Tanzania was first undertaken by the German East Africa Company, which was established in 1885. In 1891 the German government took over the company's territory, and the entire area was occupied by 1897. Brutal treatment of indigenous tribes led to the Maji Maji Revolt of 1905–7. As a result of World War I, the colony came under British rule and was renamed Tanganyika, after the largest lake in the region. In 1961 it gained independence, becoming a republic in 1962. Zanzibar also regained its independence in 1963, and its sultanate was overthrown in the following year. Tanganyika and Zanzibar merged to form Tanzania in 1964. The first president, Julius Nyerere, in his influential Arusha Declaration of 1967, called for a programme of socialist economic development, with an emphasis on self-reliance and egalitarianism, but his scheme, despite international aid, collapsed after a decade. In 1979 Tanzania invaded Uganda to oust President Idi Amin.

Modern-day Kenya was first colonized by the Imperial British East Africa Company, which was established in 1888; the company's territory was later transferred to the British government as the East Africa Protectorate, and in 1920 it became a British Crown Colony, renamed Kenya, after the highest mountain in the region. From 1903 Europeans began to settle in the highlands, taking land from the Maasai, the Gikuyu and other indigenous tribes. This settlement also induced Indian merchants to move to the interior and attracted a steady flux of further Indian immigrants, many recruited to help construct an extensive railway system. From 1952 to 1960 Kenya was placed under a State of Emergency, as the Mau Mau movement, a guerrilla group composed mostly of Gikuyu peasants, launched a violent campaign against white settlers. Kenya achieved independence in 1963 and became a republic in 1964, with Jomo Kenyatta as the first president. His party, the Kenya African National Union (KANU), dominated the country's politics for the next four decades. Rising tension between the Gikuyu and the Luo, two of the largest ethnic groups in Kenya, came to a head in the late 1960s. After Kenyatta's death in 1978, Daniel arap Moi succeeded as president, remaining so until 2002, when his regime, often accused of human rights violations and repressive measures, ended with the election of Mwai Kibaki as president.

India and Pakistan

Before European colonization, the subcontinent of India consisted of many different states, independently governed (though at times owing allegiance to one of the Mughal emperors), and with separate languages, religions and cultures. After Vasco da Gama's arrival at Calicut in 1498, the Portuguese conquered Goa (1510) and set up trading stations to monopolise the spice trade in India. In the seventeenth century the British, the Dutch and the French joined in the competition. The British East Indian Company was founded in 1600 and established presidencies in Madras, Bombay and Calcutta. In the early eighteenth century, as the power of the Muslim Mughal empire (1526–1857) declined, the rivalry between the British and the French for greater control of the territory intensified. In 1757 a British force led by Robert Clive defeated the army of the Nawab of Bengal in the Battle of Plassey, laying the foundation for the British Indian Empire. By the early nine-teenth century, the British East India Company directly or indirectly controlled all the Indian territories except Sind and Punjab, which were conquered in 1843 and 1849 respectively. In 1857 the rebellion of the company's sepoy soldiers developed into a widespread revolt against British rule (the Indian Mutiny, or the first War of Independence). After the suppression of the uprising, the company was dissolved in 1858 and India came under direct British rule as a Crown Colony. Queen Victoria was proclaimed Empress of India in 1877.

The Indian National Congress was formed in 1885 as an association of educated Indians, and soon became the leading force of India's struggle for independence. Differences of opinion within the Congress as to how to react to Lord Curzon's notorious partition of Bengal (1905–11) led to its splitting, in 1907, into a moderate group led by Gopal Krishna Gokhale and an extreme group led by Bal Gangadhar Tilak. The All-India Muslim League was created by Muslim leaders in 1906 to represent the views of the Muslim minority. The Government of India Act of 1919, which initiated a gradual introduction of self-government, was accompanied by the Rowlatt Acts of the same year, which effectively legalized the imprisonment of political suspects without trial. The campaign against these acts led to the Amritsar Massacre of 1919: General Michael Dyer's order to open fire on those attending a protest meeting, resulting in at least 400 civilian deaths, marked a pivotal moment in the Raj's history. Mahatma Gandhi, who emerged as a spiritual leader of the Indian National Congress, led a series of all-India *satyagraha*, or passive resistance, campaigns against the British rule on the principle of *ahimsa*, or nonviolence. Meanwhile, by 1940 the Muslim League, led by Muhammad Ali Jinnah, endorsed the idea of 'Pakistan', a Muslim state separate from a Hindu-dominated India. In 1947 the independence of India was achieved and the country was divided, through Partition, into two separate states, India and Pakistan. Riots and communal violence on a massive scale followed Partition, and nearly half a million were killed when more than seventeen million refugees fled across the India-Pakistan border – Muslims to Pakistan, Hindus to India. Gandhi, who sought to reconcile the two communities, was assassinated by a Hindu fanatic in 1948. Kashmir has remained a subject of territorial dispute between the two countries: the India-Pakistan War of 1947–8 partitioned the area into two, and another major war was fought in 1965. Tensions over Kashmir erupted again in the 1990s, as India launched an air strike on Muslim separatists in India-controlled Kashmir.

Pakistan originally consisted of West Pakistan and East Pakistan, separated by 1,100 miles of Indian territory. In 1971 a civil war broke out; East Pakistan, led by the Awami League and assisted by Indian forces, won and proclaimed its independence as Bangladesh. Since independence civil rule in Pakistan has been repeatedly inter-rupted by military rule. Zulfikar Ali Bhutto, who became president (later prime minister) of Pakistan after the civil war, was deposed in a coup and executed in 1979. His daughter Benazir Bhutto came to power as prime minister in 1988 and was reelected in 1993, though her regime was increasingly accused of corruption. In 1999 Pakistan was again placed under military control by Pervez Musharraf, who has recently become a key partner in the United States' 'War on Terror'.

In India, Jawaharlal Nehru, the leader of the Indian National Congress, became the first prime minister (1947–64) and the Congress became a major political party in post-independence India. In 1966 Nehru's daughter Indira Gandhi came to power as prime minister and dominated Indian politics. In 1975 she declared a State of Emergency, suspending all civil rights and imprisoning thousands of opponents, when placed under pressure to step down in the face of alleged malpractice during the 1971 election. She was assassinated by a Sikh member of her security guard in 1984, after her government's decision in 1982 to order troops into the Golden Temple in Amritsar to suppress a militant campaign by Sikhs to create an autonomous state in Punjab. In the 1990s the Hindu nationalist Bharatiya Janata Party (BJP) gained force, defeating the Congress in the 1996 election. The Congress returned to power in 2004 and Manmohan Singh became India's first Sikh prime minister.

Ireland

Ireland's long colonization by England began when Henry II landed in Ireland in 1171, proclaimed his overlordship of the island, and was supported by a decree from Pope Adrian IV. In the sixteenth century Tudor monarchs suppressed rebellions in Ireland and started the process of Protestant 'plantation' or settlement. The Protestant Church of Ireland was established by Henry VIII in 1537, though the majority of the Irish populace remained Roman Catholic. The plantation of Ulster by English and Scottish settlers began around 1610. Oliver Cromwell's punitive expedition to Ireland in 1649–50 led to the systematic confiscation of land owned by Catholics, beginning a long-lasting pattern of Protestant landlordship over Catholic tenants. William III's victory over the Catholic James II in the Battle of the Boyne of 1690 consolidated the Protestant Ascendancy, and harsher penal laws were enforced against Catholics, stripping them of basic civil rights. From 1782 to 1800 the Anglo-Irish Protestant Parliament enjoyed a brief period of limited self-government. The society of the United Irishmen was founded in 1791, aspiring to unite all Irish people, regardless of their religion, against the English, to achieve independence. In 1798 a rebellion backed up by a French invasion was instigated by Wolfe Tone, leader of the United Irishmen, but was unsuccessful. The Act of Union followed in 1801, by which the Irish Parliament was abolished and Ireland was made part of Britain. Under the Union many Irish actively participated in the British Empire, and many emigrated as settlers to the British colonies and North America.

In the first part of the nineteenth century, Daniel O'Connell, who campaigned to achieve Catholic emancipation and the repeal of the Union, emerged as a popular leader who successfully mobilized Catholic people in protest meetings. The country's all-important potato crop failed between 1845 and 1849 and Ireland suffered the Great Famine, during which more than a million people died and the ensuing emigration, during and after the famine, halved the population. In the 1850s a secret revolutionary movement known as Fenianism gained ground among Irish emigrants in the United States, out of which the Irish Republican Brotherhood (IRB) was formed in 1873. In the 1880s Charles Stewart Parnell was a leading figure in the campaign for self-government within the Union (Home Rule), and this was supported by the Liberal government in England led by William Gladstone. Two Home Rule Bills were presented to Parliament in 1886 and 1893, but both were defeated. The third Home Rule Bill was finally passed in 1914, only to be suspended because of the outbreak of World War I.

The slow process of achieving Home Rule contributed to increasing support for Sinn Féin, which was founded in 1905 by Arthur Griffith with the aim of achieving full political independence for Ireland. Meanwhile, Unionists, especially Protestants in Ulster, were rallying forces to fight against Home Rule. In the Easter Rising of 1916, nationalists, led by the IRB, seized the General Post Office in Dublin and read out the proclamation of the Irish Republic; the rebellion was quickly suppressed and sixteen of its leaders were executed. In 1919 Sinn Féin, after decisive election victories in 1918, set up the Dáil Éireann (Irish Assembly) and proclaimed independence, an act which led to the Anglo-Irish War of 1919–21. In 1920 Ireland was partitioned into Northern Ireland and Southern Ireland, and, with the Anglo-Irish Treaty of 1922, Southern Ireland was granted dominion status and became the Irish Free State. Thousands died when the Civil War (1922–3) erupted between supporters of the treaty and its opponents, who formed the Irish Republican Army (IRA) and continued to resist the partition of Ireland for more than sixty years. In 1937 the Irish Free State became a republic, changing its name to Eire. It became the Republic of Ireland in 1949, following the ratification of a new constitution.

Northern Ireland remained part of the United Kingdom, and its history has been marked by communal strife between Protestants and Catholics, and by outbreaks of paramilitary violence. Tension mounted in the late 1960s, as Terence O'Neill, prime minister of Northern Ireland (1963–9), made historic gestures to bridge the gap between the two communities, while the Catholic minority organized civil rights demonstrations; these fuelled the insecurities of the Protestant community and led to widespread riots. In 1972 a civil rights march in Derry was fired upon by British troops, killing fourteen demonstrators, an event that has come to be known as 'Bloody Sunday'. The following decades witnessed IRA bombings in Northern Ireland and the British mainland, acts of violence committed by paramilitary groups belonging to both sides of the political divide, and a militarization of the province. In 1981 IRA prisoners held in the Maze Prison, denied the status of political prisoners, went on hunger strike, capturing the public imagination. Ten of the hunger strikers died. The peace process gathered momentum with the IRA's ceasefire of 1994, following the Downing Street Declaration of 1993. In 1998 the Good Friday Agreement, aimed at paving the way for reconciliation and settlement, was reached in multiparty negotiations.

West Africa (Ghana and Nigeria)

Before the establishment of trading by the Portuguese, the West African city of Timbuktu was famed as a trading and cultural centre during the fourteenth, fifteenth and sixteenth centuries in the successive empires of Ghana, Mali and Songhai. The Portuguese visited its coastline in the fifteenth century and established trading posts for ivory, gold and slaves. Dutch, English and French traders followed and eventually replaced the Portuguese. In the seventeenth and eighteenth centuries, West Africa was a key component in a lucrative 'triangular trade', whereby slaves were 'exported' to plantations in the Caribbean, and the sugar produced there exported to Europe. The slave trade declined rapidly after Britain abolished it in 1807, and palm oil from the east coast of Ghana replaced slaves as the main 'commodity'. For most of the nineteenth century, European states ruled very little of West Africa, and their settlements were limited to the coastal area. It was represented as inhospitable and disease-ridden, and dreaded as 'the white man's grave'; an 1865 Select Committee of the House of Commons recommended withdrawal from all British settlements in West Africa, except Sierra Leone. The scramble for inner land began only in the late 1880s following the Berlin Conference of 1884. By the early twentieth century, Britain ruled Gambia, Ghana, Nigeria and Sierra Leone. A vast stretch of territory including Benin, Chad, Ivory Coast, Niger and Senegal came under French rule.

At the beginning of the nineteenth century, the Fante states of the coastal area made alliance with the British against the Ashanti, a powerful kingdom of the north, giving the British their first firm grip on modern-day Ghana. These Fante states were proclaimed the British Crown Colony of the Gold Coast in 1874, while the Ashanti kingdom, after a series of battles with the British, fell at the turn of the century and became a British Crown Colony in 1901. In 1946 the Gold Coast and the Ashanti, along with the Northern Territories and British Togoland, were brought together as the single colony of the Gold Coast. After World War II, an anticolonial movement, led by Kwame Nkrumah, gathered momentum, and in 1957 this colony became the first African state to achieve independence, renaming itself Ghana; it became a republic in 1960. Nkrumah, who by 1966 had become dictatorial, was overthrown by a military police coup in that year. After a decade of coups and countercoups, Flight Lieutenant Jerry Rawlings, in his second coup, seized control in 1981. Ghana now has a democratically elected government.

The British colonization of modern-day Nigeria began when the British captured the coastal city of Lagos in 1851, ostensibly to put an end to the dwindling slave trade. In 1861 the city was formally annexed as a British colony. After the Berlin Conference of 1884–5, which recognized Britain's sovereignty over southern Niger, the Royal Niger Company was given a charter to trade in and govern Niger and Northern Nigeria. The company's territory was transferred to the British government in 1900, and Nigeria was made a British protectorate in 1901. Nigeria attained independence in 1960 and became a republic in 1963. Its politics have from the outset been strongly affected by ethnic, religious and regional divisions, the most significant groupings being the Igbo in the East, the Yoruba in the West, and the largely Muslim Hausa-Fulani of the north. In 1967 the Nigerian Civil War broke out when, after massacres by local northerners of Igbos living in the north, the Igbo-dominated region proclaimed its independence as the Republic of Biafra; millions were killed in the fighting and as a result of starvation, and Biafra surrendered in

1970. Nigeria's economy showed signs of development in the 1970s thanks to the country's abundant oil resources, though this wealth was also a significant source of government corruption and political instability. After a series of military coups and countercoups, General Sani Abacha seized power in 1993. Under his regime his opponents were brutally suppressed, and his execution in 1995 of Ken Saro-Wiwa, writer and activist, caused an international outcry. After Abacha's death in 1998, civil rule was restored but continuing ethnic and religious tensions have caused thousands of deaths.

Select bibliography

Achebe, Chinua. 'The Role of the Writer in a New Nation'. *Nigeria Magazine* 81
(1964), pp. 157–60. Reprinted in G. D. Killam, ed. *African Writers on
African Writing*. London: Heinemann, 1978, pp 7–13.

A Man of the People. London: Heinemann, 1966.

Arrow of God. London: Heinemann, 1974.

Morning Yet on Creation Day. London: Heinemann, 1975.

'Contemporary Literature', in Saburi O. Biobaku, ed., *The Living Culture of
Nigeria*. London: Nelson, 1976, pp. 47–51.

Things Fall Apart. London: Heinemann, 1976.

Anthills of the Savannah. London: Heinemann, 1987.

Hopes and Impediments: Selected Essays, 1965–87. Oxford: Heinemann,
1988.

Home and Exile. New York: Random House, 2001.

Collected Poems. New York: Anchor Books, 2004.

Ahmad, Aijaz. *In Theory: Classes, Nations, Literatures*. London: Verso, 1992.

Forms/Figures/Formations. London: Verso, 1996.

Aidoo, Ama Ata. *Dilemma of a Ghost*. Harlow: Longman, 1965.

Anowa. London: Longman, 1970.

'Ama Ata Aidoo' (Interview with Maxine McGregor), in Dennis Duerden
and Cosmo Pieterse, eds., *African Writers Talking*, New York: Africana
Publishing, 1972, pp. 19–27.

Our Sister Killjoy: or Reflections from a Black-eyed Squint. Harlow: Longman,
1977.

'To Be a Woman', in Robin Morgan, ed., *Sisterhood is Global: The
International Women's Movement Anthology*. Garden City, NY: Anchor
Press/Doubleday, 1984, pp. 258–65.

'Ama Ata Aidoo' (Interview with Sarah Chetin). *Wasafiri: Journal of
Caribbean, African, Asian and Associated Literatures and Film* 6/7 (1987),
pp. 23–7.

'Ama Ata Aidoo' (Interview with Adeola James), in James, ed., *In Their Own
Voices: African Women Writers Talk*. London: Heinemann, 1990, pp.
9–27.

'Ama Ata Aidoo – In Conversation'(Interview with Sarah Modebe). *New
African* 288 (September 1991).

No Sweetness Here and Other Stories, Afterword by Ketu H. Katrak. New York: Feminist Press, 1995.

Anderson, Benedict. *Imagined Communities: Reflections on the Origin and Spread of Nationalism.* London: Verso, 1983.

Anderson, Linda. *Autobiography.* London: Routledge, 2004.

Appiah, Kwame Anthony. *In My Father's House.* New York: Oxford University Press, 1992.

    Cosmopolitanism: Ethics in a World of Strangers. New York: W. W. Norton, 2006.

Arnold, Matthew. *On the Study of Celtic Literature.* London: Smith, Elder, 1891.

Ash, Ranjana. 'The Search for Freedom in Indian Women's Writing', in Susheila Nasta, ed., *Motherlands: Black Women's Writing from Africa, the Caribbean and South Asia.* London: The Women's Press, 1991, pp. 152–74.

Ashcroft, Bill, Gareth Griffiths and Helen Tiffin. *The Empire Writes Back.* London: Routledge, 1989.

    , eds. *Key Concepts in Post-Colonial Studies.* London: Routledge, 1998.

    The Post-Colonial Studies Reader. London: Routledge, 1995.

Balaswamy, P. 'A Post-Modern, Provocative, Metropolitan Mother India: Aurora Zogoiby of Rushdie's *The Moor's Last Sigh*', in Rajeshwar Mittapalli and Joel Kuortti, eds., *Salman Rushdie: New Critical Insights.* 2 vols. New Delhi: Atlantic Publishers, 2003, II, pp. 52–64.

Banham, Martin (with Clive Wake). *African Theatre Today.* London: Pitman Publishers, 1976.

Baraka, Imamu Amiri (LeRoi Jones). *Raise, Race, Rays, Raze: Essays Since 1965.* New York: William Morrow, 1972.

Barber, Karin, ed. *Africa's Hidden Histories: Everyday Literacy and Making the Self.* Bloomington: Indiana University Press, 2006.

Barnes, John, ed. *Joseph Furphy.* St Lucia, Queensland: University of Queensland Press, 1981.

Baugh, Edward. 'The Poem as an Autobiographical Novel: Derek Walcott's "Another Life" in relation to Wordsworth's "Prelude" and Joyce's "Portrait"', in C. D. Narasimhaiah, ed., *Awakened Conscience: Studies in Commonwealth Literature.* New Delhi: Sterling, 1978, pp. 226–35.

Benjamin, Walter. *Illuminations.* Trans. Harry Zohn. New York: Schocken, 1969.

Bennett, Louise. *Jamaica Labrish*, with notes and Introduction by Rex Nettleford. Jamaica: Sangster's Book Stores, 1966.

Berndt, Ronald M., trans. 'Song Cycle of the Moon-Bone', in Les A. Murray, ed., *The New Oxford Book of Australian Verse.* Melbourne: Oxford University Press, 1986, pp. 239–46.

Berry, James. *Fractured Circles.* London: New Beacon Books, 1976.

    Lucy's Letters and Loving. London and Port of Spain: New Beacon, 1982.

Bery, Ashok. *Postcolonial Poetry and Cultural Translation.* Basingstoke: Palgrave Macmillan, 2007.

Bhabha, Homi. *The Location of Culture*. London: Routledge, 1994.
   'Re-Inventing Britain: A Manifesto', in *British Studies Now (Re-Inventing Britain: Identity, Transnationalism, and the Arts)* 9 (April 1997). London: The British Council, 1997. Reprinted in *Wasafiri* 29 (Spring 1999), pp. 38–43.
   'Foreword: Remembering Fanon : Self, Psyche, and the Colonial Condition', in Franz Fanon, *Black Skin, White Masks*, Liberation Classics. London and Sydney: Pluto, 1986, pp. vii–xxvi.
Bhatt, Sujata. *Point No Point*. Manchester: Carcanet, 1997.
Blake, Ann. 'A "Very Backward Country": Christina Stead and the English Class System', in Ann Blake, Leila Gandhi and Sue Thomas, eds., *England Through Colonial Eyes in Twentieth-Century Fiction*. Basingstoke: Palgrave Macmillan, 2001, pp. 104–15.
Blixen, Karen. *Out of Africa*. London: Jonathan Cape, 1964.
Boehmer, Elleke. 'Stories of Women and Mothers: Gender and Nationalism in the Early Fiction of Flora Nwapa', in Susheila Nasta, ed., *Motherlands: Black Women's Writing from Africa, the Caribbean and South Asia*. London: The Women's Press, 1991, pp. 3–23.
   Colonial and Postcolonial Literature. Oxford: Oxford University Press, 1995.
   Stories of Women: Gender and Narrative in the Postcolonial Nation. Manchester: Manchester University Press, 2005.
Boland, Eavan. *Outside History*. Manchester: Carcanet, 1990.
   'Outside History'. *PN Review* 17:1 (September/October 1990), pp. 21–8.
   'The Woman, the Place, the Poet'. *PN Review* 17:3 (January/Febuary 1991), pp. 35–40.
   The Lost Land. Manchester: Carcanet, 1998.
Booth, Howard and Nigel Rigby, eds. *Modernism and Empire*. Manchester: Manchester University Press, 2000.
Bourke, Angela, et al., eds. *Field Day Anthology of Irish Writing*. 5 vols., IV and V. Cork: Cork University Press, 2002.
Brace, M. 'Question Marks Over the Empire's Decision', *The Independent*, 10 September 1994, p. 26.
Brathwaite, (Edward) Kamau. *The Arrivants*. London: Oxford University Press, 1973.
   History of the Voice: The Development of Nation Language in Anglophone Caribbean Poetry. London: New Beacon Books, 1984.
Brennan, Timothy. *Salman Rushdie and the Third World: Myths of the Nation*. Basingstoke: Macmillan, 1989.
   At Home in the World: Cosmopolitanism Now. Cambridge, MA; London: Harvard University Press, 1997.
Brown, Lloyd. *Women Writers in Black Africa*. Westport, CT: Greenwood Press, 1981.
Brown, Stewart, ed. *The Art of Derek Walcott*. Bridgend: Seren Books, 1991.
Burnett, Paula. *Derek Walcott: Politics and Poetics*. Gainesville: University of Florida Press, 2000.

Carroll, Clare and Patricia King, eds. *Ireland and Postcolonial Theory*. Cork: Cork University Press, 2003.

Castle, Gregory, ed. *Postcolonial Discourses: An Anthology*. Oxford: Blackwell, 2001.

Childs, Peter and Patrick Williams, eds. *An Introduction to Post-Colonial Theory*. London; New York: Prentice Hall, 1997.

Chinweizu, et al. *The Decolonization of African Literature*. Washington, DC: Howard University Press, 1983.

Clarke, Marcus. *Stories*. Ed. Michael Wilding. Sydney: Hale & Iremonger, 1983.

Conrad, Joseph. *Heart of Darkness*. London: Penguin, 1973.

Cooper, Carolyn. 'Noh Lickle Twang: An Introduction to the Poetry of Louise Bennett'. *World Literature Written in English* 17:1 (1978), pp. 317–27.

    'Caribbean Poetry in English: 1900–1976'. *World Literature Written in English* 23 (1984), pp. 414–16.

Corcoran, Neil. 'The Invention of Australia', *Times Literary Supplement*, 22 August 1986, p. 919.

Corkery, Daniel. *Synge and Anglo-Irish Literature*. Cork: Cork University Press, 1966.

Cullingford, Elizabeth Butler. *Gender and History in Yeats's Love Poetry*. Cambridge: Cambridge University Press, 1993.

    Ireland's Others: Gender and Ethnicity in Irish Literature and Popular Culture. Notre Dame: Notre Dame Press, 2001.

Curtin, Philip D. *The Image of Africa: British Ideas and Action, 1780–1850*. Madison: Wisconsin University Press, 1964.

Curtis, L. Perry, Jr. *Anglo-Saxons and Celts: A Study of Anti-Irish Prejudice in Victorian England*. Bridgeport, CT: Conference on British Studies, 1968.

    Apes and Angels: The Irishman in Victorian Caricature. Washington, DC: Smithsonian Institution, 1996.

Dangarembga, Tsitsi. *Nervous Conditions*. Emeryville, CA: Seal Press, 1989.

De Blij, H. J. and Peter O. Muller. *Geography: Realms, Regions, and Concepts*. Chichester: John Wiley & Sons, 1997.

DeCaires Narain, Denise. *Contemporary Caribbean Women's Poetry: Making Style*. London: Routledge, 2002.

Desai, Anita. *Clear Light of Day*. London: Vintage, 2001.

Docherty, Thomas. 'The Place's Fault', in Ondrej Pilný and Clare Wallace, eds., *Global Ireland*. Prague: Litteraria Pragensia, 2005, pp.13–32.

Donnell, Alison. *Twentieth Century Caribbean Literature: Critical Moments in Anglophone Literary History*. London: Routledge, 2006.

Döring, Tobias. 'The Passage of the Eye/I: David Dabydeen, V. S. Naipaul, and the Tombstones of Parabiography', in Alfred Hornung and Ernstpeter Ruhe, eds., *Postcolonialism and Autobiography*. Amsterdam: Rodopi, 1998, pp. 149–66.

    Caribbean-English Passages: Intertextuality in a Postcolonial Tradition. London: Routledge, 2002.

Doumerc, Eric. 'Louise Bennett and the Mento Tradition', *ARIEL: A Review of International English Literature* 31:4 (October 2000), pp. 23–31.

Dunbar, Paul Laurence. *The Complete Poems of Paul Laurence Dunbar*, with an Introduction by William Dean Howells. New York: Dodd, Mead, & Co., 1920.

Edwards, Ruth Dudley. *Patrick Pearse: The Triumph of Failure*. London: Faber and Faber, 1979.

Eliot, T. S. *Collected Poems, 1909–1935*. London: Faber and Faber, 1936.

Elliott, Brian, ed. *The Jindyworobaks*. Brisbane: University of Queensland Press, 1979.

Emecheta, Buchi. 'Culture Conflict', *New Society*, 6 September 1984, p. 249.

Evaristo, Bernardine. *Lara*. Tunbridge Wells: Angela Roy Publishing, 1997.
    The Emperor's Babe. London: Hamish Hamilton, 2001.

Fanon, Frantz. *Black Skin, White Masks*. Trans. Charles Lam Markmann. New York: Grove Press, 1967.
    The Wretched of the Earth. Trans. Constance Farrington. New York: Grove Press, 1968.

Field, Barron. 'The Kangaroo', in Les Murray, ed., *The New Oxford Book of Australian Verse*. Melbourne: Oxford University Press, 1986, pp. 6–7.

Figueroa, John. '*Omeros*', in Stewart Brown, ed., *The Art of Derek Walcott*. Bridgend: Seren Books, 1991, pp. 193–213.

Foster, Roy. *Paddy & Mr Punch: Connections in Irish and English History*. London: Penguin, 1995.

Franklin, (Stella Maria Sarah) Miles. *My Brilliant Career*, with a Preface by Henry Lawson. Edinburgh: Blackwoods, 1901.

Fraser, Robert. *Lifting the Sentence: A Poetics of Postcolonial Fiction*. Manchester: Manchester University Press, 2000.

Friel, Brian. *Translations*, in John Harrington, ed., *Modern Irish Drama*. London and New York: W. W. Norton, 1991, pp. 340–74.

Fulford, Sarah. 'Eavan Boland: Forging a Postcolonial History', in Glenn Hooper and Colin Graham, eds., *Irish and Postcolonial Writing*. Basingstoke: Palgrave Macmillan, 2002, pp. 202–21.

Gandhi, Leela. '"Ellowen, Deeowen": Salman Rushdie and the Migrant's Desire', in Ann Blake, Leela Gandhi and Sue Thomas, eds., *England Through Colonial Eyes in Twentieth-Century Fiction*. Basingstoke: Palgrave Macmillan, 2001, pp.157–70.

Gikandi, Simon. *Reading Chinua Achebe: Language and Ideology in Fiction*. London: James Currey; Portsmouth, NH: Heinemann, 1991.

Gilbert, Helen and Joanne Tompkins, *Post-Colonial Drama: Theory, Practice, Politics*. London: Routledge, 1996.

Gilbert, Sandra and Susan Gubar. *The Madwoman in the Attic: The Woman Writer and the Nineteenth-Century Literary Imagination*. New Haven: Yale University Press, 1979.

Gilroy, Paul. *The Black Atlantic: Modernity and Double Consciousness*. Cambridge, MA: Harvard University Press, 1993.

Gitzen, Julian. 'The Truth-Tellers of William Trevor'. *Critique: Studies in Modern Fiction* 21:1 (1979), pp. 59–72.

Gorra, Michael. *After Empire: Scott, Naipaul, Rushdie.* Chicago: University of Chicago Press, 1997.

Gregory, Lady Augusta. *Our Irish Theatre.* New York: Capricorn Books, 1965.

Gurnah, Abdulrazak. *Paradise.* London: Hamish Hamilton, 1994.

'Writing and Place' (transcript of *Strangers in a Strange Land,* BBC Radio 4, 2001). *Wasafiri* 42 (Summer 2004), pp. 58–60.

'An Idea of the Past'. *Moving Worlds: A Journal of Transcultural Writings,* Special Issue 'Reflections', 2:2 (2002), pp. 6–17.

Gwynn, Stephen. 'An Uncommercial Theatre'. *Fortnightly Review* (December 1902), Reprinted in Justin McCarthy, ed., *Irish Literature.* 10 vols. Chicago: DeBower-Elliot, 1904, Vol. X, pp. xiii–xxv.

Hall, Stuart. 'Cultural Identity and Diaspora', in Patrick Williams and Laura Chrisman, eds., *Colonial Discourse and Postcolonial Theory: A Reader.* Hemel Hempstead: Harvester Wheatsheaf, 1993, pp. 392–403.

'When Was "the Post-Colonial"?: Thinking at the Limit', in Iain Chambers and Lidia Curti, eds., *The Post-Colonial Question.* London: Routledge, 1996, pp. 242–60.

Hamner, Robert, ed. *Critical Perspectives on Derek Walcott.* Washington, DC: Three Continents Press, 1993.

Hariharan, Githa. 'The Conversation with Githa Hariharan' (Interview with Arnab Chakladar). www.anothersubcontinent.com./hariharan.html.

Harris, Wilson. *Palace of the Peacock.* London: Faber and Faber, 1960.

Tradition, the Writer, and Society: Critical Essays. London: New Beacon Press, 1967.

'The Frontier on Which *Heart of Darkness* Stands', in Robert Kimbrough, ed., *Joseph Conrad: Heart of Darkness.* New York: Norton, 1988, pp. 263–8.

Selected Essays of Wilson Harris. Ed. Andrew Bundy. London: Routledge, 1999.

Hawkins, Maureen S. G. 'The Dramatic Treatment of Robert Emmet and Sarah Curran', in S. F. Gallagher, ed., *Women in Irish Legend, Life and Literature.* Gerrards Cross: Colin Smythe, 1983, pp. 125–37.

Head, Bessie. *A Question of Power.* London: Heineman, 1974.

The Collector of Treasures and Other Botswana Village Tales. London: Heinemann, 1977.

Heaney, Seamus. '. . . English and Irish'. *Times Literary Supplement* (24 October 1980), p. 1199. Reprinted in John Harrington, ed., *Modern Irish Drama.* London and New York: W. W. Norton, 1991, pp. 557–9.

Opened Ground: Poems 1966–1996. London: Faber and Faber, 1998.

Hegel, G. W. F. *Introduction to the Philosophy of History.* New York: Dover Publications, 1956.

Henderson, Ian. 'Gender, Genre, and Sybylla's Performative Identity in Miles Franklin's *My Brilliant Career*'. *Australian Literary Studies*, 18:2 (October 1997), pp. 165–73.

Heywood, Annemarie. 'The Fox's Dance: The Staging of Soyinka's Plays', in Biodun Jeyifo, ed., *Modern African Drama*. New York: W. W. Norton, 2002, pp. 552–60.

Holden, Philip. 'Imagined Individuals: National Autobiography and Postcolonial Self-Fashioning'. *Working Paper Series* 13. Singapore: Asia Research Institute, National University of Singapore, 2003.

Hooper, Glenn, and Colin Graham, eds. *Irish and Postcolonial writing*. Basingstoke: Palgrave Macmillan, 2002.

Howes, Marjorie. *Yeats's Nations: Gender, Class and Irishness*. Cambridge: Cambridge University Press, 1996.

Huggan, Graham. *The Postcolonial Exotic: Marketing the Margins*. London: Routledge, 2001.

Hutcheon, Linda. *The Canadian Postmodern*. Toronto: Oxford University Press, 1988.

The Politics of Postmodernism. London: Routledge, 1989.

Ingamells, Rex. 'Australia', in *The Jindyworobaks*, ed. Brian Elliott. Brisbane: University of Queensland Press, 1979, pp. 22–5.

Innes, C. L. *The Devil's Own Mirror: Irish and Africans in Modern Literature*. Washington, DC: Three Continents Press, 1990.

Women and Nation in Irish Literature and Society, 1880–1935. Hemel Hempstead: Harvester Wheatsheaf, 1993.

'Modernism, Ireland, and Empire: Yeats, Joyce and their Implied Audiences', in Howard Booth and Nigel Rigby, eds., *Modernism and Empire*. Manchester: Manchester University Press, 2000, pp. 137–155.

and Caroline Rooney. 'African Writing and Gender', in Paul Hyland and M. H. Msiska eds., *Writing and Africa*. London: Longman, 1997, pp. 193–215.

Ismond, Patricia. *Abandoning Dead Metaphors: The Caribbean Phase of Derek Walcott's Poetry*. Barbados, Jamaica, Trinidad and Tobago: University of West Indies Press, 2001.

Jaggi, Maya. 'Glimpses of a Paradise Lost', *The Guardian* (24 September 1994), p. 31.

James, C. L. R. 'Introduction to Tradition and the West Indian Novel', in Wilson Harris, *Tradition, the Writer, and Society: Critical Essays*. London: New Beacon Press, 1967, pp. 69–75.

Jameson, Fredric. 'Third World Literature and the Era of Multinational Capital'. *Social Text* 5 (1986), pp. 65–88.

JanMohamed, Abdul R. and David Lloyd, eds. *The Nature and Context of Minority Discourse*. New York and Oxford: Oxford University Press, 1990.

Jekyll, Walter. Preface in Wayne Cooper, ed. *The Dialect Poetry of Claude McKay*. New York: Harcourt, Brace & World, 1972.

Johnson, James Weldon, ed. *The Book of American Negro Poetry.* New York: Harcourt, Brace & World, 1931.

Joyce, James. *A Portrait of the Artist as a Young Man.* New York: Viking, 1964.
  A Portrait of the Artist as a Young Man. Harmondsworth: Penguin, 1975.
  Ulysses. Harmondsworth: Penguin, 1986.

Kay, Jackie. *Adoption Papers.* Newcastle upon Tyne: Bloodaxe Books, 1991.
  Trumpet. London: Macmillan, 1998.

Kearney, Richard. *Myth and Motherland.* Belfast: Dorman, 1987.

Kendall, Henry. 'Bell-Birds', in G. A. Wilkes, ed., *The Colonial Poets.* Sydney: Angus & Robertson, 1974, pp. 102–3.

Keown, Michelle. *Postcolonial Pacific Writing: Representations of the Body.* London: Routledge, 2005.

Kiberd, Declan. *Inventing Ireland.* London: Jonathan Cape, 1995.
  'Introduction', James Joyce, *Ulysses: Annotated Student Edition.* London: Penguin, 1992, pp. ix–lxxx.
  Irish Classics. London: Granta Books, 2000.

Kilroy, James. *The 'Playboy' Riots.* Dublin: Dolmen, 1971.

King, Bruce. *Derek Walcott and West Indian Drama.* Oxford: Oxford University Press, 1995.
  The Internationalization of English Literature: Oxford English Literary History, Volume XIII. Oxford: Oxford University Press, 2004.

Kingsley, Charles. *His Letters and Memories of His Life: Edited by His Wife.* 2 vols., London: Henry S. King, 1877.

Kureishi, Hanif. *The Buddha of Suburbia.* London: Faber and Faber, 1990.

Lamming, George. *In the Castle of My Skin.* Ann Arbor: University of Michigan Press, 1994.
  The Pleasures of Exile. London: Michael Joseph, 1960.

Landry, Donna and Gerald MacLean, eds. *The Spivak Reader.* New York and London: Routledge, 1996.

Lazarus, Neil. *Resistance in Postcolonial African Fiction.* New Haven, CT: Yale University Press, 1990.
  , ed. *The Cambridge Companion to Literary Studies.* (Cambridge: Cambridge University Press, 2004.

Lloyd, David. *Anomalous States: Irish Writing and the Post-Colonial Moment.* Durham, NC: Duke University Press, 1993.

Longley, Edna. *The Living Stream: Literature and Revisionism in Ireland.* Newcastle upon Tyne: Bloodaxe Books, 1994.

Loomba, Ania. *Colonialism/Postcolonialism.* 2nd edition. London: Routledge, 2005.
  et. al., eds. *Postcolonial Studies and Beyond.* Durham, NC: Duke University Press, 2005.

McCallum, John. 'Irish Memories and Australian Hopes: William Butler Yeats and Louis Esson'. *Westerly: A Quarterly Review,* 34:2 (June 1989), pp. 33–40.

McLeod, John. *Postcolonial London: Rewriting the Metropolis.* London: Routledge, 2004.

McCormack, W. J. and Alastair Stead, eds. *James Joyce and Modern Literature.* London: Routledge & Kegan Paul, 1982.

McGill, Robert. *The Mysteries.* Toronto: McGill and Stewart, 2004.

McGonegal, Julie. 'Postcolonial Metacritique: Jameson, Allegory and the Always-Already-Read Third World Text'. *Interventions* 7:2 (July 2005), pp. 251–65.

Marechera, Dambudzo. *House of Hunger.* London: Heinemann, 1978.

Martin, S. I. *Incomparable World.* London: Quartet Books, 1996.

Maslen, Elizabeth. 'Stories, Constructions, and Deconstructions: Abdulrazak Gurnah's *Paradise'. Wasafiri* 24 (Autumn 1996), pp. 53–7.

Mathews, P. J. *Revival: The Abbey Theatre, Sinn Fein, The Gaelic League and the Co-operative Movement.* Cork: Cork University Press/Field Day, 2003.

Matthews, S. Leigh. '"The Bright Bone of a Dream": Drama, Performativity, Ritual, and Community in Michael Ondaatje's *Running in the Family'. Biography* 23:2 (Spring 2000), pp. 352–71.

Mavia, David. ''Nyof, Nyof' and 'Shifting Visions of English Language Usage in Kenya', *Kunapipi: Journal of Postcolonial Writing,* 27:1 (2005), pp. 121–3; 124–9.

Meaney, Geraldine. 'Myth, History and the Politics of Subjectivity: Eavan Boland and Irish Women's Writing'. *Women: A Cultural Review* 4:2 (Autumn 1993), pp. 136–53.

Melville, Pauline. *The Ventriloquist's Tale.* London: Bloomsbury, 1997.

Merguerian, Gayane Karen and Afsaneh Najmabadi. 'Zulaykha and Yusuf: Whose "Best Story"?'. *International Journal of Middle Eastern Studies,* 29:4 (November 1997), pp. 485–508.

Michael, Magali Cornier. 'Rethinking History as Patchwork: The Case of Atwood's *Alias Grace'. Modern Fiction Studies,* 47:2 (Summer 2001), pp. 421–47.

Montefiore, Janet. *Feminism and Poetry.* Revised edition. London: Pandora, 1994.

Moore-Gilbert, Bart. *Postcolonial Theory: Contexts, Practices, Politics.* London: Verso, 1997 (reprinted 2000).

, Gareth, Stanton and Willy Maley, eds. *Postcolonial Criticism.* London: Longman, 1997.

Morash, Christopher. *A History of Irish Theatre, 1601–2000.* Cambridge: Cambridge University Press, 2002.

Morgan, Sally. *My Place.* London: Virago, 1988.

Morris, Mervyn. 'On Reading Louise Bennett, Seriously', *Jamaica Journal* 1:1 (1967), pp. 69–74. Reprinted in Alison Donnell and Sarah Lawson Welsh, eds., *The Routledge Reader in Caribbean Literature.* London: Routledge, 1996, pp. 194–7.

Mühleisen, Susanne. *Creole Discourse: Exploring Prestige Formation and Change across Caribbean English-Lexicon Creoles.* Amsterdam and Philadelphia: John Benjamins Publishing Company, 2002.

'What Makes an Accent Funny, and Why? Black British Englishes and Humour Televised,' in Susanne Reichl and Mark Stein, eds., *Cheeky*

Fictions: Laughter and the Postcolonial. Amsterdam and New York: Rodopi, 2005, pp. 225–43.

Murray, Les A. *Persistence in Folly: Selected Prose Writings.* Sydney: Angus & Roberston, 1986.

The Paperbark Tree: Selected Prose. Manchester: Carcanet, 1992.

Collected Poems. Manchester: Carcanet Press, 1998.

ed. *The New Oxford Book of Australian Verse.* Melbourne: Oxford: Oxford University Press, 1986.

Naipaul, V. S. *The Mimic Men.* London: André Deutsch, 1967.

The Middle Passage. Harmondsworth: Penguin, 1969.

The Overcrowded Barracoon. London: André Deutsch, 1972.

A Bend in the River. London: André Deutsch, 1979.

The Enigma of Arrival. London: Penguin, 1987.

Nandy, Ashis. *The Intimate Enemy: Loss and Recovery of Self Under Colonialism.* Delhi: Oxford University Press, 1983.

Nash, John. '"Hanging Over the Bloody Paper": Newspapers and Imperialism in *Ulysses*', in Howard Booth and Nigel Rigby eds., *Modernism and Empire.* Manchester: Manchester University Press: 2000, pp. 175–96.

Nasta, Susheila, ed. *Critical Perspectives on Sam Selvon.* Washington, DC: Three Continents Press, 1988.

'Setting Up Home in a City of Words: Sam Selvon's London Novels', in A. Robert Lee, ed., *Other Britain, Other British.* London: Pluto, 1995, pp. 48–68.

Home Truths. Fictions of the South Asian Diaspora in Britain. London: Palgrave Macmillan, 2002.

'Abdulrazak Gurnah, *Paradise*', in David Johnson, ed., *The Popular and the Canonical: Debating Twentieth-Century Literature 1940–2000.* London: Routledge, 2005, pp. 294–343.

ed. *Motherlands: Black Women's Writing from Africa, the Caribbean and South Asia.* London: The Women's Press, 1991.

Newell, Stephanie. *West African Literatures: Ways of Reading.* Oxford: Oxford University Press, 2006.

Ngugi wa Thiong'o. *The Black Hermit.* London: Heinemann, 1968.

A Grain of Wheat. London: Heinemann, 1968.

Homecoming: Essays on African and Caribbean Literature, Culture, and Politics. London: Heinemann, 1972.

Petals of Blood. London: Heinemann, 1977.

Detained: A Writer's Prison Diary. London: Heinemann, 1981.

Writers in Politics. London: Heinemann, 1981.

'On Writing in Gikuyu'. *Research in African Literatures* 16:2 (Summer 1985), pp. 151–56.

Decolonising the Mind: The Politics of Language in African Literature. London: James Currey, 1986.

and Micere Githae-Mugo, *The Trial of Dedan Kimathi.* London: Heinemann, 1976.

Oakley, George ('Evelyn'). Review in the *Colonial Monthly* [October 1869], quoted by Ken Goodwin, 'Henry Kendall', in *Dictionary of Literary Biography, Volume 230: Australian Literature, 1788–1914*. A Bruccoli Clark Layman Book. Ed. Selina Samuels. Detroit: Gale Group, 2000, pp. 193–207.

O'Brien, Flann. *At Swim-Two-Birds*. London: Penguin, 1967.

O'Casey, Sean. *Three Plays*. London: Macmillan, 1969.

Olney, James. *Metaphors of Self: The Meaning of Autobiography*. Princeton: Princeton University Press, 1972.

  Tell Me Africa. Princeton: Princeton University Press, 1973.

Ondaatje, Michael. *Running in the Family*. London: Picador, 1982.

  Anil's Ghost. London: Picador, 2000.

Parker, Michael and Roger Starkey, eds. *Postcolonial Literatures: Achebe, Ngugi, Desai, Walcott*. Basingstoke: Macmillan, 1995.

Parry, Benita. *Postcolonial Studies: A Materialist Critique*. London: Routledge, 2004.

Patke, Rajeev S. *Postcolonial Poetry in English*. Oxford: Oxford University Press, 2006.

Petersen, Kirsten Holst and Anna Rutherford, eds. *A Double Colonisation: Colonial and Post-Colonial Women's Writing*. Sydney and Oxford: Dangaroo Press, 1986.

Philip, Marlene Nourbese. *She Tries Her Tongue, Her Silence Softly Breaks*. Charlottetown, Prince Edward Island: Ragweed, 1989.

Phillips, Caryl. *The Final Passage*. London: Faber and Faber, 1985.

  Cambridge. London: Picador, 1992.

  Extravagant Strangers: A Literature of Belonging. London: Faber and Faber, 1997.

  The Nature of Blood. London: Faber and Faber, 1997.

  A New World Order: Selected Essays. London: Vintage, 2002.

Powell, Erica. *Private Secretary (Female)/Gold Coast*. New York: St Martin's Press, 1984.

Press, John, ed. *Commonwealth Literature: Unity and Diversity in a Common Culture*. London: Heinemann, 1965.

Pritchard, Katharine Susannah. *Coonardoo*. Sydney: Angus & Robertson, 1975.

Procter, James. *Dwelling Places: Postwar Black British Writing*. Manchester: Manchester University Press, 2003.

Punter, David. *Postcolonial Imaginings*. Edinburgh: Edinburgh University Press, 2000.

Quayson, Ato. *Postcolonialism: Theory, Practice, or Process?* Oxford: Polity Press, 1999.

Ramazani, Jahan. *The Hybrid Muse: Postcolonial Poetry in English*. Chicago: University of Chicago Press, 2001.

Ranasinha, Ruvani. *Hanif Kureishi*. London: Northcote House, 2002.

Randawha, Ravinda. *A Wicked Old Woman.* London: The Women's Press, 1987.

Rao, Raja. *Kanthapura.* New York: Grove Press, 1963.

Renan, Ernest. *The Poetry of the Celtic Races.* Trans. William Hutchison. New York: Collier, 1910.

Rogers, Philip. 'No *Longer at Ease:* Chinua Achebe's "Heart of Whiteness"', in Michael Parker and Roger Starkey, eds., *Postcolonial Literatures: Achebe, Ngugi, Desai, Walcott.* Basingstoke: Macmillan, 1995, pp. 53–63.

Rousselot, Elodie. *Re-writing Women into Canadian History: Margaret Atwood and Anne Hébert.* Canterbury: University of Kent PhD dissertation, 2004.

Rushdie, Salman. *Midnight's Children.* London: Picador, 1982.

'The Empire Writes Back With a Vengeance', *The Times* (London), 3 July 1982, p. 8.

The Satanic Verses. London: Viking, 1988.

Imaginary Homelands: Essays and Criticism 1981–1991. London: Granta, 1992.

The Moor's Last Sigh. London: Jonathan Cape, 1995.

Salman Rushdie Interviews: A Sourcebook of His Ideas. Ed. Pradyumna S. Chauhan. Westport, CT: Greenwood Press, 2001.

and Elizabeth West, eds. *The Vintage Book of Indian Writing, 1947–1997.* London: Vintage, 1997.

Ryan, Ray. *Ireland and Scotland: Literature and Culture, State and Nation, 1966–2000.* Oxford: Oxford University Press, 2002.

Sahgal, Nayantara. 'The Schizophrenic Imagination', *Wasafiri* 11 (Spring 1990), pp. 17–20.

Rich Like Us. New Delhi : HarperCollins, 1999.

Said, Edward. *Orientalism.* (1978). Revised edition. Harmondsworth: Penguin, 1991.

'Yeats and Decolonisation', in Terry Eagleton, Fredric Jameson and Edward W. Said, with an Introduction by Seamus Deane, *Nationalism, Colonialism, and Literature.* Minneapolis: University of Minnesota Press, 1990, pp. 69–95.

Culture and Imperialism. London: Chatto & Windus, 1993.

Sartre, Jean-Paul. *Black Orpheus.* Trans. Samuel Allen. Paris: Présence Africaine, 1956. First published as 'Orphée noir', in L. S. Senghor, ed., *Anthologie de la nouvelle poésie nègre et malgache de langue française.* Paris: Presses Universitaires de France, 1948, pp. ix–xliv.

Selvon, Samuel. *The Lonely Londoners.* London: Longman, 1956.

Moses Ascending. London: Heinemann, 1984.

Senghor, Léopold. *Ethiopiques.* Paris: Editions de Seuil, 1956.

Sidhwa, Bapsi. *Ice-Candy-Man.* London: Penguin, 1989.

'Interview with David Montenegro' ('Bapsi Sidhwa: An Interview'). *Massachusetts Review* 31:4 (Winter 1990), pp. 513–33.

Silva, Neluka. 'The Anxieties of Hybridity: Michael Ondaatje's *Running in the Family*'. *Journal of Commonwealth Literature* 37:2 (June 2002), pp. 71–83.

Smith, Michael. 'Interview with Michael Smith by Mervyn Morris (extract)', 'Me Cyaan Believe It', in E. A. Markham, ed., *Hinterlands: Caribbean Poetry from the West Indies and Britain*. Newcastle upon Tyne: Bloodaxe Books, 1989, pp. 275–83; 284–6.

Smith, Vivian. 'Poetry', in Leonie Kramer, ed., *The Oxford History of Australian Literature*. Oxford: Oxford University Press, 1981, pp. 269–426.

Sorabji, Cornelia. *Love and Life Behind the Purdah*. London: Fremantle & Co., 1901.

Soyinka, Wole. 'The Future of African Writing'. *The Horn* (Ibadan) 4:1 (June 1960), pp. 10–16.

The Interpreters. London: André Deutsch, 1965.

'Death at Dawn', in Gerald Moore and Ulli Beier, eds., *Modern Poetry from Africa*. Revised edition. Harmondsworth: Penguin, 1968, pp.145–6.

A Dance of the Forests and *The Road* in *Collected Plays I*. London: Oxford University Press, 1973

Season of Anomie. London: Rex Collings, 1973.

The Lion and the Jewel in *Collected Plays II*. London: Oxford University Press, 1974.

Death and the King's Horseman. London: Eyre Methuen, 1975.

Spencer, W. Baldwin and F. J. Gillen, *The Arunta: A Study of a Stone Age People*. London: Macmillan, 1927.

Spivak, Gayatri Chakravorty. *In Other Worlds: Essays in Cultural Politics*. London: Methuen, 1987.

'Can the Subaltern Speak?', in Cary Nelson and Lawrence Grossberg, eds., *Marxism and the Interpretation of Culture*. Basingstoke: Macmillan, 1988, pp. 271–313.

The Post-Colonial Critic: Interviews, Strategies, Dialogues. Ed. Sarah Harasym. London: Routledge, 1990.

Outside in the Teaching Machine. London: Routledge, 1993.

'Three Women's Texts and Circumfession', in Alfred Hornung and Ernstpeter Ruhe, eds., *Postcolonialism and Autobiography*. Amsterdam: Rodopi, 1998, pp. 7–22.

A Critique of Postcolonial Reason: Toward a History of the Vanishing Present. Cambridge, MA, and London: Harvard University Press, 1999.

Stead, Christina. *Ocean of Story: The Uncollected Stories of Christina Stead*. Ed. R. G. Geering. Melbourne: Viking, 1985.

A Web of Friendship: Selected Letters 1928–1973. Ed. R. G. Geering. Pymble, Australia: Angus & Robertson, 1992.

Stein, Mark. *Black British Literature: Novels of Transformation*. Columbus: Ohio State University Press, 2004.

Stewart, Douglas. *Ned Kelly*. Sydney: Angus & Robertson, 1943.

Synge, J. M. *Plays, Poems, and Prose.* London: J. M. Dent, 1949.

   The Collected Letters. Ed. Ann. Saddlemyer (Oxford: Clarendon Press, 1983).

Thieme, John. *Post-Colonial Studies: The Essential Glossary.* London: Arnold, 2003.

Todd, Loreto. 'Reviews: Louise Bennett, Selected Poems, edited by Mervyn Morris'. *World Literature Written in English* 17 (Spring 1984), pp. 414–16.

Todd, Richard. *Consuming Fictions.* London: Bloomsbury, 1996.

Trevor-Roper, Hugh. *The Rise of Christian Europe.* London: Thames & Hudson, 1965.

Trevor, William, 'The Art of Fiction No. 108' (Interview with Mira Stout.) *Paris Review* 110 (1989), pp. 118–51.

   Miss Gomez and the Brethren, London: Bodley Head, 1971.

Wake, Clive and John Reed, eds. *Senghor: Prose and Poetry.* London: Oxford University Press, 1965.

Walcott, Derek. *Dream on Monkey Mountain and Other Plays.* New York: Farrar, Straus and Giroux, 1970.

   Remembrance and Pantomime: Two Plays. New York: Farrar, Straus and Giroux, 1980.

   Omeros. London: Faber and Faber, 1990.

   Collected Poems, 1948–1984. London: Faber and Faber, 1992.

   'The Figure of Crusoe', in Robert Hamner, ed., *Critical Perspectives on Derek Walcott.* Washington, DC: Three Continents Press, 1993, pp. 33–40.

   'The Antilles: Fragments of Epic Memory', in Alison Donnell and Sarah Lawson Welsh, eds., *The Routledge Reader in Caribbean Literature.* London: Routledge, 1996. pp. 503–7.

Wali, Obianjunwa. 'The Dead End of African Literature'. *Transition* 10 (1963), pp. 13–16.

Walmsley, Anne. *The Caribbean Artists Movement, 1966–72.* London: New Beacon Press, 1992.

White, Patrick. *Voss.* Harmondsworth: Penguin, 1980.

Whitlock, Gillian. *The Intimate Empire: Reading Women's Autobiography.* London: Cassell, 2000.

Wilkes, G. A. *The Colonial Poets.* Sydney: Angus & Robertson, 1974.

Williams, Patrick and Laura Chrisman, eds. *Colonial Discourse and Postcolonial Theory: A Reader.* Hemel Hempstead: Harvester Wheatsheaf, 1993.

Wilson, Edmund. *The Wound and the Bow.* Cambridge, MA: Houghton Mifflin Company, 1941.

Wright, Derek. *Ayi Kwei Armah's Africa.* London: Hans Zell, 1989.

Wright, Judith. *Preoccupations in Australian Poetry.* Melbourne: Oxford University Press, 1966.

   Born of the Conquerors: Selected Essays. Canberra: Aboriginal Studies Press, 1991.

   Collected Poems 1942–1985. Manchester: Carcanet, 1994.

Yeats, W. B. *Autobiographies*. Dublin: Gill and Macmillan, 1955.
  Uncollected Prose. Ed. John Frayne. New York: Macmillan, 1970.
  Yeats's Poems. Edited and annotated by A. Norman Jeffares. London: Macmillan, 1989.
Young, Robert J. C. *Postcolonialism: An Historical Introduction*. Oxford: Blackwell, 2001.
  Postcolonialism: A Very Short Introduction. Oxford: Oxford University Press, 2003.
Zell, Hans, Carol Bundy and Virginia Coulon, eds. *A New Reader's Guide to African Literature*. Revised edition. New York: Holmes & Meier, 1983.

Index

Printed in Great Britain by
Amazon.co.uk, Ltd.,
Marston Gate.